Narrative of the Peninsular War

Narrative of the Peninsular War
The Experiences of an Aide-de-Camp and Officer in the 29th (Worcestershire) Regiment During the Napoleonic Wars in Spain & Portugal
by Andrew Leith Hay

First published under the title
Narrative of the Peninsular War

Leonaur is an imprint of Oakpast Ltd
Copyright in this form © 2013 Oakpast Ltd

ISBN: 978-1-78282-110-6 (hardcover)
ISBN: 978-1-78282-111-3 (softcover)

http://www.leonaur.com

Publisher's Notes

The views expressed in this book are not necessarily those of the publisher.

Contents

Preface	7
Arrival in Spain	13
Defeat of the Spanish Armies	80
Surrender of Badajos	112
Death of General Crauford	164
Lord Wellington Assembles His Army	179
Battle of Vittoria	240
Pampeluna Blockaded by the Allies	290
Termination of the Peninsular War	296
Appendix.	330

Preface

Before presenting this narrative to the public, some apology may be considered necessary, after the numerous works that have already appeared on the subject, and the period elapsed when the personal observations of an officer engaged in the scenes described may be supposed to possess either novelty or extensive interest. Unrestrained by these considerations, the author has published the substance of journals,—his constant companions during campaigns which he had the honour to serve under Sir John Moore and the Duke of Wellington; hoping that, in some respects, he may be enabled to rescue from oblivion scenes that have escaped the observation or notice of abler commentators. He has also been instigated by an anxious desire to record the deeds of officers who, respected during life, have passed from this world, and are now forgotten, except by personal friends, or those companions who, regretting their untimely fall, identify their memories with scenes never to be forgotten.

There is also, in the weakness of his nature, a vanity prompting this popular disclosure of occasions in which he participated, and to which feeling time brings no diminution. The recollections of years passed in the active and exhilarating service in Spain must ever indelibly exist in his mind, as being, if not the happiest, certainly the most interesting period of his life.

Strongly impressed with these sentiments, constantly reading the works on the Peninsular War, with which the press has for years teemed, and wherein he imagined there existed some instances of misconception, and many of unintentionally erroneous information, he has referred to his notes, which he believes to be correct, and knows to be authentic; and, after a lapse of years, has prepared them for publication.

If, in so doing, he has fortunately in any respect added claims to the already deservedly established reputation of the officers and soldiers of the Peninsular Army, if the tribute of an eyewitness to many occasions of distinguished conduct on the part of those who sealed with their blood the pre-eminent glories of the British Army, shall in the slightest degree tend, by recording their deeds, to illustrate their memories,—he must feel satisfied and happy in having made the attempt.

Owing to particular circumstances, opportunities were afforded him of witnessing the varieties of service during the struggle more generally than most other officers of a subordinate rank; and it happened that he had from its commencement resolved to preserve a regular diary of observations. Aware that, in many instances, the minor events detailed in the following narrative may be considered trivial or devoid of interest, it may also be supposed that he has too much indulged in personal records. To the first, he must plead in extenuation an enthusiastic feeling inherent in his mind, which induces him to consider the slightest incident that occurred during the war worthy of being recorded; to the second, he has only to say, that the vanity and weakness of human nature must have drawn him into an error, which he has endeavoured, as far as the nature of a narrative would permit, to avoid.

The Peninsular contest has become a theme so frequently discussed, that familiarity with details, and an impression of its forming but one incident in the great drama of the French revolutionary wars, have in our day somewhat tended to withdraw attention from the military situation Great Britain there re-established among the nations of Europe.

To recapitulate what the French Imperial troops were, or even give a summary of their achievements, is unnecessary; it never can be forgotten by the present generation, either the awe inspired, or the fixed impression of distrust, with which we were committed to conflict on the Continent of Europe against the victorious legions of Napoleon: nor will history fail to do justice when recording the deeds of the Duke of Wellington and his army,—an army that recovered the character of the nations of Europe, broke the spell, induced others to believe they might be successful, and established an imperishable reputation by overcoming and constantly vanquishing that brilliant force, whose eagles, surrounded by the halo of victory, had been conducted from triumph to triumph, by the greatest soldier that ever trod this earth.

Such having been our opponents during the protracted and obstinately conducted warfare, it is not wonderful that feelings of strong excitement should result from the recollections connected with the successes of so glorious a field; and if the author of the following pages has vaunted the achievements of his companions, or has throughout maintained that on the field of battle British infantry are the best in Europe, he, in the first place, refers unbelievers to the circumstance of their having been *"les vainqueurs des vainqueurs de la terre;"* and, secondly, if conviction has not then visited the disputants of the fact, let them appear on the plain, and the truth will be forced upon them in terrible reality.

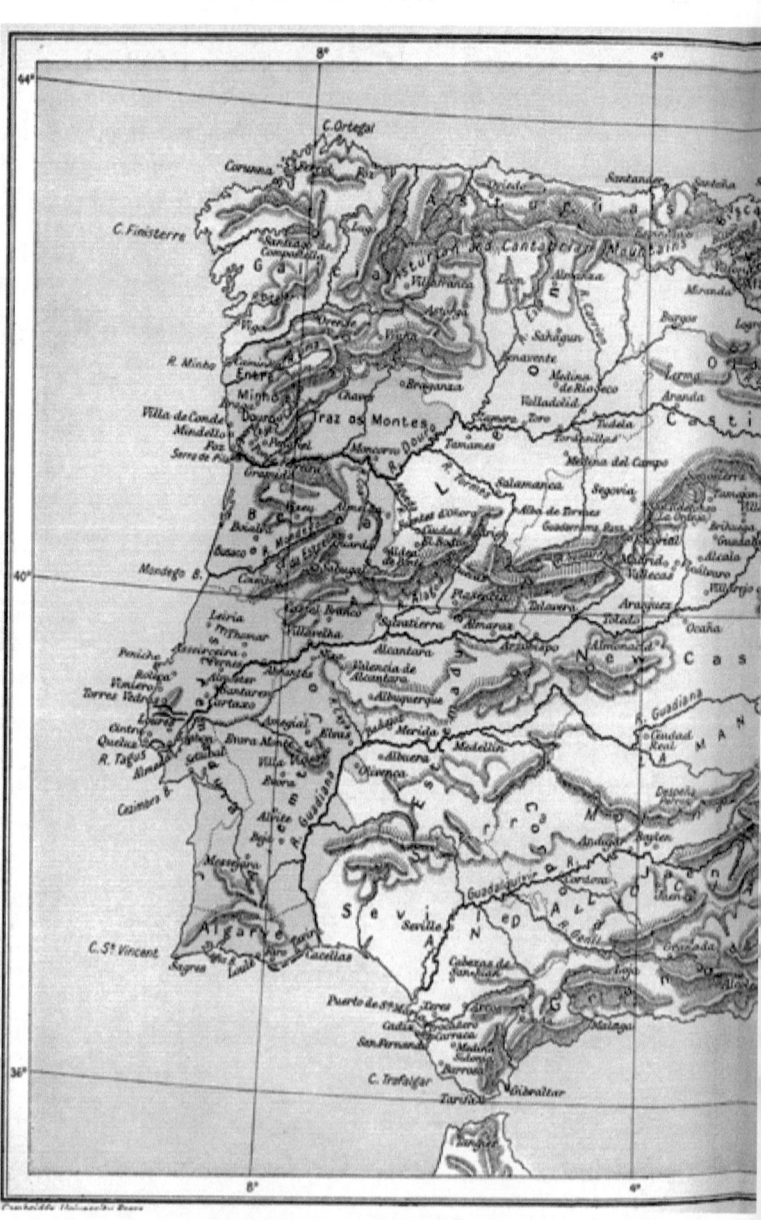

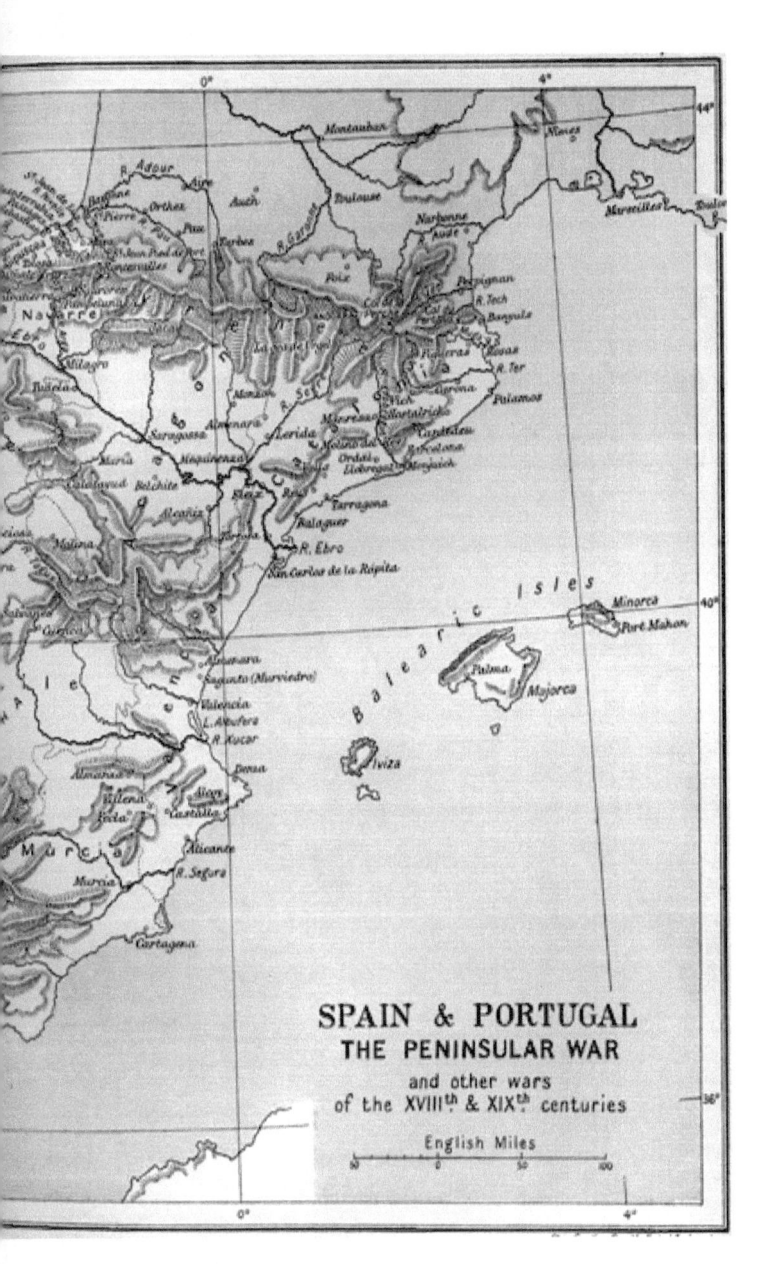

Chapter 1
Arrival in Spain

It is universally known, that the measures adopted by the Emperor Napoleon, and the disclosure of his intention to subvert the Spanish monarchy, to terminate the reign of the Bourbons, and to place one of his own family on the Catholic throne, having produced a great sensation, and excited an unexpected resistance in the minds of the inhabitants of the Peninsula, deputations were sent, early in the year 1808, from Asturias and other provinces, to England, for the purpose of soliciting the assistance of its government in resisting the attempts of the most powerful and most extraordinary man of ancient or modern times, who, supported by the victorious armies of France, wished to place the crown of Spain upon the head of a foreigner, and to overthrow the ancient laws and institutions of that kingdom.

That the British Government should at once form an alliance with the Spanish people, was the certain consequence of the appeal made to it for support; and the nation hailed with enthusiasm the commencement of a struggle, which appeared calculated to produce the only substantial and serious obstacle that had yet been opposed to the conquering genius of Napoleon,—of that extraordinary man, who rose, in a few years, from the subordinate ranks of the French Army to the throne of an empire formed by himself,—which embraced France, Italy, Holland, the Netherlands, and held in subjection the Rhenish Confederacy and the Helvetic Republic.

The revolt of the Spaniards gave, at this moment, a new aspect to the affairs of Europe. The nations appeared to derive fresh hopes, and to be aroused from the despondency which had resulted from multiplied and annihilating disasters. No sooner did the deputies appear in London, than the government actively and promptly prepared to render that assistance to the cause which sound policy dictated; and the resources of the country enabled ministers to contribute without difficulty or delay; while the undisputed sovereignty of the ocean insured a certain communication with all parts of the Peninsular coast.

A treaty of alliance being concluded between Great Britain and the Spanish people, ships were immediately despatched, consisting of the *Seine*, Captain Atkins; *L'Aigle*, Captain Wolfe; *Unicorn*, Captain Hardyman; and *Iris*, Captain Tower; laden with arms, ammunition, and specie; and every means adopted to increase the confidence felt by the leaders of the insurrection. British officers were sent to the northern provinces for the purpose of reporting upon the actual state of the country, to afford assistance in organising its military resources, and suggest measures best calculated to enable a nation—upon which the light of patriotic and noble feeling had just dawned—successfully to resist foreign subjection, although enforced by armies deemed invincible, and conducted by the greatest man of the age. Among the British officers thus employed, Major-General Leith was ordered to proceed to Santander, having received instructions to report upon the state of the armament in the Asturias, in Biscay, Guipascoa, and Las Montañas de Santander. The author of the following pages left England as his *aide-de-camp*, and sailed from Portsmouth on the evening of the 17th August, 1808.

On the morning of the 22nd, the *Peruvian* brig-of-war made the coast of Spain, and, as the vessel approached the land, the mountains of Asturias appeared in the distance; the wild and varied country, wooded to its summits, exhibiting scenery of striking grandeur and interest. From the crew of a Spanish fishing-boat, information was obtained that we were considerably to the westward of Santander—our destined port. The brig was consequently directed to the east, and coasted along the bold and beautiful shore.

In the evening, a squadron of British frigates was perceived, and a fresh breeze soon brought the *Peruvian* within signal distance. Captain Atkins, the senior officer, was then on shore, conferring with the bishop, who had taken a lead, and acted a conspicuous part, in opposition to the French usurpation.

The Bishop of Santander, in appearance or in manner, but little realized the impression which the vaunted firmness and patriotism of the warlike ecclesiastic had produced in England; but, when compared to the other specimens of Spanish military and civil authority, with whom we were soon destined to become acquainted, it is, probably, unjust to deny him a place somewhat removed from the insignificance that became apparent to the British officers, who had left England impressed with an exalted idea of the Spanish character.

The bishop had shewn considerable energy. His opinions were sincere and undoubted. Nominated regent of the province of Las Montañas, the declaration he had published established his reputation as a zealous partisan and strenuous advocate of the cause of Spanish independence. Thus situated, he was considered by the British Government as a proper person with whom to communicate. General Leith was instructed to attend to his suggestions as to the state of the country under his immediate control, and the organisation and supply of the armies collecting in the northern provinces, or who had already taken the field, in resistance to the dominion of France. The Conde de Villa Neuva, at this period, was general-in-chief of the province; and perfect cordiality appeared to exist between the military and civil jurisdictions.

The *conde*, an old officer, had formerly been in the Spanish Guards. He was a sensible, and, to a certain extent, a well-informed man, and, without doubt, in times of internal peace and inactivity, had occupied a very respectable place in Spanish society. His appearance, however, did not exactly correspond with the highest notions of modern military costume; and, as he was the first Spanish officer of rank we had seen, the impression was unfavourable.

Neither the bishop nor the *conde* possessed any certain information as to the situation or movements of the enemy, nor were they positive that a Spanish force of any description intervened between the quarters of the French Army and Santander. This, at first, appeared an extraordinary circumstance; but, when we subsequently became acquainted with the confidence and apathy of the Spanish character, it no longer excited surprise.

Santander is very favourably situated as a place of mercantile importance. Its spacious harbour is protected from the north-west by a promontory, at the eastern extremity of which is Cape Mayor. The cathedral is not a building of great magnitude or magnificence; nor is the palace of the bishop, although large and commodious, remarkable either for its elegance or splendour. The town is, however, of considerable extent, and some of the buildings, particularly those upon the quay, are spacious and handsome.

The principal line of communication from Santander to the interior of the country, is that of Reynosa, and from thence, by Burgos, to Madrid; and it being considered of importance to possess authentic information of the situation of affairs in that direction, I was ordered to proceed for the purpose of obtaining it.

Perfectly unacquainted with the language, and having been only three days in the country, this appeared a service of some inconvenience and difficulty. My instructions were, to proceed by the pass of Escudo to Reynosa, where it was conjectured I should find General Ballesteros (afterwards so distinguished during the Peninsular War), in the command of a body of Asturians. I was to be accompanied by a Spanish captain of the name of Villardet; twelve soldiers of the regiment of Laredo, to which he belonged; and an old man, who was to act as an interpreter.

The assembling of this *formidable* cavalcade occasioned a considerable sensation in the town of Santander, and, although late in the evening, a crowd collected to witness our departure. A large and handsome black horse bore the person of the Spanish captain, who was enveloped in his cloak, and whose lank and sallow visage was surmounted by a hat of no ordinary dimensions. A mule, caparisoned with all the usual cumbrance of Spanish saddlery, was prepared for me; and as, for the first time, a pair of horse-pistols graced my saddle-bow, and a *cortège* appeared ready to accompany me, I mounted with exultation, and derived no ordinary satisfaction from the feeling that I was the hero of this great expedition.

In the midst of these preparations for departure, an incident of a ludicrous description rather lessened the importance, and detracted from the gravity, of the occasion. When the old interpreter proceeded to mount the mule destined to transport him, the solemnity and silence of the scene was suddenly exchanged for the most discordant noise and the most clamorous disturbance. The master of languages, who apparently had neglected the study of equitation, unfortunately for him, had been provided with the only vicious mule in company, which, the moment he ascertained the burden that was intended for him, proceeded with his heels to disperse the crowd, to the terror and annoyance of some, and the amusement of others; nor did he desist from this violent exercise until he had prostrated his rider on the street.

A struggle then ensued between the interpreter and his friends; the former strenuously objecting to any further attempt in subduing the refractory mule; the latter, having a becoming anxiety for his safety and comfort, as eagerly urging another essay, and prophesying, with considerable apparent likelihood, that, upon a second attempt, he would find himself most steadily and agreeably carried. The contest terminated in favour of the interpreter, who, being mounted upon a more tractable animal, we proceeded upon our journey.

After travelling sixteen miles, we arrived at a village, where the muleteers insisted upon refreshment both for themselves and their quadrupeds. The *posado*, or inn, at which we halted, was, like most others in the north of Spain, of the worst description, the principal part of the house being appropriated to the accommodation of the horses and mules. At daybreak we were again in motion, and, travelling through a very romantic and beautiful country, the road conducted in narrow valleys, bounded by hills, which were covered to their summits with trees of the most luxuriant foliage. Occasionally, the valleys extended, and the country became less mountainous and more cultivated. In the course of the forenoon, we perceived smoke ascending from a wood in our front, and, upon arriving at it, found an advanced post of three hundred Asturians, all peasants, who had recently enrolled themselves, and who were but indifferently armed. From the commandant, I learned that General Ballesteros was at Reynosa; and having travelled as expeditiously as the nature of my escort would permit, reached his quarters in the evening.

The appearance and manner of General Ballesteros was very superior to that of any military man I had yet seen in Spain: young, active, and intelligent, he at once impressed a stranger with the idea that he was an efficient, and likely to become a distinguished officer. His promotion had been very rapid, the revolution having occasioned his removal at once from the subaltern ranks of the Spanish Army to that of major-general. He had been for some time at Reynosa, in command of a body of Asturians, amounting to between four and five thousand men, who had not yet been incorporated with either of the Spanish armies. The general communicated to me the information he possessed relating to the position of the enemy's troops, and the movements that had recently taken place in his cantonments. The headquarters continued to occupy Vittoria; and nothing had occurred which indicated any immediate intention on the part of the French Army to resume offensive operations. No force of any description had approached Reynosa; and his situation there appeared to be, for the present, secure and undisturbed.

Thus ascertaining that Santander was in no immediate danger of a visit from the enemy, I prepared to retrace my steps, and, having procured post-horses, galloped at midnight through the streets of Reynosa, preceded by the postilion. The stillness of a beautiful night was only interrupted by the challenge of the Spanish sentinels as we passed their several posts, and enlivened by the sound of bells attached to the bridle of my companion's horse; the wild song in which he occasionally indulged; the distant noise; the mirth of travelling muleteers; and the rush of waters falling over their rocky channels, in the ravines and closely wooded valleys through which the road is conducted.

The only pace the Spanish post-horse ever attempts is either a walk or a gallop; and as the postilion invariably precedes the traveller, and checks his horse into the former at his option, and without any previous indication of his intention, the transition from the rapid to the slow pace is attended with a species of shock not agreeable to the person unprepared for this mode of proceeding. Notwithstanding this and other annoyances, riding post in Spain is, upon the great routes, where the horses are good, a certain and tolerably expeditious mode of performing a journey. At six in the morning we reached Torre la Vega, and, at nine, arrived at Santander.

It being evident that no event of importance was soon likely to occur in the province of Las Montañas, the general resolved to reembark and proceed to Gihon and Oviedo, for the purpose of ascertaining the state of efficiency of the armament in the Asturias.

On the morning of the 29th, the *Peruvian* anchored in the Bay of Gihon, one of the most exposed on the north coast of Spain: unprotected, by the formation of the land, in any direction, the whole swell of the Bay of Biscay rolls in with uninterrupted force, and renders it, particularly in northerly winds, a roadstead of great danger. The weather had been moderate for some time, and at the anchorage we found the *Iris* frigate and *Albicore* sloop-of-war.

Gihon had been for a considerable time the station of a British Consul, and, at this period, Mr. Hunter held that office. He had long resided in Spain in similar situations, and his knowledge of the country, and of the manners and customs of its inhabitants, eminently qualified him for the service. On landing, we learnt that the arrival of General Leith had been intimated, and quarters had been prepared for him in a large old mansion near the town.

There is nothing very remarkable in the appearance of Gihon. It is a tolerably extensive seaport town, but in every respect inferior to Santander; nor is the scenery in its immediate neighbourhood so bold and picturesque as that on the other parts of the Asturian coast.

The *château* we were destined to inhabit was an ancient fabric of great extent, the property of a nobleman, and bearing every appearance of neglect and rapid decay. We entered through a large and massive gateway, leading into a spacious court, surrounded by stone pillars, the capitals of which, considerably worn and defaced, were entwined with grapes and wild shrubs of various kinds; while, at their base, weeds grew in undisturbed luxuriance. In the centre of the grass-grown court was a spacious draw-well, bearing every appearance of long disuse. A handsome staircase conducted us to numerous apartments, perfectly habitable, but alike conspicuous for their great extent and dearth of furniture. Such was the first residence of a private gentleman, and at the same time a person of rank, that we had seen in Spain.

The day after our arrival at Gihon, General Miranda and a deputation from the Junta of Asturias came for the purpose of escorting the General to Oviedo, and on the following morning we proceeded to that city. Oviedo, the ancient Ovetum, and the capital of Asturias, is situated in a romantic and beautiful valley, surrounded by rich and variegated scenery. On approaching from the north, the view is grand and extremely picturesque: the lofty spire of the cathedral forms a conspicuous object; and the background of distant mountain gives a variety and importance to the scene.

Our reception at Oviedo was of the most friendly description. Nothing could exceed the cordiality with which all classes appeared to witness the arrival of British officers. All former feelings of irritation, even those universally produced by the taking of the frigates previous to a declaration of war, and the more recent but more just misfortune brought upon the country by the destruction of its fleet at Trafalgar, seemed buried in oblivion. England, and the people of Great Britain, had become the theme of their enthusiastic admiration; and instead of regarding us as the inhabitants of a nation with whom they had recently been carrying on war, they seemed to feel they had only restored the relations between the countries that had been for a period obstructed, but which they considered ought naturally ever to exist.

The members of the Provincial Junta were assembled to receive the general; and many of them, including the general-in-chief Açevedo, the Marques de Campo Segrado, the Conde Toreno, General Ponté, and the Visconde de Campo Grande, accompanied him to the Casa de Regencia. General Açevedo, an elderly man, apparently not very energetic, and extremely short-sighted, had been appointed to the command of the Asturian contingent. He was on the eve of departure for Llanes, a town upon the coast, where the new levies were to be assembled, and where he expected to be placed in command of 10,000 men.

At this period of the war, the French Army was cantoned on the Ebro. General Blake, with the army of Galicia, was at Leon, and it was supposed he would immediately advance. He was to be reinforced by General Açevedo's corps and that of the Marques de la Romana, daily expected to arrive on the north coast of Spain, after having effected its escape from the control of the French emperor.

General Blake's force was numerically considerable, but deficient in equipment; the infantry undisciplined and ill armed, and many of the regiments composed entirely of recruits, ill officered, and inefficient. He had a very small body of cavalry, and the artillery alone seemed to be in a serviceable state. This was evidently not the description of force with which a general-in-chief would be anxious to take the field against such troops as composed the armies of the enemy. But General Blake appeared to have no feeling of this kind: he went headlong to the line of operations; and the result was, as might have been expected, most disastrous.

I must here notice some of the officers employed by the British government on missions to the Spanish armies. This is rendered necessary, in consequence of the superficial, and, in many respects, undeserved remarks, published upon the subject in Lieutenant-Colonel Napier's *History of the Peninsular War*.

That author, in enumerating the officers sent to Spain, has omitted to mention persons who had other claims to confidence than those derived from "their acquaintance with the Spanish language;" an allegation evidently made in ignorance of the fact: nor is he correct in stating that "there was no concert among them, for there was no controlling power vested in any, but each did that which seemed good to him."

Of these officers, I have to mention the names of Major Lefebure of the royal engineers, afterwards killed at Matagorda; of Colonel Jones, whose services, experience, and judgment, are so well known to the army, and whose authority upon the events of the Peninsular War is at least equal to that of the gallant author himself; of Colonel Paisley, and of Colonel Birch; all of whom were under the orders of General Leith; and it may be asserted, without fear of contradiction, that, in point of zeal, intelligence, military knowledge, or sound judgment, four more distinguished persons could not have been selected from any army.

To employ officers for the purpose of obtaining information, was certainly a very natural primary measure on the part of government; nor is it probable that authentic intelligence could have been so well obtained by any other method. These officers, however much the author above mentioned has been misinformed, were active and zealous, constantly moving from one point to another, and visiting the different Spanish armies as circumstances of interest occurred in the prosecution of the war, or had reference to the general plan of operations which ought to have been adopted.

To have selected persons qualified to give unerring advice or accurate information upon the various details of continental warfare, would have been difficult in the state of practical knowledge then possessed by the British Army. Not to have viewed the Spanish insurrection with some degree of enthusiastic partiality, must have bespoken a want of those feelings upon which the successful issue of the war in a great measure depended; and it would have said little for the rational calculation of individuals who had seen, for a length of time, the Spanish monarchy a prey to misrule and to decay, had they expected to find, without regeneration or improvement, the military establishments alone effective, and armies ready to take the field, worthy of what the Spanish infantry had once been.

It is evident that this was impossible; and I can safely aver, that no such opinion of the Spanish armies was ever entertained by many of those officers whose military foresight and civil sagacity is brought forward and commented upon by the gallant author above mentioned. To read his account of the missions to the several provinces, it would appear that a more useless, inefficient, weak, meddling set of persons, never were employed to mar a great cause. There may have been an excess of zeal, there may have been some of these officers less useful or less intelligent than others; but to include the whole, with the exception of Lord William Bentinck and Major Cox, in one sweeping and unqualified, unmerited censure, appears as little worthy of history as it probably will hereafter be considered of notice.

Having ascertained the state of forwardness of the preparations made by the Junta of Asturias to arm and equip the troops destined to reinforce General Blake, General Leith, accompanied by Captains Lefebure, Jones, and Paisley, of the royal engineers, left Oviedo, and proceeded to Gihon; from whence he travelled along the shores of the Bay of Biscay to Llanes, the headquarters of General Açevedo, and from thence, by San Vicente de la Barquera and Santillaña, to Santander, where he received intelligence of the occupation of Bilbao by a division of the Gallician Army. This event occurred on the 20th, when the Marques de Portago, with the 4th division, dislodged General Monthion, who retired to Durango without attempting any serious defence.

At this period, General Blake's headquarters were at Frias. His army occupied an extended, and, from the nature of the country, a very unconnected position. The advance of his left must have been with the intention of moving his whole army in that direction; but, executed as it was, the march of one division upon Bilbao, previous to a simultaneous alteration in the position of the others, and consequently placing the troops so advanced in an isolated state, without support, and in close contact with the enemy, was one of great danger and miscalculation. Nothing could have been easier than accomplishing the destruction of the 4th division; and it is difficult to assign a satisfactory reason for the cautious and feeble attack subsequently made by the Duke of Elchingen, he being in command of a force adequate to the successful encounter of the whole Gallician Army, instead of a single division.

When the occupation of Bilbao became known at Santander, Captain Atkins, with the *Seine* and *Cossack* frigates, sailed to the eastward, and appeared off the bar, expecting that the Biscayan peasantry would rise and join the patriotic cause; but the tenure upon which the Spanish troops held possession of the town was not of a description to inspire confidence; nor did the general commanding hold out a prospect of being enabled to maintain his post, and by so doing protect the inhabitants from the consequences resulting from the return of the French Army, the reappearance of which would, of course, be attended with more serious exaction, if the population appeared in open hostility.

In consequence of some arrangements with the bishop, General Leith was prevented from immediately going to Bilbao: he therefore ordered me to proceed to that town, and in an hour after our arrival at Santander I was on my route. Having travelled all night, passed through Santoña, Castro Urdiales, Laredo, and Portugalete, I crossed the ferry at the Convent of San Nicolas, a league from Bilbao, which is from thence approached by an excellent road, leading along the banks of the river through a rich and beautiful valley.

Bilbao is a very fine town, built with great regularity, the streets spacious, well paved, and the buildings large and handsome. The environs are highly cultivated and picturesque; the town lies low, but is surrounded by great variety of ground, the neighbouring hills being wooded to their summits. There is a cheerful and active appearance about its inhabitants, and it has every advantage from its beautiful and, commercially speaking, convenient locality. The river is navigable up to the town, which has long been the most considerable mercantile place upon the north coast of the Peninsula.

The occupation of Bilbao had occasioned a considerable sensation at the French headquarters, and an important movement was the result. Marshal Ney, with his whole *corps d'armée*, broke up from Logroña, and, having rapidly marched the distance, appeared in front of Bilbao upon the 26th.

Previous to the arrival of this force, no attempt had been made by General Monthion to recover possession of the town, nor had he in any manner disturbed the quarters of the Spanish division; but the position of the armies rendered it beyond doubt that the enemy would without delay check the progress of troops already so far in advance of his right flank, and an approaching attack was consequently expected.

On the morning of the 26th, Captains Lefebure and Jones reconnoitred the roads in the direction of the enemy's troops, and returned with information of his advance. The consternation and alarm of the inhabitants increased hourly, and the town exhibited a scene of great bustle, many persons preparing to depart; anxiety and terror depicted in the countenances of some, while a sullen and determined demeanour bespoke the resolution of others to remain with their families, and submit to the exactions they had every prospect of being subjected to, more especially as the Spaniard appeared invariably to suppose that any indication of dislike to their re-appearance, or any zealous demonstration of regard for his own military countrymen or their allies, was certain of being known, appreciated, and punished by the French.

About noon, it was reported that the enemy was within a league of the place. Even the Spanish staff was roused into activity, and the same men, who less than a week previously had driven a brigade of the enemy from the town, and then sunk into a state of apathy and forgetfulness, inexcusable even at a station removed a hundred miles from the seat of hostilities, began to recover their energies; and, in justice to them, it must be admitted, that the arrangements made for resisting the attack of an overwhelming force were, if not judicious, certainly timely.

About one o'clock, the inhabitants were thrown into the greatest consternation by unfounded rumours that the enemy's cavalry had entered the town. Nothing could more strongly prove the feeling excited by the terror of that event than the scene which immediately ensued. A more perfect panic could not well be imagined. The street was instantaneously crowded by the people, who rushed past uttering the wildest screams. They were accompanied by horses, mules, cars loaded with furniture, and by cattle and sheep; and, without pausing to investigate the truth or incorrectness of the report, were flying to gain the road to Portugalete.

General Leith, accompanied by the officers of his staff, proceeded to join the Marques de Portago, who was upon an eminence to the right of the Durango road, where had been placed two pieces of cannon. Upon rising ground, to the left of the road, were posted a column of infantry and three pieces of artillery. A battalion of grenadiers occupied a height still further to the right, and another defended the bridge at the entrance of the town.

Having made this disposition of his force, the *marques* awaited the approach of the enemy now in sight, and whose *tirailleurs* were observed descending into a valley at the distance of about two miles from the Spanish position. Three columns of infantry, with a considerable body of cavalry, advanced by the Durango road. It was evident that the enemy approached with caution; no attempt was made to press the Spanish division; but officers were sent forward to reconnoitre,—a service they performed with great boldness.

The Spanish artillery tried the range of their guns against the nearest column of the enemy's troops, but without any effect. Soon after, the French cavalry manoeuvred to the left of the Spanish position. The exposed state of that flank, and the superior force already displayed, now made it prudent to retreat. The general officers present agreed upon the impossibility of maintaining their ground against the force displayed; and the cannon having been placed in front of the column, the whole retired by the road of Valmaseda, unmolested by the enemy, and arrived at that place without sustaining any loss,—a very inexplicable circumstance, and one of peculiarly good fortune; for, had a rapid attack been made, the defeat and dispersion of the fourth division, and capture of its artillery, would have been the inevitable result.

A considerable quantity of powder having been landed at Portugalete for the use of the troops and the Biscayan levies, I was ordered to proceed to that place, and endeavour to get it removed, and then cross the country to Valmaseda.

The weather, which had been fine during the earlier part of the day, had changed. Rain fell in torrents, adding to the misery of the different persons who, escaping from Bilbao, covered the whole extent of the road to Portugalete. On it were to be seen the Spanish merchant and his family toiling through the deep mud; the unattached Spanish officer, who had displayed his uniform during the absence of the enemy, but no longer appeared to consider its being worn by him as a reason for comfortable reflection; the English amateur, who had visited Bilbao full of curiosity and warlike enthusiasm, but who, unprepared for the reverse of the picture, was now to be seen struggling onwards to a place of safety, drenched with rain, lightly clad, indifferently shod, and perfectly miserable.

At Portugalete, I was informed that the powder above mentioned was at Santurse, a league distant from the former; and, without delay, proceeded to that village, where I found the launches that contained it aground, and no possible means of transport by which its removal could be effected. It became an object of considerable importance to prevent so large a quantity as 400 barrels falling into the hands of the enemy. There being every prospect of his immediately sending detachments to intercept the ammunition and supplies, in progress from the British shipping to the Gallician Army, promptitude of arrangement became more necessary. To leave the powder in charge of the Spanish guard appeared to ensure its being captured.

When considering what was most advisable in this emergency, I observed in the crowd a Spaniard of the name of Felix Blanco, an officer who had accompanied the general to Bilbao, and whose manly appearance and fierce sombrero gave hopes that he would have led into contact with the French, but whom, I regret to state, I had passed among the fugitives. Whether it was to be attributed to his superior powers of pedestrianism, or to his early departure, I cannot decide; certain it is, he was very near the head of the column.

Although this hero, who displayed on his hat a very splendid riband, on which was inscribed "*Vencir o morir por Fernando VII.*," was not exactly the person to be selected for the defence of a post; still, taking into consideration the dislike he appeared to entertain to the sight of anything in the shape of an enemy, I considered him a person who would certainly use every exertion to expedite departure previous to his arrival; and as the launches afforded him the means of escape, as well as a plausible motive for again appearing in his native town, without having carried into effect the martial intentions with which he had left it, I felt convinced that he would strain every nerve to execute this important service.

After instructing Don Felix to proceed to sea as soon as the state of the tide made it practicable, I left Santurse, and, at three o'clock in the morning, passed to the right of the French corps which had bivouacked in advance of Bilbao. I entered the village of Valmaseda, and again joined the Marques de Portage's division, the soldiers of which were apparently as unconcerned as if no enemy was near. They were straggling about the streets, which were crowded, and blazing in all directions with the fires that had been kindled. Notwithstanding the inclemency of the weather, groups of military and peasants were to be seen; the former recounting the events, and the latter listening to the adventures, of the preceding day.

It continued to rain without intermission, and nothing could be more comfortless and wretched than the situation of the troops; still there was an uncomplaining appearance, that bespoke them well calculated to endure hard- ship and privation. No murmur of dissatisfaction escaped from the soldier, either at the exposed state of his quarters or the inclemency of the weather. He appeared to be cheerful and resigned; and, smoking his cigar, seemed in the midst of a scene which custom or nature had rendered familiar.

General Leith, accompanied by Captains Jones and Doyle, had proceeded to Frias, where he expected to find General Blake. I remained at Valmaseda on the 27th; and very early the following morning was on the road to Urantia. The rain, which had been incessant during the former day and night, continued to fall, and increased the difficulties of a bad mountain-road.

The road from Urantia towards Frias leaves the village of Angulo to the left, near to which place it ascends to the *plateau* of Old Castille by a precipitous and singularly conducted track, called the *Peña de Angulo*. The rocky heights rise perpendicularly from the plain, and the only route by which they can be ascended is, in most places, cut from the solid rock. The causeway, winding up its face, and approaching the summit, is extremely steep, and the turns in it sharp and narrow. A more dangerous road cannot well be conceived, no obstruction being in any part opposed to the consequences of a slight deviation from the beaten track.

Nothing can exceed the picturesque beauty of the scenery at this point. The country is wooded in the most luxuriant manner; and from the rocky heights, mountain torrents fall in all directions. But, having reached the summit of the pass, the aspect of the country is immediately altered; the varied and luxuriant valleys of Biscay are exchanged for the bleak plains of Castille.

At a league and a half in advance is the village of Quincoçes, which had become the headquarters of the Gallician Army. General Leith, having taken another route, had gone on to Frias; and I was the first person General Blake had seen who had been present with his fourth division upon the 26th. He appeared to have no certain information as to the occurrences upon his left, and exhibited an unpardonable degree of ignorance in a general-in-chief, more particularly as there was nothing to obstruct his communication with the division, and as an important movement had taken place two days previous, at a distance of not above forty miles.

Rumours of a very exaggerated nature had reached him concerning the retreat of the Marques de Portago from Bilbao; but no effort appeared to have been made to ascertain their foundation; no official report of any description had been received, and a division of his army might have been annihilated, forty-eight hours previously, without his having the slightest notion of the fact. Little as I knew of military arrangements, and the conduct of armies, this was to me an inexplicable circumstance, and augured ill for the future success or well-directed combination of the army of the left.

General Blake, the descendant of an Irish family, had, previous to the Revolution, been a colonel of infantry in the Spanish Army, from which rank he at once rose to the command in chief; and, although under the orders of General Cuesta at the battle of Rio Seco, he was at the head of a separate army, and, upon the removal of that general, held the supreme command in the north of Spain. He appeared at this period to be about fifty years of age, soldierlike in his person and address, with a manner that indicated firmness and resolution.

The first regiment I met at Quincoçes was one of Gallician grenadiers, a very fine body of men, better clothed and appointed than any of the Spanish troops I had previously seen. Two of the officers of this corps invited me to partake of their quarters, which I most readily acceded to; for, crowded as the village was, there appeared a slight prospect of getting cover of any description, and the rain continued as incessant as ever.

The following morning presented no improvement in the state of the weather. The wind blew loud and cold as it swept across the dreary plain upon which Quincoçes is situated, which, from its altitude and want of shelter, appeared to combine every requisite for being one of the coldest inhabited spots in Spain. In the evening, General Leith arrived, and took up his quarters in the wretched village of Lastres de la Torre, where also was the second in command of the army, General Cahigal.

It had been asserted, that in his intercourse with the British officers who previously visited him, General Blake displayed a reserve and dislike, and that he appeared to have no cordiality of feeling towards our countrymen; but whether it was that he considered General Leith possessed of additional means for supplying him with money and with arms, or whether the former impression had been ill-founded, I cannot determine; certain it is, he exhibited no appearance of jealousy at the presence of the general. He was very communicative; all their interviews passed without any difference occurring; and they parted with every appearance of cordiality.

On the morning of the 1st of October, Captains Birch and Carrol left Lastres, on their route to General Cuesta's army, and General Leith set out for Santander.

After leaving Lastres de la Torre, the road takes nearly a northerly direction, and descends gradually the whole way to Villasanta, a small village surrounded by wood. In it we found a hospitable friar of the convent of Oña, in whose house the general took up his quarters for the night. It formed a contrast to those we had lately inhabited, being arranged in the most perfect manner, according to Spanish ideas of comfort. Instead of unglazed windows, the friar, with a proper estimate of the cold situation in which his habitation was placed, had his house well supplied with glass, and double latticed, his rooms matted, and his *braseros* plentifully supplied with charcoal.

The following day, having passed through Laredo, crowded with fugitives from Bilbao, whose apprehensions had carried them thus far from the enemy, we crossed the ferry at Santoña, and arrived at Santander, where everything appeared in the same quiescent state as formerly. The return of the general had been precipitated by the receipt of information, that the troops of the Marques de Romania would be landed at Santander. The circumstances attending the escape of this force from the Island of Rugen are so well known, that it is unnecessary here to recapitulate them.

On the morning of the 8th, the *Defiance*, seventy-four guns, convoying a fleet of transports, with part of the division from the north, appeared in sight. The delight of the inhabitants, when made acquainted with this circumstance, was unbounded. They rushed in crowds to the quay, and expressed the greatest anxiety for the approach of the shipping.

As it was probable that Captain Hotham would immediately leave the coast, after seeing his convoy safe into harbour, I was ordered to proceed on board the *Defiance*, and communicate with that officer; but after setting over the bar, the boat encountered so heavy a sea, and it blew so hard, that the Spanish crew declined proceeding; and, without regret, I assented to their returning, more especially as the ship was at such a distance as to render my getting near her at all a very improbable circumstance.

Towards evening the wind moderated, the transports entered the harbour; and soon after the Conde de San Roman, Brigadier-General Caro, with some of the superior officers, landed, and communicated with General Leith.

The Marques de la Romana had gone to London, and his division was under the temporary command of Brigadier-General the Conde de San Roman, colonel of the regiment of Princessa. It consisted of four very strong regiments of infantry, a detachment of artillery, two regiments of dragoons, and two of hussars.

The regiments of Princessa and Zamora formed, previous to the Revolution, a portion of the regular infantry of the Spanish Army. They were clothed in white, and extremely well appointed, with the exception of their arms, which were old and inefficient. The two other infantry regiments bore the names of Balbastro and Valencia, and were equipped as light troops. The heavy cavalry of the division comprised the regiments Del Rey and Infante, and the hussar regiments were those of Villaviciosa and Almanza, clothed in green, and very brilliant in appearance. Unfortunately, when escaping, these regiments had, from necessity, abandoned their horses. This rendered them consequently inefficient, and incapable of taking a part in the operations of the Gallician Army, with which they were destined to act, and to which, from its deficiency in cavalry, they would otherwise have been a most useful reinforcement.

The journey of the Marques de la Romana to London, at this juncture, was an unfortunate circumstance; for, had he accompanied his division to Santander, and at once assumed the command of the army of the left, previous to any very important movement taking place, by superseding General Blake, he might have averted the fatal consequences, and counteracted the errors which that general subsequently committed. Whether the *marques* would have commanded with more science or greater judgment cannot now be determined; but he possessed one advantage of no slight importance in the struggle then going forward. It consisted in having the confidence not only of the troops, but of the people. Long accustomed to consider his name with respect, the Spanish population never doubted either his capacity, or the sincerity of his intentions, in opposing the French domination; and his recent conduct in bringing back some of the best regiments of the army to assist in fighting the battles of their country, confirmed the previously entertained favourable opinion.

On the other hand, General Blake had recently risen to command, was untried as a general, and did not possess the confidence of a majority of his countrymen in the north of Spain. Thus circumstanced, and being aware how much the war was one of prejudice and popular opinion, he might consider himself compelled to advance, and fight, when his army was not in a state to warrant the assumption of an offensive attitude; whereas, under similar circumstances, Romana might with impunity have taken the responsibility either of inactivity, or of retreat.

Upon the 12th, a *Te Deum* was performed by the Bishop of Santander, in commemoration of the arrival of the troops; at which ceremony were present, the British officers then at Santander, the Conde de Villa Neuva, and most of the officers of the Marques de la Romana's division. The cathedral was crowded, and the scene grand and impressive.

The situation of affairs in the Peninsula at this moment appeared to the vain, confiding, and credulous Spaniard, prosperous in the extreme; and it was ludicrous to hear the only speculation advanced by some, and those otherwise intelligent people,—namely, whether the French Army would be permitted to escape? Perfect and uninterrupted success appeared to them certain; and infallibility was considered the attendant of their unorganised, and ill-appointed armies. To a dispassionate observer, there was every prospect of a very different result, and every indication of the probability of those disasters, which are in a great degree to be attributed to the unfounded confidence above noticed, added to the circumstance of the Spanish armies' manoeuvring in direct opposition to every sound principle of military tactic.

The French Army, although reduced in numbers, was composed of veteran soldiers, perfectly equipped, long accustomed to service, complete in every arm, and commanded by experienced and distinguished officers. Concentrated in a plentiful country, having its communications with France open and uninterrupted, it was cantoned so as to ensure the assembling of a large force upon any point where its assailants appeared to press. From 45,000 to 50,000 men were under arms, exclusive of the garrisons; and, by intercepted intelligence, it became known, that reinforcements to the amount of 66,000 infantry, and 8000 cavalry, would join its ranks on or before the 10th of November. These troops, part of the grand army from Germany, had traversed France with great rapidity; and the Emperor Napoleon himself was on the route for Spain.

If ever practicable to have struck a decisive blow against the French Army previous to its being reinforced, the movement of Marshal Ney from Logroña to Bilbao, afforded the opportunity. Had the different Spanish armies then simultaneously moved, and attacked the enemy, weakened by the absence of the corps forming his centre, a serious impression might have been made. General Blake, by a rapid movement to his right, could, without difficulty, have co-operated in a joint attack; while the third and fourth divisions of the Gallician Army might either have followed his line of march, or remained in observation of the Duke of Elchingen's corps at Bilbao.

But nothing so well timed or rational was attempted by the Spanish generals. Their armies were either stationary or moved slowly, and only became active when the enemy was in such force as to render all their efforts perfectly unavailing. To the other errors committed by the Spaniards in the conduct of the war, is to be added the loss of valuable time; nor can the government of Great Britain be exempted from merited censure in that particular.

Following up the retreat of Joseph Bonaparte from Madrid, and taking advantage of the fortunate result of Castaños's campaign in Andalusia, before the impression thereby created had ceased to be important, and before Napoleon had it in his power to strengthen his armies in the Peninsula, was the sound and rational policy of the Spanish Government and its powerful ally. Instead of adopting such immediate and vigorous measures, they permitted the armies to remain inactive, not improving in discipline, and little in equipment, until the enemy was sufficiently strengthened to render all attack abortive. Then, indeed, the Spanish authorities shewed a decided inclination to precipitate their troops into contact with prepared and powerful adversaries; and the consequences became as disastrous as the result was certain. As to the British government, if an army was to be sent into Spain as an auxiliary force, essentially to benefit the cause, it ought to have been concentrated, and advanced to the line of operations, by the 1st of October.

General Blake had moved his headquarters from Quincoçes to Valmaseda, and from thence, upon the 12th, advanced to occupy Bilbao with three divisions of his army. Marshal Ney had previously returned to the Ebro, leaving General Merlin, with 8000 men, in Bilbao; but, upon the advance of the Spanish divisions, being greatly outnumbered, he evacuated it, and retired to Zornosa. The Marques de la Romana's division continued inactive at Santander, notwithstanding its having been supplied with British arms, and perfectly equipped for the field.

On the morning of the 14th October, the troops were drawn up on the Plaza de San Francisco. It was the first time that the division had assembled under arms since landing, and its appearance was soldierlike and effective. Being the birthday of Ferdinand the VIIth, the air resounded with expressions of loyalty; and the enthusiastic cheering of the great crowd assembled, left no doubt as to the sincerity of feeling in the cause. Historians may endeavour to misrepresent the real feeling of the inhabitants of the Peninsula, and may accuse those officers who possessed other means of judging than could be obtained by marching through the country with their regiments, of being blinded by flattery and attention; but the pertinacity with which the Spanish people combated misfortune, and the unconquerable resolution with which they endured misrule,—the patient sufferance with which they bore years of constant distress, and supported circumstances of unceasing exaction, will prove to future times that there was truth in their professions, and sincerity in the cordiality of their hatred to the French.

General Blake remained inactive at Bilbao from the 12th to the 24th of October, upon which day he advanced for the purpose of attacking the enemy at Zornosa. His previous movements had been directed to the left; and it was evidently his intention to advance still further on that flank, and thereby turn the right of the French Army. In prosecution of this object, the division from the north would have been a most important reinforcement; and it might have been either transported to Bilbao, or marched to that place previous to the movement against Zornosa; but, instead of that plan being adopted, upon the very day the Gallician Army advanced towards Durango, Romana's division was marching upon Reynosa, completely in rear of the line of operations, and further removed from a junction with the main body of the army than it had been at Santander.

It was three o'clock on the evening of the 24th before General Blake attacked the enemy at Zornosa, and then very feebly. The French supported a fire of light troops in front of the town until dark, and the Spaniards, although greatly superior in force, made no impression. During the night, General Merlin placed his troops in position on the road to Durango, and the following day was passed in skirmishing, without any serious affair taking place.

During these operations, the army from Germany had reached the Spanish frontier, and reinforcements to a great extent had joined the ranks of the enemy. If the advance of General Blake under former circumstances was rash and dangerous, it now amounted to absolute madness. It was rushing to inevitable destruction; and broken, disheartened, and dispersed as his army soon became, it is a reflection upon the tactic and the energy of the enemy that any portion of it was suffered to escape. He could not be in ignorance that columns of the grand army covered the route from Bayonne to Vittoria, and that, instead of manoeuvring to surround a weakened and dispirited force, he had to encounter the best troops on the continent of Europe, soon to be again commanded in person by the master-spirit of the age. Even after the advance to Zornosa, the Spanish general might have changed his line of operations with safety and effect. Instead of following- General Merlin, had he retired upon the evening of the 25th to Bilbao, and from thence, by Valmaseda, to the Ebro, he might have assembled his army, and either formed a junction with other portions of the Spanish force, or continued on the defensive until circumstances changed, or events decided that some chance of success might attend his operations.

In direct opposition to any line of conduct; either so prudent or judicious as this would have been, General Blake continued to persevere in the movement he had commenced; and, as if aware of his own weakness and inability to make an impression even against one division of the French Army, he continued inactive from the 25th to the 31st,—thereby giving Marshal the Duke of Dantzic time to assemble a force at Durango of above 20,000 men, with which, on the morning of the latter day, he attacked the Spaniards, overthrew them without the slightest difficulty, and drove them back upon Bilbao. The Spaniard continued his retreat, and arrived at Nava, upon the River Salcedon. Marshal Lefebvre terminated the pursuit at Guenes; and, having left a division of his corps at that place, he retired with the main body to Bilbao. Napoleon had not yet assumed the personal command in Spain; a circumstance that accounts for the delay which occurred in completing the destruction of General Blake's army.

The Marques de la Romana not having arrived at Santander, and it being possible he might have landed at Coruña, and proceeded direct to the capital, I was ordered to Madrid; and at nine o'clock on the evening of the 29th October was on the road to Reynosa with dispatches for that general, for Mr. Frere, and for Lord William Bentinck. After having passed through Reynosa, Burgos, and Lerma, I arrived at Aranda de Duero. The route from Reynosa to Aranda is uninteresting in point of scenery; the country, in many places, flat, bare, and but indifferently cultivated. The olive, which is a dull, unpicturesque tree, is almost the only one that interrupts the sameness that characterises the plains of Old Castille.

The Duero runs close to the town of Aranda, and is there crossed by a very handsome bridge, upon the great road to Madrid, which continues through a plain to the post station of Onrubia, from thence to Fresnillo de la Fuente and Castillejo.

In the evening I approached the Somasierra, and entered the pass over the celebrated barrier of the Castilles. It was midnight before I ascended the mountain, which was covered with snow to a considerable depth, that had recently fallen. The wind blew loud, and the cold was extreme. The road winds through ravines for a considerable distance, and, gradually ascending, it is neither very steep nor ill conducted.

The village of Somasierra is situated high on the mountain. The houses, when I passed, were covered with snow to a degree almost rendering them imperceptible. Where the village is situated, the hill descends precipitously to the west of the road; and upon this slope, probably for purposes of shelter, the houses are built. Snowed up as the whole scene at this time was, the low and insignificant town, with its flat roofs, appeared, from the height above, to be but a part of the mountain side. Having crossed the *sierra*, the route to Madrid passes through a country little varied in scenery, and neither picturesque nor luxuriantly cultivated. The villages, as the road approaches the capital, improve in appearance and extent; but no alteration in the aspect of the country, either in improved cultivation or ornamental scenery, in-

MADRID

dicates the neighbourhood of a great city.

At the distance of a league from Madrid, to the left of the road, is Chamartin, the residence of the Duque del Infantado. It is situated in a wood, very limited in extent; nor are the grounds about it either varied or beautiful. The house resembles, in size and appearance, an English gentleman's residence of the second or third class; and is consequently not on such a scale of *grandeur* as it might be supposed would have satisfied the luxury and magnificence of the great family of Infantado.

Madrid is so situated as not to be seen at a great distance when approached from the Alcobendas road, in consequence of the plain which extends from that village having a gradual ascent; and it is only upon gaining the summit, at the distance of about half a league, that the domes and spires of the capital become visible. No villas, rows of trees, fountains, public walks, or well-frequented footpaths, extend in this direction. The plain is sterile and uncultivated; nor is it until close under the walls of the city that the slightest attempt at ornamental shade has ever been attempted. Then, indeed, the scene is changed; and after passing the amphitheatre for the bullfights, on the right, and the Prado on the left, the traveller arrives at the splendid Puerta de Alcala, and enters the spacious and elegant street of that name.

Madrid differs from most other towns of equal magnitude. It has no suburb; and the moment the wall is passed, the palaces of the court appear in all directions. As a commercial city, it never could be of importance. The inland situation, and absence of any navigable river, rendered that impossible. The inhabitants, consequently, in its days of prosperity, consisted of the court, of its followers, and of artisans and tradesmen to supply them with the necessaries and the luxuries of life.

From a census of the population, taken by order of Carlos IV. in 1797, it contained at that period 167,607 inhabitants, being an increase of 20,064 souls in the course often years; the census of 1787 making the number within its walls only 147,543. Estimating the increase at the same ratio for the subsequent ten years, it would, in 1807, have contained nearly 188,000 people. Since then the population has decreased; consequently, the modern capital of Spain never contained 200,000 inhabitants. The town is about a mile and three quarters in length, and a mile and half broad; its greatest extent being from the Puerta de los Embaxadores to the northernmost gate, and its narrowest part from the Puerta de Alcala to the Palacio Nuevo. Madrid is encircled by a wall, and domineered by a height, upon which the Retiro is placed, and which is only separated from the town by the southern part of the Prado, or great public walk.

The Prado, shaded by trees, planted in rows, and of great beauty and magnitude, is also embellished by fountains. It is a noble public walk, to which, in the evening, a great portion of the population resort, sometimes crowding it to excess. At other periods of the day, it has rather a deserted appearance; but it is at all times a great ornament to the city.

Of all the gates of Madrid, the "Puerta de Alcala," built during the reign of Carlos III., is the finest. It is a noble entrance to a town, and forms one of the most distinguished ornaments of the Spanish capital. The Puerta de San Vicente, close to the Manzanares, is the entrance nearest to the Palacio Nuevo. It is also a handsome gateway, and was erected in the same reign.

The Alcazar, or Royal Palace, is supposed to have been originally founded by Alphonso VI., the fifty-ninth Catholic king of Spain, and to have been destroyed by an earthquake. Henry II. rebuilt it; and the fourth king of that name enlarged and adorned it.

The Emperor Charles V., the greatest name in Spanish history, who was partial to Madrid, from having experienced the salutary effects produced by its climate, the quality of the water, and purity of the air, determined, in the year 1537, to remodel and enlarge the palace,—a work which was in a progressive state when he resigned the crown to his son, Philip II., giving him, at the same time, strict injunctions to have it completed. Philip III. and Philip IV. contributed to its improvement. The most eminent architects were employed; and in adorning the interior, the most celebrated painters and artisans of the age found scope for their varied talent. In the reign of Carlos II., the palace continued to receive further embellishment; but this perfected work, the result of the united exertions of so many ages and so many kings, of so much ingenuity, and such endless expense, became the victim of accident, and was consumed by fire in the year 1734.

Philip V. resolved to restore the palace on a scale of magnificence beyond that of any similar class of building in Europe. He consequently ordered a model to be submitted to his approbation by an architect of the name of Juvarra, who had rendered himself celebrated in Italy, particularly at Turin, by the splendour of the edifices there erected in conformity to his designs. Under Juvarra's auspices a model was framed, and approved of, which is still in existence. It was constructed to combine every quality of extent and decoration calculated to satisfy the intentions of the king, and at the same time suited to the situation upon which the palace was to be erected, it being the determination of Philip to place the Palacio Nuevo exactly upon the site of the Alcazar.

While the preliminary arrangements were yet incomplete, the architect died, and his pupil, Saqueti, was employed to carry the great work he had projected into effect. After considerably altering Juvarra's plan, and rendering it, as he considered, better calculated for the situation, Philip gave his final approval to the design; and upon the 7th April, 1737, the work commenced.

The four fronts of the Palacio Nuevo extend each 470 feet, and the height of the building, from the base to the cornice, is 100 feet. It is built of white Colmenar stone, which, preserving its purity of appearance, gives to the building a light and brilliant effect. The columns and pilasters are of the Doric and Ionic orders. The height of the palace is at all points the same, nor is any portion of the roof perceptible. The cornice is surmounted by a balustrade, with pedestals at intervals. Upon these were once placed statues of the kings of Spain, from Ataulfo to Ferdinand VI.; but having been removed, urns were substituted, and the royal arms, carved in stone, decorate the eastern entrance. In the interior of the great court were statues of the Emperors Trajan, Adrian, Theodosius, and Honorius; but it appears that some enemy to statuary had once held predominant influence at the Spanish court, for these have also been removed, and pillars of marble occupy their sites.

There are six principal entrances to the edifice, five of which are on the south and one on the eastern front. The inner court is 140 feet square, with an open portico that surrounds it, and forms the support of a gallery, from whence communicate the apartments of the royal family and the rooms of state. The interior decorations of the palace are superb; and it contains a very fine collection of pictures by the most eminent masters of the Italian, Spanish, Dutch, and Flemish schools.

The fresco painting throughout the palace is very finely executed; and some of the ceilings by Mengs are considered as the *chefs-d'œuvre* of that master. Of these, the apotheosis of Hercules and of Trajan are very splendidly designed. Of the numerous and valuable pictures, the portraits by Velasquez form a conspicuous and brilliant portion.

The Conde Duque d'Olivarez, by that master, is one of his most spirited and grandest pictures. He has there given life and action to a very heavy class of horse, and seated the favourite minister upon his back with peculiar firmness and grace. Philip III., Philip IV., and their queens, also by the chief of the Madrid school of Spanish painters, are fine pictures; as, indeed, are all those from the hand of Velasquez, who, for elegance of design, taste in his compositions, brilliancy in colouring, and all the higher requisites of the art, has seldom been equalled, and never surpassed. Titian and Vandyke can alone be compared to him as portrait painters; and his historical pictures are even more celebrated. Mengs considered his great picture of General Pescara receiving the keys of a Flemish fortress, as the *chef-d'œuvre* of Velasquez.

The picture by Titian of the Emperor Charles V. is worthy of particular notice. It is a noble portrait. That of Philip II., and his infant son, is a grand composition. In it the king is represented as holding up his son to fame, personated by an allegorical figure descending, in the act of presenting a palm branch and a crown. In a scroll, are the words "*Majora tibi;*" and the signature of the painter is "*Titianus vicelius equis Cæsaris fecit.*"

The martyrdom of San Lorenzo, by Luco Giordano—Susanna and the Elders, by Paul Veronese—the martyrdom of St. Bartholomew, by Spagnoletto—the descent from the Cross, by Mengs—Ulysses discovering himself to Achilles at the court of Licomedes—Judith with the head of Holofernes, by Tintoretto—and two children, by Guido Rheni, are all fine specimens of the masters. The collection is also rich in the works of Vandyke, Tiepolo, Rafaelle, Bernino, Coreggio, Brughel, Wouvermans, Murillo, Leonardo da Vinci, Nicolas Poussin, Marati, Albert Durer, Andrea Sachi, Teniers, Annibal Caracci, and Andrea del Sarto.

The model, by Don Philip Juvarra, is preserved in the Royal Armoury, an extensive building, situated at the eastern side of the place on which the Palacio Nuevo stands. Had the design been carried into full effect, the palace would have been unequalled in grandeur and extent.

The Manzanares is a very inconsiderable stream, but its banks are beautifully wooded. It was the frequent pastime of the dull court of Carlos IV. to pass in the evening through the gate of San Vicente, from whence the line of carriages, preceded by those of the royal family, drove at a slow pace along the shaded road upon the river side towards the bridge of Toledo, and afterwards returned to the palace by the route they had previously taken.

The Prado is situated at the lower end of the Calle Alcala. At its southern extremity is the Puerta de Atocha, and at the other the palace of Bueno Vista, built by the Duchess of Alba, and by her sold to the Prince of Peace. The Calle Alcala is much the finest street in Madrid, varying in width, and having a considerable ascent. The western extremity is not visible from the Alcala gate; but it extends to the Puerta del Sol, where the Calle Mayor commences, and, running nearly in a direct line, intersects the town diagonally at its narrowest point.

The residences of the nobility are, in general, very splendid, and well calculated to contain the great number of retainers and domestics that, previous to the Revolution, appertained to the establishments of many of the grandees. It is stated that the Duque de Medina Celi formerly had upwards of eight hundred persons either belonging to his household, or supported exclusively by his munificence. Representative of the first family in Spain, he was also the richest of all the grandees, having a revenue of fifteen millions of *reals*.

The houses of the Prince of Peace, of the Duques de Osuna, Infantado, Hijar, Lerida, and Frias, of the Marquesses de Sant Jago, Villafranca, and Santa Crux, of the Condes Altamira, Rivella Gigeda, and Fernan Nuñez, are the most remarkable private edifices in Madrid.

The Casa del Campo, situated upon the opposite bank of the Manzanares, is not, either from the size of the building, its interior decoration, or the beauty of the park in which it is placed, worthy of notice. It was, however, a favourite residence of Carlos IV., who, like other members of the Bourbon family, was an enthusiastic sportsman. The bronze equestrian statue of Philip III., by Bologna, in the gardens of this hunting seat, is much and justly admired. The only other statues of any celebrity at Madrid, are those of Philip IV. and of the Emperor Charles V., in the gardens of the Retire.

The Royal Academy of San Fernando, or Cabinet of Natural History, is situated on the highest part of the Calle Alcala, and was originally intended to comprise schools for painting, sculpture, and architecture, with a repository for specimens of the natural history of the world. The building is not imposing in its appearance. It possesses very little external ornament; and although one of the most modern, it is the least conspicuous, of any public edifice in Madrid. The interior is well adapted for the purposes intended. The lower story contains the schools. The gallery, with casts from the ancient statues, is spacious and handsome: it is completely filled with them, arranged in perfect order, and so numerous as to produce a grand effect.

In the picture gallery is the celebrated Titian Venus, considered one of the finest works of that master. The Ascension, by Rafaelle, the Virgin, the Judgment of Paris, the Susanna and the Elders, by Rubens, are amongst the genuine pictures of this collection. There are also many copies after the great masters.

The cabinet of natural history contains a very extensive collection of fossils, ores, anatomical figures, animals, birds, and fishes, apparently well arranged, and in perfect preservation: in it is also a great variety of Jewish, Grecian, Moorish, and Roman vases; in addition to which are specimens of all the richest and rarest jewels, set in different forms, and studded, as ornaments, on the most beautifully wrought vases and goblets. This collection is, upon particular days, thrown open to the inspection of the whole population; and when I visited it, the rooms were crowded with Spanish soldiery, and persons in the lower ranks of society.

The Opera House, called Los Caños del Peral, is small, and not calculated for any great display of spectacle, but well adapted for music. Previous to the Revolution it was a fashionable place of resort, and possessed the attraction of the most celebrated singers in Europe.

The Spanish theatres Del Principe and De la Crux are named from the streets in which they are situated: both are spacious, and well adapted for representation. The Principe is the most modern, and is, in some respects, superior to the other. These are the only theatres of Madrid, and they are apparently sufficient to accommodate the portion of the public having a taste for histrionic display. Popular pieces, alluding to the various scenes which had occurred since the commencement of the war, were exhibited; but even these failed to produce crowded houses, although nothing could be more enthusiastic than the expressions of delight with which the auditory beheld the Siege of Valencia portrayed, or the applause that accompanied the appearance of a most outrageous representation of the union between Great Britain and Spain, depicted by a flaringly coloured transparency, in which figured his Majesty George the Third and the amiable Fernando Septimo, locked in a close embrace!

In pursuance of the object with which I had visited Madrid, after having ascertained that Mr. Frere, the British Minister, had not yet arrived, I proceeded to the house of the Duchess of Osuna, and delivered the despatches to Lord William Bentinck. His Lordship questioned me very particularly upon the state of affairs in the north; and, regarding the strength and position of the French Army, it was quite evident that the Spanish Government either had not the means of obtaining accurate information from the immediate scene of action, or, having become possessed of it, did not impart what they knew to the confidential and intelligent person then acting for the British government. Lord William Bentinck knew with certainty nothing as to the real state of the war on the Ebro, nor had he been made acquainted either with the force of the enemy, or of the Spanish armies, now in progress to become the assailants, and who were advancing with misguided confidence to certain destruction.

On the evening of the 7th, Mr. Frere arrived. He directed me to remain until after his first interview with the Central Junta, then at Arunjuez, where he proposed going the following day. Numerous reports occupied the public attention during the short period of my residence in Madrid, and daily assemblages of the people took place at the Puerta del Sol to discuss the popular topics of the day, and to criticise with unsparing seventy the conduct of the generals in command,—particularly Castaños, who was supposed by the mobility to have exhibited either supineness or treason; they *wisely calculating* that the person who had gained the battle of Baylen, and occasioned the surrender of the army of Dupont, could, without hesitation or difficulty, have driven the main body of the enemy across the Pyrenees, or led them captive to Madrid!

Tolerably accurate information at last reached the capital as to the arrival of the grand army in Spain, and reports were circulated that the enemy had advanced to Burgos; but no incidental particulars were either known or fabricated. The quiet and security that had for a short period blinded the inhabitants of Madrid was destined soon to give place to other scenes; and from the 10th November disastrous events followed each other in rapid succession, until confidence became annihilated, and all ranks awakened to a sense of the real situation of affairs, and to see through the false data upon which a partial success had induced the Spanish government to proceed.

From the information now received by Lord William Bentinck, it became very problematical whether I should be enabled again to join General Leith at Santander; but having received his lordship's instructions to proceed to the north, and Mr. Frere having given me charge of his despatches for England, I left Madrid upon the morning of the 10th, and, having posted all night, arrived at noon the following day at Aranda de Duero, where I met with convincing proofs of the French Army having resumed the offensive. The town was crowded with

Spanish soldiery; and I soon ascertained that the army of Estremadura, the headquarters of which were now in Aranda, had been defeated near to Burgos on the preceding day.

The Conde de Belvedere, having received intelligence of the enemy's advance, assembled the main body of his army at the village of Gamonal, and sent forward the Mariscal de Campo Henestrosa, with a column of infantry, cavalry, and artillery, to Villa Fria. Henestrosa soon came in contact with the light cavalry of the French Army, and beat them back; but, with true Spanish confidence, instead of ascertaining the. real nature of the attack, or the force brought against him, he followed up what he considered an advantage gained, and before he was aware, had become committed with a greatly superior body, by which he was forced back upon the army posted at Gamonal.

The Walloon and Spanish guards fought for some time with considerable determination and coolness, but the arrival of the Duke of Istria with the cavalry, put a period to the action. The Spanish cavalry did not await the issue of a charge; but, upon being approached by that of the enemy, turned and fled in all directions, leaving the flanks of the army completely unprotected. Even with well-disciplined and experienced infantry, this would have been a serious position of affairs; but with the class of troops forming the Estremaduran army, the effect was instantaneous and conclusive; the whole gave way, the French entering Burgos *pêle-mêle* with the fugitives.

As is invariably the case with undisciplined troops, the Spaniards entertained an overstrained impression of the resistless effect of an attack of cavalry. A kind of panic always attended the appearance of that description of force, nor did they overcome the feeling during the course of the Peninsular War. It had subsequently fatal results in more than one action, where the conduct of the infantry was otherwise steady, and such as for a time to balance success even with the imperial troops themselves.

The Emperor Napoleon had from Vittoria directed the movement executed by Marshal Soult with the second corps. The imperial headquarters arrived at Briviesca on the evening of the 9th, and a night march from that place brought the Duke of Dalmatia in contact with the Spaniards on the morning of the 10th, as above stated.

Napoleon with his guards followed the movement of the second *corps d'armée*, at the same time having ordered forward the Duke of Istria with an overwhelming force of heavy cavalry to complete the impression he did not doubt would be made by Marshal Soult. The

Spaniards suffered very severely in the action, and their broken infantry continued to be sabred without intermission through the city of Burgos, now deserted by its inhabitants, and given up to plunder.

On the 8th, Burgos had contained a population following their different avocations in apparent security; it was also crowded with Spanish troops: everything appeared cheerful, and calculated to inspire confidence. Upon the 10th it was deserted, and occupied solely by the dead bodies of its countrymen, while the rush of fugitives, and the crash of pursuing cavalry, gave at intervals a dreadful variety to the scene, rendered more awful by the incessant fire of artillery, and the noises produced by the work of pillage, which had commenced in all directions. The Conde de Belvedere, upon ascertaining the total defeat of the corps under Henestrosa's command, fell back with precipitation, and continued his retrograde movement until he reached Aranda, on the morning of the 11th, having then retired sixty miles from the field of battle.

Nothing could exceed the confusion and bustle which attended the arrival of this disorganised and tumultuous host. The streets became crowded with the soldiery; horsemen were to be seen passing in all directions; strings of mules, carrying off families with their effects; peasants anxiously listening to details of what had, and what probably would, occur; and all order or discipline apparently having received a fatal shock from the events of the preceding day.

The square or *plaça*, in which the Conde de Belvedere was quartered, I found occupied by a crowd, evidently in a state of great excitement. This was occasioned by the detection of a Spaniard, said to be employed as a spy, and who had been taken in the act of procuring information. The crowd was so dense, that to penetrate into the square was impracticable; I, therefore, determined patiently to await the result. The culprit had been conveyed to the part of the *plaça* fronting the general's quarter, and soon after, some officers, one of whom was the Conde himself, appeared at a balcony, and addressed the populace.

The noise and incessant clamour from beneath, prevented his being heard at any distance; but I was informed his address was directed with a request to the enraged multitude that they would spare the life of the offender until he might be regularly tried and punished. This temperate appeal appeared not to have the slightest effect; on the contrary, greater agitation seemed to prevail, and when looking with anxiety for the finale of this singular scene, without any indication of instantaneous action, or any alteration in the position of the people, and while the *conde* and his staff were still in the balcony, I perceived the ponderous swords of some Spanish dragoons hacking at what it could not for a moment be doubted was the person of the unfortunate spy. There was no shriek, no sound of lamentation heard; the deed was done; the Conde and his officers entered the window from whence they had appeared, and the crowd gradually and quietly dispersed.

The Conde de Belvedere, a very young man, perfectly unaccustomed to command, had been left in charge of the Estremaduran army at this most critical moment, a circumstance in unison with the other arrangements of the Spanish government, and by which a general, in whom no confidence could be placed, was permitted to hold the temporary command of an army critically situated at one of the most important periods of the war.

Probably no talent or science could have obstructed the advance of the French Army; but it appears most inexcusable to have exposed this body of troops, particularly upon the great route to the capital, without its being conducted by an officer capable of manoeuvring under such circumstances; for it is evident, upon every rational military principle, that the Estremaduran army ought not to have been committed at Burgos. Nothing was to be gained by an action, even if success, in the first instance, had been the result; for Marshal Soult, driven back, would have retired upon the army led by the Emperor, marching in his rear, and which must have overwhelmed the Spanish troops; whereas, in the more probable event, that of defeat, they had no reinforcements upon which a retrograde movement could bring them; nor was there a single battalion to join the ranks between Aranda and the Somasierra.

Had the Estremaduran army retired upon the advance of the enemy, it might have formed a junction with the troops from the south, and, placed in position on the Somasierra mountain, contested that very strong ground, and occasioned, at all events, a great loss to the enemy. Disheartened and weakened by its disasters at Burgos, its artillery taken, troops dispersed, its cavalry absolutely unserviceable, and wandering over the face of the country, it was no longer formidable in any respect. By this injudicious affair, some of the best Spanish infantry became shaken in discipline and in confidence to a degree never restored during the long and arduous struggle in which they subsequently became engaged.

The Conde de Belvedere imparted to me the information he possessed as to the movements of the enemy. He informed me of his intention to retire, and that he only remained at Aranda for the purpose of assembling the fugitives, and enabling those who had escaped by lateral lines of road to rejoin their colours. The *conde* made a great case of the desperate resistance of General Henestrosa's corps; and as some excuse appeared necessary for anything like disaster having befallen the Spanish troops, he wished to attribute the defeat of the 10th to treason. How or where that existed, he did not explain; and probably to have done so satisfactorily would have been difficult.

Before leaving Aranda, I wrote to Lord William Bentinck, informing him of these reverses. The route by Burgos being effectually obstructed, determined me to proceed to the left, and, by making a *détour*, avoid the country occupied by the enemy's troops, and regain the coast. With this object in view, on the morning of the 12th, I mounted a post-horse, and took the road to Sotillo, on which were numerous parties of dispersed soldiery moving towards Aranda to rejoin their respective regiments.

As I proceeded towards Palencia, various reports were in circulation concerning the motions of the enemy, but all agreeing in the unwelcome intelligence that he was very rapidly advancing.

Part of Marshal Soult's corps had entered Lerma on the night of the 11th, and it was reported that French cavalry had been seen in the direction of Palencia. Calculating on the probability of this latter rumour not being authentic, and anxious to make as short a circuit as possible, I continued my journey, and having passed through Sotillo and Tortoles, arrived at Cabeça Nabero, without having obtained any certain information as to the more immediate quarters of the enemy; but at Baltanas, two leagues in advance, the *alcalde* informed me that his cavalry were at Torquemada, also at Palencia, and that his advanced posts were at the distance of a short league. Under these circumstances, I considered the only safe proceeding was to return to Cabeça Nabero, and at twelve o'clock at night, again entered that village.

Some of the fugitive hussars of Valencia, dispersed after the affair of Gamonal, had arrived there from Burgos, and six of them offered to accompany me on the following morning, in any direction removed from the track of the French Army. Valladolid appeared, under the circumstances, to be the nearest route, not obstructed by the presence of the enemy's troops, that could now be adopted in proceeding to the north, and at daylight on the 13th I sallied forth, escorted by the hussars, in the direction of that city. As we proceeded, constant reports of the proximity of the French cavalry were in circulation;

but so contradictory, and apparently exaggerated, that I determined to persevere until some certain information could be obtained. Having passed through the villages of Castilla de la Pena and Esgavillas, after travelling for nine hours during heavy rain, we arrived at Tudela on the Duero. Remote as this day's journey was from the scene of action, the roads continued to be strewed with dispersed soldiery from Gamonal.

The *cura* of Tudela received me with great kindness and hospitality. His house became the receptacle of numerous visitors, anxious to obtain intelligence as to the probability of the enemy's approach. That he already occupied Valladolid they had ascertained, and the *cura* informed me that nearly the whole population of the town were prepared to make their escape whenever a visit from the French became certain.

As we were only two leagues from Valladolid, it became important to investigate the nature of the information which the inhabitants of Tudela had obtained of the enemy's movements. I was soon satisfied upon this subject, from the terror that appeared to prevail, as well as the apparent bustle and activity, indicating the necessity felt by all classes to prepare for immediate departure.

Never did the people of Tudela pass so anxious or sleepless a night. Constantly moving about, its inhabitants looked forward to daybreak with unceasing alarm, and frequent were the visits of consultation paid to the *cura*, who appeared to have great influence, and to possess their entire confidence.

At six o'clock in the morning, my Asturian servant rushed into the room in a state of great alarm, informing me that the French cavalry were said to be close to the town. A very few minutes elapsed before I was across the Duero, having passed the bridge amidst a crowd of the inhabitants forming a most singular cavalcade, men, women, children, cattle, sheep, horses, and cars, covering the whole road, and flying in the utmost confusion. The Valencian hussars, with an *alertness* highly praiseworthy in that class of light cavalry, had, the previous night, marched to the rear, without any intimation of such being their intention, or having had the civility to request that I should accompany them.

Having extricated myself from the line of march adopted by the population of Tudela, I proceeded to Valdestillas, where post-horses were to be procured; and after passing through Rueda, recrossed the Duero by the bridge of Tordesillas. The inhabitants of that town appeared perfectly tranquil, expressing no alarm on the subject of French visitation; nor had they heard of the enemy's cavalry having penetrated into the district in their vicinity. Under these circumstances, I had hopes of having turned the part of the country subjected to his inroads, and of being permitted to proceed upon my journey without difficulty or obstruction.

Late at night, I left Tordesillas, posted to Beja, from thence to Villar de Fraydes, to Villalpando, to San Estevan, and to Villa Nueva del Campo. In the course of this route, no intelligence of the enemy was obtained. It, therefore, appeared probable that the utmost extent of his advance had been to the neighbourhood of Palencia and Valladolid, and that, consequently, I might now, with safety, take a road more to the right, and a nearer line to the point at which it was my object to arrive. I, therefore, struck across the country, and in the evening arrived at the village of Veçilla, where I again experienced the hospitality of the Spanish clergy, taking up my quarters in the house of the Cura de Santa Maria.

At six o'clock on the morning of the 16th, accompanied by two peasants and my servant, I took the road to Villada, on which we had not proceeded above a league, when, through the mist, horsemen appeared upon the road advancing directly towards us. We immediately halted, and soon ascertained they were dragoons. Upon perceiving us, they retired with precipitation. Supposing them to be a patrol of the enemy's cavalry,—for, doubtful as was the light, the brazen *casque* and streaming horsehair proclaimed without doubt the country to which they belonged. I lost not a moment in following their example in the opposite direction, and galloped back to Veçilla. The extremely dense mist and darkness of the morning must have deceived these soldiers as to the quality of the party they encountered; for of the four, I was the only armed person, and that very slightly, my friends the hussars having relieved me from the encumbrance of my pistols during our journey from Cabeça Nabero to Tudela.

After this certain indication of the enemy's troops being scattered over the whole face of the country, I abandoned all hopes of being enabled to return to Santander, resolving to adopt the most direct route to Leon, and to be regulated as to future proceedings by the information I should receive in that city.

The cavalry I had heard of in every direction since leaving Aranda was ascertained to be the force under the Duke of Istria, despatched immediately after the affair at Gamonal to suppress the insurrection, as it was termed, and strike terror into the minds of the inhabitants of Old Castille. Unresisted—for no troops opposed their advance—these horsemen swept over the face of the country. The towns through which they passed were either deserted, or the inhabitants subjected to heavy contributions. All thoughts of contending against them vanished; and the impression made was even greater than the circumstances warranted. Nor was this to be wondered at. The people, who, a few days previously, had been led to expect information of the flight or annihilation of the French Army, if they heard at all of what had recently happened, obtained the intelligence from dispersed soldiery, whose descriptions were, of course, frequently charged with exaggeration; and before they had time to recover from the shock received by the communication of these reverses, the enemy's cavalry was at their gates.

At this period of the war, Sir John Moore was at Salamanca with the main body of the British Army, Sir David Baird at Astorga, and General Hope, with the artillery and stores, making an unnecessary and dangerous *détour* by Talavera de la Reyna, the Escorial, and the Guadarama pass.

From Veçilla, I regained the great road at Mallorga; from thence proceeded to Mansilla de las Mulas, and at twelve o'clock at night entered Leon.

The city of Leon, and capital of the kingdom of that name, is beautifully situated between the rivers Vernesga and Torio, which, forming a junction to the south of the town, fall into the Esla between Mansilla and Valencia de Don Juan. Leon was founded by the Emperor Trajan, and derives its name from one of the Roman legions. It is irregularly built, the streets narrow, and ill-paved, and the houses generally insignificant in appearance; but it possesses a magnificent cathedral, founded by Don Ordoña, second king of Leon. It was destroyed by the Moorish king Almanzor, at the close of the tenth century, but restored by Don Pelayo, who directed the works, which, in the end of the twelfth and beginning of the thirteenth centuries, led to the completion of the present splendid edifice.

The building is of the most florid style of Gothic architecture: nothing can be more beautiful than the rich and elaborate carving of the western and southern entrances, the former of which is the principal portal. The windows, of stained glass, are of great magnitude, extending nearly the whole height of the cathedral, and giving to the interior a very grand effect.

There is an old Spanish saying, illustrative of the peculiar style of the different cathedrals:

Toledo en riqueza,
Compostela en fortaleza,
Y Leon in sutileza:

Thus giving Leon pre-eminence in the delicacy and beauty of the work.

The principal buildings, exclusive of the churches and convents, are the houses of the Duque de Uçeda, the Conde de Luna, and the Marques de Caraçena. The walls of Leon are very ancient, but have been repaired, and in some places rebuilt, in more modern times. One of the gates of the city is called Del Castillo, having been erected in 1759, near to the site of the once celebrated state prison of that name.

At Leon, some of the officers of the British commissariat had arrived, and Colonel Nicolay of the Staff Corps, employed by Sir David Baird to procure information, was at Mansilla: but from none of these persons was to be obtained the slightest intelligence of the Marques de la Romana; nor had they heard the result of the operations of the Gallician Army, upon which, of course, his motions, as also those of General Leith, must in a great measure have depended. In this state of uncertainty, it appeared to me most important to proceed direct to the coast of Asturias, and send Mr. Frere's despatches by the earliest conveyance to England.

On the evening of the 18th November, I left Leon, with the intention of crossing the mountains to Oviedo. The view from the heights, on the road to La Robla, looking back upon the plain on which the city is placed, is very beautiful, the country being rich in cultivation, and luxuriantly wooded.

From La Robla to Buiza, the road is extremely bad, frequently intersected by mountain torrents, which, being swollen by the heavy rain that had fallen, became, in some instances, nearly impassable.

After leaving Buiza, the road leads over one of those passes so frequent in the North of Spain, but that of Pajares exceeds in roughness and intricacy all those I had previously travelled. To the difficulties of this mountain track, were, on this occasion, to be added an extremely dark night, and a violent storm of wind and rain, rendered doubly irksome by the impossibility of urging the wretched horse I rode into a pace calculated speedily to overcome the misery of this most tedious and apparently interminable stage. At last, however, after having had more than one roll amongst the rocks, and with the prospect of occasionally accompanying some of the mountain streams into the valleys to which they were rushing with great rapidity, I arrived at the town of Pajares, having been seven hours and a half in travelling sixteen miles.

On arriving at Oviedo, the *procurador*-general of the province, and General Ballesteros, informed me of the disasters that had befallen the unfortunate army of the left; that it had been completely defeated; that Generals Açevedo, Requelmè, and the Conde San Roman, had been killed; that the survivors had dispersed, and sought safety by flight into the mountains of Leon,—the *procurador*-general declaring, with a countenance combining an expression of solemnity, melancholy, and despair, that the whole was to be attributed to the treason of General Blake! I had heard so much of the treason attributed to Spanish generals, whenever a remarkable occurrence was to be accounted for, that this communication passed unquestioned. As usual, an thing like a correct statement of facts was not to be obtained; even the intelligent General Ballesteros appeared to know that defeat had overtaken the Gallician Army: but as to authentic detail, he was in perfect ignorance.

Having failed in obtaining any positive information at Oviedo of the route either of the Marques de la Romana, or General Leith, it was unnecessary for me to delay in that city. In the evening, therefore, I rode to Gihon, where, having delivered the despatches to Mr. Hunter, to be by him transmitted to Mr. Canning, I once more took the road by the coast towards Santander, and arrived at Villaviciosa. On the route, in advance of that village, I met the Baron Almendarez, with the four cavalry regiments of the division from the North, who informed me, that when he marched from Santander, General Leith was still there. This determined me to proceed in that direction; but upon reaching Colunga, I obtained certain information of his having quitted that town.

The next report that met me was his having gone by Infiesta to Oviedo. It was possible he might have taken this mountain road; at all events, it was quite unnecessary for me to proceed to Santander; and I resolved to strike across the country in hopes of joining him on his route.

The town of Infiesta, in the centre of the great chain of the Ariales, is beautifully placed in a valley on the bank of the Ribadecella River.

The mountains ascend precipitously to the north, but are luxuriantly covered with chestnut, and other trees of great magnitude and richness of foliage. It is difficult to conceive scenery more varied and picturesque, than that through which the road from Colunga to Infiesta is conducted.

General Leith had neither arrived at, nor passed near to, that place. Disappointed and uncertain what course to adopt, I at last resolved upon returning to Oviedo; and, in consequence, made strenuous application to the *alcalde* for horses. Whether his authority was slight, or he was lukewarm in attending to the requisition, I cannot determine, but certainly the delay was greater than I had yet experienced any where under similar circumstances.

At length the horses were produced, and after sunset we were on the road to Oviedo, guided by a peasant, who, either from ignorance, or the darkness that prevailed, lost the road, and conducted us to the bank of a river, which he had previously informed me it was necessary to ford. After having travelled about a league from Infiesta, not doubting his knowledge of the route, and being in front of the party, I urged my horse into the stream; nor was it long before it became proved to be anything but a ford into which I had been erroneously led; for, after several plunges, the horse lost his footing, and it was with difficulty that he regained the bank from whence he had entered. The guide made many protestations of regret, but as he had cautiously abstained from following my example, in entering the river, it is not improbable that he had some slight idea of its depth; at the same time not exactly agreeing with me in the estimate formed of the value of my safety, provided he recovered his horse, which, under all circumstances, he had a fair prospect of succeeding in.

La Pola, the nearest village on the route, was four leagues distant. The night excessively cold. I was drenched with water; the guide apparently uncertain where he was, and the darkness such that no object could be distinguished at any distance. Few situations in the annals of travelling can be conceived less enviable. To discover a habitation of some description became most desirable. That there were such in the neighbourhood the peasant declared to be his belief. After proceeding a short distance, it was with no slight degree of satisfaction I discovered a light, not far removed from the bank of the river, which, when approached, proved to come from the window of a cottage. The inmates of this humble dwelling received us with the utmost cordiality and kindness. Our appearance at that late hour must have occasioned considerable surprise, as well as distrust, but the moment the reason for it was explained all restraint appeared to have vanished, while every effort was made by these poor peasants to render their habitation as comfortable as possible.

The arrival of General Caro, at Oviedo, on the 24th of November, at last put me in possession of certain information. From him I learnt that the Marques de la Romana and General Leith had gone to Leon by Potes—that the remains of the Gallician Army were there assembling—and that, without doubt, I should meet them in the neighbourhood of that city.

At ten o'clock at night I once more left Oviedo, passed the Puerta de Pajares under more favourable circumstances, both of light and the state of the atmosphere, than formerly, and the following evening had the satisfaction of joining the *marques* and General Leith at the palace of the Bishop of Leon.

Thus terminated a journey of above 900 miles, in the course of which a considerable portion of the country had been traversed under circumstances that enabled me to ascertain the sincere feeling of the people. It is but justice to state, that in the whole course of it I met with but one sentiment as to the war; that I was everywhere treated with kindness, and my progress facilitated, even under circumstances where individuals suffered inconvenience from their horses or mules being put into requisition. Unaccompanied by any British subject, I passed in safety at all hours of the day and night. Nothing could have been easier than to have terminated my career, and carried the despatches to the enemy, without the event ever being ascertained, notwithstanding which my progress was unimpeded in any one instance; nor, with the exception of the river scene, near Infiesta, was my safety ever compromised. I mention this as a creditable circumstance to the inhabitants of the Peninsula, and in contradiction to the statements often recorded, unjustly in my opinion, of the want of faith, of supineness, and of perfidy, in the Spanish people.

The Marques de la Romana had unfortunately arrived too late to take the command of his army; he had the mortification to find it had been completely defeated. The first troops he met were flying in the greatest disorder, dispersing in the mountains, half-famished, without shoes, many wounded, and all in a state of misery and exhaustion.

It was out of the question to attempt the reorganisation of the Gallician Army anywhere near the enemy. The only chance, therefore, was to indicate a rallying point considerably to the rear, there once more to collect the fugitives into the appearance of an army. With this object, the *marques* had retired to Leon, where his exertions were strenuous and incessant. Unfortunately, the brunt of the actions fought by General Blake had fallen upon the veteran soldiers of the division from the north, few remaining of those fine regiments that had been restored to their country by the man, who, of all others, posterity will admit, conducted himself invariably, during the struggle, with a firmness, an integrity, a prudence, and a courage, worthy the best days of the Spanish monarchy, or the noblest records of patriotism.

The Marques de la Romana appeared at this date to be aged about fifty. Short in stature, without any great look of ability, his countenance, although it did not indicate the firmness of his mind, had an expression of much amiability of disposition. I was present at his first interview with General Blake, after the disasters of his army: it was conducted by the Marques with the utmost mildness; no expression of irritation or disappointment escaped him, the only restraint appearing on the part of the defeated general.

Ever since the affair of Durango, on the 31st of October, the army of the left had been subjected to a series of reverses, having been closely followed up by Marshal the Duke of Belluno in the direction of Espinosa, and by the Duke of Dantzic in that of Villarcayo.

General Blake occupied a strong position at Espinosa, where he had at last concentrated his whole army, with the exception of the fourth division, which had previously been cut off, and forced back upon Portugalete. In this situation he was attacked by the Duke of Belluno on the 10th, but, after fighting the whole day with very equivocal success, the position was in some points maintained.

On the following day the French marshal renewed his attack: the Asturian infantry gave way: their example was followed by the left of the army: the battle was irretrievably lost: the whole fled with rapidity in the utmost confusion, leaving their cannon, ammunition, and baggage, in the hands of the enemy. Never was victory more complete; from that instant the Spanish force, as an army, ceased to have existence. All that remained was a tumultuous mob, half-famished, without officers, many having thrown away their arms, and all being dispirited and wretched to a degree.

Thus, by the combinations of the Emperor Napoleon, the Spanish armies of the centre and the left were attacked and overwhelmed at the same moment. These operations, however, formed but a subordinate part of the plan he had arranged for the campaign. While Marshals Soult and Victor were destroying two Spanish armies at different points, General Castaños was on the eve of being attacked and defeated; the most important movement of the whole—the march upon Madrid—being carried into effect by the emperor himself.

It was when these events had occurred, or were rapidly arriving at consummation, that a British auxiliary force arrived in Spain. One month earlier, it might have produced the most powerful as well as most beneficial effect; but the time was past. A body of really good troops, co-operating with the Spanish armies, and vigorously attacking the French before they became reinforced, might have totally changed the aspect of affairs; but what great impression was to be expected from 30,000 British taking the field against the enormous strength of the enemy, particularly after the total discomfiture of every Spanish force with which they were destined to act, or by joining whom they might in any degree assimilate in numbers to those opposed?

On the 13th October, Lieutenant-General Sir David Baird arrived at Coruña. The same day of the following month Sir John Moore, with the advance of his army, entered Salamanca. General Hope, with the artillery, two regiments of light cavalry, and 3000 infantry, was in the neighbourhood of Madrid on the 22nd November. Such were the arrangements as to time and combination of movement with which commenced the operations of Sir John Moore's army.

Very nearly a month was lost in consequence of the *détour* which want of information had occasioned General Hope to make on his march to Salamanca; while false intelligence induced Sir David Baird to retire from Astorga to Villafranca. Where promptitude was important, nothing could be more unfortunate than these false movements.

It was on the 27th November that General Leith left Leon to join the British Army, having received orders to that effect. Upon that day the head-quarters continued at Salamanca; Sir David Baird was at Astorga, with his corps cantoned to his rear upon the Coruña road; General Hope at the southern entrance of the Guadarama pass. Fortunately, the Duke of Dantzic with the fourth *corps d'armée* had not yet occupied it, although in full march for that purpose. Had he done so, it would have been impracticable for General Hope to have formed a junction with the main body of the British Army, and the whole must have retired on Portugal.

This is a tolerably convincing proof, that during the Peninsular War the leaders of the French Army were not always possessed of the best information. Much has been written on the conduct of Spanish authorities, British agents, and others, in not affording prompt or accurate intelligence: it perhaps never was in any country more difficult to procure. The victorious enemy, the defeated Spanish general, the favoured ally, were all subjected to this serious inconvenience; nor was it until a later period of the war that a more perfect and certain detail of events was ever obtained. The improvement in gaining information, and a better regulated scheme of ascertaining the validity of reports, was one consequence of experience in campaigning.

The Duke of Dantzic with his whole corps, marching diagonally across the country to the Guadarama mountains, might without difficulty have intercepted the British convoy, had he been aware either of its situation or its strength.

Lieut.-General Lord Paget had joined the army with the 7th, 10th, and 15th hussars. The *élite* of no army could produce three more brilliant regiments of their class, either as to appearance and equipment, or the really gallant spirit with which they were inspired. Their superiority over the cavalry of the enemy was more conspicuous in this, than in any other of the Peninsular campaigns. The headquarters of Lord Paget were at Astorga on the 1st of December.

Astorga, the ancient Asturica Augusta, was formerly a place of great strength, and is surrounded by a wall, having every appearance of antiquity. Near to the city is the ruined castle of the Marques de Astorga, a building of great extent, and apparent baronial importance. The cathedral is neither celebrated for its elegance nor magnitude, being in every respect very inferior to that of Leon.

On the 2nd of December, General Leith set off to join his brigade, consisting of the Royal, 26th, and 81st regiments, at Villafranca. The weather was now very inclement, and as we ascended the mountains from Astorga, the cold became extreme. The spacious and well-conducted Camino Real winds gradually up to the wretched village of Manzanal, from whence the road descends to Torre. Both these places were completely crowded with troops. It was with the utmost difficulty that accommodation could be obtained, without dislodging some of the officers of two regiments in possession of the only tolerable house. This, however, through the exertions of Colonel Nichols, and Major Wood, of the 14th regiment, was accomplished.

At daybreak we continued to descend into the valley leading towards Villafranca. The road is extremely good; the scenery wild and beautiful. Villafranca del Bierzo is a considerable town, very romantically situated, watered by a clear stream of some magnitude. It is surrounded by rising ground, clothed with the finest wood. The Plaza Mayor is large and regular, both in its area and buildings; it is superior to the square of most Spanish towns of a similar class. At the southern entrance, the first house on the left is the *château* of the Marques de Villafranca, a very spacious, but apparently neglected building.

On the 4th of December, the brigade continued its retreat towards the coast; it halted that night at Herrerias; the 5th at Nogales; the 6th at Constantin and Sobrado. On the 7th we arrived at Lugo (the Lucus Augusti of the Romans), which is one of the most considerable towns of the province. It is surrounded by an ancient wall, having towers at certain distances around its whole extent. It is the seat of a bishopric, and is situated on the River Minho, the principal stream that waters the kingdom of Gallicia. The retreat of Sir David Baird's corps terminated at Lugo. Upon the morning of the 9th, orders were received to march back with the least possible delay to Astorga.

The situation of the British Army was now destined to undergo a very important alteration. After having determined to retire from the Spanish territory, the general-in-chief, yielding to circumstances, to the pressing solicitations of the Spanish authorities, and to the bold opinions of the British minister, resolved to make a dangerous effort for the country which he had been sent to assist, but which *reasonable* persons expected he was to liberate.

The circumstance which more immediately produced this change of plan was the resistance threatened by the town of Madrid, the nature of which was communicated to the British head-quarters in a very exaggerated shape. Unfortunately, the fall of the capital soon became known; but having once resolved, Sir John Moore was not to be shaken in his determination. He ordered Lord Paget, with the cavalry of Sir David Baird's corps, to his front; and without waiting for the arrival of its infantry, marched forward in the direction of Valladolid, where he expected to assemble a large portion of his force on the 16th.

When the army moved from Salamanca, it was in the contemplation of its general to advance upon Burgos, thereby to obstruct the communications of the French Army at Madrid. No circumstance can more strongly prove the want of information as to the position and strength of the different corps of the enemy, than this fact; for, without detaching a single battalion from the army commanded in person by the emperor, 40,000 French, with a large force of cavalry, could have been assembled on the plains of Old Castillo. It was under a false impression of the British Army having retired upon Portugal that Napoleon advanced upon Madrid. Had he been aware of its real situation, to march in that direction would have been his first movement; nor was it until in possession of the capital that he received certain information of Sir John Moore having united his different corps, and being in the act of commencing offensive operations.

On the 13th of December, the headquarters left Salamanca. The British general advanced unaided by, or in communication with, any Spanish force, excepting the remains of the army of the left, under the Marques de la Romana, who continued to occupy Leon with that weak and inefficient force;—this, with about 5000 Asturian recruits under General Ballesteros, that had not yet been engaged, being the only Spanish force now in the field in the whole north of Spain. Sir John Moore had no friendly corps to protect his flanks—no reinforcements to expect. He commanded an army, brilliant in appearance, yet. weak in numerical strength; but upon that, and that alone, was dependence to be placed for the successful result of a very bold advance against a superior enemy in his front, a corps nearly as strong as his own upon his right flank, and the whole army of the emperor unoccupied, and ready to move against him whenever he had penetrated into the country.

In stating that a superior force was in front of the British Army, it must not be supposed to apply to the *corps d'armée* of Marshal Soult alone, but included that of the Duke of Abrantes, then between Vittoria and Burgos. The most inexplicable part of the enemy's operations at this moment was the persevering march of the Duke of Dantzic, the object of which originally was to proceed by Badajos, and intercept the retreat upon Lisbon. For this purpose he had moved diagonally across the country, towards the Guadarama, the advance of his cavalry being at Arevalo on the 30th of November. It is inconceivable that General Hope should have passed within a few leagues, without the event having been reported, or the direction taken by his column ascertained. Had the French marshal, judging that the British were not retiring, then halted, watched the motions of Sir John Moore, and marched direct upon Astorga, when the British had already crossed the Esla, the consequences might have been most disastrous.

The situation of the several corps of the French Army, when Sir John Moore advanced from Salamanca, was as follows:—The Duke of Dalmatia at Sahagun, Saldanha, and the villages in that neighbourhood on the River Carrion—Marshal the Duke of Treviso moving upon

Zaragosa—the Duke of Abrantes, with the eighth corps, at Vittoria Marshal Lefebre, with the fourth corps, beyond the Guadarama— Marshal Lasnes upon the Ebro—and the Emperor Napoleon, with the Imperial Guard, the first and sixth *corps d'armée*, at Madrid.

At Alaejos, an intercepted despatch made Sir John Moore acquainted with the true situation of Marshal Soult's corps, as also of that commanded by the Duke of Abrantes, composed of the same troops that had capitulated at Lisbon in the month of August, and were now rapidly advancing to the line of operations. It also communicated the tranquillity of Madrid, after having opened its gates to the emperor; and the false impression at the French headquarters as to the position or intentions of the British Army. This intelligence produced an immediate alteration in the plan of the campaign.

Instead of continuing his movement upon Valladolid, the British general turned short to his left, crossed the Duero, and, on the 15th, established his headquarters at Toro. Sir David Baird's corps was now in communication with the main body of the army. General Hope had effected a junction with it; and the whole force was in a very concentrated situation. The cavalry had frequent affairs with the enemy's posts, in which they were invariably successful. A strong proof of the inertness with which the French troops at times acted, is to be deduced from the circumstance of no less than ten regiments of their cavalry being at this moment in the neighbourhood of Valladolid, without having ascertained the movements of the British. It was from three deserters that Napoleon first learned the important fact of their advance towards the Esla.

Sir John Moore arrived at Castro Nuevo on the 18th, continued his march by Villalpando and Valderas to Mallorga, which became headquarters on the 20th. Upon the junction of the troops from Portugal and Coruña, an alteration occurred in the formation of the army.— Sir David Baird was placed in command of a division, while General Manningham, from the temporary command of a division, returned to his former brigade. Major-General Leith was by this arrangement removed to that consisting of the 51st, 59th, and 76th regiments.

At Lugo, General Leith had been attacked by sickness, which prevented his accompanying the troops upon their second advance from that place, rendering it a matter of uncertainty when he would be enabled to proceed. I was extremely anxious to be with the army, and he yielded to my wishes on the subject. On the morning of Sunday the 18th, I mounted a post-horse, and rapidly followed the track of the army. Having passed through Villafranca, Astorga, La Baneza, Villamañan, and Valencia de Don Juan, I pursued my course uninterruptedly day and night to Mallorga, the headquarters of the British Army.

It was late at night, on the 20th, when I arrived; the town was crowded with troops; not a house unoccupied, or a quarter to be procured. From this dilemma, rendered doubly serious by the intense cold that prevailed, I was relieved by a fortunate *rencontre* with my friend Captain Patrick, who invited me to his lodging, which, although a poor and comfortless habitation, was luxurious when contrasted with my previous situation—wandering about the streets of a Spanish village on a wearied post-horse, late at night, and the ground covered with snow!

On the morning of the 21st, Lieutenant-General Lord Paget marched from Melgar, with two regiments of hussars, in hopes of surprising General Debelle's brigade of dragoons at Sahagun. His Lordship accompanied the 15th. General Slade, with the 10th, marched direct upon the town. The escape of some men from one of the enemy's patrols announced the approach of the 15th; this gave him time to mount and form in the vicinity of the town. Disregarding the disparity of numbers, Lord Paget resolved to attack without waiting for the 10th; and, confident in the support of that gallant spirit which had characterised the British hussars since their arrival in Spain, he manoeuvred to charge with effect, and without delay. General Debelle very inconsiderately awaited the attack, instead of meeting it,—his line keeping up a fire of carbines on the assailants; but the impetus given to the fresh and high-bred English horses, and the resolution embodied in the brave soldiers that conducted them, was irresistible; the French line was borne down by the torrent, and retired in disorder; two *Chefs d'Escadron*, with 170 other officers and privates, were made prisoners this short but brilliant affair.

On the night of the 21st, the division of Lieutenant-General Sir David Baird advanced from its quarters, and, at ten o'clock, marched in the direction of Sahagun. The column moved from Mallorga with the artillery in front; the depth of snow, with some intricacies of the road, rendered more serious by the darkness, occasioned frequent halts, during which the excessive cold was severely felt. It was two o'clock in the morning before General Manningham's brigade had accomplished a march of eight miles. At daylight, it again proceeded, arriving at Sahagun early in the forenoon of the 22nd. The weather continued very inclement, but the numerous convents afforded shelter to the troops.

The commander of the forces received, during the 22nd and 23rd, various reports of an unfavourable description; first, that Marshal Soult had been reinforced; secondly, that the Duke of Dantzic had halted at Talavera, and was to discontinue his march towards Badajos; thirdly, that Napoleon was advancing against him. Even under these adverse circumstances, he persevered in his intention of beating up the quarters of the 2nd corps upon the Carrion. The general officers received their instructions, and, at eight o'clock in the evening, the troops were formed in two columns, ready to march against the enemy; but upon the receipt of a second despatch from the Marques de la Romana, placing the approach of the emperor beyond doubt, Sir John Moore reluctantly abandoned all intention of a further advance, the march of the troops was countermanded, and they returned to their cantonments.

The intelligence thus received was of the greatest importance. The march upon Carrion would undoubtedly have compromised the safety of the army. Not only the most probable, but the most to be desired result of that movement, namely, the defeat of Marshal Soult, would but have added to its dangers and difficulties. Had Marshal Soult retired when assailed by the British force, it is probable that its general, being in ignorance of the rapid movement making against him from the Escorial, would have advanced in pursuit; this must have rendered his situation still more critical. In either case, the time lost could not have failed to occasion the destruction or capture of the army.

The judgment with which the commander of the forces yielded to these circumstances, the promptitude with which he checked the advance of his army, and the accuracy with which he calculated the exact moment when retreat became not only a measure of expediency, but of absolute necessity, appear to be the greatest proofs of capacity for command exhibited during the campaign.

On the morning of the 25th of December, the retreat commenced. The weather had completely changed on the preceding day; a rapid thaw succeeded the snowstorm, rain fell in torrents, rendering the roads deep to a degree that impeded the march of the troops, artillery, and baggage. At night, Sir David Baird's division, composed of the Guards, Lord William Bentinck's and General Manningham's brigades, occupied Valencia de Don Juan; on the morning of the 26th, the passage of the river Esla was effected. There was but one boat, of a ponderous description, extremely ill managed, and very slow in its operations; the crossing of the soldiers alone by this conveyance would have occupied the whole day, while the rapid rise of the river rendered it important to gain the right bank with the least possible delay. It having been ascertained that a ford a little lower than the ferry was still practicable, over it great part of the infantry, with the carriages of every description, were passed.

It is difficult to conceive a more gloomy scene. The weather continued as bad as possible, and the pouring rain was rendered more galling by a piercingly cold wind. The animals of burden, the followers of the army, with the women and children accompanying a column of 8000 men, added to the confusion. Many were seen struggling in the rapid stream that rolled past, while groups on either bank watched their progress. Nothing could be more comfortless than the appearance of all present; but notwithstanding the overturning of cars, the refractory exertions of mules, the terror of the women, and vociferation of the Spaniards, the whole reached the right bank of the Esla without any lives being lost, or any serious accident having occurred. The passage of the river was fortunately timed; for, before night, the flood had increased to a degree that would have rendered it impracticable.

The commander of the forces, with the other divisions of infantry, had marched upon Benevente, crossing the Esla, on the morning of the 26th, by the bridge of Castro Gonzalo. Sir David Baird halted on the 27th, the troops of his division occupying Toral, Villamor, and Villamañan.

Upon the British cavalry being withdrawn from Sahagun, the Duke of Dalmatia advanced in pursuit of the army. Fortunately, that pursuit was not conducted in the most rapid manner; for when the delay occasioned by attempting to remove the magazines from Benevente is considered, as also that Sir David Baird's division was nearly six days between Sahagun and Astorga, it does not appear either difficult or improbable that the French marshal, taking, as he did, the direct route by Mansilla and Leon, might have reached that point previous to the British Army. This has always appeared to me to have been the greatest danger attending the retrograde movement from Sahagun; for the unfordable state of the Esla, and destruction of the only bridge upon that river between Mansilla and its junction with the Duero, retarded the advance of Napoleon. On the other hand, Marshal Soult obtained undisputed possession of the bridge of Mansilla, and had nothing in his front to prevent his advancing *tête baissée* on the communications of the British with Gallicia.

It was on the 21st that Napoleon, then at Madrid, received information of Sir John Moore's march against his second *corps d'armée*. His resolution, and the carrying it into effect, was like lightning,—the flash was no sooner visible than the thunder rolled; the influence of his mighty genius was instantaneously felt; no delay was permitted to take place; the troops were immediately in motion, and their great leader rushed to retrieve the errors of his lieutenants. On the 24th, he was at Tordesillas, one hundred and twenty miles from Madrid, after having passed his army across the ridge of the Carpentanos, deeply covered with snow, under circumstances that would have effectually obstructed the advance of an ordinary man. The difficulties were such, that the artillery officers, preceding the column of infantry, considered them insurmountable, and were returning down the southern ascent of the Guadarama mountain when met by the emperor.

This retrograde movement was occasioned by the increased violence of a hurricane, blowing hail and snow with, as they believed, resistless force. In addition to the report of his officers, the Spanish peasants declared the passage to be attended with the greatest danger. Napoleon ordered his troops to follow him, and immediately proceeded to place himself at the head of the column. Accompanied by the *chasseurs à cheval* of the guard, he passed through the ranks of the infantry; then formed the *chasseurs* in close column, occupying the entire width of the road; when, dismounting from his horse, and directing the regiment to follow his example, he placed himself in rear of the leading half-squadron, and the whole moved forward. The men, by being dismounted, were, with the exception of those immediately in front, more sheltered from the storm, while the dense mass trod down the snow, and left a beaten track for the infantry, who, no longer obstructed in the same degree, and inspired by the presence, as well as the example of Napoleon, pushed forward, and the whole descended to Espinar.

The emperor, with Marshal Ney's corps, reached Valderas on the 28th; the troops were excessively fatigued, having performed an almost unparalleled march. Still he continued to urge them on, holding forth the certain destruction of the British Army as an accession to their glory, and a reward for their toils and their exertions. From Valderas he sent forward General Lefebre-Desnouettes, with the *chasseurs* of the guard, to press the British rear, and communicate intelligence as to its movements. In the execution of this duty, the General arrived on the left bank of the Esla, opposite to Benevente, on the morning of the 29th. The bridge of Castro Gonzalo had been destroyed. No body of troops appeared, some scattered patrols of cavalry being alone discernible upon the plain. Deceived by these indications of retreat, General Lefebre, having discovered a ford, passed the Esla.

Colonel Otway of the 18th Hussars, who commanded the British piquets, made the best disposition for resistance. Having assembled them, he skirmished, maintaining his ground, and frequently charging the advanced squadrons of the enemy. These encounters continued, with various success, until the arrival of the 10th Hussars, supported by which regiment, the piquets made a decisive attack. The French chasseurs regained the Esla at full speed, closely pursued by the assailants; but instead of breaking their ranks, and dispersing in their flight, they continued in a compact body; and having judged the situation of the ford with accuracy, plunged in, and succeeded in regaining the opposite bank. In this affair, which was well contested on the part of the enemy, he sustained a loss of one hundred and thirty officers and men, killed, wounded, and prisoners. Among the latter was General Lefebre. The French regiment here engaged was the same with which Napoleon had forced through the snows of the Guadarama, and for which he had a particular favour.

No further attempt to cross the Esla was made by the French Army during the 29th. In the evening, Lord Paget evacuated Benevente with the cavalry, and retired to La Baneza, both of which towns were the following day visited by Marshal the Duke of Istria, at the head of nine thousand cavalry. The bridge at Castro Gonzalo was repaired during the 30th, and the infantry of the French Army passed it in the course of the night.

On the same day, Lieutenant-General Hope's division passed through, and Sir David Baird's entered Astorga. The weather had again changed; the cold was excessive, and the appearance of the atmosphere indicated an approaching storm. The whole British force was, at this date, with the exception of the reserve and the cavalry, either in Astorga or on the route to Villafranca.

The Marques de la Romana, unable to contend with Marshal Soult, had retired from Leon on his approach, arriving at Astorga with the purpose of crossing the route of Sir John Moore, to retire with his shattered and inefficient force to the valley of the Minho. Nothing could be more wretched than the appearance of the Spanish troops that arrived at Astorga; disease and starvation seemed to struggle for mastery in the annihilation of life. Some of the worn-out wretches, half naked, stretched on the ground, and in the agonies of death, presented a picture of squalid and extenuated misery not to be described.

The British troops finally abandoned Astorga on the 31st. The reserve, commanded by General Edward Paget, formed the rear of the column of infantry, and with it was the commander of the forces, Lord Paget, with the cavalry, continued close to the enemy.

At Bonillos, General Robert Crawford, with 3000 light infantry, struck off to the left, taking the route by Orense to Vigo. Two reasons have been assigned for this division of force; first, that it was to lessen the difficulties of the commissariat, and, secondly, to secure the left flank of the army. The first may be defended. There appears to have been no necessity for the second. If the left flank was insecure, it could only become so from lateral roads, by which the troops from Astorga might have turned the line of march of the retreating battalions; but to separate from these, and proceed direct for the valley of the Minho, through a distant country, where no enemy had existence, was an extraordinary mode of securing the uninterrupted march of the army.

It was between Benevente and Astorga that the emperor was overtaken by a courier from Paris with despatches communicating the hostile dispositions of the Austrian Government, and the certainty of an approaching declaration of war. This was the most important despatch, either with reference to the existence of the powers of Europe or his own personal views, that Napoleon ever received. From it may be dated every subsequent disaster that befell him; it saved Spain, divided his power, periled his invincibility, and, by a combination of circumstances, occasioned losses and produced misfortune, that laid the foundation for the Russian war, and finally induced the Emperor Alexander to adopt the bold measure of singly taking the field against the man whom, after Erfurt, he willingly would have conspired against, but did not openly dare to do so.

This alarming communication had an immediate effect upon the emperor. The pursuit he was anxiously urging, with the utmost celerity, no longer appeared to possess his undivided thoughts. Germany distracted his mind; he was, in idea, upon the banks of the Danube, accompanied by his faithful, his indefatigable guard. Of the numerous army collected at Astorga, he placed twenty thousand infantry, four thousand cavalry, and fifty pieces of cannon, under the orders of Marshal Soult, directing him to pursue and compel the British either to surrender or embark. The Duke of Elchingen, with his corps, received orders to march in support of the above. There are two routes from Astorga to Villafranca del Bierzo. The one by Bembibre is the most modern, and the best conducted; the other, by Ponteferrada, is the more direct, but worst road. They meet at the village of Calcabelos. The former was the line adopted by the British, the main body of the enemy pursued by the latter.

The Camino Real, upon which the retreat was conducted, is an excellent road, causewayed where necessary, spacious in all parts, frequently level with the streams rushing through the valleys, and nowhere so steep as to occasion the slightest difficulty to carriages of any description. Favourable as this route would appear for the progress of an army, many circumstances occasioned it to be otherwise when passed by Sir John Moore. In the first place, the severity of the weather, with the rapid transitions from frost and snow to rain, and then again to ice, had broken up its surface and rendered it very deep; the disrepair was, of course, much increased by the march of troops, accompanied by cars, horses, mules, and all the encumbrances of an army. The order of retreat in which the British Army moved from Astorga was, first, General M'Kenzie Fraser's division; then General Hope's, followed by that of Sir David Baird; lastly, the reserve and the cavalry.

A division of French dragoons accompanied each of the columns moving by Ponteferrada and Bembibre. General Franceschi, with the light cavalry, advanced by a valley to the extreme left, with an intention of gaining the main road to Coruña, and coming in front of the retreating force;—an unaccountable movement in such a country as Gallicia, perfectly unsuited as it is to the operations of cavalry. If a column of *voltigeurs*, unencumbered, and marching with the rapidity of French soldiers, had accompanied him, great annoyance might have resulted; but General Franceschi marched on unsupported by any other arm. This might have succeeded against undisciplined troops, but had he placed his hussars and *chasseurs* as a barrier to interrupt British infantry and artillery, the consequence would have been his being speedily blown out of the way.

On the morning of the 1st of January, the commander of the forces, with the reserve, entered Bembibre. Exposure to inclement weather, inexperience in making the best of untoward circumstances, fatigue, and other causes, had occasioned irregularities in the line of march; but these were inconsiderable, until the stores at Bembibre became ransacked. This fatally shook the discipline of the regiments; from that town may be dated the really serious aspect of the retreat.

The weather, from the commencement, had been severe; the roads not impracticable, but distressingly fatiguing; the men loaded with heavy knapsacks, great-coats, canteens, ammunition, and their arms; the route knee-deep in some places; a violent wind beating alternately snow, sleet, or rain, directly in their faces; such was the situation of the infantry soldier during the greater part of this memorable retreat; added to which, he had become irregularly and but scantily fed.

At Calcabelos, where, as previously stated, the Ponteferrada and Bembibre roads join, a smart skirmish took place upon the 3rd. It was on that occasion alone that the French shewed anything like enterprise in the pursuit. Incited probably by a temporary confusion, occasioned by retreating cavalry patrols and straggling soldiers, General Colbert very inconsiderately charged. The consequence was a serious tiraillade from the neighbouring vineyards, which effectually checked the pursuers, and deprived the French Army of a very popular and gallant officer: a ball struck him in the forehead, and he dropped dead from his horse.

General Hope's division halted at Lugo upon the 5th. The town was completely occupied by the troops. A more motley scene than that presented within the walls of Lugo at this time can scarcely be imagined. The place is naturally dull. It now assumed an appearance of great activity, of endless bustle; not that of festivity or of commercial importance, but the feverish impulse induced by terror, inconvenience, injury, and annoyance, on the part of its inhabitants; of comfortless endurance, of all-powerful selfishness, of contemptuous disregard to all feelings but their own, on that of many of its visitors.

On one side was to be seen the soldier of every rank who had secured a habitation to shelter him, but whom duty or inclination occasioned to wander through the crowds of people and deeply mudded streets of the town; on the other, the disconsolate person that made his appearance after the *alcalde's* ingenuity had been stretched to the uttermost in procuring quarters for the troops already arrived, and whose *personal friends* had been subjected to the unusual order for admitting strangers. The pitiableness of his case was either to be discovered by a resigned and woeful visage, or by certain ebullitions of temper destined to waste themselves in the desert air.

Next were to be seen the conductors of baggage toiling through the streets—their laden mules almost sinking under the weight of ill-arranged burdens swinging from side to side; while the persons, in whose charge they had followed the divisions, appeared undecided which to execrate most, the roads, the mules, the Spaniards, or the weather. These were succeeded by the dull, heavy sound of the passing artillery; then came the Spanish fugitives from the desolating line of the armies. Detachments with sick or lamed horses scrambled through the mud; while, at intervals, the report of a horse-pistol knelled the termination to the sufferings of an animal that a few days previously, full of life, and high in blood, had borne its rider not against, but over, the ranks of Gallic chivalry. The effect of this scene was rendered more striking by the distant report of cannon and musketry, and more gloomy by torrents of rain, and a degree of cold worthy of a Polish winter.

Hitherto the reserve, with detachments of hussars, had alone been in contact with the enemy. It now became the intention of Sir John Moore to assemble his force, and to check the advance of Marshal Soult. On the evening of the 6th, General Hope's division marched in advance of Lugo, and bivouacked on a position where the whole army was to be concentrated on the following day. The troops were permitted to take up their ground without any annoyance from the enemy. The position occupied by the British was much elevated, and exposed to a piercing north-west wind. Rain fell without intermission; the ground, covered with underwood, was wetted to a degree; neither hut nor tent to shelter from the elements; the only heat to be procured was flitting, comfortless, and uncertain; the glimmering, pale, expiring fires of the enemy were alone seen at intervals, proving the slight chance we had of producing a brighter blaze; the wet broom emitted dense clouds of smoke that loaded the atmosphere, and almost appeared to give weight and substance to the falling rain.

Such was the situation of all ranks in the bivouac at Lugo! Morning dawned; the rain became less violent. The men, suffering from the effects of cold and wet, were without bread, with difficulty preparing some flour and water to appease their craving appetites. Everything was dreary and comfortless, except the presence of the enemy. There was excitement in that, and not a murmur of complaint was heard.

In the position above mentioned, General Hope's division occupied the left, having General Hill's brigade on its right, Colonel C. Crawfurd's in the centre, and General Leith's on the extreme left of the British line. The rest of the army extended to the right, where it was protected by the river Minho. Early on the morning of the 7th, the enemy shewed a large force of cavalry; apparently arriving from the rear in very extended order, they moved to the left of the French position. It was evident the number of troops directly in front had been greatly increased. Cannon were brought to the verge of the ravine which separated the two armies; but as the southern side did not domineer the British position, there was little risk of much impression being made, and the British artillery were immediately placed to silence them. Discharges of cannon were heard at intervals. The light troops skirmished in the ravine, but no serious attack had yet been made; about noon the firing towards our left became more serious, and it was evident a reconnoissance of some importance was meditated. Five pieces of cannon opened upon General Leith's brigade; a column of infantry at the same moment passed the ravine, drove in the outposts, following them rapidly up a road leading directly to the centre of our position.

The light companies were thrown out in front, and the regiments stood to their arms. The soldiers engaged on the slope of the ravine in extended order, were soon forced back, retiring in some confusion. That the attack was not to be repulsed by the fire of sharp-shooters alone was evident; the light companies were consequently assembled, met the enemy when near the summit, poured in one discharge, and rushing forward with the bayonet, drove all before them. Brigade-Major Roberts, and the author of these pages, accompanied the light infantry, who continued in pursuit until they reached the commencement of the ascent upon the opposite side.

The road, or lane, up which the French attacked, was flanked by walls, and overhung with trees, being also so narrow as to occasion considerable confusion in the *mêlée* which took place. Filled with smoke from the incessant and vivid fire of the parties, it was almost impossible to distinguish friend from foe, but our people cheered; and, rushing forward, occasioned great loss to the enemy. When leading the pursuit into the ravine, Major Roberts was wounded, and compelled to retire. Sir John Moore was present during the latter part of this affair, and expressed himself satisfied with the manner in which the attack had been repelled. During the remainder of the day, no attempt was made by the French marshal to molest his adversary; the weather continued very inclement, and darkness came on, accompanied by a storm rivalling in violence that of the former night.

On the morning of the 8th, the troops were formed along the whole extent of the line anxiously awaiting an expected attack. The commander of the forces early appeared at the left of his army, certainly the most vulnerable point of his position his centre being placed upon unattackable ground, his right not to be turned. No movements became visible in the enemy's lines. The Duke of Dalmatia hesitated to bring on an action, for which he had ascertained his opponent was wishful and prepared. I can never look back to the scenes in front of Lugo without a feeling of regret that the battle was not there fought, nor ever bring to recollection the gallant bearing of the troops, under all their miseries, without admiration of the spirit that appeared to animate them, and must have led to certain victory.

After passing the morning in anxious expectation, and giving up hopes of an attack, Sir John Moore, to deceive the enemy as to his immediate intention of further retreat, ordered the infantry to erect huts, which was instantly obeyed. Before it became dark, habitations of various descriptions covered the British position. These were abandoned at ten o'clock in the evening, when, in silence, the whole army filed off to the rear, by different routes leading towards Lugo.

Although considered, under the circumstances, to be advisable, this night-march became a most serious evil. It was excessively dark, the wind blew loud, and hail showers superseded the preceding rains. The track, by which General Leith's brigade marched, was of the roughest and worst description, as may be conjectured from the fact, that untired men took five hours in travelling as many miles, namely, the distance from the position to the city of Lugo. Without halting in that town, the whole moved forward; but even daylight did not materially improve the state of affairs. The storm raged with increased violence; the country, after passing Lugo, becoming more level, the wind, hail, and sleet, swept resistless across the plains. It was with difficulty, at particular points of the route, that I could prevail upon my horse to face the tempest; at last, the straggling and confused column reached the villages of Guitteriz and Valmeda.

These towns were perfectly inadequate to afford accommodation and shelter for the infantry. They were fully occupied by the cavalry, the commissariat, and the staff. The regiments were consequently marched off the road, and halted in some fields to its right, without even a tree to defend them from the blast, the ground streaming with water, the rain and sleet descending in torrents. To men worn down with fatigue, hunger, and want of sleep, this short rest afforded slight comfort. When the order arrived to stand to their arms, and set forward, they rose unrefreshed, footsore, weak, and depressed. A second night's march completed the disorganisation; the whole road presented a mass not of battalions, but one continuous line of stragglers, mixed in confusion, without reference to regiment, brigade, or division, pressing onward to the best of their physical ability, but having lost sight of their officers and their colours.

The state of the weather was at this time peculiarly unfortunate. After leaving the position at Lugo, a forced march became absolutely necessary. The nature of the country through which he had to pass, left Sir John Moore no alternative, but to press on, and avail himself of the advantage gained by the start he had obtained. This was rendered more imperative by the possibility of cavalry acting against him when circumstances had diminished the efficiency of the brilliant force he once possessed of that description. Had the weather been more favourable, the halt at Guitteriz might have been prolonged without compromising the safety of the army; but as it was, the only wise measure seemed to be urging on the infantry to Betanzos; and there halt for the period requisite to assemble the scattered portions of his force, leaving the indefatigable Reserve to bring up the rear, as they had hitherto done in the most soldierlike and gallant manner.

On the morning of the 10th, we arrived at Betanzos, with the headquarters of the regiments, some of whom had not fifty men with their colours. During the course of the day, however, many joined their ranks, and the alteration produced by a short intermission from fatigue was highly creditable to the soldiers. The battalions that on the morning of the 10th entered Betanzos reduced to skeletons, marched from thence on the 11th strong and effective; the column, composed of all the infantry of the army which ascended the road towards Coruña, was orderly in appearance, and perfectly unlike what could have been expected to reform from the *débris* of an army, which but the preceding day had exhibited an alarming state of demoralisation and exhaustion.

On the 11th, a favourable change had taken place in the state of the weather; the sun shone upon the troops; and as the column ascended the winding road from Betanzos, it presented a very brilliant appearance, more particularly when contrasted with that of the preceding day. It was at Betanzos, and not at Coruña, that the real hardships of the retreat terminated.

Lieutenant-General Hope's division occupied on its arrival the suburb of St. Lucia, extending along the western shore of the harbour of Coruña. In these quarters the troops remained until after dark on the evening of the 12th, when they marched to a position two miles in front of the town, on the Betanzos road. The enemy's fires covered the heights on the opposite side of the River Mero, extending from the village of El Burgo to the ocean. We had the broad and swampy river between us, perfectly unfordable, and the bridge at El Burgo had been destroyed. The night of the 12th was consequently passed without annoyance.

General Hope was on the extreme left, being much the strongest ground of the position that had been selected by the commander of the forces, and, from its elevation, the least exposed to the sweeping effects of artillery. On the highest part of the ground, through which the road from El Burgo passes, General Hill's brigade was posted; on his right, General Leith; and a short distance to the rear, prolonging the line to the left, the brigade of Colonel Catlin Crawford; the advanced posts were placed in the valley in front of this line, extending to the village of Palavio Abaxo.

The following morning everything appeared quiet; the night had passed without rain, a serene and cloudless sky gave promise of more genial weather; nothing seemed likely to produce any immediate excitement, when the sound of the explosion of four thousand barrels of powder burst upon the astonished ear. It is impossible to describe the effect. The unexpected and tremendous crash seemed for the moment to have deprived every person of reason and recollection; the soldiers flew to their arms; nor was it until a tremendous column of smoke, ascending from the heights in front, marked from whence the astounding shock proceeded, that reason resumed its sway. It is impossible ever to forget the sublime appearance of the dark dense cloud of smoke that ascended, shooting up gradually like a gigantic tower into the clear blue sky. It appeared fettered in one enormous mass; nor did a particle of dust or vapour, obscuring its form, seem to escape as it rolled upwards in majestic circles.

A lesser quantity of powder had been first exploded; but the reports succeeded each other nearly instantaneously. Whether from oversight, or supposing our posts sufficiently removed to prevent the danger of accident, I cannot determine, but no notification having been sent to General Leith, a sergeant of the 51st regiment, and two other men belonging to the piquets of his brigade, were killed at a considerable distance from the magazine.

On the forenoon of the 13th, the division of Lieut.-General Sir David Baird marched into the position; General Manningham's brigade forming on the right of General Leith's, Lord William Bentinck on his right, and the Guards in reserve.

It was not until the 14th that the bridge of El Burgo was sufficiently repaired to admit of the enemy passing the river. The moment it was so, Marshal Soult pushed a considerable body of infantry and cavalry across. On the 15th, he ascended the range of heights directly above the northern branch of the Mero, and on which the ruined magazine was situated. To cover this movement, and protect the right flank of his columns, three pieces of cannon and a howitzer were advanced to the angle of the road above the village of Palavio Abaxo; these soon after opened upon the left of the British line, but without producing any effect. The whole ridge was soon covered with French troops.

The weather was clear and beautiful, every movement of the enemy being discernible from the high ground. During the course of the day the piquets were often slightly engaged, and towards evening a more serious affair was occasioned by the zeal of Colonel Mackenzie, of the 5th regiment, who was killed in attempting to cut off two guns considerably advanced, and annoying the troops to the left of the position. The assembling of the French Army on its bold and commanding ground had scarcely been completed, when the fleet destined to convey the British from the shores of Spain made its appearance. The line-of-battle ships and transports were seen gliding along the coast towards the harbour of Coruña; but it was too late to commence an action, and darkness overspread the British force, without any attempt being made by the enemy to render unavailing the means of removal it now possessed.

At daybreak on the 16th, the enemy's drums beat to arms, but no firing at the advanced posts denoted an immediate attack; when the heights became perfectly visible, the enemy were discovered quiet, without any hostile formation. It was, however, an anxious period; a battle must in all probability take place. It was not to be expected that an uninterrupted embarkation would be permitted; and, situated as we were, one half-hour was a sufficient space of time to bring 40,000 men into close and deadly conflict.

Sir John Moore was early in the midst of the troops, and from the rocky eminence in front of General Hill's brigade, closely examined the whole range of the enemy's position. Contrary to all calculation, the early part of the day was passed without any offensive movement taking place. The commander of the forces, wearied of looking out for an attack, which did not seem intended, rode to the town, to give his final instructions for the embarkation, which was rapidly proceeding in the harbour; all the civilians of the army, the sick, the wounded, the dismounted cavalry, and most of the cannon, had been conveyed to the shipping; the infantry, and a small force of artillery alone, remained upon Spanish ground.

The inactivity of the French Army on the morning of the 16th appeared inexplicable, more particularly as a battery had been formed during the night, for the evident purpose of supporting an attack. Had it been placed merely to fire upon the encampment of the troops, it would, of course, have commenced at daylight; instead of which, during the forenoon not a single discharge issued from it. This was the more unaccountable, that in a very few hours darkness would prevail, only to be dispelled when every British soldier was beyond its reach. The battery, situated on a rocky height to the left of the French position, was armed with eleven pieces of cannon of large calibre; it domineered and swept the whole valley below.

At last the anxiously expected moment arrived; the enemy got under arms along his whole line; his columns were speedily formed; and about two o'clock he descended into the valley, threatening the centre and left, while a serious attack on the right had the twofold object of turning or forcing back the weakest point of the British position. Artillery, placed along the whole ridge on which the enemy had stood, now opened on the British line. He had forced back the advanced posts, and Sir David Baird's division received that of General Mermet, which had poured like a torrent down upon the village of Elvina. Fortunately, Sir John Moore had left Coruña, and was on horseback when the report of an immediate attack reached him; he arrived on the field at this critical moment. The scene now became one of the utmost animation.

When the battle commenced, being in the lowest part of the ravine, it was completely filled with smoke. Above, on either side of the valley, was to be seen the hostile array, spectators of the contest. The sun shone bright, glittering arms bristled the steep declivity; the rolling fire of artillery and musketry was constant, loud, and uninterrupted; the centre became warmly engaged. It appeared that the work of death was extending to the left. The commanding situation of the enemy's cannon was severely felt. Nothing checked their rapid fire. Immovable, they poured from the heights showers of balls; they had no opposed batteries to silence, no position to alter.

Unassailed, and in security, their conductors had alone to consider the selection of those points where, by a judicious direction, the fire might be most effective. Lord William Bentinck's brigade had from the first to resist an attack, made with all the spirit, the rapidity, and violence, natural to French troops. It had not only to maintain its ground, but to counteract the effect of a flank movement, which was executed, but ill supported, on the part of the enemy. The village of Elvina, of no importance to the security of the British position, but, being directly in the line of advance adopted by the left column of the enemy, became the seat of violent contest, terminating in its possession by the 50th regiment.

It was in the act of directing and encouraging the regiments of this brigade that the commander of the forces was mortally wounded. In the midst of a fire of musketry of the hottest description, he was also exposed to the effects of the great battery, directly over, and pointed at, this part of the field. A ball struck him from his horse, inflicting a wound of so dreadful a nature, that it is matter of surprise vitality could survive the instantaneous consequences of such tremendous injury. Thus fell, supporting the honour of his country, this truly excellent and gallant soldier!

It is neither my intention nor my wish to enter into the controversial opinions so often delivered upon the conduct of his last campaign, further, than to state a firm conviction that his talents, his energies, or his motives, are far above the reach of calumny, more particularly when clothed in all the grovelling and subservient infamy of party purpose.

The fall of Sir John Moore placed General Hope in command of the army, the battle proceeding with unabated fury. The Guards were brought up to support Lord William Bentinck; General Paget, with the Reserve, turned the left flank of the enemy. General Fraser, still more to the right, and nearer Coruña, had not yet been engaged, nor had any part of General Hope's division. The enemy's column above Palavio remained stationary, but that under General Merle vigorously attacked the British centre, without, however, succeeding in making any impression.

After the left of General Manningham's brigade had been for some time engaged, General Leith was ordered to advance one of his battalions to relieve the 81st regiment, which had not only suffered severely, but nearly exhausted its ammunition. He marched down the 59th, taking up the ground under a very heavy fire of musketry, which wounded Colonel Fane, and six other officers. A successful charge with the bayonet put a period to these volleys in our immediate front. It was now nearly dark; the firing on the right had ceased; in all directions it appeared to die away, when a warm tiraillade issued from the village of Palavio. Colonel Nichols, with the 14th regiment, had been sent to drive the enemy from thence; this he accomplished without difficulty, and in doing so, terminated the battle.

The British position was unshaken. General Paget, by a judicious movement, had endangered that of the enemy; darkness alone prevented the complete *déroute* of the French Army. Cut off from the St. Jago road by the advance of the Reserve, having that of Betanzos on which alone to retreat, with the difficulty of passing his army, in a state of confusion, across the superficially repaired bridge at Burgo, the Duke of Dalmatia might have been totally routed, could the advantage gained have been followed up immediately after the battle. It was a fortunate circumstance for his army that he deferred the attack to so late an hour; for, had light permitted, two British divisions of fresh troops would have poured upon his left, where the broken and defeated division of General Mermet would, without difficulty, have been forced back upon the centre, also defeated.

Only one of the French infantry columns remained unengaged; the numerous and fine division of General Hope, by rapidly advancing through Palavio towards El Burgo, would have completed the confusion, and might have prevented the passage of the Mero by the enemy. During this supposed state of affairs, the corps of Sir David Baird, of which some regiments had been but slightly engaged, could have remained on the ground where the battle was fought, and have kept up the communication with Coruña.

At the close of this action, there was not the same exhilarating feeling, the same excitement, that usually attends a victory. No pursuit, no trophies, nor any prisoners, at once to attest the services and the fortune of the army. The situation of the soldiers, and their various occupations, were the same as on the preceding night, while darkness prevented any traces of the action from being perceptible. A stillness prevailed for hours. The repose of the camp was only interrupted by the formation of the troops at midnight, when the whole, with the exception of the piquets, marched towards the harbour.

The enemy, unconscious of the departure of the army, continued immovable until daybreak, when the deserted position became visible. He then crossed the line of what had been the British ground, and, without delay, formed a battery upon the northern point of that range of heights where General Hope's division had been encamped; these, extending past the village of Airis, slope gradually towards the

San Diego point, at the southern extremity of the harbour. Before this battery opened its fire, most of the infantry were embarked, while distance from the shipping rendered its effects little dangerous. The only chance of serious accident was produced by the precipitation of some masters of transports, who, unaccustomed with such salutations, shewed the greatest anxiety to get as speedily as possible beyond their reach: cables were cut, sails set, and confusion evident on board many of the merchantmen.

The line-of-battle ships remained steady at their anchorage, the crews regardless of the balls passing over their decks or through the rigging. At last, the *Norge*, of seventy-four guns, lying nearest to the San Diego point, opened her battery, as if to convince the enemy it was fortunate for him that such a space intervened.

At this time, either four or five transports were aground: others had run foul of, and disabled, each other. One struck on the rocks near to the citadel, and almost immediately upset; the troops were, by great exertion, removed. Gradually the other vessels sailed, the harbour became less crowded, the wind was favourable, the arrangements of the navy were admirable, and the departure of the armaent from the shores of Spain, and from a land-locked harbour, took place without the loss of many lives; the only consequences resulting from the enemy's efforts to annoy being the destruction of the few transports wrecked in the harbour, and burnt by the British navy.

Soon after daylight on the 17th, General Leith's brigade was conveyed to the shipping; the boats of the men-of-war rapidly performed this service. The indefatigable officers of the navy carried on the embarkation with all the celerity resulting from discipline. The consequence was, that the service was far advanced before the French battery opened. It might otherwise have done considerable execution against boats crowded with men, and covering the whole surface of the water.

When passing the citadel of Coruña, on our way to the *Zealous*, of seventy-four guns, we perceived, in the nearest bastion, Colonel Graham and one other officer superintending a ceremony which we could not doubt was the interment of the brave commander of the forces. There was something unusually melancholy in this scene, and in the reflections it occasioned. Nothing around seemed calculated to enliven it. The embarkation going forward had none of the exhilaration attending an operation naturally accompanied with so much of activity, life, and spirit; all seemed sombre and depressed; we were flying from the land, which was left in the undisturbed possession of troops vanquished on the preceding day, but now preparing to fire the last taunting discharges against soldiers whom fortune appeared to have frowned upon, even in victory.

Under these circumstances, were committed to the earth the remains of Sir John Moore—a man whose memory, friends, political writers, sycophants, and interested persons of all descriptions, have visited with injustice; one party holding up his last campaign as a matchless specimen of military tactic; another, for party purposes, endeavouring to affix to his conduct the errors committed by others,—all the misfortunes occasioned by adverse and uncontrollable circumstances; while some are prepared to maintain that he was betrayed by the Spaniards, unsupported by the British Government, and left to the resources of his own mind, which alone saved the army he commanded. The character of Sir John Moore is fixed upon a less perishable basis. It will live in history, armed with all the advantages to be derived from disinterested testimony impartially given,—founded on facts and rational conclusions, not subjected to the erring opinions either of his contemporaries, or his companions in arms.

With reference to the much-complained-of conduct of the Spaniards, I have to remark, without dread of contradiction, that it was throughout distinguished by good faith, but, at the same time, rendered apparently equivocal from characteristic negligence, want of energy, and deficiency in the moral power to be alone derived from free institutions and an enlightened aristocracy.

A great portion of the difficulties occasioned by want of cordial assistance in procuring means of transport, are to be attributed to two causes; namely, ignorance in, drawing forth the resources of a country, having yet to learn the method of compelling friends to assist, and at the same time to consider themselves obliged, or the total absence of all arrangement by the authorities of that country. To expect that the Spanish peasantry were to rush from their houses, and supply the wants of the soldiers with the only provisions they possessed for their families—who might, in consequence, be left in the midst of the mountains, in the depth of winter, to starve—was imagining friendly feeling carried to an unnatural extent, and just as likely to happen, as it would have been, in the event of Napoleon having invaded Britain, that an English yeoman should have earnestly requested one of the soldiers of his own country to accept of the last morsel of bread he either possessed, or had the means of obtaining for his children. The misfortunes of Sir John Moore's army were occasioned by inexperience in campaigning, by an ignorant commissariat, by bad roads, and dreadful weather, but never by the enemy.

The fleet having been collected off the harbour of Coruña on the morning of the 18th, the admiral made the signal for proceeding, when eleven line-of-battle ships, with the whole of the transports, steered for the shores of England,

CHAPTER 2

Defeat of the Spanish Armies

On the evening of the 2nd July, 1809, the *Champion* frigate, Captain Henderson, anchored in the Tagus.

On my way to join the 29th regiment, I had embarked at Portsmouth with Captain Henderson, and accompanied him to Guernsey, where he took under convoy a fleet of transports, having on board the second battalions of the 34th, 39th, and 58th regiments, which he now saw in safety to their place of destination. It was late when we entered the river, and darkness prevented our enjoying a view of the beautiful scene. At daybreak, however, the city of Lisbon appeared in all the majesty of its picturesque and grand situation, while the stately river bore on its waters the ships of many nations. Close to where we anchored was the *Barfleur*, of ninety-eight guns, bearing the flag of Admiral Berkeley, commanding, in appearance, as in reality, every vessel that floated on the noble Tagus.

Line-of-battle ships, frigates, and smaller vessels of war, were discernible in every direction; the light, serviceable, and elegant rigging of the British navy contrasting with the slack, slovenly, or loaded cordage of all other description of shipping. The Russian men-of-war, detained at the period of the convention of Lisbon, dismasted, and moored above the town, presented the very *beau idéal* of hulks, while the large and handsome Portuguese frigates, anchored on the Almada side of the river, seemed in a state of preparation to carry from their native shores the persons to whom such emigration might become a matter of interest or necessity, in the event of a French Army again occupying Lisbon. A large fleet of transports were at anchor; boats passed in all directions; vessels arriving or departing gave life and variety to a scene of the most animated, varied, and interesting description.

Lisbon, when seen from a distance, were it not for its situation and splendid river, is not, as a town, either grand or beautiful. Unlike other great cities, it derives no ornament from spires or domes, with the exception of that of the Estrella convent. The sameness in the appearance of its buildings is unbroken; but its varied situation, the inequality of the ground on which it stands, rising at once from the banks of the Tagus, its great extent, the light colour of the stone with which it is built, the luxuriant appearance of the surrounding country—altogether give it an unequalled aspect of importance.

At this period, not a French soldier remained in Portugal. The second invasion of that country had been repelled, and the army of Sir Arthur Wellesley, after having driven the Duke of Dalmatia from Oporto across the frontier, had marched to commence offensive operations in Spanish Estremadura. This was one of the bright and apparently prosperous epochs of the Peninsular War.

The Spanish armies, defeated, but not discouraged, were numerous, improved in equipment, in some measure accustomed to active warfare; the British Army had just terminated a short but brilliant campaign; the frontier fortresses were in possession of the allies; the *morale* of the French Army had been shaken, while its numbers were diminished by the departure of the Imperial Guard, and other troops for Germany, and the casualties attendant upon the unpopular and dangerous service on which it was employed. Ten British battalions had just arrived in the Tagus. The season was beautiful. Uninterrupted supplies poured in, at the same time, from England and America. The governments of the three countries seemed determined zealously and cordially to prosecute the war.

Napoleon was at Vienna; his brother Joseph acted as generalissimo of the French arms in Spain, Marshal Jourdan as his chief of the staff. The other marshals employed in the Peninsula were without confidence in the military judgment of these persons; they were also jealous of each other,—a feeling to which the ablest of them was subjected. Such was the situation of affairs when Sir Arthur Wellesley established his headquarters at Plasencia, on the 8th July, 1809.

The brigade of General Robert Crawford, composed of the 43rd, 52nd, and 95th regiments, left Lisbon to join the army. Three finer battalions never took the field; nor did their conduct upon any occasion ever belie the promise held out by their discipline, their robust healthy appearance, brilliant equipment, or distinguishedly military air.

From the moment of my arrival in Portugal, it naturally became an object of intense interest to join my regiment. Fortunately, I met

Distant Castello branca

at Lisbon Captain Tucker, of the 29th, who, impressed with similar feelings, agreed to adopt the most rapid mode of joining the army. We procured a post-order to facilitate our progress, and, having determined to proceed as far as Villada by water, embarked on the morning of the 14th, to row up the Tagus.

The right bank of the river is covered with olive-trees, the ground rather elevated, and extremely picturesque. Villada, situated thirty-six miles from Lisbon, is a miserable village, and the country near to it flat and uninteresting. We there left the boat that had conveyed us from the capital, and commenced the journey by land. It was very late when we arrived at Santarem, where considerable difficulty occurred in procuring a lodging. As might naturally be expected, the inhabitants were not particularly anxious to disturb their families at one o'clock in the morning, for the purpose of welcoming perfect strangers, nor had they been by inspiration expecting an arrival, or ready to receive us.

Probably all this was indicative of apathy, want of energy, and bad faith. Whatever *rational* motive may be assigned for the circumstance, we had to support the inconvenience, and were left to divine the reason of such conduct, without being empowered to obtain redress. Having travelled through the rich and fertile valley of Golegao, we arrived next morning at Abrantes, one of the most beautifully situated towns in Portugal. Seated on an eminence overhanging the Tagus, it commands one of the most extensive and varied prospects to be imagined.

Abrantes is a town of considerable size. The convent of San Antonio, to the north, forms a striking object, and is seen at a great distance. In the evening we again proceeded, gradually forsaking beautiful scenery for that of a more wild and dreary cast. Late at night, we reached Penascoso. From thence to Vendas Novas the road is extremely bad, the country continuing bleak and uncultivated. Having passed Perdigao, apparently the seat of poverty and misery, we arrived at Castello Branco. From thence to the frontier of Spain, no feature of particular interest attracts notice. The road passes through Idanha Nova and Salvaterra. The latter town, built upon very high ground, overlooks the River Erjas, forming the boundary of the kingdoms. Directly opposite to Salvaterra, also upon precipitous and elevated ground, stands the ruined castle of Penafiel, which appears to have been erected as a watch-tower for the Spanish border.

Zarza Mayor, seated in a valley, is in every respect contrasted to those towns we had lately seen in Portugal. It is built with regularity; the houses having an appearance of cleanliness and comfort. Coria, situated on the right bank of the River Alagon, is the seat of a bishopric. It is surrounded by an ancient wall. The cathedral is the most diminutive, the least remarkable building of its class, that I have ever seen in Spain.

The Alagon at Coria is a large and deep river, running through a flat country, beautifully wooded, and in many places in a high state of cultivation. A bridge of seven arches connects the town with the river, over which, however, there is no bridge. This gives rise to the Spanish saying, that Coria is a town with "*Puente sin Rio, y Rio sin Puente.*"

Late at night, after a day's journey of fourteen Spanish leagues, we arrived at the city of Plasencia, a large town in the centre of fertile plains, surrounded by mountains. Plasencia must ever be celebrated, from the circumstance of the Emperor Charles V. having selected it as the place of retirement, to which he dedicated the last years of his eventful and brilliant life; nor does it appear, that, in the whole extent of his Spanish territories, a more favourable spot could have been chosen, either with reference to climate, beauty of situation, or retirement of position. If ever there was a retired city, it is Plasencia. Its cathedral is a fine building, but not of first rate magnificence.

The British Army having advanced in the direction of Madrid, the sick alone remained at Plasencia. On the morning of the 20th, we proceeded on our journey, crossed the mountains in front of the town, and descended into the valley of the Tietar, from whence, having passed the village of Majadas, the route traverses immense forests of oak, frequently close to the banks of that romantic and beautiful river. We crossed the Tietar by the temporary bridge of Bazagona, arriving at mid-day near the Casa de las Llomas, beautifully situated on an eminence in the centre of the forest, the river winding through the extensive valley, its banks covered with the noblest trees, luxuriant in foliage, affording shade, and coolness, and relief from the effects of a meridian sun. To the left, and in the distance, appeared the lofty range of mountain, separating Estremadura from the province of Salamanca, surmounted by the Sierra de Gredos, with its summits clad in perpetual snow. A more splendid scene can scarcely be imagined. Nothing could be finer than the bold outline of the mountains, or more magnificent than the broad dark shadow, which, descending from their precipitous and rocky sides, overspread forest scenery that appeared interminable.

Oropesa we found unoccupied by the allied troops, but there received information of a slight affair having taken place with the rear of the French Army. It, therefore, became important to proceed with the least possible delay; and, at two o'clock on the morning of the 23rd, we joined the 29th regiment in camp, near Talavera de la Reyna. Having dismissed the horses we had brought from Oropesa. Captain Gauntlet's tent afforded us shelter. Wrapped in our cloaks, we reposed until half-past three, when the regiment got under arms.

The immediate vicinity of the enemy rendered it probable that the slightest forward movement would bring us in contact; nor did the orders of the preceding night in any respect remove the impression, that we were likely to be engaged. My travelling companion and myself, therefore, had a good chance of being in fire, before we had time to consider our relative situations in the regiment, where we were posted, or, in short, anything except marching forward. There was a novelty and bustle in the situation, that gave it interest; nor had we time to receive those instructions which the etiquette of the service render necessary, until the parade was dismissed, which was soon after the result of its being ascertained that no immediate advance was contemplated.

Talavera, situated on the right bank of the Tagus, was at this period the headquarters of Sir Arthur Wellesley, and General Cuesta. Above 50,000 British and Spanish troops occupied the neighbouring encampment. In front, on the high grounds to the left of the River Alberche, was the *corps d'armée* of Marshal the Duke of Belluno.

The 29th regiment, brigaded with the 48th, and 1st battalion of detachments, under Brigadier-General Richard Stewart, formed part of the division of Major-General Hill. This brigade, until the evening of the 27th, occupied the olive groves in front of the town, upon the immediate left of the road to Santa Olalla and Madrid.

The 23rd passed without any important event occurring. The allied army continued at Talavera; nor were the enemy's troops withdrawn from the position.; in front. It appears difficult to account for this delay in, attacking so inferior a force; as regimental officers, we knew nothing with certainty, except what we personally witnessed, or read in the orders of the army; all else was rumour, exaggeration, surmise, or error. We were told that old General Cuesta declined fighting on Sunday. If he did assign that reason, it could only have been in bitterness and derision; but from whatever motive, the combined army permitted Marshal Victor to withdraw his corps uninjured, which he effected during the night. Early on the morning of the 24th, the whole army moved to attack his position. It was found unoccupied.

Sir Arthur halted the troops under his orders, upon this fact being ascertained; but the Spanish general, with characteristic arrogance, singly dashed forward in pursuit. His columns passed the Alberche in rapid succession, as if they were alone to be obstructed by the iron barrier of the Pyrenees. General Hill's division retraced its steps, occupying the same ground on which it had previously been encamped. The state of the campaign to an uninformed spectator appeared extraordinary. The army, previously acting in concert, was now separated, the least effective part being in pursuit of the enemy. Part of the British force had crossed the Alberche, and was ten miles in advance of Talavera, while the remainder continued perfectly quiet, enjoying demi-starvation upon the banks of the Tagus.

The 29th regiment, at this time commanded by Colonel White, had suffered on many occasions since its arrival in the Peninsula.[1] Reduced in numbers, its colours were still defended by gallant and highly disciplined soldiers. A long-established and excellent regimental system was calculated to outlive the contingencies of frequently changed command, or the blanks occasioned by the fall of old and experienced soldiers. It would have demanded as much misapplied energy to have effectually broken down its discipline and appearance, as it does the best or soundest judgment to eradicate the fatal effects of a long standing bad system in battalions, even where the dregs, the recollections, and the consequences, alone remain.

During the 25th, we heard nothing of the Spanish Army, but on the following day the report of artillery announced its return,—not unaccompanied. The cannonade was distant, but evidently becoming less so. Runaways and stragglers passed to the rear; the weather was very fine; from the vicinity of the Santa Olalla road we derived great amusement: it was covered by a succession of groups, habited in various costumes.

On the morning of the 27th, we learned that part of General Cuesta's army had passed to the rear; while battalion after battalion formed a continuous line of march in the same direction. From amidst clouds of dust, disorderly chattering assemblages of half-clad, half-armed men, became occasionally visible; again, regiments marching in perfect order, cavalry, staff officers, bands of musicians, flocks of sheep,

---

1. *With the 29th Regiment in the Peninsula & the 60th Rifles in Canada, 1807-1832* by Charles Leslie also published by Leonaur.

and bullocks; artillery, cars, carriages, and wagons, varied the animated, confused, and singular scene on which we gazed,—forgetting for the time that all this was intimately connected with our very existence. The Spanish Army, notwithstanding this confusion, had not the appearance of being pressed by the enemy in its retreat; nor did the scene we now witnessed differ much from that it would have presented, under more favourable circumstances. The battalions marched in their best order; but with all this qualification, it was still a Spanish Army,—ill commanded, ill appointed, moderately disciplined, and in most respects inefficient. In the line of march, I perceived the Villaviciosa hussars, and accosted one of the soldiers who had accompanied General Leith during the campaign of 1808. He informed me of the Baron Almendarez having been wounded, and taken in the affair of Santa Olalla on the preceding day.

After the Spanish Army had ceased to march past us, we returned to the quiet of the olive grove. Cannon and musketry were heard at intervals, but no order to move had yet arrived. Several officers of the 29th were assembled, when the Spanish General O'Donahue rode up from the direction of the Alberche. He appeared in a state of considerable excitement, stating we probably were not aware of the enemy having crossed the river, and that he would be upon us without delay. This information was received in a manner little according with his own apparent feelings on the occasion. We merely thanked him, adding, that when it was necessary to get under arms, orders to that effect would of course be communicated. Another hour elapsed,—when the firing became so close and constant, that we began to consider it extraordinary that orders were not received.

At last, however, the brigade got under arms, and marched to the left, passing both Spanish and British troops in line, who already occupied the position defended by them on the following day. As we moved left in front, the 29th, being the senior regiment, was in rear of the column,—the 48th leading. In this formation we advanced about half way between the town of Talavera and the eminence then unoccupied, but which was evidently, from its locality and importance, destined to become the left, as also the strongest part of the position.

The brigade halted for a short time near to the division of Brigadier-General Alexander Campbell, in rear of an unfinished Spanish redoubt. The evening was far advanced when we again moved towards the hill. The firing, as we pressed forward, appeared heavy and incessant in the direction of the Alberche. Regiments of General

M'Kenzie's division, retiring, passed us diagonally, falling into the line. It was now nearly dark. We were approaching the base of the hill, when a sharp fire issued from the leading regiment, which, although assailed in its progress, continued to advance.

The 29th was formed in column of companies, at quarter distance. The 48th and battalion of detachments met with a formidable resistance, and were driven back at this critical moment, upon which the safety of the army depended. The 29th was ordered to advance at double quick time. The leading company crowned the summit previously to receiving the enemy's fire. A considerable body of French were now in possession of the height. Their numbers rapidly increasing, the drums beat the *pas de charge*; while at intervals voices were heard, some calling out they were the German Legion, others not to fire. It was so dark that the blaze of musketry alone displayed the forms of the assailants.

The leading company of the 29th poured in a volley when close to the bayonets of the enemy. The glorious cheer of British infantry accompanied the charge which succeeded. The rest of the regiment arrived in quick succession, forming on the summit a close column, which speedily drove everything before it. The enemy was pushed down the hill, abandoning the level ground on its top, thickly strewed with dead bodies or wounded men. No second attempt was for some time made to carry this most important point. The 29th remained in possession of the ground, lying on their arms in the midst of fallen enemies. The furred *schakos* of a dead French soldier became my pillow for the night.

The heavy fire of musketry, the darkness, the apparently obstinate nature of the dispute for the possession of the hill, the uncertainty of the result, all occasioned great anxiety at head-quarters. Sir Arthur Wellesley himself rode to the spot, to which he immediately ordered up artillery; and the early part of the night was employed in drawing cannon to the height. After they had been placed in battery, a stillness for some time prevailed. About midnight this was suddenly interrupted, by firing towards Talavera;—not the straggling, desultory, yet distinct reports of light troops, but a roll of musketry that illuminated the whole extent of the Spanish line. It was one discharge; but of such a nature that I have never heard it equalled. It appeared not to be returned, nor was it repeated. All again became silent. A false alarm had occasioned this tremendous volley; but we were too distant to ascertain what had produced the violent irruption, or how many of our allies had thrown away their arms, and fled, after having delivered a fire sufficiently formidable to have shaken the best and bravest troops.

For hours nothing seemed to interfere with the stillness of the night, until the rattling of gun-carriages in our front bespoke preparation for renewed hostility at daybreak. It was evident from the sound that cannon were placing in position, at no great distance, and immediately opposite to the height we occupied. Whether occasioned by the noise of this operation, from officers reconnoitring, or cavalry patrols advancing near to our posts, is uncertain, some straggling shots were fired, occasioning a momentary *alerte*; but no enemy appearing, the cause of alarm was speedily explained and forgotten.

Just before daybreak was an anxious moment; and when the first glimmering light appeared, the attention of all was naturally riveted upon the enemy's position, to ascertain what troops were opposed, where his cannon were placed, and to what extent we were to be assailed. Twenty-two pieces of artillery had their mouths directed towards us. They were posted upon elevated ground, but by no means of equal height to that on which we stood, having, however, the whole face and summit of the hill well within range. To the right of the French cannon were perceived columns of infantry. A renewed battle for the hill became certain.

The 29th regiment, having carried it on the previous night, were not removed from its summit during the whole course of the subsequent operations, except in pursuit of the enemy. The formation of the brigade became consequently altered, that regiment being on the extreme left of the whole line of British infantry, while the battalion of detachments, and the 48th, were formed on the slope extending to the right, and gradually losing itself in the olive groves that covered two-thirds of the position.

When it became perfectly light, a signal gun put the enemy's columns in motion, the whole of his artillery opening almost immediately after. The incessant and violent description of cannonade prevented the British infantry from interrupting the progress of the French columns; nor did they sustain any loss whatever in the early part of their advance, coming on with a resolute and rapid pace. The 29th were ordered to lie down a short distance behind the brow of the hill, which the soldiers did with arms in their hands, ready to start up at a moment's warning. By this judicious arrangement, the regiment suffered little from the cannonade, although the enemy's practice appeared excellent, every shot either striking the ground immediately in front, or passing close over our heads.

There is at all times something grand, imposing, and terrific, in the sound of a cannonade. Here we had the astounding noise, with time to contemplate what was passing over us, without the attention being abstracted by great personal danger, or immediate effort at extrication. The effect was consequently very impressive. An old Scotch sergeant, crouching close to me, permitted his head to attain a very slight elevation, and, with a groan, said,—"Good God, sir, this is dreadful!" Without discussing the merits of our situation, I merely advised him to keep down his head,—a hint instantly adopted, without any apparent reluctance on his part, and, at the close of the affair, I was happy to find it was still upon his shoulders. At this period we had the battle entirely to ourselves, no other part of the army being engaged.

When the French columns had mounted the ascent, and were so near as to become endangered from the fire of their own artillery, a scene of great animation was exhibited. The summit, which had appeared deserted, now supported a regular line of infantry. Near the colours of the 29th, stood Sir Arthur Wellesley, directing and animating the troops.

General Ruffin had nearly surmounted all the difficulties of the ground, when a fire burst forth that checked his advance. His troops wavered. Sir Arthur ordered a charge. With one tremendous shout the right wing of the 29th, and entire battalion of the 48th, rushed like a torrent down, bayoneting and sweeping back the enemy to the brink of an insignificant muddy stream, nearly equidistant in the ravine which separated the two armies. In the pursuit, all order was speedily lost. The men advanced in small parties, destroying those of the enemy who had not ensured their safety by flight. At this moment, when the whole valley was filled with troops, in all the confusion attending the eagerness of pursuit, a column of French infantry appeared close upon our right flank, facing towards the irregular mass.

It became necessary to collect the pursuers, to form a front, and to charge these fresh assailants. This was, by great exertion, accomplished. Broken as we were, an irresistible impetus had been given, and the enemy's column followed the example of those who had mounted the hill at the *pas de charge*. So completely were these attacks repelled, that the British infantry were quietly collected in the ravine, and marched back to the height without being seriously assailed. The enemy now threw out light troops in front of his defeated 1st corps. Artillery continued to fire at intervals; but for a time nothing like serious fighting succeeded the Duke of Belluno's failure in the morning.

To the left of the British position at Talavera is a flat, extending in breadth about a mile, bounded to the north by a ridge of high rocky mountains, terminating the prospect. Upon these heights the enemy placed a number of light troops, which were, during the day, effectually kept in check by a division of General Cuesta's army. The tiraillade was incessant, probably little destructive; but it had the desired effect, no jealousy being created by the progress of the war in that quarter. In this valley to our left, but somewhat in rear of the infantry, was placed General Anson's brigade of light cavalry, consisting of the 1st Hussars of the German Legion, and 23rd Dragoons. These regiments were in line, dismounted. In rear of them, also in line, was the heavy brigade of General Fane; and in his rear the Duke of Alburquerque, with the Spanish cavalry.

After the repulse of the 1st corps, great indecision seemed to prevail in the enemy's army. His columns remained for hours immovable. During this cessation of hostilities, the troops of General Hill's division descended in parties to the stream in our front, for the purpose of procuring water, which was only obtained in small quantities, of a description that, under other circumstances, would have produced loathing; but the excessive heat of the weather, added to exertion, occasioned a burning thirst, demanding to be quenched by any possible means. This temporary calm was only the prelude to more serious conflict. Early in the afternoon, appearances again indicated renewed attack on the part of the enemy. His whole line stood to their arms. Clouds of dust marked the advance of troops against the centre and right of the British position; while the 1st *corps d'armée*, supported by a large body of cavalry, formed for another effort to force the left.

To the right of where the French artillery had been placed in the night, and on a line with them, was a small building, behind which, and to its right, was formed General Villatte's division; higher up the valley, the remains of General Ruffin's; a third division supported General Villatte, and the whole *plateau* to the rear was covered with cavalry in extended order. Some Spanish artillery had arrived upon the height: plunging into the enemy's columns, their fire was incessant, and well directed. In the midst of our troops, these men fought their guns in a manner to excite the admiration of all present; proving that Spaniards only required the confidence given by example to conduct themselves in the face of an enemy with propriety.

The scene from the hill was now of a grand description. A fire of cannon and musketry to the whole extent of the British centre and left, was of the most serious description. To those who, elevated as we were, saw every movement, this was the most anxious moment of the whole battle. Heavy columns of French infantry seemed following in succession to press upon the weakest part of the line; nor did it appear within the reach of probability that the centre could successfully resist this overwhelming force.

General Alexander Campbell, upon the extreme right of the British force, was flanked by a redoubt which strengthened his position, and became of essential importance. His troops were never shaken; they fought with the greatest gallantry, drove back General Sebastiani, and took ten pieces of cannon. Thus far the battle had proceeded without the slightest reverse.

General Sherbrooke was now vigorously attacked. His division was assailed, both in front and on its left flank, by a fire of artillery; while columns of infantry rushed up to the bayonets of the British Guards. They were instantaneously borne back in confusion. In the heat of pursuit, the Guards, as is the case with troops in all parts of the world, in every similar situation, fell into disorder. Who has ever seen an unbroken line preserved in following up a successful bayonet charge? As they advanced, the enemy's artillery fire became, of course, closer and more deadly. Fresh, and regularly formed troops, met the pursuers, and drove them back. If they were in confusion when advancing, this state of matters was not calculated to restore their formation. The Guards were driven across their former ground, and the line seemed pierced. The German Legion on their left also vigorously attacked, and, suffering severely from the cannonade, gave way. There was no reserve of infantry. One single file of Germans had stood between us and destruction. This had now disappeared. It was an awful moment; promptitude, and the inertness of the Duke of Belluno, alone saved the army.

Sir Arthur Wellesley, who, from the height, surveyed the progress of the battle, directed the 29th to go down; and the regiment was in the act of moving, when, considering probably its weakness in numbers, he ordered the 48th to proceed, and check the enemy's progress in the centre. That excellent regiment marched with the utmost rapidity, and compelled the enemy to desist from the pursuit. The Guards rallied, cheering their readiness to again press forward, the Germans recovered their formation, and the battle was restored.

During this great struggle, the troops upon the hill had remained comparatively disengaged; a fire of artillery and light troops, producing a slight effect, alone disturbing the regiment, and the numerous staff, upon its summit. The favourable termination of the battle in the centre had created a great excitement. The cheer, which had been re-echoed from the height, had scarcely died away, when a scene of another character was in preparation, again to call forth its invigorating influence.

The movements of the divisions Ruffin and Villatte had, during the contest just described, been vacillating and uncertain. Formed to all appearance determined again to attack the height, they had even advanced some distance towards its base. Their light troops skirmished closely and seriously; but nothing like the attack of the morning was again attempted. Still the right of the French Army had a very imposing appearance. In columns of attack, and supported by numerous cavalry, a serious effort was every moment to be expected. Sir Arthur Wellesley crossed with rapid step from the right of the 29th to the part of the hill looking directly down upon General Anson's brigade of cavalry, which mounted on the instant. It was immediately known that a charge would take place.

The ground upon which this brigade was in line is perfectly level; nor did any visible obstruction appear between it and the columns opposed. The grass was long, dry, and waving, concealing the fatal chasm that intervened. One of General Villatte's columns stood at some distance to the right of the building formerly mentioned. These troops were directly in front of the 23rd Dragoons. Another was formed rather to the rear, and more in front of the German hussars, on the left of the line. Such were the immediate objects of the charge.

For some time the brigade advanced at a rapid pace, without receiving any obstruction from the enemy's fire. The line cheered. It was answered from the hill with the greatest enthusiasm; never was anything more exhilarating or more beautiful than the commencement of this advance. Several lengths in front, mounted on a gray horse, consequently very conspicuous, rode Colonel Elley. Thus placed, he, of course, first arrived at the brink of a ravine, which, varying in width, extended along the whole front of the line. Going half speed at the time, no alternative was left him. To have checked his horse and given timely warning became impossible. With some difficulty he cleared it at a bound, and, on gaining the opposite bank, endeavoured by gesture to warn the 23rd of the dangerous ground they had to pass; but, advancing with such velocity, the line was on the verge of the stream before his signs could be either understood or attended to. Under any circumstances this must have been a serious occurrence in a cavalry charge; but, when it is considered that four or five hundred dragoons were assailing two divisions of infantry unbroken, and fully prepared for the onset, to have persevered at all was highly honourable to the regiment.

At this moment the enemy, formed in squares, opened his tremendous fire. A change immediately took place. Horses rolled on the earth; others were seen flying back dragging their unhorsed riders with them; the German hussars coolly reined up; the line of the 23rd was broken. Still the regiment galloped forward. The confusion was increased; but no hesitation took place in the individuals of this gallant corps. The survivors rushed forward with, if possible, accelerated pace, passing between the flank of the square, now one general blaze of fire, and the building on its left.

Colonel Elley and Major Frederick Ponsonby—officers not to be easily checked—headed the part of the regiment that had penetrated thus far; and, as if enraged at not having been enabled to make a sabre stroke at the infantry, rode forward against the cavalry drawn up in line to the rear. These *chasseurs*, either impressed with the extraordinary nature of the attack, or from some inexplicable cause, gave way before these broken, but gallant horsemen.

The situation of the 23rd was now very critical. To return directly from whence the regiment had advanced, was impracticable. By doing so, the surviving soldiers must have again sustained a close and deadly fire from the French squares; and, although the *chasseurs* had given way, another line of cavalry was in their front. To their right was the whole French Army; to their left, and in rear of the enemy's infantry, was the only possible line of escape. This was adopted. In small parties, or singly, they again regained the valley, re-forming in rear of General Fane's brigade, the advance of which had been countermanded, after the unsuccessful result of the first charge was ascertained. Fortunately for the first *corps d'armée,* no further attempt was made to carry the hill. The same repulse would probably again have attended the effort, while 6000 cavalry were in the immediate vicinity, and could have instantaneously fallen upon the broken ranks.

Eighty pieces of French cannon now thundered along the extent of the line; and as the infantry attacks failed, the circumstance appeared but to give renewed vigour to the cannonade, which was incessant and destructive. Towards evening the long grass in the valley to our left, and in front of the height, took fire; burning with great violence, and extending with rapidity. The whole surface of the flat, over which the 23rd had advanced, and the face of the hill, up which General Ruffin's division attacked in the morning, became one close continuous mass of fire and smoke. The French artillery and *voltigeurs* still fired upon the height; nor had the infantry columns of the Duke of Belluno been withdrawn. It being of importance to ascertain that no more serious attack was imperceptibly permitted to take place, I was directed by Colonel Bathurst, the military secretary, to station myself near the cannon on the summit, and report the enemy's motions. These guns were now silent; and the 29th regiment, a short distance to their rear, removed from the effects of the enemy's fire.

The grass being excessively dry, burnt with astonishing rapidity,—the whole face of the country over which the conflagration extended, soon forming one black scorched mass, studded with bodies of the dead or wounded. After serious attack had ceased on all parts of the line, and even the light troops had become more distant, Sir Arthur Wellesley was seated, with some officers of his staff, upon the south-eastern ridge of the hill, observing the retiring columns of the enemy, when a musket ball struck him on the breast with sufficient force to give a severe and painful blow, without penetrating. It would be idle to descant upon the destinies depending on the degree of impetus possessed by this small portion of lead!

Worn down with long exertion and fatigue,—exhausted from want of food,—oppressed by heat,—tired by the duration of a struggle that appeared interminable,—the approach of night was not unwelcome. The enemy had been repulsed at all points, but no pursuit to any extent had been attempted; and when darkness closed upon the armies, it was uncertain that the following day would not produce a renewed effort on the part of the enemy. The fire of cannon had not yet ceased, nor was it until the close of twilight, that the dull sluggish sound of artillery, when heard alone at intervals, or at a distance, seemed to knell the close of this sanguinary but most interesting battle.

The 29th regiment, reduced by the fall of one hundred and eighty-six officers and soldiers, bivouacked for the night on the same spot as the preceding. Great firmness to grapple with responsibility, self-possession to rise above adverse circumstances, a vigorous mind to decide promptly and correctly, brave troops, and the good fortune of being indecisively and injudiciously opposed, brought Sir Arthur Wellesley through the Battle of Talavera.

No generals, possessed of the experience and character of Marshals Jourdan and Victor, ever committed more errors in one day; it would be difficult to point out any portion of the plan adopted by them that was not faulty and ill-conceived. What makes this more conspicuous and more remarkable is, that it was not one erroneous principle of tactics, but a succession, and that after events had proved the hopeless success of their primary arrangements, they did not correct the disposition of their force, and make a simultaneous and irresistible attack.

Having failed in obtaining possession of the hill on the night of the 27th, Marshal Victor, who is understood to have known the ground perfectly, might have passed the whole of his *corps d'armée* through the valley to the left of the British without obstruction; 30,000 men would still have been in line in Sir Arthur Wellesley's front. Secondly, the isolated attack of the British left at daylight was ill-judged and unsupported; had cavalry then been in the valley, the enemy's column, which, as it was, suffered severely, might have been annihilated.

If the French marshals, instead of attacking the flanks of the British, had borne, with a large portion of their force, upon the centre, making demonstrations sufficient to occupy the other parts of the line, they must, in all probability, have succeeded; but it is an unanswerable reflection upon generals commanding 50,000 troops, that they, having made a serious impression, permitted victory to be wrested from them by a single battalion, and that battalion detached from a point where five others, reduced in numbers, were threatened by a whole *corps d'armée*. All combination seemed at an end in the French Army. In the morning, the Duke of Belluno was defeated, the other generals looking on; in the evening, General Sebastiani met with the same fate, Marshal Victor remaining immovable.

In passing this censure upon the conduct of the French generals-in-chief at Talavera, it is but just to bear testimony to the gallantry of the troops. Upon no occasion did the enemy's infantry ever assail ours with more determined resolution, more impetuosity, or with more undoubted bravery.

A cold damp night succeeded to this excessively warm and fatiguing day. The troops remained in position without covering of any description, and without food. Never did a British Army attach less importance to such privations. Events had succeeded each other so rapidly, the whole scene was so impressive, that all else appeared forgotten; for the last thirty-six hours, a morsel of bread, with some pure water, would have been considered luxurious fare upon the hill at

Talavera.

At daybreak, it became evident that the main body of the enemy had retired from view. A corps, estimated at 10,000 men, occupied the heights of Salinas, on the left bank of the Alberche; but no other part of the enemy's army was in any direction discernible. It was no longer necessary to detain the troops in position. At nine o'clock, the 29th regiment marched from the height, to encamp in the olive-grove at its base. There was something noble in the waving colours of the British regiments, as they slowly descended from that eminence where, two days previously, they had been planted, not to be shaken by any assault, however firmly made, and which they now left covered with dead bodies, broken arms, shattered tumbrils, and the fragments of shells. As we descended, every step displayed objects proving the severity of the conflict which had taken place on the particular spot: but nowhere was there appearance of more terrific execution than on the ground of the German Legion; there, both artillery and musketry appeared to have revelled in slaughter.

The morning after the action, General Robert Craufordʼs brigade arrived, and, passing over the field of battle, took the outpost duty upon the Alberche. The town of Talavera became crowded with wounded, many of whom were in a wretched state. By the activity and energy of Mr. Guthrie, surgeon to the regiment, those of the 29th were comparatively well lodged, his hospitals presenting an appearance of great regularity and arrangement. Captain Gauntlet, who had, upon the morning of the 28th, been wounded on the right temple by a grape shot, lingered until the 30th, when he expired. The regiment accompanied his remains to the height where he fell.

The small portion of the Spanish Army that were engaged on the 28th, behaved very gallantly, particularly the cavalry regiment Del Rey, which charged, and was most useful, after General Alexander Campbell had repulsed the attack of the fourth corps; but most of General Cuesta's force remained inactive spectators during the course of the battle. The Duke of Alberquerque had no opportunity of engaging the great body of cavalry under his immediate orders; but its presence in the valley was of the utmost importance, and must have had considerable influence on the movements of the Duke of Belluno.

The inactivity of General Venegas, who was, during these operations, in the vicinity of Toledo, with twenty-five thousand men, is quite inexplicable. Great results must have been produced by a decisive and prompt co-operation on his part. He might have converted the repulse of Talavera into a substantial victory; as it was, no military situation can well be conceived more dangerous or more perplexing than that of the British general, even after the successful issue of the battle.

He was acting in concert with General Cuesta, an obstinate, jealous, imbecile old man, at the head of an army on which no great dependence could be placed. In his front, were the defeated but unbroken corps of Marshal Victor, Generals Sebastiani and Dessolles. General Venegas either could not, or would not, co-operate. In his rear, in possession of the lines of communication, north of the Tagus, were Marshals the Dukes of Dalmatia, Elchingen, and Treviso, cutting off his retreat by Plasencia, commanding the passage of the Tagus at Almarez, Ponté Cardenal, and Alcantara, and rapidly advancing upon Oropeza. Added to these circumstances, his army was difficulted in obtaining supplies. Animals for transporting the 5000 sick and wounded, that filled the hospitals of Talavera, were not to be procured.

Had the Spanish armies been composed of troops equal to the French in discipline or the knowledge of war, commanded by men cordial in their alliance, and ready to second the views of the British general, an immediate advance upon Madrid, and junction with Venegas, might have been the most judicious measure to have adopted under the extremely difficult circumstances. As it was nothing but madness could have dictated such a movement. Remaining at Talavera was also out of the question: to have done so would have been playing the enemy's game to the fullest extent.

Taking the chance of a large portion of the French Army, which had fought the battle of the 28th, being occupied by General Venegas, and Sir Robert Wilson's corps,—that the remainder could not immediately return to Talavera,—that, if they did so, General Cuesta's army ought to be sufficient to keep them in check,—was a sound view of the first part of the plan adopted. To return by the Plasencia road, and give battle to the Duke of Dalmatia, with the whole of the British Army, was the only possible method of saving its hospitals. On the morning of the 3rd of August, therefore, having left General Cuesta at Talavera, Sir Arthur Wellesley marched his army to Oropeza.

The British had scarcely disappeared from his sight, when the old Spanish general began to doubt the security of his quarters; nor were the enemy long in giving him reason to suppose that the sooner he approximated to his ally the better. The great force with which the Duke of Dalmatia was advancing, being now ascertained, must probably have prevented Sir Arthur following up his intention of giving him battle; but the arrival of the Spanish Army in full retreat made an immediate and decided movement absolutely necessary.

There was no possible safe line of operation now left on the right bank of the Tagus. One passage across that river alone remained open,—that by the Puente del Arzobispo, over which, during the 4th, the army passed, encamping in the woods on the left bank. At daybreak, on the morning of the 5th, we marched in the direction of Mesa de Ibor, halting for the night in a ravine, distant six leagues from the Puente del Arzobispo. On the 6th, the army continued its route, passing over a rugged and precipitous road. At one part of the Sierra, and for a considerable distance, to drag the artillery up by the usual means became impossible. The infantry were put to the guns, who, with considerable difficulty and exertion, forced them along the mountain road.

On this day's march, for the first time, were heard complaints from the soldiers on the subject of want of food. Toiling over these mountains, dragging the cannon, severely harassed by excessive heat, the men, conversing with each other, talked loudly of the hardships endured; but a soothing and encouraging expression was alone necessary to restore their good humour, even when assailed on the tenderest point.

General Robert Crauford's brigade had preceded the army in the direction of Almaraz, to watch the passage of the river at that important place. Fortunately, the enemy had hitherto confined his movements to the right bank of the Tagus. Had he crossed part of his force at Almaraz previous to the arrival of the British, which was perfectly possible, the situation of Sir Arthur Wellesley must, of course, have become one of increased embarrassment; but the moment he arrived at Deleytosa the safety of his army was beyond doubt: its retreat was no longer liable to obstruction. His situation at Talavera, upon the morning of the 3rd of August, was one of incomparably greater danger than that of Sir John Moore at Sahagun; but, as has previously been stated, the merit of extrication must deservedly be given to his own great military talent, his firmness of determination, his clear insight into the real state of affairs, both with regard to his allies, his enemy, the country in which he was committed, or his own numerical means; but all this must have been unavailing had he been opposed by generals of great military talent. The Battle of Talavera proved what pretension Marshal Victor had to that character; the Duke of Dalmatia was only great when acting under the immediate orders of Napoleon.

It is evident that, had it been practicable for Sir Arthur Wellesley at this period to form a correct estimate of the extent or nature of Spanish co-operation, or had he obtained information as to the real situation of Marshal Soult's army, the Battle of Talavera ought never to have been fought. It is also certain, that the error thereby committed was in a great measure remedied by the judicious arrangements of the British general, resulting from the knowledge of facts acquired subsequent to the action; and that he was, four days after the victory, placed in a more critical situation than if Marshal Victor had not again appeared upon the Alberche after the affair of Santa Olalla. Fifty thousand men, including above five thousand cavalry, with one hundred pieces of cannon, were in his rear. Nothing checked the return of the first corps, the King's Guards, or the division of General Dessolles. Thus far, to all appearance, the plan of the French Marshals had succeeded; but they knew not how to carry into full effect their own designs; and their greater enemy escaped. Fortunately the genius of Napoleon was far distant!

On the 8th, the British headquarters were at Deleytosa, a small village, seated on an eminence, in the direct road to Truxillo. On the morning of the 9th, Spanish cavalry and infantry again appeared retiring upon the track of Sir Arthur Wellesley; the bridge of Arzobispo had been forced, and General Cuesta's army was in full retreat.

We were now approaching the cultivated plains of Estremadura, which, although already subjected to the withering effects of the Spanish and French armies that had traversed them for months in succession, during the early part of the season, still afforded a prospect of those supplies that the British had lately been perfectly uncertain of obtaining.

The long fatiguing marches which followed the retrograde movement from Arzobispo, were now discontinued. Those of the 8th and 10th were short, over a comparatively flat country, and easily accomplished. The evening of the 10th, we encamped on the right bank of the Rio del Monte, near to Jaraicejo. The following day, crossing that river, the troops took up an *alignement* on its opposite bank. The situation of this camp was picturesque in the highest degree. Considerably elevated above the river, the view in front was not obstructed by the numerous splendid trees that shaded its banks; the ground sloped steeply, but not ruggedly, down to the water, which was here a broad, deep, but rather sluggish stream. To the rear of the encampment were extensive forests of cork, chestnut, or oak-trees; the road from Deleytosa to Truxillo intersecting the line of tents nearly at a right angle. On this beautiful spot we remained in perfect inactivity for some days. The Spanish Army had disappeared from our front; nor did we hear any tidings of the enemy. Nothing could be more dull or monotonous than the camp at Jaraicejo.

On the 13th, accompanied by Captain Gell, of the 29th, I rode to Truxillo. This excursion was made with an intention of purchasing provisions; but a desire, also, of varying the scene, and curiosity to visit the birthplace of Francisco Pizarro, formed additional inducements to wander.

Truxillo is a large town, commandingly situated on a height rising from a level of great extent. The view from it is extensive, grand, and varied. It appears the monarch of the plain. Upon the approach of the armies, its inhabitants had fled, but returned upon becoming acquainted with the fact that payment would in all cases be obtained from the British. This restored confidence, and founded a system of barter equally enriching to them, and useful to the army. Everything was of course charged enormously. Wine was sold in profusion. The depositaries had nearly become emptied, but ingenuity made up for the insufficiency of the supply. The Spaniards, conceiving that their allies were persons who must have wine, and at the same time would not be particular as to the quality, diluted and mixed the originally poor produce of the grape of Estremadura in such a manner, composing so horrible a description of drink, that it is only extraordinary more fatal effects were not immediately produced by its deleterious qualities.

As might naturally be expected, all parts of the camp sent forth its foragers, flocking to the emporium of Truxillo, where scenes of a ludicrous kind were constantly occurring. The stores were absolutely beset with applicants, while the struggle carried on to obtain early attention to individual demand, was extremely diverting, particularly to those whose wants had been already supplied. In the midst of this extraordinary market, all distinctions of situation vanished before the natural impulse of earnest endeavour to procure the necessaries of life. The quartermaster-sergeant, the regimental officer, the medical man, the soldier's wife, or the officer of the Guards, were alike employed in the inelegant and vulgar avocation of purchasing meat, vegetables, chocolate, groceries, or even bread!

In one part of the *plaza* was to be observed the scion of aristocracy in the act of despatching his servants after having completed the degrading service on which he had from necessity most unwillingly proceeded; in another, the more humble messenger of a subaltern's mess had just heaped upon his sinking quadruped the last deposit of his purchased store, the accompanying soldier almost lost in a forest of canteens, containing enough to poison a whole regiment.

The anxious inquiries of those arriving, as to the situation where their wants could be supplied; the careless manner of the retiring groups, intent alone upon urging to accelerated speed the animals in their charge, and having obtained the object of their own visit, treating with characteristic churlishness the questions of unfortunates arriving to pass through the same ordeal of difficulty and imposition, added to the effect of this varied scene.

The house of the Pizarro family at Truxillo is spacious and handsome, presenting an ornamented façade, and having the appearance of a distinguished residence. In the ruined church of Truxillo is placed a monument to the memory of the celebrated conqueror of Peru. The building had been dismantled by the French troops, but the marble recording the name of the town's most distinguished citizen survived the sacrilegious devastation. The Duques de San Juan, also an Estremaduran family, have a residence in Truxillo.

It was late when we returned to the camp. Either from carelessness or accident, the woods had taken fire. Smoke, and distant light, for which we could assign no reason, met us, or struck upon our sight as we approached Jaraicejo; but it was not until within half a league of the encampment, that we ascertained from whence these appearances proceeded. The forest was illuminated in all directions. The crackling of the branches, and the sheet of fire which enveloped the stems of the ilex or chestnut, had in the darkness a brilliant appearance. The trunks of these venerable trees blazed not, but, red with fire that appeared eating to their hearts, resembled innumerable pillars of light. To penetrate by the nearest tracks to the camp became impracticable; we therefore continued upon the main road, crossed the bridge, and regained the position of the 29th regiment. Fortunately, the fire had not extended to the immediate neighbourhood of our camp, and the wind drove it in a different direction.

On the 19th of August, two divisions of the army broke up from Jaraicejo, marching to the rear. On the 20th, General Crauford arrived from Almaraz. The 21st, at daybreak, General Hill's division quitted the banks of the Rio del Monte, encamping in the evening to the southward of the city of Truxillo.

The 22nd, we marched to Santa Crux de la Sierra—a beautifully situated village, at the foot of a mountain from whence it derives its name. The *sierra* is covered to its summit with myrtles, vines, mulberry and fig-trees, presenting a rich and luxuriant landscape, Near to the town is a convent of Augustine Friars. We were encamped in a wood about a mile in advance. During the forenoon, one of those accidents occurred, which in the track of armies are often erroneously attributed to design. The brushwood at the base of the mountain became kindled, the excessively dry state of the country soon spread the flame with resistless fury, taking a direction through the vineyards up the face of the *sierra*. The unfortunate peasants were seen at intervals through the smoke, endeavouring to arrest the progress of the devastation; but their efforts were unavailing. This beautiful mountain garden soon became a scathed and blackened wilderness.

Having passed the night of the 23rd near Miajadas, we marched to Medellin, encamping near to that town on the following day. Medellin is situated on the southern bank of the Guadiana, over which is a bridge of twenty arches. The town itself is uninteresting; but upon a height, rising immediately from the river, is a Moorish castle, seated upon a steep and rugged rock, like most other Spanish castles, deriving its importance and effect more from the bold altitude on which it stands, than either from its extent or grandeur of architecture. The surrounding country is unadorned by wood, bleak, and uncultivated. A plain to the south of the town bore numerous marks of having been a field of battle; nor had the four intervening months served to efface the evidences of defeat and slaughter. Fragments of uniforms, caps, bones, dead horses, cartridges, exploded shells, strewed the ground in every direction.

During a day of excessive heat the division marched from Medellin to Merida. Merida, the Emerita Augusta of the Romans, and capital of ancient Lusitania, is situated on the right bank of the Guadiana, over which is a bridge of fifty-four arches, erected by the Emperor Trajan. The town is encircled by a wall, bearing the appearance of great antiquity. Near the river it is of considerable altitude, intersected by square towers; but in many places dilapidated, and fast mouldering to decay. The ruins of the Roman aqueduct are very fine, strongly contrasting with the inferiority of a modern building erected for the same purpose. Many of the ornamental and sculptured parts of the Temple of Mars are in preservation. Of a circular form, and having been

MERIDA

of considerable magnitude, the foundation of the Temple of Minerva alone remains. Nothing is left to prove its architectural merits. In the destruction of this edifice, it is probable time has been aided by the barbarism of mankind; it is by far the most dilapidated of the Roman buildings of which any trace exists at Merida.

An arch, called by the Spaniards, the "*Arco de St. Jago*," is worthy of observation, from its magnitude, its beauty of form, and its appearance of stability after the lapse of so many years. It bears no inscription by which the date of its erection can now be ascertained; but, from the style of the building, it appears of the same era as the bridge—owing its existence to the man who of all others has left to Spain the noblest monuments of his grandeur, his taste, and munificence.

On an eminence in the town are seated the ruins of the Temple of Diana: they are to be seen from the bridge. The pillars, formed of freestone, are, of course, more defaced than the marble relics of the same age. The western colonnade is the most perfect; there the splendid Corinthian capitals are still extant, although worn and decayed. The amphitheatre, patched up with modern masonry, had been converted into an arena for the bullfights. Merida once contained a very large population. For an inland town its situation is particularly favourable. It is now much reduced; but, possessing as it does so many Roman antiquities, it must be considered an important and interesting place.

On the 3rd of September, we crossed the plain extending from Merida to Badajos, the headquarters of the division, and General Tilson's brigade occupying Montijo. A mile to the westward, nearer to the Guadiana, lies the village of La Puebla de la Calçada. In it the 29th regiment was, for the first time during the campaign, cantoned. La Puebla is a village exclusively inhabited by persons employed in agriculture,—the houses, nearly of equal importance, are all cleanly, and well constructed for the purpose of giving shelter and coolness from the excessive heat of the season. Nothing can be less interesting than the country in the vicinity of La Puebla. It is perfectly flat, without wood; the plains presenting no variety. The Guadiana, at this season an insignificant stream, steals through a chasm sufficiently deep to prevent its being seen, except when closely approached.

The town of Lobon, on the brink of an elevation directly opposite; crowns an unbroken shapeless cliff of considerable height, affording neither variety nor boldness to the landscape.

Lord Wellington's headquarters were now established at Badajos; General Sherbrooke's division being encamped near Talavera la Real, a small town on the left bank of the Guadiana. Early on the morning of the 6th, the sick of General Hill's division moved from Montijo and La Puebla, in the direction of Badajos, on their route to Elvas, now become the general hospital of the army. I accompanied these detachments, in charge of that belonging to the 29th regiment. We forded the Guadiana about two leagues in advance of La Puebla; and having passed Talavera la Real, entered a plain extending twelve miles, and terminating under the walls of the capital of Estremadura.

The first view of the city of Badajos from the Talavera road is very striking. Placed on an elevated situation, the castle rises immediately above the Guadiana, that stream washing the northern base of the rock on which it stands. The fortifications descend gradually on the low ground to the south-east of the town. Its spires and public buildings are seen successively in the distance; and to the front are plantations of olive, giving it a verdant and picturesque appearance.

The Guadiana, even in summer, is, under the walls of Badajos, a fine river. It seems to have forced an unwilling passage between the castle rock, and the precipitous bank on which Fort San Christoval stands; the chasm having the appearance of being sufficient only to admit of the unobstructed course of the river. Another Roman bridge adorns the Guadiana at Badajos, near to which is the Alameda, or public walk. Nothing that I have ever experienced in this delightful climate equalled the calm, placid, glowing, genial feeling during the twilight of a September evening on the Alameda at Badajos. The cathedral is not one of the most splendid. A large square tower is its only exterior decoration: within, it is low in the roof, and inelegant.

The route to Portugal passes out of the walls of Badajos by the Puerta de las Palmas. It then crosses the bridge, a structure six hundred yards in length, protected by a *tête de pont*, and under the fire of Fort San Christoval.

Upon gaining the right bank of the Guadiana, Elvas, with its forts, appears in the distance. The road leads through a plain, terminated by some rising ground, covered with olive-trees. Elvas, a fortified town, is so situated as to be commanded by two neighbouring heights. Upon these, however, forts have been erected. The one to the north-east of the town, constructed in 1766 by Conte Schomberg Lippe, and bearing his name, is placed on an eminence of considerably greater altitude than either the city or Fort San Lucia; it is a place of great strength, seated on the summit of a conical hill, and apparently rendered invulnerable by nature and art.

The River Caya, between Badajos and Elvas, forms the boundary of the kingdoms. Formerly most of the places on the Portuguese frontier were fortified. Elvas alone continues to possess military importance along the whole line from the Guadiana to Almeida. It is a singular fact, that two fortified towns, placed under similar circumstances, in enmity to the invading armies, only three leagues distant, should, during the course of the Peninsular War, have experienced so very different a fate. Badajos suffered from no less than four sieges; Elvas was never regularly invested.

Elvas is a large and populous town, but, being built upon a ridge, the streets are steep and irregular. The *plaza*, generally the most conspicuous, best arranged part of Peninsular towns, is in Elvas insignificant,—the buildings being of an inferior class, and its area circumscribed.

It is impossible ever to pass the Spanish frontier into Portugal without being forcibly struck with the difference, in appearance, habits, and manner, of its inhabitants,—a comparison little favourable to the latter. To invariable inferiority in personal appearance is added the impression created by a language apparently keeping pace with the reduced physical stature of the utterer—the noble, sonorous Castillian being converted into a mongrel, mincing tongue. The high bearing of the Spaniard, which has survived ages of misrule and degradation, is not to be met with in his Lusitanian neighbour. The Castillian and Moorish blood flowing in his veins, still gives him an external that belies the insignificance which despotism and ignorance have too frequently rendered triumphant in his character.

The *sojourn* of the British Army on the plains of Estremadura soon produced the most injurious effects. Sickness rapidly spread through the different corps of which it was composed. Typhus fever obtained more than usual influence over the constitutions of its victims: the hospitals were crowded. Elvas became one great receptacle of disease. Without any visible cause, certainly without overstrained exertion, the army was encumbered with 10,000 sick. The regimental hospitals teemed with cases beyond the reach of removal; every succeeding day added to the list. The month of September passed without any circumstance occurring to draw our attention from the sameness and perfect want of interest that prevailed; no movement of the troops, no approach of the enemy, no prospect of departure from the sandy plains, on which we appeared fixed to witness only the ignoble death of the best and bravest soldiers.

It is for historians to detail, with all their impartiality and sound judgment, the reason for this waste of life; for an humble narrator of events and circumstances which he witnessed, it is sufficient to state, that neither then nor since, having dispassionately considered the matter, have I ever been enabled to discover a sufficient reason for Lord Wellington subjecting his army to this mortal and, apparently, unnecessary infliction.

On the 4th of October, Lord Wellington reviewed General Hill's division on the plain of Montijo. The brigades of Generals Tilson, Richard Stewart, and Catlin Crauford, consisting of ten battalions of infantry, were in line. The regiments present were the 29th, the first battalions of the 3rd, 48th, and 57th, the second of the 28th, 31st, 34th, 39th, 48th, and 66th.

The succeeding month produced no variation in the situation of the army, either as to active employment or the withdrawal of the regiments, even for a short period, from the influence of disease with which the quarters in Estremadura were so fatally impregnated. The general hospital continued at Elvas. The cases became more virulent, the mortality increasing, while each succeeding day brought additional victims from the crowded regimental medical establishments. Nothing could be more gloomy than the prospect; change of season and of temperature alone appeared likely to check the progress of the evil.

Not having escaped from an attack of typhus fever, and being thereby prevented from immediately resuming regimental duties, a medical board recommended my removal to Lisbon. Leave of absence was consequently obtained, and on the 18th of November, accompanied by Captain Tucker, also an invalid, I commenced a journey towards the capital of Portugal.

Few districts of the Peninsula are more richly wooded or highly cultivated than the six leagues that intervene from Elvas to Estremos. The latter, a considerable town, is situated in the centre of extensive plantations of olive.

The Praça, or great square, of Estremos, is spacious, unpaved, and inelegant. It contains several convents, one of which is inhabited by nuns, so rigid in their seclusion, that no persons, with the exception of their attendants, ever obtain access within its walls. The citadel, seated on a rock, surrounded by the city, commands a most extensive and beautiful prospect of the valley in which it is placed. Numerous country-houses, with whitened walls, afford relief and cheerfulness to the widely extended landscape; while the rising grounds, surmounted by watch-towers or distant convents, give variety and interest to the scene.

The country, as we advanced, became less rich and luxuriant, having a bolder aspect, more broken, mountainous, and picturesque. Near to Montemor the scenery is a combination of cultivation and wildness. From Vendas Novas to Aldea Gallega the road passes through a great extent of moor-ground, varied at intervals by forest scenery, not confined to woods having neither extent nor magnitude of timber to give them importance, but presenting, at particular points, no visible termination in the one case, and noble specimens in the other. The causewayed road, the morass, or the barren heath, at the same time impressing with a view of nature, either monotonous, repulsive, or neglected, is contrasted with the bold, rugged, luxuriant features of the cork-tree, in all its magnificent, though frequently solitary state.

The view of Lisbon from Aldea Gallega, and in passing the ferry, is very striking. The variety of ground, the whole extent of the city, the beautiful adjacent country, with the river and shipping, form a scene at once grand and picturesque. A light boat, and fair wind, soon transported us across the great basin of the Tagus; which river, confined by the precipitous bank of Almada, directly opposite to the town, appears to have forced out this noble estuary, to prove its grandeur and importance.

Lisbon, at this period, had the appearance of the capital of a British colony; the embassy, the navy, and the troops of that nation, seeming in undisturbed possession of the city. The Portuguese soldiers, commanded and disciplined by British officers, looked more the partisans of their powerful ally than the military force of the country to which they belonged. Everything was apparently subjected to the control of the great power whose assistance could alone prevent the French armies from obtaining possession of the soil, and subduing the vindictive and turbulent feelings of its inhabitants. Even the jealousy natural to the people was subjected to the perfect sway obtained over their destinies and their opinions. Not a murmur escaped indicative of their stifled feelings, forming a combination of respect, hatred, and fear. The latter part of the year 1809 had been employed by the officers attached to the Portuguese regiments, in organising and training their respective corps,—a duty uninterrupted by the presence of an enemy, and executed with great assiduity, ability, and success.

During the inactivity of the British Army in Spanish Estremadura, the enemy had directed his efforts against the Spanish troops, having the temerity to approach the capital, and to encounter his disciplined battalions in the open field. The army of General Venegas was totally defeated by General Sebastiani at Almonacid; while the largest Spanish force ever collected in one army during the war, commanded by General Ariesaga—a man equally incapable, presumptuous, and rash—was totally overthrown at Ocaña.

ABRANTES

CHAPTER 3

Surrender of Badajos

Towards the close of the month of December 1809, General Hill established the headquarters of his division at Abrantes, Lord Wellington, with the main body of the army, having marched towards the Douro. General Fane's brigade of heavy cavalry remained, with the second division, on the banks of the Tagus.

Abrantes, naturally a strong place, surrounded by a ruined wall, had been, in some measure, fortified by the British engineers. It is a very important post, commanding the passage of the Tagus, over which river a bridge of boats had been constructed. Abrantes is a large and populous town, confusedly built, containing but few good houses, the streets being steep, narrow, and irregular. Placed on the very summit of the eminence, it is exposed to the wind from every quarter; the cold in winter is consequently extreme.

On the 5th of January, General Richard Stewart's brigade marched to Punhete, a small town beautifully situated at the junction of the Zezere with the Tagus. The scenery is wild and romantic, the adjacent country being covered with wood.

Punhete is built upon a peninsula. Abrantes, although two leagues distant, forms a fine feature in the prospect; the Tagus winds majestically through the valley, while the large white sails of the boats, passing in rapid succession, and appearing at intervals from among the trees, give life and gaiety to the scene.

At the distance of a league from Punhete is the village of Tancos, near to which, on a rock in the centre of the Tagus, stands the ruined castle of Almiroh. From the gardens of the convent of San Antonio, situated on the banks of the river, the castle has a picturesque and striking effect.

The enemy, taking the first favourable opportunity, from the change of season, to advance into the plains of Estremadura, were now in force at Merida, having troops at Montijo, La Puebla, and the neighbouring villages, threatening Badajos and the Portuguese frontier. General Hill, in consequence of these movements, received orders to cross the Tagus, and occupy Portalegre. General Tilson's brigade broke up from Abrantes, crossing the bridge of boats, on the 15th: Generals Richard Stewart's and Catlin Crauford's, on the following day. On the 18th, the whole division was assembled at Portalegre.

On the morning of the 19th, General Hill ordered me to proceed to the Spanish Army, from thence to communicate the movements of the enemy in his front. It was late in the afternoon when I arrived at Arronches, on the road to Alburquerque, where the 2nd division of the Marques de la Romana's army was then quartered. The route from Arronches leads through a wild, uncultivated country, overgrown with gum-cistus, and intersected by innumerable paths, branching off in all directions. Not having adopted the precaution of taking a guide, the tracks that beset me became bewildering,—even the bold, rocky, not to be mistaken site of the Castle of Alburquerque, did not assist in directing a selection; for the road which appeared leading towards it frequently turned abruptly to either side, penetrating into the interior of the luxuriant brushwood, in many places of a height to obstruct the view, that, when obtained, only prove the traveller had been pursuing a directly opposite course to what he intended.

For two hours, no human being, or habitation of any description, presented itself: it became dark; nor did there seem a prospect of extrication from this wilderness, when, fortunately, a light glimmered through the thicket. It proceeded from the habitation of some goatherds, who, upon being summoned, made their appearance. Astonished at that hour to see a stranger in the unfrequented vicinity of their hut, and alarmed at the circumstance, these peasants became for a time incommunicative. At last, however, one of their number, influenced by bribery, agreed to conduct me on the road leading to Alburquerque.

General Carlos O'Donnell, with his division, consisting of 4500 infantry, 700 cavalry, and some artillery, occupied the town and neighbourhood; his advanced posts being three leagues in front on the route to Caceres, and at Villar del Rey, on that of Merida.

The following day I accompanied General O'Donnell to his advance upon the Aliseda road. This post was commanded by Don Carlos de España, then Colonel of the Tiradores de Castilla.

Don Carlos, a Frenchman by birth, of the ancient family of Foix,

The castle of Almiroh on the Tagus

and brother to the Marques d'Espagne, had, upon taking arms in the Spanish cause, altered his name to España—a precaution calculated to facilitate his advancement in a country where everything bearing affinity to France was for the time considered with hostility and abhorrence. He was active, intelligent, and brave, without difficulty becoming distinguished in an army deficient in the former qualities, however much individually they might possess the latter. Don Carlos had been favourably noticed during the former campaign, when his regiment formed part of the force under the command of Sir Robert Wilson.

On the 23rd, General O'Donnell and myself rode to Villar del Rey, where we remained some hours with the brigadier-general commanding. When about two leagues advanced on our return, a dragoon overtook the general, with information that the enemy had entered soon after his departure, that the Spaniards had been driven out, and that the town was in possession of the French cavalry.

This was one of the frequent foraging expeditions of the enemy, made solely for the purpose of levying contributions, or procuring provisions. These were generally undertaken by forces proportioned to the size of the towns, or the vicinity of hostile troops. In the present case, being aware of a Spanish division occupying that part of the country, the column sent to Villar del Rey was of unusual strength, consisting of a division of infantry—the brigade of light cavalry of General Soult, with five pieces of cannon.

No intention of attacking General O'Donnell, or forcing him from his quarters at Alburquerque, appears to have been contemplated by this movement. Having possessed Villar del Rey for the night, the French column exacted as much as was practicable, and threatened more. The enemy retired on the following morning, when 700 Spanish infantry, with a squadron of dragoons, again obtained quiet and undisputed possession of the town. The 2nd *corps d'armée* at this period had troops in Montijo, La Puebla, Cordovilla, Lobon, and La Roca, the latter being distant two leagues from Villar del Rey.

The divisions of the Marques de la Romana's army arriving from the Sierra de Francia, had crossed the Tagus, and were marching to occupy a line extending along the frontier, having Alburquerque on its left, with Campo Mayor as the headquarters.

The policy of the Marques Romana had, for some time, invariably been to act upon the defensive. Taught by experience to estimate the real quality of the troops which he commanded, a mountain warfare seemed alone adapted to his means, and, at the same time, best calculated to harass and wear out the French soldiers, who, in every person, civil or military, beheld a foe. He successfully maintained this system in Gallicia, where, although frequently a fugitive, and never enabled to keep his ground when formidably attacked, he contrived to support a guerilla species of warfare, more fatal to the French armies than any they had yet encountered. During his absence, when called to the seat of government, the command of the army of the left devolved upon the Duque del Parque, one of those men destined to control others, without having any of the requisite qualities to ensure success.

The Battle of Tamames—the solitary instance during the war of a Spanish force, unassisted, defeating an enemy of not very disproportioned strength—gave a temporary *éclat* to his military character, soon to vanish before subsequent errors, crowned by the circumstance of fighting a general action at Alba, with the River Tormes rolling between the divisions of his army.

The information received daily at General O'Donnell's quarters of the enemy's movements, was not of peculiar interest. It merely detailed the alteration of position for the purpose of levying contributions, which was the constant practice in the French Army during the whole Peninsular War. Rarely supplied with magazines, with a commissariat acting only upon principles of exaction, it became part of the duty performed to march and obtain supplies,—not, indeed, by sacking the towns and villages, which would at once have annihilated the sources from whence they derived subsistence, but by taking as much as possible, without incurring the risk of forcing emigration, or preventing a future visit from being in some degree attended with success.

On the 5th of February the weather suddenly changed; the air became cold; rain fell for days without intermission; the rivers were flooded; the Guadiana unfordable in any situation. This produced an immediate change in the French quarters, only tending to remove their troops further from Alburquerque.

The 9th and 10th, the weather again became fair, the floods subsided, and the rivers became passable. A French detachment, 1000 strong, crossed the River Aljucen, and marched upon Caceres, to levy contributions on the richest town of Spanish Estremadura.

Information having reached General O'Donnell that the enemy's detachment had taken up its quarters in Caceres (no other French troops being within several leagues of that town), he resolved to march and dislodge it. On the morning of the 12th, advancing with 2500 infantry and 300 cavalry, he halted for the night near Aliseda. On the 13th, he arrived at Arroyo del Puerco, from whence he again proceeded, encamping, at one o'clock in the morning of the 14th, within six miles of Caceres. It is a singular proof of the situation in which the French armies were placed in Spain, that so intelligent an officer as General Foy should have remained in ignorance of the approach of a column that had taken upwards of forty-eight hours in advancing eleven leagues,—which had passed the night within a league and a half of his quarters, and might, with common energy or conduct, have completely cut him off.

At daybreak, the Spanish troops were again in motion. General O'Donnell marched direct upon the town, the cavalry and Tiradores de Castilla preceding the column. Caceres is situated at the eastern extremity of the *sierra* of that name, over which the road to Aldea del Caño passes, presenting very strong ground for obstructing the march of troops. Some infantry were detached by a road to the right to occupy these passes in the mountain.

When close to the town, the cavalry came in contact with the enemy's posts; the French cavalry and infantry were soon after perceived ascending the heights on the Aldea del Caño road. Don Carlos de España pressed forward with as much celerity as possible; his light troops covering the broken ground to the right. A smart skirmish immediately commenced. Leaving the town on his left, he fired on the flank of the French column, hoping that the infantry detached to the western extremity of the *sierra* would arrive in time effectually to obstruct the retreating force.

General Foy, now aware of his danger, and thinking only of securing his retreat, marched rapidly on. Having a number of *voltigeurs* extended over the high ground on his right flank, these kept up a continued and well-directed fire, which effectually checked the near approach of the Spanish infantry; and when Don Carlos arrived at the descent from the mountain, he had the mortification to discover, instead of a disputed passage, as had been intended, that the French column had obtained an uninterrupted egress from the defiles of the *sierra*, and was proceeding in perfect order along the plain.

Although past the only place where such troops as the Spaniards could have fatally intercepted him, the French general was far from having secured the retreat of his column without its being subjected to serious loss. He had to traverse a level extending for many leagues, without the least variation in the ground; not a tree, or a building of any description to shelter his troops, or to afford the slightest assistance in checking the pursuit; added to which, the River Salor intersected the plain. That stream could be passed only at a narrow bridge, where his column must of necessity alter its formation, and where it might have been advantageously attacked.

He was saved by the inferior quality of the troops opposed. Not all Don Carlos's exertions, not his animating example, while the drums beat, and *"vivas"* resounded, could induce the Spaniards to close with the enemy. They pursued, indeed, keeping up a constant fire, frequently too distant to have much effect, at other times becoming so galling as to induce General Foy to throw out his light troops and cavalry skirmishers to a still greater distance in rear of his column and on its flanks. At length he reached the bank of the Salor. Don Carlos perceived that the moment had arrived when he could, by vigorously pressing on his rear, seriously inconvenience the enemy; he therefore renewed his efforts to accelerate the pursuit, and ordered the Spanish cavalry to charge the French when in the act of filing across the bridge. They advanced a short distance; but the enemy's *chasseurs à cheval* soon checked their ardour, by appearing in line to receive them.

General Foy restored his original formation the moment he had passed the river, notwithstanding the same irregular, though constant, fire being kept up by the Tiradores de Castilla. After having persevered in the pursuit for a distance of three leagues, Don Carlos requested I would return to General O'Donnell, who was with the main body of the infantry, report to him what had occurred, and receive instructions as to his future movements. He then desisted from following the enemy, who soon disappeared.

General Foy conducted his retreat very judiciously. His column preserved a compact and soldierlike form; nor did he appear for a moment diverted from his object,—that of withdrawing from an isolated and dangerous situation, where he was assailed by a very superior force. The only loss sustained by the Spanish division was in the Tiradores de Castilla, which corps had about thirty men killed or wounded; that of the enemy was more considerable.

In the evening, Don Carlos and myself entered Caceres, his regiment and the cavalry being quartered in the town. General O'Donnell retired at night to Arroyo del Puerco. I became the guest of the Marques de Santa Marta.

After arranging for the accommodation of the troops, the next point was proving the extent of gratitude the Junta of Caceres would evince for relieving them from the presence of the enemy. In conformity to his instructions, Don Carlos directed that council to be assembled, and to it I accompanied him. The opening of the conference consisted in a declaration on the part of the military authority, that without support from the towns, particularly such as Caceres, the Spanish armies could not carry on the war of resistance, upon which their temporal and spiritual comfort and happiness depended.

This was answered by professions of gratitude, patriotism, and poverty, on the civil side. The next step was to state a demand for shoes, accoutrements, and money; astounding no doubt, but received with a degree of coolness and unconcern, proving the extent to which custom can reconcile even the most unwelcome requisitions. The civil authorities now argued on the score of inability; there were no shoes, no accoutrements, and but little money. After a warm discussion, it was admitted that there were some means; but taxing their extent was, if possible, a more perplexing difficulty than the former.

At last, after considerable dexterity, some liberality, a great portion of bold demand, only to be palliated by being a public measure, and various indications of the contribution being more produced by fear than any other feeling, it was settled that 30,000 *reals* should issue from the coffers of Caceres on the following morning. I am thus particular as to this negotiation, in order to give some idea of the situation in which the inhabitants of Spanish towns were constantly placed during the progress of the war. If the above picture appears to others not so serious as it did to me, I have to add that the parley was between friends and countrymen,—leaving them to judge how much the situation must have been *improved* on the arrival of starving Frenchmen, probably infuriated against the whole population, by some recent act of summary vengeance on unfortunate stragglers, or wounded soldiers of their army.

On the morning of the 15th, I left Caceres, overtaking the Spanish division near Aliseda. General O'Donnell had proceeded to Alburquerque, where his troops were again assembled on the following day, The inhabitants of Caceres enjoyed but short-lived tranquillity in consequence of our visit; for on the 22nd, eight hundred French cavalry arrived, plundered the town, retiring in the evening towards Truxillo.

The distance from Alburquerque to Portalegre not being great, I made frequent excursions to see General Hill, and to receive his orders. On the 29th, I received information from General O'Donnell of the enemy's advance in force to Caceres, Arroyo del Puerco, and Malpartida; at the same time General Hill heard of French troops, supposed to be of the sixth corps, having passed the Puerto de Baños, and entered Estremadura Alta. He directed my immediate return to Alburquerque, where I learnt that Don Carlos España, now a brigadier-general, had advanced to Aliseda with three regiments of infantry, and that the French troops from Malpartida and Arroyo had encamped on the opposite bank of the Salor, at the distance of half a league, the advanced posts being in close contact.

On the 30th, I joined Don Carlos, in his camp on the heights behind Aliseda. The enemy had again retired to his cantonments without making any attack. At daybreak we were on horseback to reconnoitre: nothing appeared, except some cavalry patrols, who retreated on being fired at. At nine o'clock the peasants brought information of the cavalry having left Arroyo; and about midday it was ascertained that the second corps had marched from Caceres in the direction of Merida.

The moment the enemy disappeared from his front, General España broke up from the cold bleak heights of Aliseda, sending his infantry back to the headquarters of the division, while we proceeded for the purpose of ascertaining the real direction of the enemy's motions, and, accompanied by a squadron of cavalry, again entered Caceres. The Marques de Santa Marta, kind and hospitable under all circumstances, notwithstanding the serious visitations he had been subjected to, received us most cordially. General Reynier had been quartered in his house.

The whole of the second corps, consisting of the divisions of General Merle, Comte Heudelet, and the light cavalry brigade of General Soult, had been quartered in Caceres, or the towns in its immediate neighbourhood.

It was evident that the rapid movement now made by General Reynier had some more important object than a mere change of quarters; it was supposed to be connected with a combined effort to annihilate the army of General Ballesteros, which had given considerable annoyance to the French force in Andalusia. The night of the 31st, General Reynier's advance reached Cordovilla, while his infantry halted at Aldea del Caño. The day following, part of his corps crossed the Guadiana at Merida, moving upon Almendralejo, on the direct road to Santa Olalla and Seville.

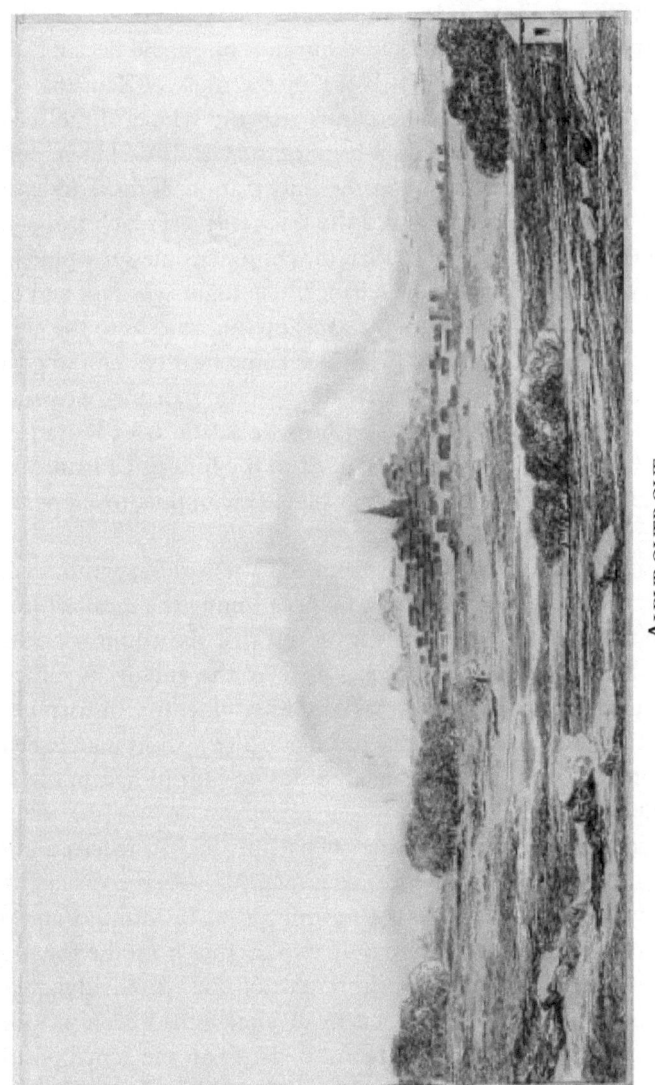

Alburquerque

On the 3rd, a despatch was received from General O'Donnell, acquainting Don Carlos of the Marques de la Romana having appointed him to the command of a corps destined to move upon Merida, for the purpose of creating a diversion in favour of General Ballesteros; that 1000 light infantry, with 200 cavalry, had been detached to La Roca, there to await his orders; and adding, that the more expeditiously he joined these troops, and put them in motion, the better. Late in the evening we marched for La Roca, by the route of Zangana.

It was not satisfactorily ascertained that the whole of the second *corps d'armée* had quitted the right bank of the Guadiana; but, in pursuance of orders, and relying upon the information of those by whom they had been given, we followed the track of the French troops, accompanied by a squadron of cavalry, in whose steadiness it would have been folly to have placed great reliance. The night was dark and cold. We occasionally questioned the peasants on our route as to the enemy, but heard no tidings of any of his troops being near enough to try the courage of the Castillian cavalry. At three in the morning we reached Zangana: at daybreak were again on horseback, and at La Roca found General O'Donnell, who had advanced to the ford of La Lamia, with three regiments of infantry and four pieces of cannon, to support the movement on Montijo.

Instead of advancing into the plains of Estremadura, without being opposed, and creating a diversion, by occasioning the recall of troops gone on other service, it was soon proved that the country north of the Guadiana continued to be occupied by the enemy, in sufficient force to prevent the Spaniards making either extensive or formidable inroads. The corps of Don Carlos had made a very short march, before a dragoon overtook its commander, ordering him to halt until General O'Donnell came up.

Subsequent to General España's departure, he had received information of the enemy being in force at Merida,—that a cavalry skirmish had taken place early in the morning near to Montijo, and that the French advanced posts were only two leagues from the town.

Under these circumstances, although not considered advisable to send infantry into the plains so far in advance as had been proposed, it at the same time became important to ascertain the actual position and force of these newly arrived enemies. For this purpose, Don Carlos's detachment of cavalry was augmented to two hundred and fifty; with it we proceeded to Montijo.

The place was quiet, but its inhabitants expressed great anxiety and alarm, in consequence of the visit they had in the morning received, which they doubted not would be repeated. The cavalry were piqueted in rear of the town, the roads patrolled; and we remained undisturbed for the night.

The slight affair which had taken place in the morning was very characteristic of the warlike habits of the country. The same men who invariably gave way when opposed in open day, (and with reference to the Spanish cavalry, the experience of the Peninsular War proves that to have been the case,) were not far distant from the enemy, whose presence in this instance they had every reason to expect. In such a state of apathy or unconcern were they, that thrusts of the Polish lances broke their slumbers. They were apparently as regardless of danger as the best and most experienced troops; and must have known that danger was near, yet adopted no precaution to avert it. They retired not out of reach of observation, but quietly and contentedly slept upon the plain, until trampled upon by the enemy's horsemen! These same men, shewing this disregard of peril, and recklessness of safety, would probably have turned their backs and fled, if assailed by their opponents face to face; a proof that the inhabitants of some countries can sleep away their fears.

For some days we remained at Montijo, taking precautions to ascertain the approach of the enemy, being always on horseback an hour before daylight, and having patrols upon the roads in every direction. At length information arrived of Marshal Soult having marched from Valverde and Don Alvaro,—his cavalry crossing the Guadiana two leagues from Merida—the infantry of his corps moving by the right bank of the river to Medellin. Subsequent intelligence announced his having withdrawn from the latter, that his headquarters had moved from Don Benito to Villa Nueva de la Serena, and that no troops, either of his or any other French corps, continued to be cantoned on the right bank of the Guadiana between Medellin and Badajos.

By this movement on the part of the French general, the whole extent of the fertile province of Estremadura, to the north of the Guadiana, was left in possession of the Spanish armies, Badajos becoming the headquarters of the Marques de la Romana. At this period the author of these pages quitted the Spanish Army, returned to General Hill's headquarters, and from thence proceeded to Lisbon, where he again became *aide-de-camp* to General Leith, recently arrived from England to join the army.

Nothing can more strongly prove the vacillating conduct of the

The Castle of Zagala

enemy, nor any thing be adduced more decidedly to place beyond the reach of controversy, the inertness, deficiency in judgment, occasional despondency, and frequent temerity, of the Spanish Government, than the situation of all parties at the present moment. In the first place, the French armies in Spain were directed by a weak and erring person, possessing none of the talent of his brother; commanding, without capacity; a king, without a people; a *generalissimo*, neither respected nor obeyed.

To no set of men was this fact more evident than the French marshals, who, despising the military judgment from whence the orders emanated, felt prepared if possible to evade them; and their own high reputation induced their taking the responsibility of doing so. Thus, at the same time, one *corps d'armée* was acting in conformity to the orders received from Madrid, while another, destined to co-operate, was adopting a directly different sphere of action, according to the caprice or obstinacy of its commander. In addition to this course of proceeding, in itself enough to ensure the discomfiture of armies, is to be considered the jealousy of each other constantly bursting into publicity among these generals, by whom, and through whose exertions, it has been ingeniously supposed the Emperor Napoleon accomplished in other countries his unparalleled successes.

Next is to be considered the actual situation, and what had been the co-operation or assistance given by the army of Lord Wellington. The true estimate of the preparations for a favourable reception of that assistance, appears to rest with the undisputed fact, that, after such a lengthened period of professions, of experience, of means, or of opportunities, to have perfected, by well-arranged combination, both in equipment and in discipline, an effective army, no force deserving that name had been organised.

But, even admitting that the government could not be responsible for the quality of the troops, and that the British general was soon convinced of their perfect inability to perform the duties of a regular army, even then he would have kept the field, had it been possible to induce the Spanish authorities to use the slightest exertion for the maintenance of his troops. That was not to be obtained. The threat of withdrawing found the Central Junta as inactive, as inefficient, or as treacherous, as ever.

Disappointed in every anticipated assistance,—having won a battle the result of which was, being obliged to abandon his hospitals and the cannon he had taken,—his troops nearly starved, escaping most imminent danger, being beset by an auxiliary force, which, instead of assisting, served but to consume the produce of the country, and make the supply of his own army more precarious and more difficult;— such had been the situation of Lord Wellington, and it was under such circumstances, with reference to all parties hitherto engaged, that he retired from Spain. It was with an army reduced by sickness that the British general had now to defend the Portuguese frontier, having left the battle upon the Spanish territory for a time to be fought by the troops of the country, the guerillas, and the enemy;

The British Government, it must be admitted, had made great efforts in its assistance to the Spanish cause. Armies had appeared, whose qualities will be most correctly appreciated by reference to their achievements. By them battles had been won, but under such disadvantageous or unfortunate circumstances as to increase respect for the troops, without greatly strengthening the impression of benefit derived from their co-operation. Little had yet been accomplished in forming that stupendous power which the talent of Lord Wellington, and the successes of his army, ultimately created. He was, at this crisis of the war, a popular and distinguished general, directing the army of a great country, opposed on the part of the Spanish Government by some degree of jealousy, and a weight of self-sufficient inactivity and misrule.

Great himself in military resource, he was thwarted in the expected exertions of his allies, and unfortunate in the well-intentioned but ignorantly applied efforts of the British ministry; it remained for a series of events, for an improved policy on the part of those furnishing the means, and for an uninterrupted course of distinguished conduct in his army, to create the glorious situation he afterwards filled in the estimation of the government and the people on whose territory he was fighting the battle of independence. There were two degrees of character to be won from the universal voice of the Spanish nation: that Lord Wellington and the British Army were not inferior to their own generals or their own troops; secondly, that they were in every respect superior. The first had been wrung from the most determined advocates of Castillian pre-eminence. The latter, that of decided superiority, was alone conquered by such a chain of events as it will be my endeavour subsequently, though imperfectly, to detail.

The result of the Battle of Wagram having again restored peace to Germany, 100,000 men reinforced the French armies in Spain. Thus possessed of the means by which the character of the war in the Peninsula was once more destined to be varied, the Emperor Napoleon directed the invasion of Portugal, not, as had been the case on two former occasions, by one corps, but by an army composed of a large portion of his disposable force, commanded by an officer whose name was sufficiently conspicuous in the annals of the French Revolutionary army to carry with it an impression only inferior to that of Napoleon himself. But there existed another motive for this inroad,—that of forcing the British troops from the Peninsula. Napoleon at once perceived the infinitely greater interests depending upon that measure than the mere fact of bringing superior force to vanquish an army numerically weak, or the depriving Spain and Portugal of its assistance.

He foresaw the danger to his own situation and views created by the presence of Lord Wellington's army on the continent of Europe. At Vimiera, Coruña, Oporto, and Talavera, the French had ascertained the quality of their island opponents. To crush such troops when inferior in numbers was within the reach of probability; permitting them undisturbedly to receive reinforcements, or to be joined by equally good troops, hitherto employed on other service, was unlike the policy of such a man as Napoleon; but above all was the impression resulting from the presence of a British Army, giving confidence to the Spanish cause, protracting the struggle, forming the nucleus of future strengths to be marshalled against him. It was this influence which he especially wished to destroy.

The Marshal Prince d'Essling was appointed general-in-chief of the Army of Portugal, composed of the 6th corps, under Marshal Ney; the 8th, commanded by General the Duc d'Abrantes; the 2nd, by Comte Reynier, and the cavalry corps of General Monbrun. It was not considered necessary to withdraw General Reynier from the frontier near the Tagus until after the first offensive operations had been carried into effect. These consisted of the sieges of Ciudad Rodrigo and Almeida, which were carried on exclusively by the 6th corps.

The siege and capture of Ciudad Rodrigo formed the most important event of Marshal Massena's preparatory operations. The investment took place early in June, the garrison surrendering on the 10th of July. The town was defended with considerable firmness and perseverance on the part of the Spaniards; nor was it until the Duc d'Elchingen had made his arrangements for assaulting the breach, then considered practicable in the body of the place, that the governor capitulated. The opinion of the French Army was against the mode in which the attack had been conducted, the loss sustained by the assailants being very considerable, and the time taken to reduce a place not of the first order, considered disproportioned to the means employed.

Vizeu had for some time been the headquarters of Lord Wellington. In its vicinity were cantoned, the 1st, 3rd, and 4th divisions of his army, with a large proportion of the cavalry; and in advance, upon the Coa, was the light division, with some Portuguese infantry, detachments of British cavalry, and the troop of horse-artillery commanded by Captain Ross. At Portalegre was the corps of General Hill, and at Thomar that of Major-General Leith.

During the year 1809, and the commencement of that following, the Portuguese army had been disciplined and equipped. The appearance of the regiments had rapidly improved, many of them becoming incorporated with the divisions of British infantry. It only remained to be ascertained whether their conduct in the field, or capacity for military movement, kept pace with their now really soldierlike demeanour.

On the 14th of July, General Leith assumed the command of ten thousand infantry and cavalry at Thomar. This corps, destined in the first instance to observe the line of the River Zezere, was in reserve to that of General Hill. Its movements in great measure depended upon those of General Reynier, still in Spanish Estremadura, whose operations were of course more closely watched by the troops nearer to the frontier.

The second *corps d'armée* crossed the Tagus about the 20th of July, occupying Plasencia, Galisteo, and Coria. Its cantonments changed as provisions became difficult to obtain, advancing towards the frontier of Portugal, or again penetrating to the base of the Sierra de Gredos, until the moment arrived when the Coa was to be passed, and the whole army to advance in one concentrated movement upon Lisbon.

General Hill had for some time been altering his quarters in conformity to the changeable habits of the enemy. Wherever General Reynier appeared, the British general was in his front. This became a measure, with reference to the invasion of the country, of positive importance; although it was ultimately proved, that no idea of entering the Portuguese territory on more than one line was ever contemplated by the French generals. The nearest approach to the frontier at this time made by the second corps, was the advance of a regiment of infantry, with two squadrons of cavalry, to Salvatierra, from whence, after plundering the town, they again retired to Zarza Mayor.

General Reynier's motions appearing directed towards the north, General Hill crossed the Tagus with the whole of his infantry at Villa Velha, marching upon Castello-Branco; from whence he penetrated into the mountains towards Guarda, occupying Atalaya and Alpedrinha.

During these movements General Leith continued at Thomar, a town beautifully situated in Portuguese Estremadura, on the right bank of the River Navansi—a stream running into the Zezere, near to Punhete. On an eminence, close to the town, and domineering it to the westward, stands the convent of Christ, grandly situated, surrounded with luxuriant scenery; in itself a building of great magnitude, variety, and richness of architecture. The ruins of a Moorish castle, and very extensive aqueduct, add to the picturesque effect of this most conspicuous and noble monastery.

Thomar was founded by Galdim Paez, grand-master of the Knights Templars, in 1145. On the left bank of the river is the site and remains of the Roman town of Navansi, built in the 852nd year of the Christian era. The church of Santa Maria do Olival, at Navansi, is said to be the most ancient building of a similar description in Portugal. It contains a very handsome monument to the memory of the first Bishop of Funchal, erected in 1525. The convent of the Order of Christ is on a very magnificent scale, commanding a prospect of the whole surrounding country. The building has evidently been erected at different periods; the additions made from time to time proving the date by the various species of architecture peculiar to the age.

The cloisters, completed in the reign of Philip III., are massive and spacious; the chapel, erected during that of Don Manuel, King of Portugal, is remarkable as well for the beauty of its external ornament as its interior decoration. It is of a circular form, having an altar in the centre, opposite to which is a lofty arch, forming the entrance to the choir, an oblong square, elevated above the body of the church the walls are covered with paintings on panel, from subjects in the New Testament. In a private chapel is a picture by Rafaelle; in addition to which, that of Friars of the Order of Christ receiving the rules from St. Benedict, and two others representing the taking of Santarem from the Moors, and their final overthrow at Campo d'Ourique, are conspicuous ornaments of the chapel. The number of friars in the convent is reduced to twenty-five. Formerly, it contained above one hundred. They possess the land contained in the circuit of half a league, and have a revenue of 150,000 *crusadoes*. During the first invasion of Portugal by General Junot, the French levied a contribution of 20,000 *crusadoes*, which was paid by this opulent monastery in twenty-four hours. At Thomar is a cotton manufactory, on a large scale, originally established by the celebrated Marques de Pombal.

General Reynier's headquarters were at Zarza Mayor on the 22nd. Upon the morning of that day, a party of French cavalry, sixty in number, having penetrated to Ladoira, in advance of Salvatierra, were met by Captain White, in command of a troop of the 13th Light Dragoons, and one of Portuguese cavalry, who charged them with such success, that the whole of the enemy's detachment was either killed or made prisoners, without the loss of a single man on the part of the allies. Major Vigoureux of the 38th regiment, who had been sent in advance by General Leith, for the purpose of obtaining information, was with Captain White, and assisted in the discomfiture of the enemy.

On the 23rd, the headquarters of Lord Wellington were at Alverca; the following day the enemy crossed the frontier. It was on the morning of the 24th July that the invasion of Portugal in 1810 really commenced. On that day, an affair of a serious description took place between the light division, the only British troops now on the Spanish territory, and the 6th corps of the French Army, accompanied by three thousand cavalry. On this occasion, the light division became engaged under most critical circumstances. Very inferior in every arm, with the rapid and unfordable mountain stream of the Coa in his rear, having one only line of retreat over a narrow bridge, General Crawford was attacked by a force sufficient to have occasioned his total destruction. Never was there a more favourable opportunity presented for proceeding *tête baissée*, as the French term it, than occurred on this occasion; but it happened not to be the description of service on which, against British troops, they shewed the greatest enterprise.

The arena for a really vigorous French attack is one that few other troops would enter,—at all events with equal alacrity, equal spirit, or with the same apparent determination. In mounting steeps defended by troops—in making attacks in large bodies, where a great crisis is at issue in forcing on under fire, until all difficulties, but the personal, the close conflict with his opponent, has been overcome—the French soldier appears to be unequalled; but when perseverance has placed him on equal ground—when he apparently has obtained a chance of successfully terminating his attack, he becomes no longer formidable: and appears paralysed by the immediate presence of his opponents—a strange and inexplicable result of so much gallantry, such gaiety, so much recklessness of danger, only to be accounted for by the supposition that the physical composition of the people does not permit the effervescence to subsist beyond a certain exertion, that, if unchecked, might have continued buoyant, but being resolutely met, becomes depressed and vanquished.

The siege of Almeida, and the unfortunate accident of the magazine exploding, which placed that fortress in possession of the enemy, were the next events that distinctly marked the progress of the campaign. Almeida, prepared for defence, numerously garrisoned, and in every respect calculated to make a protracted resistance, having so prematurely fallen, was a very fortunate circumstance for the French Army. The favourable season of the year, its erroneously supposed perfect preparation for active operations, the non-arrival of reinforcements to the allied army—all added to the importance of carrying a place, that, under ordinary circumstances, must have occasioned a delay of a month or six weeks' duration, supposing it to be assailed as Ciudad Rodrigo had previously been.

During these events, the division of General Leith continued to occupy Thomar and its neighbouring villages. On the 4th of September, an express announced the retirement of the headquarters from Celorico. Lord Wellington, at the same time, communicated the approach of the enemy, his advance having driven in the allied piquets at Alverca and Freixadas. Gouvea became the headquarters of the allied army.

The affair of posts at Alverca and Freixadas was the consequence of a change of quarters in the *corps d'armée* of the Duc d'Elchingen, on the line of his ulterior advance, but not the forerunner of an immediate attack on the part of the enemy; nor did the French general-in-chief appear prepared to take advantage of the unexpected fall of Almeida. Nearly three weeks elapsed, after the reduction of that fortress, before he seriously moved forward. This must be admitted to have been an error of Marshal Massena. The time occupied in reducing Ciudad Rodrigo ought to have sufficed for the completion of his arrangements. The absence of General Reynier's corps, when Almeida fell, may have occasioned the delay; but that affords no excuse: he only awaited orders to join him, and was unobstructed in doing so; nor does there appear a sufficient reason for delaying that junction after commencing the last siege necessary to undertake before advancing upon Lisbon. What is the utility of fortunate accident in a military point of view, unless immediate advantage can be taken?

It has always appeared to me a most brilliant feature in this cam-

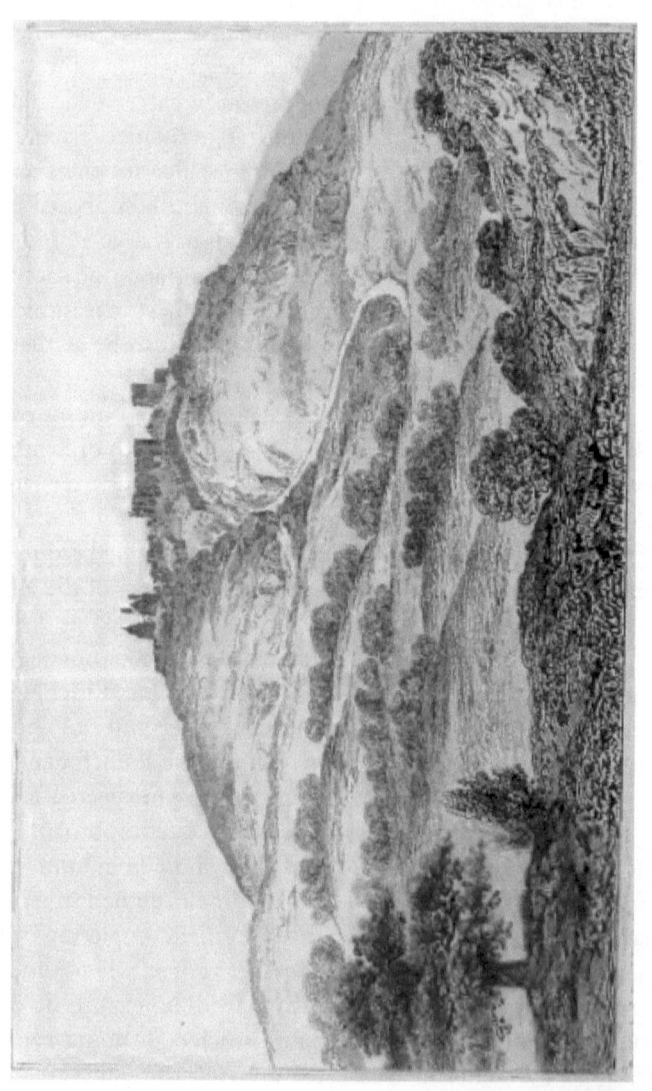

Guarda

paign of Lord Wellington, and one presenting a remarkable contrast in the maturity of arrangement of two distinguished men. A very formidable enemy's army threatened the country which the British general was destined to defend. It reduced one fortress, and laid siege to another; when, contrary to all human calculation, accident at once occasioned the fall of the latter: the consequence was, that Lord Wellington being prepared for all contingencies, the premature reduction of Almeida did not essentially annoy him, while his antagonist was unprepared promptly to follow up the advantage naturally arising from the circumstance.

At length the Prince d'Essling, having reduced the encumbrances of his army, abandoned many of the unwieldy ambulances hitherto accompanying it, and left a corps under General Gardanne in the vicinity of Almeida, marched on the 15th of September, to carry into effect the ultimate objects of the campaign. The 2nd and 6th *corps d'armée* took the direction of Guarda and Celorico, the 8th marched on Pinhel. As if to initiate the French commander into the species of warfare he was about to encounter, the convoys, following his army at the distance of a day's march, were attacked by parties of militia and *ordenança* at this early period of the invasion.

The line of advance adopted by the "Army of Portugal" being now placed beyond doubt, Lord Wellington ordered Generals Hill and Leith to march upon the Mondego, with the least possible delay. The latter consequently moved his corps from Thomar to Cabaços on the 18th, the following day was at Espinhal, and on the 20th at Foz d'Arouse.

Lord Wellington, having retired his army by the left bank of the Mondego, was prepared either to dispute the strong ground of the Sierra d'Estrella, or to cross the river, and occupy the Sierra de Alcoba, affording a formidable position; without forcing which, Marshal Massena's direct route to Coimbra became obstructed.

So well-timed was the junction of the different corps of the British Army, that Lord Wellington's third division, under General Picton, occupied the quarters of Foriera on the 20th; these becoming next day the cantonments of the corps from Thomar, commanded by General Leith, while at the distance of one day's march was General Hill; all moving to the same point, without interference, confusion, or delay. On the 22nd, General Leith's corps was stationed at Sobriera and Casa Nova. On the following morning he crossed the Mondego at the Barca de Conselha, halting at Peña Cova for the night. Having during the 24th encamped near the church of Nuestra Senhora de Monte Alto, he moved into the position of Busaco on the morning of the 25th, occupying the extreme right of the ridge, with his flank on the Mondego, on the opposite bank of which was the whole corps of General Hill, extending to the Ponte de Murcella.

The Sierra de Busaco, after the army of Lord Wellington and the corps from Thomar had extended along its ridge, was not fully occupied; the commander of the forces therefore directed General Hill to cross the Mondego, and form on the extreme right of the position. To give space for this alteration, as also to condense the *alignement*, General Leith was ordered to move to his left. This was considered the least vulnerable part of the position, consequently the main body of the army had previously been extended from the San Antonio de Cantora road to the junction with the Sierra de Caramula.

To form some idea of the great extent of the position at Busaco, it is only necessary to state, that after 50,000 men had been placed upon it, a space of nearly two miles intervened from the left of General Leith's corps to the right of the 3rd division, standing next in line. General Picton defended the San Antonio de Cantaro road; General Hill was in force on the extreme right; the left of the position was fully occupied. The only troops considered disposable were those of General Leith, admirably placed both with reference to what was supposed probable, and what did occur. If the right of the army should be attacked, he was close at hand to support that point; if the San Antonio road became the line of attack, he was equally prepared to march in aid of General Picton. His own ground was considered not liable to assault, the ascent being particularly steep; nor did any roads intersect it coming from the direction of the French Army.

The 26th was a beautiful day, with bright sunshine; nor can anything be conceived more enlivening, more interesting, or more varied, than the scene from the heights of Busaco. Commanding a very extensive prospect to the eastward, the movements of the French Army were distinctly perceptible; it was impossible to conceal them from the observation of the troops stationed along the whole range of the mountain; nor did this appear to be the object of the enemy. Rising grounds were covered with troops, cannon, or equipages: the widely extended country seemed to contain a host moving forward, or gradually condensing into numerous masses, checked in their progress by the grand natural barrier on which we were placed, and at the base of which it became necessary to pause.

Peña Cova

In imposing appearance as to numerical strength, I have never seen anything comparable to that of the enemy's army from Busaco; it was not alone an army encamped before us, but a multitude: cavalry, infantry, artillery, cars of the country, horses, tribes of mules with their attendants, sutlers, followers of every description, crowded the moving scene upon which Lord Wellington and his army looked down.

Some French officers, who have written upon the subject, admit the intention of creating an erroneous impression as to the strength of the French Army, and blame Marshal Massena for having subsequently displayed his force in order of battle, before such a position as Busaco, where it became impossible to support the delusion,—the separation from non-combatants at once proving the real strength of the army, in direct opposition to the supposed important object of confirming an exaggerated estimate as to the irresistible means employed for the subjugation of Portugal.

The evening of the 26th closed upon the allies finally arranged in position; after dark, the whole country in front was illuminated by the fires of the French Army. The 6th and 8th corps of the enemy had arrived in front of the position by the routes of Casel de Maria and Mortagoa, the 2nd by that leading to San Antonio de Cantaro.

On the forenoon of the 26th, I was directed to advance in front with a squadron of Portuguese cavalry, and report the movements of the enemy on the roads close to the right bank of the Mondego, directly communicating with the valley of Larangeira. In the execution of this service, we proceeded two leagues without encountering an enemy, the French advancing by roads more to their right, and only extending to the left when immediately in front of the sierra. As we rode forward, a cannonade and fire of musketry was heard in the direction of St. Combadao, where the Duc d'Elchingen and General Reynier were forcing back upon the position the advance of the allied army.

The scene presented during this short *reconnaissance* was of the most interesting description. Passing through a very picturesque and beautiful country, we occasionally descended to the banks of the Mondego, or ascended the eminences, from whence was discernible the enemy's line of march on the right, at intervals enveloped in dust and smoke. To the rear was the imposing line of mountain occupied by the allied army, luxuriant woods, fertile valleys: great excitement, and a brilliant atmosphere, added to the effect of the whole.

The Duc d'Elchingen, on arriving at the base of the Sierra de

Busaco, was impressed with an opinion as to the unattackable nature of the ground; but Marshal Massena, after reconnoitring, determined to try its strength. At daybreak, on the 27th, reports of cannon were heard in the direction of the convent of Busaco. These were at first audible but at intervals; they soon after became incessant, accompanied by heavy discharges of musketry. The line of the mountain, irregular in its course, intersected by ravines, varying in height, forming the convex of a circle, from where we were stationed, prevented the slightest prospect of the part of the position attacked.

It soon, however, became evident, from the sound of the firing, that General Picton was also engaged; but, although nearest to us in the line, his troops, and those by whom the 3rd division was assailed, were alike hidden from our view.

In the immediate front of General Leith's corps, no hostile movements were perceptible; he, therefore, with the concurrence of General Hill, put his division in motion, marching by his left along the summit of the ridge intervening between the ground on which he had encamped the preceding night and the San Antonio de Cantaro road.

On approaching the right of General Picton's position, the whole sierra presented a crowd of light troops, masses of British and French infantry, and a very warm contest in full progress. At this moment, the enemy had penetrated to the very summit of the mountain; the outnumbered light infantry of General Picton were severely pressed. When the smoke dispelled, that at intervals enveloped the whole extent of the face and crest of the ridge, the highest rocks appeared in possession of the French *voltigeurs*: one officer was particularly conspicuous, on the very highest point; cheering, and waving his *schakos*, he urged on his comrades, then climbing the ascent.

A column of the enemy now appeared gaining the *plateau* on the mountain top, with its head directed so as to ascend diagonally to the line of the allied army, by which its left flank was exposed to the troops arriving from the right of the British position.

Colonel Barnes's brigade of General Leith's corps, composed of the Royal, 9th, and 38th regiments, had been advanced to the head of the column, and consequently first came in contact with the enemy; the 9th regiment, commanded by Colonel Cameron, being the leading battalion, when about a hundred yards distant, wheeled into line, firing a volley, the effect of which was terrific; the ground was covered with dead and dying, not new levies or mercenaries, but the *élite* of the

French Army. This destructive fire being followed up by an immediate charge, the enemy gave way, rushing down the steep face of the *sierra* in the utmost confusion; nor did his troops attempt to rally until on the same ground from whence they had advanced to this most unsuccessful and murderous attack.

On the same space of ground has seldom been seen such destruction as overtook the division of the 2nd corps on this occasion.

Previous to this signal repulse, the other division of General Reynier's corps had in a similar way been driven from the *sierra*, by the 3rd division, after an attack equally gallant and hopeless.

The battle to the left of the convent, and sustained exclusively by the light division and General Pack's brigade, closed with brilliant success on the part of the allies.

General Loison's division of Marshal Ney's corps, with one brigade of the division Marchand, had attacked these troops; while the other brigade of General Marchand, and the entire division of General Mermet, were formed in mass at the base of the mountain, in readiness to support the first attack. The 8th *corps d'armée*, in reserve, was prepared to move forward at a moment's warning.

The French cavalry were stationed near a village to the right of General Reynier's bivouac on the night of the 26th, and to the rear of the whole army.

General Simon's brigade, at the head of the division Loison, advanced with great resolution, notwithstanding the difficulties encountered: nor is it light praise to bestow upon any troops, when it is admitted that they made great progress for a time under all the disadvantages of a very steep ascent, a heavy cannonade, and such troops as the light division to oppose. At last they were forced back, having sustained enormous loss, and, with the two other brigades forming the column, were bayoneted back from whence they came. General Simon was wounded and taken.

The column advancing on the road from San Antonio de Cantaro, repelled, as formerly stated, by the right of the 3rd division and Colonel Barnes's brigade, made the attack under very desperate circumstances. When it commenced to ascend the sierra, no troops to the left of the road were visible on the summit; consequently, in pressing forward, with all the characteristic activity, alacrity, firmness, and incessant progress of a French attack, the attention of officers and soldiers was diverted from whence the real clanger ultimately proceeded. When not obscured by the constant fire kept up in advancing, the men were seen pressing forward, loading with trailed arms, but not halting for a moment. On one of these occasions, the flank of at least 5000 men became exposed to view; into that flank was the fire of Colonel Barnes's brigade deliberately discharged, searching its ranks from left to right. It is difficult to imagine any circumstances under which musketry could be more annihilating: the result proved that it was so.

There was something exhilarating to a degree in the whole day of Busaco: as it advanced, a bright sun shone on the armies; no event had occurred to counteract the full tide of success attending the defensive warfare adopted by Lord Wellington. Strength of position, with great firmness of purpose, had enabled the allies to repel very serious attacks with comparatively trifling loss; the glacis of the mountain-barrier on which we stood was heaped with bodies of the enemy. The innumerable host that had been displayed on the previous day were checked; while the soldiers, brave and skilful enough to have mounted the summit of such a position, were repulsed, and driven back upon their disheartened comrades. General Foy received one of his numerous wounds upon this occasion.

General Graindorge, commanding a brigade of the second corps, was killed, as were many superior officers. The general of division, Merle, was severely wounded. The French regiments that suffered most from the attack of Colonel Barnes's brigade were the 2me and 4me legère, the 15me, 17me, 36me, and 70me of the line.

One of the results of this action, and certainly not the least important, was ascertaining that the Portuguese troops would conduct themselves well under fire,—that their behaviour, when opposed to the enemy, was consistent with their highly improved and soldierlike appearance; nor did a single instance occur, during this first trial, in which their firmness could be questioned. Wherever their battalions met the enemy, the contest was supported with credit to themselves, and to those British officers, who, in the course of a difficult, frequently unpleasant duty, had, by perseverance, military knowledge, and great exertion, created such troops from the materials presented by the Portuguese army, when purely national in its habits, its officers, its insubordination, and its insignificance.

A stronger proof of the power or effect of discipline cannot be adduced in the history of armies, than was exhibited by these soldiers during the course of their subsequent service under Lord Wellington. They became excellent troops, equal to contend with the French infantry; under *ordinary circumstances*, acting with the same energy and bravery as their island allies: no higher praise appears just or necessary.

The 8th Portuguese regiment, commanded by Colonel Douglas, was particularly distinguished. By that corps, in conjunction with the 45th and 88th British regiments, the most successful attack of the day was repulsed. Placed as they were on very commanding ground, the loss sustained by these regiments, being nearly equal to that of all the other corps of the army combined, proves the serious nature of the contest from which they had acquired such merited distinction.

The troops continued in expectation of renewed assault during the day, but no movement indicated any intention on the part of the enemy to renew the costly experiment he had already made. Light troops skirmished near the base of the mountain; on its summit the most perfect confidence was established: a feeling seemed to prevail that no efforts could shake the allied army, or force its position.

Before dark, General Leith's corps withdrew from the eastern face of the ridge, taking up its bivouac at the commencement of the descent, looking towards Coimbra, but near to the summit; about a hundred yards lower down the slope were assembled a considerable number of the French wounded, who, although removed from the immediate scene of action, had not yet been transported to the rear. The bright day we had enjoyed closed with a night of extreme cold, rendering the situation of these men much to be commiserated; wounded, laid on the heath, without any description of covering, their complaints were loud and incessant, accompanied by entreaties to remove them from the rigour of the bleak mist that now shrouded the sierra, attended by a piercing wind.

An hour before daybreak, on the 28th, the troops were in line: mist continued to hang on the mountain: all remained quiet during the whole extent of the position; nor when light appeared, did any sound proclaim the approach of a renewed attack.

A flank movement alone remained for the adoption of the French Army, with any prospect of success. Circumstances rendered even that very precarious; forcing the position was not to be accomplished. There existed one road, the occupation of which by the allies, was a matter of uncertainty at the headquarters of the Prince of Essling, intelligence received from the peasantry inducing the French marshal to hope that it remained open. General St. Croix was sent, with two regiments of dragoons, to reconnoitre and report. He ascended to the summit on the route by Avilans do Cima to Sardao, without encountering an enemy; and returned with the information, which at once determined the movement. The whole army was directed, in one column, upon this road, led by the cavalry, with the brigade St. Croix at its head.

At ten o'clock on the forenoon of the 29th, the *sierra* was passed without the slightest opposition, the army descending into the plain on the Coimbra side of the mountain.

The route thus, of necessity, adopted by Marshal Massena, considerably lengthened his distance to Coimbra: while the allies, descending from the sierra by the more direct roads, without difficulty arrived, previous to the enemy's approach, on the great line leading to Lisbon.

On the morning of the 29th, General Hill marched in the direction of Espinhal and Thomar, the main body of the army descending the right bank of the Mondego. General Leith's corps encamped near Diantura, a village one league from Coimbra. From thence it proceeded, on the 30th, to the Quinta de San Jorge, the country residence of the friars of Santa Cruz at Coimbra, beautifully situated on the left bank of the river, surrounded with orange-groves and vineyards. From observations of Portuguese scenery, I should be inclined to select the valley of the Mondego at Coimbra as the richest and most beautiful portion of the kingdom.

At the Quinta de San Jorge we were joined by General Hay, who assumed the command of the brigade hitherto under the orders of Colonel Barnes.

The French Army found the city of Coimbra, as it had previously done Vizeu, perfectly deserted; the houses closed against them; the inhabitants wandering over the face of the country, or crowding the roads leading to Lisbon. This emigration, produced, in great measure, by the instructions of Lord Wellington, was of incalculable inconvenience to an invading army, moving without magazines, consequently depending for subsistence on the countries through which it advanced. Instead of beholding a large population, to be subjected to intimidation and reluctant discovery of the stores in their possession, they found the bare walls of the houses, while the depositaries of grain, or provisions of any description, fell but unfrequently and accidentally into their power.

The column of march of the allies, on the 1st of October, presented an extraordinary scene, the varieties of which it is impossible minutely to describe; but when it is explained, that the route was absolutely and continuously covered during its whole extent, some idea may be formed as to its unusual aspect. It was not only troops of all arms, attended by the incumbrances or followers of an army: it was not peasantry, removing with their families; it was not the higher orders of society, travelling conformably to their rank; it was not the furniture, grain, cattle, of an extensive line of country, passing from one station to another,—but it was all these combined, pressing forward in one varied, confused, apparently interminable mass.

On the 2nd, Leiria became the headquarters of the army. General Leith's corps halted at Boa Vista, the following morning passing through the former town, and proceeding to the villages of Carvalho and Carvalhal.

During the progress of depopulation which the country at this period underwent, the friars of the great convent of Batalha deserted their residence; and when General Leith, with the officers of his staff, arrived, one solitary inhabitant was discovered in charge of the building, and the relics of former ages contained within its splendid walls.

Batalha, founded in commemoration of the victory gained at Algiberotti in 1386, by the first John, king of Portugal, is situated in a valley, surrounded by hills covered with wood. These are not of great altitude, but prevent a distant view of the monastery. On being approached, the building is displayed, rising from luxuriant groves of orange-trees. It is of great extent, very irregular, but presenting an exterior both grand and impressive.

The long galleries and spacious cloisters of the convent were now seen under peculiar circumstances; the deep obscurity, the deserted aspect of the building, imparted a melancholy feeling. The silence that prevailed added to the gloom and solitude of the scene. It was only interrupted by the distant sound of voices, which at intervals struck upon the ear, as the British officers, from curiosity, explored the recesses of the building. It could not fail to occur, when wandering through the deserted convent, what a change a few hours had produced; how much the habits and the practice of centuries, with reference to its absent possessors, had been overturned by events with which they were apparently not immediately connected. For hundreds of years the Dominican friars had occupied these walls, only torn from them by death.

An even course of monastic life had closed on generations of men, without their existence as a body having been violently assailed. The advance of the French Army, combined with the orders of superior civil and military authorities, had, for a time, broken up an establishment, that it appeared nothing but a revolution in the Catholic church, or in the state, was at all likely to endanger. Families deserting their homes, escaping in confusion and distress, exhibited the devastating influence of war; but the dissolution of a great fraternity such as Batalha, was an impressive instance of the uncertainty of all situations in countries subject to the incursions of an enemy.

Batalha, on the previous day, had been filled with its usual inhabitants, in all the bustle of preparation for departure, uncertain when they might return; equally so as to the fate of the building,—consequently removing, by all possible means, everything either valuable or portable, except the kingly remains, the swords, and armour deposited in the chapel,—these being left to the sacrilegious mercy of the French array.

The interior of the chapel is very chaste and beautiful. In it were exposed to view the remains of John II., King of Portugal. The coffin being open, the embalmed figure was subjected to the inspection and touch of the strangers present. It presented a singular appearance after the lapse of so many years,—the flesh of the face yielding to the pressure of the hand,—the teeth and nails perfect; the skin and flesh had disappeared from the head and other parts of the face. On the cheeks alone did it remain undecayed. Time had not worn or defaced the habiliments in which the body had been deposited. Altogether, it had in some respects more the appearance of recent decease than the relic of inanimate mortality for four hundred years.

The swords and helmets of the First and Second John were also exhibited by the only remaining brother of the convent, as also the original charter of the monastery. These latter relics were conveyed by General Leith to the San Domingos convent in Lisbon, which many of the fugitive brethren of Batalha had adopted as their temporary residence. Having passed the night of the 3rd in the convent, General Leith moved his corps on the following morning, concluding the day's march at the village of Frugiuli, where he halted during the 5th.

The French Army, detained by want of provisions, and also by the arrangements necessarily made for establishing its hospitals at Coimbra, did not move from that town and Condeixa until the 5th, when the whole advanced upon Leiria. This delay, added to the previous advantage, as to progress on its route, obtained by the allied army, prevented the troops from suffering during the retreat any harassment, either in the length of marches, or from being pressed by the pursuing enemy. Slight affairs of cavalry alone occurred. These were invariably favourable to the allies; nor was it until a large proportion of the Prince of Essling's army arrived at Alenquer, that any affair of importance took place. The 2nd corps, and the cavalry under General Monbrun, advanced from thence upon Villa Franca, while the 8th took the direction of Coral. Lord Wellington retired part of his army by the route of Alcobaça and Caldas, by which also a great proportion of the fugitive population approached the capital.

On the 6th, General Leith's corps marched to Quinta de Torres; on the 7th, to Ribaldeira. Soon after leaving the former, very early in the morning, we for the first time saw the Brunswick Oels regiment, which, on its route to join the army, had bivouacked on the line of march, a short distance in advance of the Quinta. A dense fog covered the face of the country, dispersing at intervals, so as to make objects discernible when not far removed. The appearance of the Brunswick corps under these circumstances was peculiarly novel and picturesque. The long black clothing of the men,—their *schakos*, bearing in front the emblems of mortality,—the waving horsehair that streamed in the wind, were increased in magnitude and effect by the misty curtain that at times admitted to view these unusually gaunt figures.

At daybreak, on the 10th, we marched to the village of Enexara dos Cavalleros. A day of more incessant heavy rain, accompanied by a gale of wind, has seldom been witnessed. The aspect of the country was bleak and dreary. The roads very deep, and the troops confined to quarters from whence they were little tempted to come forth; for, when the soldiers were obliged to face the storm, their own feelings, and the appearance of drenched, miserable-looking passengers, served as an incentive to regain the shelter of their crowded habitations.

On the evening of the 12th, the 8th *corps d'armée* attacked part of Sir Brent Spencer's division in Sobral. The consequence was the evacuation of that town by the allies, in rear of which the advanced posts of the 1st division were established. Alenquer became the headquarters of the French Army.

On the 14th, the state of the weather had greatly improved. The morning was cloudless, succeeded by a day of bright sunshine. Encouraged by these appearances, and curious to observe the position of the enemy, accompanied by Lord George Grenville, I rode to the advanced posts. We left our horses in the ravine which separated the heights, on which was the position of the allied army, from a rising ground where a breastwork had been thrown up to protect a post occupied by part of the 71st regiment, and about one hundred and fifty yards removed from which was a French work, constructed of casks, doors, and planks, brought from Sobral. Behind this the enemy's infantry were perceived, but apparently quiet. For some time we continued to observe the different detachments more immediately opposite. Between the breastwork and the temporary redoubt of the enemy, extended a level field, on which neither a tree nor obstruction of any description presented itself. The French soldiers were observed looking from behind the casks, but not a shot was fired by either party.

Our attention was soon after attracted to the road leading from Alenquer into the town of Sobral. A crowd of officers on horseback, detachments of cavalry, dragoons with led horses, and all the *cortège* of a general-in-chief, appeared upon it. The drums beat; the troops in rear of the village got under arms: still no movement was perceptible in the post to which we were immediately opposed. It was, however, evident that a *reconnaissance* of some importance was contemplated; nor did it appear probable the troops would be permitted long to continue in their present inactive state.

Marshal Massena, the Duc d'Elchingen, and General Junot, ascended to a height a short distance to the north of the town, where they dismounted, near a windmill, and became seated, apparently reconnoitring the position opposite. Soon after their arrival, a rocket was fired from the cask redoubt, succeeded by the unmasking of some light guns, which were instantaneously discharged against the breastwork of the 71st.

We had previously been kneeling, looking over the embankment, which was struck near its crest by the shot fired. The British detachment continued protected until after the first musketry discharge of the enemy, on receiving which, the men started up, making a deadly return to the comparatively harmless volley. The French infantry, after this preamble, rushed forward with their usual impetuosity, reaching the embankment unchecked, when the 71st, with Colonel Reynell at their head, springing over the work, not only bayoneted the enemy back to his intrenchment, but drove him from thence into the town. During the progress of this affair, Colonel Cadogan, perceiving the detachment of his regiment engaged, joined it, and was wounded.

The enemy continued to persevere to the right and left of the redoubt from whence he had been repulsed, the nature of the ravine, penetrating to its rear, and in some places covered with wood, admitting the chance of forcing the allies to retire, by operations tending to turn the ground on which they were posted. These manoeuvres were effectually checked by the German Legion on the right, and the light companies of General Cameron's brigade to the left. The fire of light troops near Sobral continued for some hours, gradually dying away towards evening. On the morning of the 15th, Sir Brent Spencer's division was withdrawn from its advanced situation, and the *videttes* or piquets of the allied army alone remained assailable, without attacking the position itself.

At this period, some gun-boats, manned by the navy, were sent up the Tagus, under the command of Lieutenant Frederick Berkeley. Stationed opposite to Alhandra, firing in all directions wherever an enemy appeared, they harassed and annoyed the parties sent either to reconnoitre or to occupy the villages on the right bank of the river. An accidental shot from one of them killed General St. Croix in the act of descending into a road apparently protected from the effects of the cannonade, but where he was nearly cut in two by a *recochet* ball. On many occasions distinguished for his bravery and address, he was much regretted by the French Army.

The first position of the enemy, when established in front of the lines, was as follows:—The 2nd *corps d'armée* was placed a short distance in rear of Villa Franca, having its left on the Tagus, with its right extending towards Arruda; a brigade of light cavalry was posted at Porte de Mugem to keep up the communication with Santarem. General Monbrun, with most of the cavalry, was on the Zezere, watching the motions of the garrison of Abrantes, and protecting the rear of the army. The headquarters continued at Alanquer. The 6th corps was in position at Otta, with the exception of the division Loison, which, placed on the road between Alanquer and Sobral, kept up the communication between General Reynier and the Duke of Abrantes.

The brigade of dragoons attached to the 8th corps was placed to the right of Caxieras, observing the numerous routes leading from Alenquer to Torres Vedras, and from the latter to Villa Franca, by Sobral and Arruda. The division of General Solignac was placed rather more to the left, for the purpose of threatening the valley of Arruda. The *videttes* and advanced posts were close to those of the allies, while along the whole extent of the position, from Sobral to the Tagus, beacons were erected by the French Army. On the 7th of October, only two days after the departure of the French Marshal from Coimbra, Colonel Trant, with a force of Portuguese militia, entered that town, capturing the enemy's hospitals, containing 5000 sick or wounded.

The large body of troops employed in the invasion of Portugal having, of course, weakened the already shaken French domination in Spain, it became unsafe for the corps of Marshal the Duke of Treviso to continue in the country which it had for some time occupied, in communication with, and supported by, General Reynier. He, therefore, retired from Zafra and Los Santos, crossed the Sierra Morena, forming a junction with the army of the south, commanded by Marshal Soult, and holding in subjection the kingdoms of Andalusia. In this movement, Marshal Mortier was followed by General Ballesteros, who advanced to the neighbourhood of Castillo de las Guardias. At the same time, the Marques de la Romano marched from Spanish Estremadura by Alemtejo, to reinforce Lord Wellington. The leading division of his army, under General Carlos O'Dounell, crossing the Tagus on the morning of the 14th, arrived on that day at Cabeça de Montachique.

Reinforcements having arrived from England, Lord Wellington altered the formation of his army, to which two divisions of infantry were now added. The corps hitherto commanded by General Leith, formed principally of Portuguese, was broken up, and the 5th division, composed of the brigades of Generals Hay and Dunlop, with the Portuguese troops of General Spry, placed under his orders.

The British regiments of this division were, the Royal, 4th, 9th, 30th, 38th, and 44th.

The 3rd and 15th Portuguese infantry of the line and 8th Caçadores formed the brigade of General Spry. To each of the British brigades of this division was attached a company of the Brunswick Oels corps.

The fortified positions to cover Lisbon, and, in the event of necessity, protect the embarkation of the army, were commenced in the autumn of 1809. The plan originated with Lord Wellington: the execution of it was intrusted to Colonel Fletcher, and the British engineer officers then in Portugal.

These lines, so celebrated under the denomination of Torres Vedras—so influential in the circumstances of the war—so justly calculated to raise the military reputation of the commander of the forces, and to prove the scientific acquirement, the deep practical knowledge, of the officers employed in completing them, must ever be considered as the noblest specimen of a fortified position rendered perfect by human art,—disproving at once the previously received opinion, strengthened by the experience of other times, against the possibility of rendering such ground defensible, when assailed by unfettered and concentrated attack.

In giving a brief account of the lines in front of Lisbon, I must state, that the detail is not derived solely from defective personal observation, but is sanctioned by the authority of an officer eminently qualified to give a just representation of their varied defences.

In order to give some idea of the natural means of defence, or of communication, it is necessary to explain, that the Peninsula, at whose south-eastern extremity Lisbon is situated, is crossed by two sierras, extending, with various altitudes and abruptness, but with partial interruptions, from the Atlantic to the Tagus. Through the passes in these mountains, and the low ground bordering the Tagus, four roads from the interior to the capital are conducted,—namely, by Mafra, Montachique, Bucellas, and near to Alhandra. These sierras run nearly parallel, at a distance of from six to nine miles; the point of the line nearest to Lisbon being close to the Tagus, between Via Longa and Quintella.

Of these lines of defence the most complete, the least subjected to the dangerous effects of flank movements, as well as the most continuous in its inaccessible features, and uninterrupted capability of defence, is that nearest the capital, or the second line, as it has been generally denominated, extending from the village of Ribamar, near the mouth of the Rio Lorenzo, to the pass of Mafra—from thence to the Cabeça de Montachique, then to the steep and formidable pass of Bucellas, having to its right the Sierra de Serves, descending precipitously into the plain, at a distance of two miles and a half from the Tagus. The latter space appeared the only vulnerable part of this formidable position. To it the attention of the executive officers was particularly directed, every means which art could devise being adopted to strengthen any point that presented the slightest capability of being converted into an obstacle to the enemy's progress.

In front of Via Longa, upon an eminence rising from the plain at a short distance from the river, six redoubts were constructed, so situated, in consequence of the nearly circular formation of the *plateau*, as to command the approaches in every direction within range of their artillery. Three of these immediately domineered the great route from Alhandra to Lisbon, to the right of which, upon a knoll, in front of the town of Povoa, another work was formed, sweeping the communication in the direction of Quintella. On the bank of the Tagus, a redoubt, armed with four twelve-pounders, terminated the line at its eastern extremity. Fifty-nine redoubts, containing 232 pieces of cannon, estimated to require 17,500 men to garrison them, protected the weaker points, enfiladed the roads, or swept the ascent to the escarped mountains in the range of this extended position, occupying a front of twenty-two miles.

The front line, and that on which the allied army was placed subsequently to the Battle of Busaco, was first intended more as one of isolated posts capable of protracted defence, some of which must have been forced before the main position could have been assailed, than, as it afterwards became, an uninterrupted extent of strengthened ground, sufficiently formidable to induce Lord Wellington there to receive the expected attack of the French Army. The left of this chain rested on the Atlantic, at the mouth of the Rio Zizandra, which holds its course parallel to, and a short distance in front of, the position between Torres Vedras and the sea. From Torres Vedras, for seven miles in rear of the valley of Runa, and extending towards Monte Agraça, was the weakest part of this line. There the exertions of the British engineers were unceasingly directed in aid of the natural defences, and to render the country in all respects as impracticable as possible for an invading army.

On the *sierra* of Monte Agraça, in rear of Sobral, was constructed a redoubt of great magnitude, armed with twenty-five pieces of artillery, and prepared for the garrison of a thousand men. This formidable work, from its commanding and centrical situation, was the constant daily resort of Lord Wellington. There he came every morning, and continued until it was ascertained that no hostile movement had taken place, and until light permitted a *reconnaissance* of the enemy's troops encamped opposite. From the redoubt on Monte Agraça, the line continued, crossing the valleys of Arruda and Calhandriz, until it rested on the Tagus at Alhandra.

Nature and art had rendered the ground from Calhandriz to the river particularly strong; but, to make the defences still more formidable, and to form an intermediate obstruction, redoubts were thrown up extending to the rear, nearly at right angles with the front line. These swept the whole portion of the valley by which a column of infantry must penetrate, even had it succeeded in forcing an entrance into the ravine. Sixty-nine works of different descriptions fortified this line: in these were mounted three hundred and nineteen pieces of artillery; the troops required to garrison them were upwards of 18,000 men; and the extent, in a direct line from flank to flank, twenty-five miles.

In the progress of constructing these very numerous, varied, and complicated defences, Colonel Fletcher, the chief engineer, was removed to the headquarters of the army then on the frontier, where his services were deemed essential: consequently, on the 6th of July, 1810, the command of the department in the lines devolved upon Captain J. T. Jones, to whom is justly to be ascribed the merit, not only of perfecting the previously traced out or contemplated works, but of having suggested and completed many of the most scientific, useful, and laborious obstructions during the extent of this stupendous barrier. Of these, as an example, may be cited the gigantic work of escarping the mountain near Alhandra for a connected distance of nearly two miles, rendering its crest an impenetrable curtain, presenting a natural wall from fifteen to eighteen feet in altitude, not accessible to human assault.

In the line occupied by the allied army, and in front of which the enemy abandoned all hopes of success, Captain Jones had ample scope for his scientific and indefatigably zealous exertion. As above stated, this position was in the previous design neither so connected, nor so generally strengthened, as that of Mafra and Bucellas; but when the army arrived from Busaco, it had become, although not perfect, a continuous line of support, daily gaining strength from the unremitted exertion of the engineers, assisted by the labours of the troops.

It has by some persons been erroneously supposed, that the regular army was, in the event of attack, to occupy the redoubts, and other works in the lines, or, at all events, that a large proportion of the troops would of necessity defend these temporary fortifications. In the calculation of probable circumstances, no British soldiers, with the exception of artillery, would have acted within their walls. Some Portuguese infantry, with the militia and *ordonanza*, were destined to compose the garrisons; while the whole allied army, numerous, brilliant in equipment, high in spirit, confident in its great commander, was prepared to move in every direction, to cover the summits of mountains, to descend into valleys, or to pour in torrents on any luckless column that, with diminished numbers, might have forced past the almost impenetrable obstacles of this grand position.

It is neither chimerical to advance, nor inconsistent with reality to believe, that the battle of Busaco saved the French Army. Had it not been fought, the Prince of Essling must have attacked the lines; and where is the person in either army that could now candidly doubt the result of such an attempt? When I say, must have attacked, it does not appear incredible that the same energy, equal confidence, and the same bravery, that could imagine, or execute, the attack at Busaco, would have made a fruitless attempt of a more fatal description in front of Lisbon, had it not been for the salutary lesson received upon the Sierra de Alcoba.

In addition to the works thrown up in either line, or in the intervening points of communication, rivers were obstructed in their course, flooding the valleys, and rendering the country swampy and impassable; trenches were cut from whence infantry, perfectly protected, might fire on the advancing columns of an enemy, these being also flanked by artillery, sweeping the approaches to them in every direction. Mountains were scarped as above stated; abattis of the most formidable description, either closed the entrance to ravines, impeded an approach to the works, or blocked up roads in which deep cuts were also marked out for excavation; routes conducting from the front were rendered impracticable; others within the lines, either repaired, or formed to facilitate communication, to admit the passage of artillery, or reduce the distance by which the troops had to move for the purposes of concentration or resistance; bridges were mined, and prepared for explosion.

Telegraphs, erected at Alhandra, Monte Agraça, Socorra, Torres Vedras, and in rear of Ponte de Rol, rapidly communicated information from one extremity of the line to the other. These signal stations were in charge of seamen from the fleet in the Tagus, under the command of Lieutenant Leith, of the *Barfleur*. To complete the barriers, palisades, platforms, and planked bridges, leading into the works, fifty thousand trees were placed at the disposal of the engineer department, during the three months ending on the 7th of October, 1810.

The cannon in the works were supplied by the Portuguese Government. Cars, drawn by oxen, transported twelve-pounders where wheels had never previously rolled. Above 3000 officers and artillerymen of the country assisted in arming the redoubts, and were variously employed in the lines. At one period, exclusive of these, of the British engineers, artificers, or infantry soldiers, seven thousand peasantry worked as labourers in the completion of an undertaking only to have been accomplished under the most favourable circumstances, both with regard to cordiality of assistance, neighbouring arsenals, a British fleet in the Tagus, constant uninterrupted communication with a great capital, a regular remuneration to the labourers, an anxious and deep interest in the exclusion to be accomplished by the assistance of the works in progress, and, above all, an intelligence and firmness in command, that could at the same time extract the greatest benefits from these combinations, and urge exertion where it appeared to relax.

The allied army, on arriving in the lines, was placed as follows:

In the great redoubt on Monte Agraça was stationed General Pack, with his brigade of Portuguese infantry. The fifth division, under General Leith, was encamped on the reverse of the heights directly in rear of that work. General Hill's corps occupied the position of Alhandra; to its left, the light division, commanded by General Crauford, extended through Arruda, to Monte Agraça. The first, fourth, and sixth divisions, under Sir Brent Spencer, Generals Cole and Campbell, were at Zibriera, Ribaldiera, and Runa; their right being in contact with General Leith, and their left with General Picton, who, with the third division, occupied Torres Vedras, and guarded the line of the Zizandra.

The cavalry were stationed at Mafra on the second line, and in the villages to the extreme left of the position, where, or in the intermediate space, they could alone be serviceable in the event of attack. The Spanish corps of the Marques de la Romana was stationed at Enexara dos Cavalleros.

The works had received their garrisons, stores, and ammunition; districts were formed under the separate charge of the engineer officers; guides were attached, to the divisions of the army,—everything was in the highest state of preparation to receive the enemy, whose advance was day after day anxiously expected. That these expectations were destined never to be fulfilled, will be recorded as a lasting memorial of the military knowledge and sound judgment of Marshal Massena, more worthy of his reputation as a general than any previous or subsequent event that occurred during the campaign.

It is stated by Colonel Jones, and was believed at the time, that the Duke of Abrantes urged the general-in-chief to permit him, with a division of his corps, to assault the great redoubt of Sobral before daybreak. Had he done so, the first encounter would have been with General Pack, an officer equally brave and determined; nor could he have been more than momentarily engaged with him when the fifth division would have crowned the summit of the ridge, and ensured, not his discomfiture only, but, in all probability, the annihilation of the attacking column.

During the period of the French Army continuing in the immediate front of the lines, the allies were invariably under arms every morning long before daybreak. Frequently in the course of the first ten days, dense fogs prevailed, rendering objects at any distance imperceptible, until the mist dispelled, which it usually did, gradually, after sunrise. On these occasions, Lord Wellington remained in the redoubt on Monte Agraça receiving the reports of the night, by sound alone enabled to judge whether the enemy was moving in advance. The few musketry shots sometimes heard early in the morning, proceeding from the French piquets feeling their way in the mist, occasioned some degree of anxiety to ascertain whether the firing continued, or assumed a more serious noise. This never was the case; nor was there the slightest attempt made to assail any of the works, or an endeavour to penetrate the line during the wide extent of its range.

Deserters arrived daily from the enemy's *alignement*, reporting the distress and scarcity which therein prevailed; and it being now evident that the Prince of Essling would not attack the allies, the period of his departure became the only matter of speculation. At length, urged by necessity, on the morning of the 14th November, the enemy broke up from his encampments in the immediate front of the allied army. The huts in which the French Army had endured inactivity, disappointment, disease, inclement weather, and every species of privation, were deserted. Marshal Massena, compelled by the state of his army, retired from a position, the occupation of which, for such a length of time, without the possible chance of circumstances becoming more favourable, can never, on any sound military principle, be defended.

On arriving in front of the position, of the natural or artificial strength of which he was probably in perfect ignorance, he must at once have become convinced of the defensive intentions of Lord Wellington, and the means he possessed of carrying them into terrible effect. Having ascertained this fact, no satisfactory reason can be assigned for bivouacking in the months of October and November, close to an army which he very properly had not the temerity to attack.

In reverting to the conduct of the Prince of Essling, it maybe urged that he had expectations of being reinforced to an extent warranting an attempt to force the intrenched position of the allies. Subsequent events proved this to have been out of the question.

It may also be questioned whether change of position, having for its object an endeavour to turn or endanger the fortified camp of his opponent, might not have afforded reason for delay. Nothing of the kind was attempted. The French Army continued in a state of apathy and inactivity; the posts were relieved, but no other indication of military movement, no disturbance of any description, varied the monotonous daylight observation of one army, or the listless inaction of the other. Military annals do not record a greater contrast in the real situation of two hostile armies, close to each other, but unwilling to engage, than was exhibited in front of the capital of Portugal.

The allies, abundantly supplied in every respect, receiving provisions, clothing, and money from Lisbon, reinforced daily either by newly arrived troops, or convalescents from the medical depots. Secure and confident in their position, having the recollections of Busaco to inspire them with every rational hope as to the possible result of an attack in their present situation, were buoyant in spirit. On the other part, was an army pressed forward without reference to the principles of tactic, defeated in its first encounter, which the natural arrogance of the Imperial troops attributed more to the nature of the position than to the firmness of the people by whom it was defended.

This impression, however soothing it might have been between Coimbra and Sobral, must have vanished when a still more formidable line of country presented itself, on which they had to encounter the same battalions. To this primary reverse attending the advance of Marshal Massena's army are to be added, the difficulties occasioned by the absence of magazines in an enemy's country, the exposure to cold, damp, rainy weather—to the progress of disease, but, above all, the feeling produced on minds no longer occupied with hopes of glory, or dreams of plunder. These had all vanished: desertion became frequent; and Lisbon, more distant from their grasp, less likely to be subjected to their spoliation, than when the march commenced from Almeida.

Lord Wellington, having ascertained the nature of the retrograde movement made on the 14th, advanced his troops on the track of the French Army. Sir William Erskine's brigade of the 1st division passed through Sobral on the 15th. The only human being remaining in that town was a wounded soldier of the 71st British regiment. On the 16th, the 5th division marched in advance. The whole of the 1st division, General Pack's Portuguese brigade, and the light division, were already on the route to Santarem. Unfortunately for the operations of the army, the weather had become more than usually boisterous and inclement; the rain fell incessantly, rendering the roads, already injured by the passage of the enemy's army, rough, deep, and all but impracticable.

On the 18th, the fifth division marched to Alenquer. The condition in which we found the town, left not a doubt that the enemy had completed its demolition out of pure wantonness. It is not to be supposed, that the state in which we found it was the same wherein the headquarters of Marshal Massena had been satisfied to reside during the preceding month. General Leith inhabited what had been the quarters of the general-in-chief, left in a most dilapidated and disgraceful state. The enemy owed us some dislike for the discomforts to which depopulating the country had subjected him; but there could be no excuse for this pitiful mode of venting ill-humour, held in contempt by those against whom it was directed, and proceeding, of course, from the soldiers alone, was a reproach to the discipline of the army to which they belonged.

On the 19th, we marched through Azambuja, left in a state of ruin not inferior to the other unfortunate towns on the route. The houses in many instances were unroofed, doors and windows burnt, the interiors as uninhabitable as malignity or ingenuity could make them. In the evening, the division arrived at Cartaxo. In the course of this day, we met some hundreds of prisoners taken by the leading divisions of the army. The appearance of these men was wretched in the extreme. Disease and want had reduced them to a state of exhaustion and weakness, rendering them incapable of supporting the fatigues of a lengthened march, commenced with barely sufficient physical power to attempt the exertion.

Lord Wellington had intended to dislodge the enemy from his position at Santarem, on the 19th; but his arrangements not being completed, in consequence of delay in the arrival of some artillery destined to support the attack made by General Pack, the whole operation was postponed until the following morning, when the fifth division received orders to participate in the service.

Before detailing the offensive movements contemplated by Lord Wellington, it is important to explain the change that had occurred in the position of the French Army.

When the Prince of Essling determined on retiring to Santarem, the line of the Zezere, and Thomar, he commenced by ordering the sixth corps to break up from Otta. Marshal Ney fixed his headquarters at Thomar, with the left of his *corps d'armée* near the Zezere,—his right being beyond Ourem. General Loison occupied Golegao with his division and a brigade of dragoons. General Monbrun marched with most of the cavalry to the neighbourhood of Leiria. Torres Novas became the headquarters. The hospitals and civil departments of the army moved to Santarem.

The eighth corps marched soon after dark on the evening of the 14th. At 7 o'clock, General Clausel removed the posts along the line, assembling his division at Sobral, from whence he took the route conducting to Alenquer.

General Solignac, at the same hour, collected his posts, forming his division in close columns on the *plateau*, domineering the valley of Arruda. The brigade of General Ferret was ordered not to move in retreat until the whole of General Junot's corps had passed the defile leading to Alenquer. A brigade of cavalry closed the line of march.

On the 17th, the eight corps marched to Pernes, while that of General Reynier continued in position on the formidable heights of Santarem.

The town of Santarem is encircled by plains, through which the Rio Mayor, and other minor streams, flow into the Tagus. To the south, the town is elevated on ground rising precipitously from the Tagus; in all other directions it is alone approachable through morasses, rendered additionally difficult by the overflowing of the rivulets intersecting them.

The route from Cartaxo crosses the Rio Mayor near to Santarem, the bridge being approached in either direction by a walled causeway, leading through the swampy ground upon its banks, elevated several feet above the level of the plain, and 400 *toises* in length. Behind a strong abattis, formed of large trees placed across the road, was stationed the advanced post of the second corps; a rising ground, close to the extremity of the causeway, on the Santarem side, was armed with artillery, commanding its whole extent; the approach to the position was further defended by intrenchments, and trees cut down, rendering it extremely difficult of access. General Reynier considered his position so formidable, that he did not deem it important to destroy the bridge.

Notwithstanding these serious appearances, Lord Wellington seemed determined to attack the second corps on the morning of the 20th. General Hay's brigade of the 5th division, with General Pack's Portuguese brigade, were ordered to ford the Rio Mayor above the town, turn the enemy's right, drive in his posts, and advance until established on the heights, there to await for subsequent orders. The 1st division, under Sir Brent Spencer, and two brigades of the 5th, commanded by General Leith, were to proceed in columns along the causeway, until across the river; then to quit the road, leap the wall to its left, and having formed on the plain, march direct to the enemy.

The light division to force across the Rio Mayor, near to its junction with the Tagus, and, with a brigade of light cavalry, manoeuvre on the enemy's left flank.

Before daybreak we marched to carry into execution these movements. It had rained constantly during the night; the roads were deep to a degree. As the divisions approached the high ground on the right bank of the Rio Mayor, the weather improved, the rain ceased to be violent; the troops halted on the eminence domineering the western extremity of the causeway, from whence every preparation for defence made by the enemy was clearly discernible.

The demonstrations made by the allies alarmed General Reynier, notwithstanding his previously established confidence in the strength of his position. The troops under Generals Hay and Pack appeared marching to carry into execution what he most dreaded, an attack on his right flank. In ignorance as to the means possessed by these officers of crossing the Rio Mayor, he was unaware of the security afforded by the accidental flooding of the river, which, against a corps unprovided with pontoons or apparatus for constructing a bridge, presented a sufficient obstacle. The force in his immediate front, apparently on the eve of debouching to carry the bridge, had a formidable appearance; while the light division defiled along the bank of the Tagus. General Clausel's division of the 8th corps, the nearest infantry with whom he could communicate, was four leagues distant. Under all these circumstances, General Reynier prepared for retreat: the sick, the wounded, and the equipages, were sent to Golegao; he at the same time despatched information to the Duke of Abrantes, and the general-in-chief, as to the critical nature of his situation.

The 1st and 5th divisions of the allied army, crowning the heights as above stated, remained in anxious suspense, expecting every moment to hear the troops to their left engaged. The enemy appeared equally intent in watching the progress of events; but nothing was destined to result from what had every semblance of being the immediate prelude to a very serious contest. The causeway could not have been forced without great loss; nor was it possible for Lord Wellington to ascertain so immediately the exact position of the remainder of the French Army as to judge how far it was practicable to dislodge the 2nd corps by flank movements alone. Conjecture was, however, at an end, upon the abandonment of all intention to attack being communicated. General Hay's brigade rejoined the division, which retired to Cartaxo, where General Cameron's brigade, with the German Legion,

PUNHETE FROM THE OPPOSITE BANK OF THE TAGUS

were also quartered for the night.

During these operations, in consequence of the enemy having re-established a bridge over the Zezere at Punhete, General Hill's corps was passed across the Tagus at Villada, by the boats of the fleet at Lisbon. The possibility of the French Army obtaining supplies from the Alemtejo was thus effectually counteracted.

The 5th division marched from Cartaxo on the morning of the 23rd, adopting a route to its right of the great road to Lisbon, and being quartered for the night in the villages of Aveiro de Baxo and De Cima. We inhabited the Quinta of the Condes de Aveiro—a large house, situated in a valley, surrounded by all the neglected luxuriance of Portuguese scenery. The French had bestowed an unusual degree of violence upon the unfortunate Quinta; not a window in the spacious building was left in a perfect state; refining in mischief, the sashes had been thrown open to reduce the consumption of labour or of time in completing the work of destruction.

On the 24th, the division moved to Alcoentre. The French Army now occupied a portion of the territory best calculated to supply its wants; the valley of Golegao, that of Thomar, and on the right bank of the Zezere, being not only one of the most fertile parts of the kingdom, but in those districts the system of emigration and removing property had not been so generally or systematically carried into effect as on the line nearer the coast, by which the enemy had advanced after the Battle of Busaco.

Possessing this district from whence to derive his supplies, Marshal Massena subsisted his army by means of its own exertions in procuring food; a system of foraging was established with great care as to detail, and carried into practice not in one direction alone, but over the whole extent of country in rear of his cantonments. As the grain and cattle of the nearer districts became exhausted, the daily marches of the detachments were of course more extended and more harassing, occasioning irregularity in the supply of food; while the soldiers, subjected to constant fatigues, suffered from a season of itself calculated to produce aguish complaints, and to engender sickness; the effective strength of the army rapidly diminished, nor did there appear any immediate prospect of reinforcement or relief.

The communications of the French general, either with Spain or France, were effectually obstructed, leaving him in ignorance as to the progress of events, or the wishes of the emperor on the future conduct of a campaign now proceeding under very different prospects from those he had been induced to anticipate.

Early in December, General Gardanne, with a large convoy of clothing and provisions, escorted by 3000 infantry, with three squadrons of cavalry, entered Portugal, for the purpose of conveying these supplies to the army of the Prince of Essling. Having penetrated to Cardigos, within three leagues of being in communication with the French troops on the Zezere, he, from some inexplicable cause, became alarmed, retraced his steps, and returned into Spain, pursued by the militia and *ordinanza*.

During the month of December, slight variation occurred, either in the position of the armies, or the nature of the war; the only occasions on which the troops came in contact, resulting from efforts made to obstruct the foraging parties sent from the right of the enemy's line into the country in front of Obidos.

In upwards of twenty slight affairs, Captain Fenwick, of the Portuguese service, had from Obidos harassed, defeated, and captured parties of the enemy, in all of which he had exhibited a combination of enterprise, gallantry, and judgment. Having, with eighty militia of the garrison under his orders, attacked a similar number of French grenadiers at a village near Alcobaça, he was mortally wounded when in pursuit of the flying enemy. To have been so frequently and invariably successful in the command of Portuguese militia against French troops, even in minor affairs, was a proof of no ordinary military talent.

In consequence of the report made by General Foy, who had been sent to Paris soon after the arrival of the army at Alanquer, General Drouet, with the 9th *corps d'armée*, was ordered to make a reconnaissance, penetrate into Portugal until in communication with Marshal Massena, ascertain the state of his army, and, having accomplished this service, return to the Spanish frontier. General Drouet, having left his cavalry in the neighbourhood of Almeida, and one division of his corps, under General Claparède, at Guarda, advanced with the other, and the division of General Gardanne, by Ponte de Murcella, upon Pombal, where he communicated with the right of the French Army. This march for a time disencumbered the flank and rear of the enemy of militia detachments, that had previously occasioned great inquietude and annoyance, but who were, of course, unequal to a contest with 10,000 regular infantry.

The French marshal prevented General Drouet from retracing his steps, and prevailed upon him, until despatches were received from Paris, to continue as a reinforcement to the army of Portugal. He, consequently, placed the troops under his orders at Leiria, thus strengthening and extending the right of his line; after which he moved this corps to the left, and it was cantoned on the banks of the Tagus. The arrival of this reinforcement, the certainty of the enemy having constructed bridge equipages at Punhete, for the purpose of passing the Tagus, and the advance of Marshals Soult and Mortier, with the disposable force, from Andalusia on the Guadiana, were all calculated to create uneasiness at the allied headquarters.

The general of artillery, Eblé, had with great exertion completed upwards of a hundred and fifty pontoons, with all the necessary apparatus for constructing two bridges across the Tagus, having already placed one over the Zezere at Punhete, and another at Martinchel. At this period the allied army was cantoned as follows: The headquarters, with the guards, and General Cameron's brigade, occupied Cartaxo; the German Legion, Aveiro de Baxo; Sir William Erskine's brigade, Alcuntrinha; General Picton's division, Alcoentre; General Leith's, Torres Vedras; General Cole's, Azambuja; General Campbell's, Alenquer; and the cavalry extended in advance, or to the left of the position.

On the 19th of January, the Duke of Abrantes, at the head of five thousand infantry and three hundred cavalry, left Alcanhede, at five in the morning, marching direct upon Rio Mayor, through which town he drove the allied piquets. This reconnaissance was made under an impression that a large force had been collected at or near Alcoentre, for the purpose of debouching on the right of the French Army; upon ascertaining that the information received was erroneous, the troops returned to their cantonments, the only result being the dangerous wound received by the general-in-chief of the 8th corps. The Duke of Abrantes, having advanced to an eminence in front of his light troops, that he might more narrowly inspect the position or force of the allies, was fired at by the retiring *videttes*, and seriously wounded. A carbine ball fractured the bridge of his nose, close to the forehead, lodging in the right cheek-bone, from whence it was extracted on the following day.

On the 23rd, the Marques de la Romana died at Cartaxo; the last act of his military life was, detaching the troops under his orders for the purpose of endeavouring to check the operations of the Duke of Dalmatia in Spanish Estremadura. General Mendizabel was intrusted with the conduct of this service, in the execution of which he gave unquestionable proofs of perfect incapacity. He had for some time been manoeuvring in the country on the left bank of the Guadiana, and to reinforce him the Spanish infantry from the Tagus were directed.

On the 30th of January, Marshal Soult commenced the siege of Badajos, by opening a parallel against the Pardaleras, one of its outworks. The Spanish garrison, being accidentally under the orders of a man of firmness and energy, prepared for a vigorous defence; nor did it appear doubtful that a considerable delay must be occasioned, as well as loss to the enemy, before he obtained possession of so strong a fortress. The Duke of Treviso conducted the siege, which was urged with all possible despatch, but received a partial interruption from a sortie made by the garrison on the 3rd of February. Two thousand infantry, with three squadrons of cavalry, forcing back the workmen and guard of the trenches, filled in twelve *toises* of the parallel; this was, however, soon repaired, and, on the evening of the 11th, the Pardaleras was carried by assault.

General Mendizabel, having encamped on the right bank of the Gebora, with his left flank protected by Fort San Christoval. watched the progress of the siege. From this very favourable position he was unfortunately induced to move, by a fire of shells from the enemy's works on the opposite side of the Guadiana. Thus, to escape a minor inconvenience, abandoning the safeguard of the fort, and marching to his left, where the flooded state of the rivers alone protected him. For some days they were impassable; but on the waters subsiding, Marshal Soult determined to strike a blow against a force he neither dreaded, nor, upon military principles, could disregard.

On the night of the 18th, the French troops marched, forded both rivers, overthrew the Spanish Army, capturing its artillery, camp equipage, and baggage; no rout could be more complete; the whole were either killed, taken, or dispersed, the fugitives obtaining shelter within the walls of Badajos or Elvas. Don Carlos de España on this, as on all similar occasions, distinguished himself; to his gallantry and exertion may be attributed the escape of any portion of this ill-fated force, with the exception of General Madden's brigade of Portuguese cavalry, acting with the Spanish Army, which also left the field in a creditable state of formation, considering the ruin, havoc, and dispersion that surrounded it in every direction.

The tardy progress of the siege of Badajos, under circumstances that made its speedy reduction a matter of deep interest to the French marshals, proved the determined defence of the governor; the month of February passed without any immediate prospect of its fall. Unfortunately, one of those accidents occurred which, in war, are so frequently influential. General Menacho was killed by a cannon shot in the act of observing the effect of a sortie. The command of the garrison, in consequence of this much-to-be-lamented event, devolved upon General Imaz, a weak, irresolute man. The alteration in the energetic nature of the defence became immediately perceptible, and the day following that on which the breaching battery opened, the place surrendered; fortunately, however, not until after reinforcements, to the amount of seven thousand men, had arrived in the Tagus from England, and the Prince of Essling commenced his retreat.

The animating service that succeeded the decided movement in retreat of the enemy's army, I was not destined to witness, nor shall attempt to describe events in which, unfortunately, we did not participate, and that have been so frequently detailed by persons more competent to relate with accuracy what there occurred. The illness of General Leith occasioned his return to England previous to any indication of the Prince of Essling's serious intention to abandon the Portuguese territory. The *Gorgon*, of fifty guns, conveyed Sir Stapleton Cotton, Generals Leith and Colman, Lord Tweeddale, Lord James Hay, Captain Dudley, and the author of this narrative, from the shores of the Peninsula.

CHAPTER 4

Death of General Crauford

The successful and admirably conducted attack made by Lord Wellington upon Ciudad Rodrigo having terminated on the night of the 19th of January, 1812, the 5th division (again under General Leith), which had not been engaged in the active prosecution of the siege, was ordered to march into the town, and undertake the work of repairing its defences.

The reduction of the place had been effected under disadvantages of an extremely stormy and boisterous season; but, from the judicious nature of arrangements made for attack, the promptitude and foresight of the British general, the exertions of the engineers, and the bravery of the troops, possession of it was obtained without a single obstruction to the regular progress of the approaches, without a very severe loss of life, and in so brief a space of time, that all attempts at relief meditated by the French generals were rendered abortive.

It was in the act of debouching from the suburb of San Francisco to mount the breach at the head of the light division, that General Robert Crauford was mortally wounded. In him the army sustained a severe loss: stern and rigid in his notions of military duty, unrelaxing in the exaction of strictly observed discipline, those qualities were directed by a perfect knowledge of his profession, not in the minor details only, but in the more extensive and more difficult acquirements of scientific information or sound practical judgment. His personal gallantry on every occasion inspired confidence. If an error existed in his character as a soldier, it proceeded from a too ardent desire to be in constant contact with the enemy.

No sooner had Ciudad Rodrigo fallen, than Lord Wellington determined to reduce Badajos. Unremitted exertions were consequently made to complete the repairs of the former: the trenches were filled in, breaches closed up, works constructed to prevent the approach of an enemy by the upper Teson, and everything arranged to check the progress of Marshal Marmont, who had assembled a powerful army at Salamanca.

The works of Almeida being also in some degree restored, that fortress was provisioned and garrisoned. Thus the two frontier places again presented obstructions to an army invading Portugal by the province of Beira, and the battering train of the French Army had been captured in Ciudad Rodrigo.

On the 6th of March, the army moved in the direction of the Tagus; the 5th division, with some light cavalry, alone remaining on the banks of the Agueda. Precautions were taken to deceive the enemy as to the march of the allies; but the preparations for such an undertaking as that in contemplation could not be carried on without some degree of publicity. The consequence was, that the governor, General Philipon, communicated to Marshal Soult the prospect of an immediate siege. Lord Wellington moved rapidly to the scene of a still more important triumph than that recently achieved. He arrived at Elvas on the 11th, and on the 16th Badajos was invested by the 3rd division, under General Picton, the 4th, commanded by the Honourable General Colville, and the light division, under the temporary command of Colonel Barnard. Two corps of observation were placed in advance. The one, composed of the 1st, 6th, and 7th divisions, with two brigades of cavalry, was commanded by Sir Thomas Graham; it advanced to Zafra and Llerena. The other, under General Hill, formed of the 2nd division, the Portuguese division of General Hamilton, and one brigade of cavalry, was on the Guadiana, between Merida and Almendralejo.

The nearest of the enemy's troops at this time without the walls of Badajos, was the corps of General Drouet, belonging to the army of the south, which, at the period of Sir Thomas Graham's advance, occupied Villa Franca de los Barros, and Los Santos, but immediately after retired to Hornachos.

The weather, from the commencement of this important siege, was extremely unfavourable; rain fell in torrents, not only occasioning difficulty and delay in the formation of the trenches and erection of the batteries, but adding to the hardships endured by the troops, necessarily, on such a service, exposed without shelter to the inclemency of the season.

The 5th division having arrived from the vicinity of Ciudad Rodrigo, completed the investment on the right bank of the Guadiana on the 22nd of March. During the evening of that day, the river became so flooded as to carry away the pontoon bridge, and the current being at the same time sufficiently violent to obstruct the passage of the boats forming the flying bridge, this was likely to become a serious, if not insurmountable inconvenience, the supplies of ammunition and provisions being exclusively obtained by. these communications. Fortunately, the fall of the river again permitted the repair of the bridge, and the siege proceeded without further interruption.

On the 24th, the 5th division invested Fort San Christoval. On the 25th, the batteries, armed with twenty-eight pieces of ordnance, opened against Fort Picurina, the Lunette of San Roque, and to enfilade the bastions of La Trinidad and San Pedro. After it became dark, General Kempt, commanding in the trenches, carried Fort Picurina by storm. Three detachments from the troops of the 3rd division assailed the work; the garrison made a vigorous defence, but the column led by Captain Holloway of the engineers, and commanded by Captain Powis of the 83rd regiment, succeeded in forcing an entrance by escalade. The other detachments subsequently gained the rampart, and the enemy's troops were either bayoneted or made prisoners. Captain Powis was mortally wounded on the parapet of the work.

Marshal Soult tardily moved to react the same part he had performed during the progress of the siege in 1811, which terminated so unprofitably for all parties in the bloodiest of fields, that of Albuhera. On the present occasion, he advanced from Seville to Llerena, concentrating his troops, and marched with the evident purpose of endeavouring to raise the siege. In conformity to the preconcerted arrangements of the commander of the forces, Sir Thomas Graham retired before this superior force. Sir Rowland Hill's corps also fell back upon Talavera la Real, after having exploded the centre arches of the bridge over the Guadiana at Merida.

The labours of the troops, notwithstanding the heavy rains which fell during nearly the whole progress of the siege, were unremitting. Obstacles of every description yielded to the zeal and determination exhibited in all departments of the service. The consequence was, that, in an unusually short space of time, the breaches in the main body of the place were considered practicable. That the assault would have been so early given under other circumstances is very improbable. With so powerful an army, and such efficient means, delay must have afforded opportunity for rendering the success of the storm less problematical; but, in Lord Wellington's situation, it became not only the boldest, but the wisest policy to make a great effort before an equally numerous, and, within the reach of possibility, an overwhelming force, could be brought against him. He calculated the chances, went resolutely and directly to the point, and carried Badajos.

On the 5th of April, the 5th division bivouacked in rear of the Sierra del Viento, in readiness to co-operate in the assault. On the following evening, four divisions of the allied army were destined to mount the walls of Badajos, and triumphantly to accomplish a service, only to have been achieved by the best soldiers and the bravest men.

Ten at night was the hour ultimately fixed for a general attack of the place, that being considered the earliest period at which the respective arrangements, of necessity not commenced until after dark, could be completed. This delay, although unavoidable, was attended with increase of difficulty to the assailants, in entering by the breaches; for the moment the batteries ceased firing, which they did at half-past seven, the enemy, during the two and a half hours intervening, worked assiduously, covering the front of the breaches with harrows and crows' feet, and crowning their summits with *chevaux-de-frise* of sword blades.

Every means that French ingenuity could devise had been resorted to, in accumulated profusion, to render entrance by the ruined bastions impossible: retrenchments had been formed as substitutes for the battered walls—combustibles of every description placed along the parapets, to be hurled down with incessant and destructive precision—showers of shells—fire barrels, and hand grenades, added to the effects of an unceasing musketry, gave to the ditch of the bastions of La Trinidad and Santa Maria the appearance of one uninterrupted fearful torrent of fire, unequalled in the annals of modern warfare. That existence could be preserved, or that any man should have issued untouched from the effects of one or other of the missiles thus directed for the extinction of life, seemed impossible.

Beat back after repeated efforts to force an entrance, but unshrinking and determined, the brave officers and soldiers of the 4th and light divisions continued for a length of time under these annihilating circumstances, occasionally in small numbers mounting the breach, until they grappled with the sword blades, in the act of endeavouring to remove which, the bravest men were either bayoneted, killed by the musketry fire, or rolled back into the ditch upon their less adventurous, but gallant comrades.

Quis cladem illius noctis, quis funera fando
Explicet?

During this most discouraging aspect of affairs at the breaches, General Picton, with the 3rd division, had also met with serious difficulty in obtaining possession of the castle. For upwards of an hour, gallantry, perseverance, activity, and determination, had been in vain exerted to force an entrance by escalade. Ladders were placed, and ascended, but death met the successive officers or soldiers that reached the parapet. At length, by the personal exertions of the leading officers of the 3rd division, and the constant succession of fresh assailants that undauntedly ascended, an entrance was forced from the summit of one ladder, and a lodgement being at last effected, the troops rushed forward in support; resistance became less determined, and the 3rd division remained in possession of the castle.

To form and march down on the rear of the force defending the breaches, was immediately determined upon; but it was discovered that the enemy had built up or barricaded the gates in so substantial a manner, as to prevent their being forced without considerable delay, and the assistance of other implements for removing the obstructions than those in the immediate possession of the 3rd division. General Picton consequently resolved to establish the troops under his orders in the captured portion of the fortress, and await for daybreak.

An officer, conducting the party with scaling-ladders from the engineers' park to the bivouac of the 5th division s lost his way. General Leith, in consequence, had the mortification of being delayed until past eleven o'clock, before he could move to carry the escalade of the bastion of San Vicente into execution. During the interval, he attracted the enemy's attention by a false attack on the Pardaleras outwork. The 8th Portuguese Caçadores, employed on this service, kept up a galling and incessant fire from the very glacis of the work itself. At length, the ladders having been delivered to the division, the column moved towards the north-west angle of the place. General Leith, having received instructions to escalade the bastion of San Vicente with one brigade, and to support the attack with the other regiments of his division, ordered General Walker, with the 4th, 30th, and 44th, to mount the wall; the difficulty of which service may be estimated when it is explained, that the face of the bastion had an *escarpe* thirty-one feet six inches in height, flanked by artillery,—that the palisades of the covered way were entire,—the counterscarp wall nearly twelve feet deep, and in the ditch, a *cunette*, five feet six inches in depth, by six feet six inches in breadth, had been excavated.

The troops were discovered by the garrison when on the glacis, and a heavy fire opened upon them before they had forced the barrier gate; but nothing could check the progress of General Walker and the battalions under his orders, until they reached the lofty wall, at the summit of which the enemy, aware of their intention, and fully prepared, were extended deliberately and obstinately to resist men ascending singly, and on ladders upwards of thirty feet high. This does not appear the description of situation where defence could be difficult, or entrance practicable to ordinary men. At first, few of the ladders could be placed; some of them, after being reared, were thrown from the walls back into the ditch. Others, constructed of green wood, opened and separated, or were not of sufficient length, consequently the troops forced in by means of three or four only of the number originally appropriated to the service; but force in they did, and General Walker formed his brigade on the ramparts. He had been instructed to move forward, and by making a circuit of the interior of the works, to come in rear of the enemy's troops defending the breaches.

There are no means of destruction more alarming in the contemplation of mankind than mines, nor any warlike engine or preparation calculated to have the same appalling ideal effect on the minds of the soldiery. There is also in the darkness of night, and the treading hostile ground, supposed to have been prepared for every species of obstruction, something so uncertain, that it is neither to be wondered at, nor considered inconsistent with their general bearing, that, under such circumstances, the bravest troops should be seized with irresolution from the most trivial causes. The flame of a portfire struck a momentary terror into the minds of men, that artillery, musketry, walls, and the bayonets of French infantry, had failed to daunt.

Part of General Walker's brigade, mistaking this appearance for the forerunner to the explosion of a mine, broke, and were bayoneted back to the spot where they had previously surmounted difficulties which there could have been no discredit in failing to overcome. Fortunately, General Leith had advanced part of the right brigade of his division in support of that already in the town. The second battalion of the 38th regiment, under Colonel Nugent, had ascended, and were formed on the ramparts. When the circumstance above detailed occurred, that corps, being prepared, received the pursuing enemy with a volley and bayonet charge that speedily terminated all contest.

In the course of this short reverse, General Walker was dangerously wounded, and Lieutenant-Colonel Grey, of the 30th regiment, a very gallant officer, died in consequence of profuse bleeding, before assistance could be procured.

General Walker's brigade having again formed, the other regiments of the division ascended the ladders, and the whole marched on the rear of the troops defending the breaches. General Leith narrowly escaped being precipitated into the ditch by the fall of a soldier killed on the upper part of the ladder he was mounting. Having succeeded in penetrating, and dispersing his opponents, he sent an officer to report to Lord Wellington that the 5th division was in the town. His bugles sounded the advance in all directions, distracting the enemy's attention, and inducing him to believe he was to be assailed from all quarters.

Whether it proceeded from a knowledge that the castle was in possession of the allies, or an impression that further resistance was vain, the efforts of the garrison relaxed, the 5th division drove everything before it; and, having opened the communication with the bastions of La Trinidad and Santa Maria, the 4th and Light divisions, which had previously been withdrawn, again advanced, and marched into the town by the breaches. After considering the various events of this most important night, and comparing the periods at which it is authenticated that the different services were performed, it appears consistent with truth to arrive at the following conclusions:—

In the first place, had Lord Wellington alone relied upon the ordinary mode of assault, that of storming the breaches, the town would not have been taken. Had General Leith received the ladders, and escaladed soon after 10 o'clock, as was intended, he would have been equally successful, and have saved the divisions contending for entrance at the breaches, upwards of an hour of continued and tremendous loss. Had he not escaladed at all, Badajos must have fallen in consequence of the castle being carried by the 3rd division, but not until the following day, when the enemy might have given further trouble. Had the attack by General Picton failed, still the success of the 5th division ensured the fall of the place. It was, consequently, the escalade of the bastion of San Vicente that occasioned the immediate reduction of the fortress.

Of the British troops employed in the assault, the Light division had fifty-eight officers, and eight hundred and sixty-eight men; the 3rd division, fifty officers, and four hundred and thirty-four men; the

4th, ninety-one officers, and eight hundred and forty-four men; and the 5th division, thirty-six officers, and five hundred and nine men, killed or wounded. Of the light division, Colonel M'Leod, commanding the 43rd regiment, a young officer of great promise, was killed. Colonel Ridge, of the 5th regiment, was supposed to have fixed and ascended the first ladder placed against the castle wall, where he was unfortunately killed. Lieutenant Lascelles, of the engineers, fell in the ditch of the bastion of San Vicente, directing the 5th division to the point of attack.

It was at Villafranca, on the 8th of April, that the Marshal Duke of Dalmatia received information of Badajos being in possession of the allies. The object of his march being thus frustrated, he put his army in retreat on the following day, and returned to Seville.

Lord Wellington, having directed the necessary repairs to the works of Badajos, and ordered Sir Richard Fletcher to see them completed, marched his army to the north, with the exception of Sir Rowland Hill's corps, left to manoeuvre on the Guadiana, and to observe the motions of Comte d'Erlon, who continued in Estremadura with his division of the army of the South.

On arriving at Fuente Guinaldo, where, on the 25th of April, the allied headquarters were established, Lord Wellington sent Colonel Sturgeon, of the staff corps, to Badajos and Elvas, for the purpose of superintending the construction of a very ingenious repair to the fracture occasioned by the explosion of an arch of the bridge at Alcantara. The arch destroyed was of so extensive a span, and the parapet of the bridge so great a height from the bed of the river, that no repair by using timber was practicable; the gap to be passed over being ninety feet wide, and the height of the bridge, one hundred and eighty from the bed of the river. Colonel Sturgeon selected the pontoon house, in the arsenal at Elvas, as the place for forming the net of ropes destined to afford a secure passage for troops, artillery, and carriages of every description, across the chasm.

The work was commenced by placing two beams on supporters four feet high and ninety feet asunder. These were secured to the side and end walls of the building by braces and tackles, to prevent their approximating by the straining of the ropes. Eighteen cables were then stretched round them, extending from end to end; eight pieces of timber, six inches square, at equal distances, were placed upon the ropes, with notches, one foot asunder, cut on their surface to secure them; these notches were seared with hot irons to prevent the ropes from chafing. The cables were then lashed to the beams; they were netted together by rope-yarn, and chains of sleepers were bolted and laid on the network, and secured to the two beams originally placed at the extremities of the work. Planks were cut and prepared for being laid across, bored at the ends so as to receive a line destined to secure them to the sleepers and to each other.

This effective and extremely portable bridge was, on being completed, packed up for removal. The great net beams and transverse bearers were rolled up like a web of canvass, and placed on one of the pontoon carriages, which conveyed them to Alcantara. The next point was to prepare the edge of the fractured part of the bridge, and to cut channels in the masonry for the reception of the purchases.

When arrived on the spot, four strong ropes were stretched from side to side, as conductors, for passing the cable-bridge across, the beam on the south side having been previously sunk into the masonry; the whole was then stretched by windlasses erected on the opposite pier, by which means it was so tightly drawn as to prevent any great sinking, or the vibration which might render it insecure and dangerous, even when heavy weights were passed over.

This bridge, simple and ingenious in its construction, for the first time in Europe established the fact, that by cables drawn to their utmost tension, without any support whatever, the whole equipments of an army could be transported, without difficulty or danger, over a great river and very extensive chasm, while, on the approach of an enemy, the apparatus could be withdrawn, and transported to safety, without the slightest inconvenience. I cannot close the description of what has ever appeared to me a very eminent application of scientific knowledge, without noticing the person to whose varied intelligence and superior qualities more competent authorities have borne testimony. Colonel Sturgeon possessed extensive and scientific information, sound judgment, unwearied assiduity, and undaunted courage.

At the moment when Lord Wellington thus re-established his own communication across the Tagus at Alcantara, he determined to destroy that of the enemy at Almaraz, and thereby defeat the direct combination that might otherwise have rendered formidable the armies commanded by Marshals Soult and Marmont. Sir Rowland Hill received orders to execute this service, and having obtained heavy cannon and ammunition from Elvas, with part of his corps, breaking up from Almendralejo, he marched, by Truxillo, to the banks of the Tagus.

Almaraz, centrically situated, and being also on the great route from Madrid to Badajos, was the most important point at which the French armies, acting to the north and south of the Tagus, could have established a safe and constant passage across that river: to deprive them of this, secured the impossibility of Marshal the Duke of Ragusa being reinforced from the army in Andalusia or Spanish Estremadura, without the enemy's troops being subjected to a great *détour*, and a consumption of time calculated to render such co-operation of comparatively trifling avail.

To render their temporary bridge, composed of pontoons, secure from the inroads either of guerillas or Spanish regular troops, the French constructed a *tête-de-pont*; and two formidable redoubts, armed with eighteen pieces of cannon, were completed on the immediate banks of the river. On the right bank, at a short distance from the *tête-de-pont*, was Fort Napoleon, calculated for a garrison of four hundred and fifty men; Fort Ragusa, on the opposite side of the river, near the road leading to Navalraoral, was capable of containing four hundred.

Sir Rowland Hill, with great promptitude and judgment, reduced these works, without sustaining a very severe loss. Having ascertained that the pass of Miravete, the only one by which artillery could be transported, was not to be forced without considerable difficulty and delay, he resolved to leave his guns on the mountain, and adopting a path only practicable for infantry, to carry the *tête-de-pont* and Fort Napoleon by escalade. This was immediately accomplished by General Howard's brigade. The 50th, under Colonel Stewart, one of the most distinguished regimental officers of the army, accompanied by a wing of the 71st regiment, placed ladders and carried the fort; they then rushed with the fugitive garrison, *pêle-mêle*, into the *tête-de-pont*, not giving the enemy a moment to rally, or organise any systematic defence.

The French infantry crowded towards the bridge, hoping to receive shelter and protection from their companions in Fort Ragusa. Those who first succeeded in gaining the right bank, cut away the three boats nearest to that end of the bridge, by which means the survivors of the garrisons of Fort Napoleon and the *tête-de-pont* were prevented escaping: many had been drowned in the bustle and confusion, but two hundred and fifty officers and men were secured. The commandant of Fort Ragusa, panic-struck, abandoned the work, without an attempt at resistance, and marched his garrison in the direction of Navalmoral, for which dastardly conduct he was shot at Talavera de la Reyna.

Sir Rowland, having thus brilliantly carried into effect the instructions of Lord Wellington, destroyed the works, burnt the pontoons with their carriages, and then returned to Merida.

I have not, in the course of this narrative, hitherto noticed with sufficient attention, a very influential and extraordinarily constituted force, namely, the guerillas—partisans equally dreaded by the enemy, and hated by their own countrymen; a force combining many valuable qualities with great laxity of principle, frequently exhibiting undaunted courage and adventurous temerity, on other occasions shrinking from conflict, and only formidable to the unfortunate inhabitants subjected to their frequently unreasonable exactions.

The foundation of the Spanish guerilla force is to be ascribed to the nearly universal spirit of hostility to the French aggression. That feeling, strongly implanted as it was in the minds of a turbulent, naturally warlike, noble, though misgoverned, people, induced a very general desire to participate in the struggle carrying on throughout the whole extent of the monarchy. This unsettled and hostile inclination became strengthened by the circumstances under which the civilians suffered, during the devastating system of subjection to the constant visits of different armies or bodies of troops, all burdensome, and, unfortunately, at times presenting not a very distinct difference of conduct in the acknowledged enemy, the soldier of the country, or his more disciplined, but not more easily accommodated, friend and ally. It requires no additional testimony to establish the fact, that not only the armies, but the population of Spain, were in active hostility to the French.

The city, the agricultural village, the ruined convent, alike sent forth persons to swell the guerilla force. At the commencement of the war in 1808 no such bands existed; nor was it until the provincial jurisdictions had shaken the basis of regular government, and subsequent to the dispersion of the Spanish armies, that these partisans made their appearance. The dispersed and lawless Spanish soldiery found their safety dependent on forming parties sufficiently numerous to resist the authority of the *corregidors* and *alcaldes*, and to enforce demands made in parts of the country where no power, either civil or military, existed sufficiently formidable to curb their exactions, or restrain the self-created importance they did not hesitate to assume.

This system, successfully adopted in a country whose government had become a chaos, was speedily enlarged upon. The marauders chose a chief and these men, no longer contemplating a return to their regiments, became the nucleus of many a guerilla party; their military knowledge and habits, their uniform and equipment, serving as a defective model to others hitherto uninitiated. These parties soon became numerous, but a spirit of enterprise and successful command only distinguished a few of the leaders; consequently, the generality of the bands gained little in numerical strength, or were destined to arrive at great notoriety; but the most insignificant were objects of terror to the French troops, inasmuch as their vicinity rendered the slightest removal from quarters a matter of captivity or death.

Of the most distinguished guerilla leaders may be cited, the Mina's, the *empecinado*, Don Julian Sanchez, the Medico, Porlier, the *cura*, and Chaleco; these all commanded numerous and formidable bands, and were of essential service to the allied cause.

Nothing could be more motley than the usual array of the guerilla bands. Provided a certain degree of individual military appearance prevailed, no effort at uniformity of dress or appointment was considered essentially necessary. The guerilla generally became equipped with spoils from the soldiery of other countries, or a mixture of the most gaudy and tawdry dresses of his own. The flaring scarlet and light-blue jacket of an Estremaduran hussar, the *schakos* of a French *chasseur à cheval*, pistols and saddle of English manufacture, the long straight sword of the enemy's dragoon, the brown Spanish sash, and leathern cartouche belt, with an Arragonese or Catalan *escopeta*, were the not unfrequent equipments of the same brigand, as the French invariably designated them.

The *empecinado*, acting in the districts more immediately in the neighbourhood of Madrid, was more than any of the other partisan leaders in the public view. His band, conducted with great gallantry and enterprise, became the terror of the court of Joseph Bonaparte. Reports were often circulated of Don Juan Martin, and his adventurous followers, being close to the walls of the capital, when in reality he was either scouring the Province of Guadalaxara, or levying contributions at Alcala de Henares. On one occasion he penetrated to the precincts of the Casa del Campo; at another, interrupted the rural festivities of the Pardo; and when more important service became necessary, he was found at the head of a formidable body of cavalry and infantry, ready to measure swords with the regular troops of the enemy

Perfectly acquainted with the country, surrounded by friends from whom he obtained the most accurate information of the movements against him, personally brave, possessing the confidence of his party, zealous in the cause, and highly exasperated against the French, such a man could not fail to become powerful as an enemy, and by his successes, which were frequent and signal, encourage others to embark in similar modes of life.

Of the Asturian guerilla leaders, the Marques de Porlier was the most celebrated. At an early period of the partisan warfare, he exasperated the enemy by the frequency of his attacks upon the convoys and detachments on their route from Bayonne to Madrid; invariably retiring into the mountains when numerously attacked, he baffled the utmost efforts of the French generals to rid themselves of the serious inconvenience and loss sustained from the effects of his active and indefatigable exertions. Upon one occasion, two divisions of infantry, with some hussars and Polish lancers, were detached (but without success) for the purpose of annihilating his numerous and formidable band.

Having obtained timely information of the movements against him, Porlier manoeuvred to draw his enemy into the fastnesses of the Sierra de los Cameros, constantly retiring when outnumbered, occasioning considerable loss to his assailants, who, believing their own safety would be compromised by further pursuit, left the *marquesito*, as he was called, to reassemble his followers, and return to the line of communication from whence he had been driven only to prove to his enemies the impossibility of destroying a force so constituted and commanded, when aided by the zealous assistance of the population of an almost inaccessible district.

In the Province of Leon, Don Julian Sanchez commanded an enterprising band, with which he frequently surprised the enemy's posts. Moving rapidly,—ever on the alert,—not subjecting himself to conflict on equal terms, possessed of the most accurate information,—at the head of a numerous and well-mounted party, he established a renown, conveying to the French soldiery an exaggerated impression of his power, that proved highly beneficial to the cause. Don Julian evinced great zeal. He seemed to bestow his undivided attention on the discomfiture of the enemy, and was probably with less justice accused of mercenary exaction than any other guerilla chief.

From the first establishment of the Spanish guerilla force to the termination of the war, it daily rose in importance, becoming, as the struggle advanced, an increased object of annoyance and terror to the enemy. It had also obtained a firmer hold of public opinion, and was extended over the whole surface of the monarchy.

The bands of various descriptions that started into notice, as a consequence of the successes obtained by the earlier adventurers, were innumerable; many of them, insignificant in number, possessing no leader either of character or talent, meriting in every respect the French appellation so liberally bestowed by that people on the whole class. Still they were useful, inasmuch as the very name of guerilla sounded harshly in the enemy's camp, cramped the operations of his troops, occasioned a distrust and restraint seriously affecting the *morale* of the soldier, and preventing, in some degree, the undisturbed system of contribution by which alone the armies of Napoleon existed in Spain.

That little discipline or subordination existed in the minor guerilla parties, may be deduced from the fate of Martinez—a man of stern, uncompromising temper, with a degree of resolute activity that had obtained for him considerable notoriety. Having entered into some trifling- altercation with one of his *partido*, the exasperated brigand drew a pistol from his belt, and discharged it through the head of his chief!

The perfectly uncontrolled authority of the guerilla leaders gave them additional capabilities of annoyance. A partisan chieftain manoeuvred his band more with reference to the enemy's communications, than with a view of engaging him on the plain. The country in which he carried on operations was usually selected, not by superior direction, but to suit his own convenience, and in accordance with what appeared best calculated to support his predatory system, and afford scope for those minor successes against isolated detachments of the French Army, by whose destruction he derived a claim to levy contributions on his defenceless countrymen.

It was no security to a French general that these petty chiefs were understood to be at a distance from his quarters; on the contrary, it tended to give a misplaced confidence, and to encourage the wandering propensities of the soldiery, who were frequently cut off by guerillas supposed to be in another province. Whenever a chief had traversed a district, and levied contributions on the several towns within its boundaries, he marched to a different field of action, leaving its inhabitants to the *merciful protection* of some other bandit as rapacious as himself.

In the dusk of evening, I have frequently seen the horsemen of a guerilla band entering a village to take up their quarters for the night; the stillness of all around, with the perfectly quiet and unostentatious arrival of the *partido*, being strongly contrasted with the scene immediately resulting from it. First, there probably occurred great difficulty and dissatisfaction as to quarters, proper respect not being paid to the defenders of their country, arising very naturally from the people not considering those visitors of superior importance to their own families, or being inclined to resign every comfort to satisfy their unreasonable expectations.

Next came the assembly of the magistracy, to whom demands, requests, or threats, were applied, as circumstances rendered necessary, with a view to extract supplies of money, clothing, provisions, or arms. Where were the unfortunate peasants to find means of resistance? or to whom were their well-founded complaints to be addressed?—nowhere with the least probable chance of commiseration. "It was unfortunate," they were told, "hard upon the inhabitants, and to be deplored; but the nature of the war, and circumstances of the country, rendered these inflictions unavoidable: they must consequently be patiently and uncomplainingly borne."

With all this oppressive latitude, neither very temperately nor judiciously exercised by the description of people in whose hands rested the power, the guerillas, as I have previously stated, were eminently useful in harassing and weakening the enemy, and had an undoubted influence on the favourable termination of the war.

The above picture, added to every circumstance of this noble and most interesting struggle, may convey some idea of the depth of feeling which animated the Spanish people—a feeling that years of misery, constant annoyance, loss of property, and endless exaction, left unshaken and unabated.

CHAPTER 5

Lord Wellington Assembles His Army

Early in June 1812, Lord Wellington, being in possession of the frontier fortresses, assembled his army, with the exception of the corps in Spanish Estremadura, commanded by Sir Rowland Hill, and prepared to resume offensive operations. Marshal Marmont had foreseen this movement, and appears to have adopted an exaggerated idea of the force with which his opponent was about to penetrate into the interior. Alarmed by the circumstance, the French general urged the necessity of being immediately reinforced. He stated that the "Army of Portugal," although still formidable, was not sufficiently numerous to ensure a successful resistance to the approaching attack, or to manoeuvre with certainty of favourable results against the allied army.

Notwithstanding the immense armament at this period directed against the Russian Empire by the Emperor Napoleon, his troops, extended over the territory of the Peninsula, were numerous and efficient. The army immediately opposed to Lord Wellington, retaining the designation of the "Army of Portugal," commanded by Marmont, Duke of Ragusa, consisted of eight divisions of infantry, a large body of cavalry, and one hundred pieces of cannon. This force occupied the country between the Tormes and the Duero, having one division, under General Bonnèt, detached in the Asturias.

The "Army of the North," under General Caffarelli, sixteen thousand strong, occupied Biscay, Las Montañas de Santander, and Alava. The "Army of the Centre," at Madrid, Guadalaxara, and Segovia, under the immediate orders of Joseph Bonaparte, was composed of French and Spanish infantry, the latter termed *Juramentados*, in consequence of their having taken the oath of allegiance to the usurper, and from amongst whom were selected the newly incorporated royal guard. These, with the dragoons under General Trelliard, and some detachments of light cavalry, amounted to thirteen thousand men. The "Army of Arragon," ten thousand strong, had its headquarters in the illustrious city of Zaragosa.

The Marshal Duke of Dalmatia held in subjection the kingdoms of Andalusia. His army, that "of the South," formed the blockading force before Cadiz, and had Comte d'Erlon's corps at Llerena, opposed to Sir Rowland Hill, the whole amounting to fifty-five thousand combatants. The corps of the Marshal Duke of Belluno formed part of this army.

The "Army of Cataluña," commanded by Suchet, Duke of Albufera, hitherto the most successful of the French marshals during the Peninsular War, garrisoned Barcelona, Tarragona, Figueras, Valencia, and Gerona, and possessed a disposable force of twenty-eight thousand men. Such was the actual state and position of the enemy's armies when Lord Wellington passed the Agueda, on the 13th of June, with thirty-five thousand infantry, two thousand five hundred cavalry, and fifty pieces of cannon.

The 5th division marched from its cantonments in Portugal on the 5th of June, halting at Trancosa until the 8th, on which day it arrived at Freixedas and Alverca. From Alverca the division advanced to Castel Mendo, situated on an eminence overhanging the Coa, a river accompanied by one general character of scenery along the whole extent of its course; bold rocky banks invariably confine this rapid, wild, and picturesque stream.

From Castel Mendo we marched, on the 10th, to Poza Velha, and encamped in a beautiful valley, shaded by lofty trees. On the 11th, having passed through Espeja and Carpio, we arrived on the left bank of the Agueda, and were joined by the 4th division, forming, with two brigades of cavalry, the centre column of the army; the right being composed of the 1st, 6th, and 7th divisions; the left by the 3rd division, the Portuguese brigades of Generals Pack and Bradford, and one brigade of cavalry.

Upon no occasion had the allied army taken the field in a more efficient state; every description of force composing it was serviceable and well-appointed. The cavalry had recovered their condition. Experience taught the practical minutiae of active warfare. The weather was beautiful. Confidence in their leader and themselves occupied the minds of the troops; while presages of success and anticipated variety of scene imparted gaiety and buoyancy of spirit. The light division, with the German hussars, horse artillery, and detachments of British

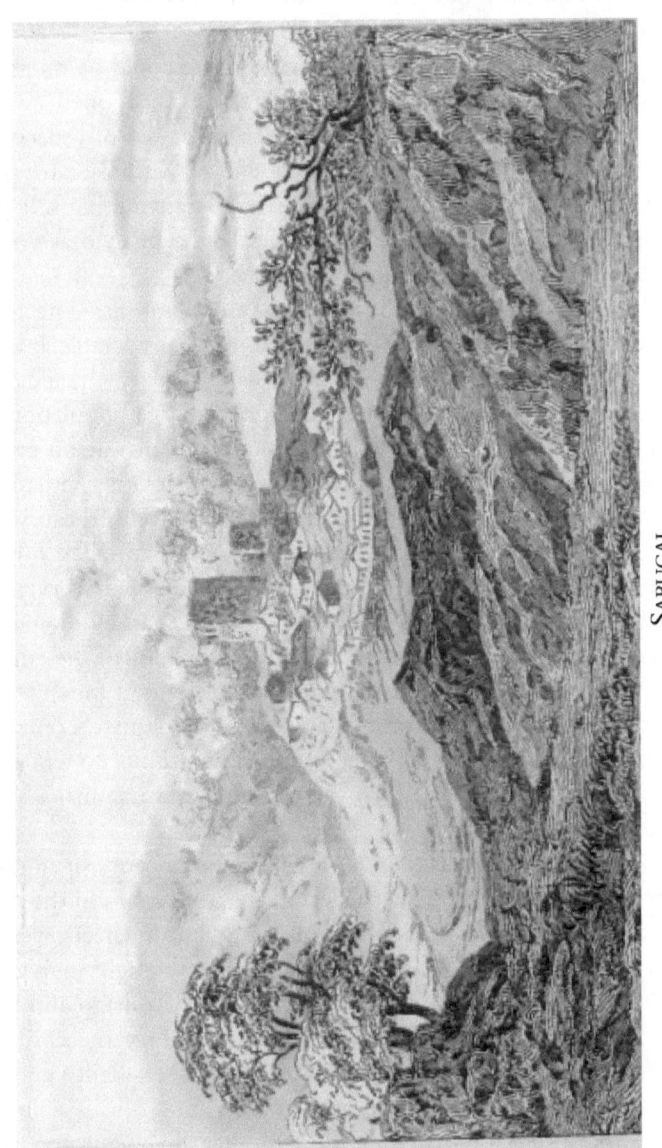

SABUGAL

light cavalry, were on the right bank of the Agueda, near to the convent of La Caridad.

The army halted on the 12th. During that day, General Leith was quartered in Ciudad Rodrigo, where we examined the renewed defences, and the different parts of the town appearing to have most severely suffered from the effects of war. Nothing could be more ruinous, dilapidated, or wretched. The destruction occasioned by two sieges in the course of eighteen months, with the results of a successful storm, had left the unfortunate town in a deserted and miserable state. Still the remaining inhabitants appeared friendly, attributing solely to the enemy losses and violence to which the allied army had, as a natural consequence of events, so much contributed.

Ciudad Rodrigo is a fortification of limited *enceinte*. The town within the walls is consequently confined and inconsiderable, but the suburbs are extensive, containing many inhabitants, which, added to those in the main body of the place, comprise a large population. Its environs presented a gloomy picture of the effects of war on everything near to an armed place subjected to such devastating visitations. The public walk deprived of the foliage that had given it beauty and shade, looked bare, sterile, and deserted; the trees had fallen for the purpose of giving scope to the uninterrupted sweep of artillery; roofless houses and battered walls presented themselves in all directions. The earth, thrown up to shelter the troops, still exhibited the rugged and bare aspect attendant on its being replaced without much attention to natural beauty or convenience. The great square contained dismounted cannon, shattered wheels, and ruined tumbrils; while the effects of bombardment had torn up and rendered unequal its formerly smooth and level area.

On the 13th, the centre column of the allied army encamped upon the Tenebron, near to Bocacara; the left at Spiritu Santa, and the right at the village of Tenebron. The day following, headquarters were at Cabrillas, the 4th and 5th divisions at Sanmuñoz; the light division at Aldegula. We found the country between Ciudad Rodrigo and Sanmuñoz, beautifully wooded, and admirably adapted for the encampment of troops, there being great abundance of water, while the trees afforded shelter from a scorching sun.

It was not until the morning of the 16th that the enemy appeared. Early on that day, I rode forward, and joined the patrols of the 1st Hussars upon the Carneiro road. About two leagues from Salamanca we encountered the advance of the French cavalry, and proceeded to drive them back. The enemy stood firm, and exchanged shots with the hussars, only retiring when the main body of that regiment debouched from the wood. He then retreated by the several roads leading to the town. The 14th, with part of the 11th Light Dragoons, and some horse-artillery, now joined the hussars. On ascending the heights, which rise gradually from the right bank of the Valmusa, several squadrons of the enemy's cavalry were perceived formed on the extensive plain reaching to the banks of the Tormes. Small detached parties occupied the several eminences immediately on the flanks of the main body, and it appeared their intention to dispute the ground until outnumbered or driven back.

The scene now became very animated and interesting. Parties were observed firing or charging in all directions. Repeated attacks were made by either force, as circumstances warranted, or as they became most numerous at the particular points. In one direction was to be seen a troop or squadron charging half their number of opponents, who, by a precipitate retreat, fell back on others, until their strength became superior, when, in turn, they for a time carried with them the successful tide of battle. The plain was covered with officers and scattered cavalry soldiers; carbines and pistols were discharged without intermission; frequent personal conflicts took place.

On one occasion, Major Brotherton of the 14th Light Dragoons, mounted upon a very small Spanish horse, crossed swords with a French officer of *chasseurs*, and continued cutting and parrying until the *mêlée* broke up the encounter. Colonel Sturgeon put to flight, and rode after, a private dragoon, who, being overtaken, surrendered without resistance.

During the progress of this protracted skirmish, although occasionally successful, the enemy was losing ground, and was finally driven within two miles of Salamanca; orders were there received to desist from further pursuit; I then returned to General Leith, who had encamped his division on the bank of the Valmusa.

At daybreak, on the 17th, the army was again in motion. Immediately after the troops had marched, proceeding in front to obtain information as to the progress of events, I passed our advance posts, and rode to the bridge of Salamanca, where were assembled some of the guerillas of Don Julian Sanchez, and a patrol of the 11th Dragoons. The enemy, on perceiving us, opened a fire of artillery from the forts, which they had constructed on the right bank of the Tormes. There being no object in continuing within range of these guns, we retired without loss, except in a horse of the 11th, killed by a cannon-shot.

Near to the bridge I met Major Brotherton, who had been in the town, where he ascertained the fact of the enemy having retired during the night, leaving garrisons in the forts; that the bridge was not destroyed; and that the houses in the immediate neighbourhood of the fortified convents having been set on fire, were then burning, which accounted for the smoke that occasionally enveloped the place.

Returning with this information, I met Lord Wellington, who sent me to General Leith, with directions that he should halt until further orders. I then followed the commander of the forces, and overtook him before he reached the. Tormes. The bridge being in possession of the enemy, the only means of getting access to the town was by proceeding up the river, and passing across at the nearest practicable spot. In the act of attempting what appeared to be a ford, a discharge of grape from Fort La Merced wounded the horse I rode. A ball entering his back close to the saddle, he immediately drooped, and appeared in the act of falling, but recovered himself, and was, notwithstanding the injury received, enabled to go on. The river became so deep, that, abandoning the attempt to pass, I returned to the left bank, and with the whole staff crossed a considerable distance higher up the stream.

Lord Wellington entered Salamanca about ten o'clock in the forenoon: the avenues to it were filled with people, clamorous in their expressions of joy; nothing could be more animating than the scene. The day was brilliant, presenting all the glowing luxuriance of a southern climate. Upwards of fifty staff-officers accompanied the British general; they were immediately followed by the 14th Dragoons and a brigade of artillery; the streets were crowded to excess; signals of enthusiasm and friendship waved from the balconies; the entrance to the *plaza* was similar to a triumph; every window and balcony was filled with persons welcoming the distinguished officer to whom they looked up for liberation and permanent relief.

Lord Wellington dismounted, and was immediately surrounded by the municipality, and the higher orders of the inhabitants, all eager to pay him respect and homage. At the same moment, the 6th division of British infantry entered the southwest angle of the square. It is impossible to describe the electric effect produced under these circumstances by the music; as the bands of the regiments burst in full tones on the ear of the people, a shout of enthusiastic feeling escaped from the crowd, all ranks seeming perfectly inebriated with exultation.

From this scene, so calculated to distract the attention of ordinary

Disatnt Salamanca

men, Lord Wellington retired to make immediate arrangements for reducing the forts. A plan of them having been produced and placed in his hands by the Spaniards, he left the adulating crowd, escaping from the almost overwhelming demonstrations of friendship and respect with which he was greeted; and before the town had recovered from its confusion and its joy, or the "*vivas*" had ceased to resound, his system of attack was decided upon, and the necessary orders for its execution issued to the troops.

Salamanca being considered by the French commanders-in-chief as a favourable situation for establishing the *dépôts* of their "Army of Portugal," preparations were made, in 1810, to strengthen some of the ruined convents, and render the otherwise, in some respects, open and defenceless town, a post, not only secure from the inroads of guerillas, but unassailable without formidable means of attack, or liable to be subjected by any force not having pretensions to the character of a regular army.

The numerous monasteries and colleges which, previously to this war of succession, adorned Salamanca, had been visited by the violence of the French Army to such a degree, that, when the allies arrived on the Tormes, thirteen of twenty-five convents were in ruins; and of an equal number of buildings belonging to the university, twenty-two had been destroyed.

From these extensive and massive buildings the enemy had selected three suited to his purpose, as much from their form and strength of masonry, as from the isolated situation they now occupied in the town; their vicinity to the bridge, which must be completely commanded by their fire, and of which two of the number had an uninterrupted view from one extremity to the other, making them at the same time very eligible.

The most considerable of these works was that of San Vicente. Situated directly between the great convent of San Francisco and the river, it rose from the old wall of the town, which, at that particular point, was lofty, and built on the summit of a precipice, the base of which is washed by the Tormes. From San Vicente towards the bridge the ground descends into a valley, on the opposite side of which it again becomes elevated; and at the distance of two hundred and fifty yards from the principal work, the ruined buildings of Gayetano and La Merced were converted into forts.

The 6th division, under General Clinton, was intrusted with the investment and reduction of these works, which, on being reconnoitred, were ascertained to be more formidable than had been supposed from previously received reports of their construction and extent. The proportion of heavy artillery now with the army was not on a scale for the reduction of any regular fortification: limited as it was, however, Lord Wellington determined to proceed, and on the night of the 17th, ground was broken before San Vicente.

From the lofty spire of the cathedral, the forts, with the operations carrying on against them, were distinctly visible, presenting a scene of great interest and variety. The convents had been loopholed, and prepared for a protected fire of musketry, which was kept up with unremitting activity: to counteract and suppress the effect of this galling tiraillade, one of the rifle battalions of the German Legion was stationed in the neighbouring buildings, and by a constant return of well-directed fire, kept that of the enemy very much under.

At daybreak of the 19th, a battery, armed with seven pieces of ordnance, opened at a distance of two hundred and fifty yards from the work; and at nine in the morning, the end wall of one part of the convent was battered down, the interior of the building becoming displayed. A spirited and incessant fire was returned by the garrison, occasioning many casualties in the ranks of the assailants. Although the convent wall had been reduced to ruins, its fall by no means facilitated the assault of the place: it became therefore necessary to vary the point of attack, and another battery was formed near to the college of Cuenca; its fire being directed to reduce the masonry of an angle of the building nearer to the Tormes than that already beat down.

The fire being directed against the lower part of the wall, its effect for some time was almost imperceptible: the convent appeared to stand unshaken from the cannonade; its loopholed wall poured forth an incessant tiraillade from every crevice; when, in a moment, on one discharge of the battery, the wall and roof of the building, with its numerous inhabitants, were precipitated to the earth with a tremendous crash; a cloud of dust and lime cleared away to exhibit a shapeless heap of ruin; while its brave garrison, stationed in that part of the building, were buried and invisible in the mass which alone appeared. The fall of this wall laid open the interior of the building much more extensively than the former had done.

The alacrity of the enemy was now exerted to the utmost: in order to counteract the effect of carcasses discharged with the object of setting on fire the other portions of the building, parties watched where they struck, and in the intervals of firing, were employed in cutting them out, and thereby preventing the destruction that must naturally have resulted, had they been left to burn amidst the wooded portions of the building. These efforts were effectual, and all attempt to set it on fire for some time appeared unattended with the slightest success.

On the 20th, intelligence was received of the approaching reappearance of the Duke of Ragusa, after having assembled a considerable force. This occasioned an immediate movement on the part of the allies: the army, with the exception of the troops carrying on the siege of the forts, was placed in position on the heights of San Christoval, with its right on the Tormes, and left extending near to Aldea Seca. The 5th division passed the night at the last-mentioned village. In the course of the evening, some skirmishing had taken place between the advancing enemy and the British cavalry, but no affair of importance occurred.

The following morning, General Leith's division marched from Aldea Seca, and formed part of the *alignement* on the fine position of San Christoval, covering Salamanca. The enemy appeared in force, bivouacking directly in front of the allies; some slight affairs were the consequence of the very proximate situation of the two armies, but nothing indicated an intention on either part of immediately proceeding to more serious conflict.

At daybreak of the 22nd, the enemy appeared in his position of the former day. To relieve or withdraw the garrisons of the forts, was the evident purpose of this advance on the part of Marshal Marmont. The ammunition for the heavy ordnance with the allied army had been nearly expended in two days' firing, without having sufficiently damaged the defences to render an assault advisable. The commander of the forces had, therefore, no other alternative left than to watch the motions of his opponent, offer him battle, and mask the works in Salamanca until additional means of reducing them were procured from the *dépôts*.

The position of the armies presented a singular contrast: the allies on high and commanding ground, from whence the slightest movement of the enemy was perceptible; the French on the plain directly below, just sufficiently distant to be out of the range of artillery, were not in sight of the town, or of those garrisons which it was their object to communicate with and succour.

Early in the morning, the French marshal reconnoitred the right of the allied position. This produced a slight affair. He was prevented from prosecuting his meditated observation, and retired, after sustaining the loss of a hundred men. Later in the forenoon, the French staff were perceived moving, with an escort, from their right, in the direction of Aldea Seca, evidently intending to ascertain the precise situation of the allied left. In this instance the Duke of Ragusa advanced so near to the position of his opponents, and removed so far from his own troops, that there appeared a probability, not only of interrupting his observations, but of intercepting his return. For this purpose, and to discourage these bold attempts at *reconnaissance*, Lord Wellington directed his *aide-de-camp*, Captain Burgh, to proceed to the quarters of the 12th Dragoons, and order two squadrons of that regiment to mount, and go forth on this service.

Accompanying Captain Burgh, we descended the sloping ground in our front, and entered a village situated towards the left of the position, where the 12th were stationed. Nothing could be more congenial to the feelings of Colonel Ponsonby than this *chasse*; the men and horses were lightened of every encumbrance, and being formed without any delay, he placed himself at their head, and at a quick pace sallied forth from the village. The scene now became animated and interesting; it was a species of great tournament, the lists of which were peopled by 50,000 men. The rapid advance of this body of light cavalry, particularly under the circumstances, excited the curiosity of the enemy; the huts in his encampment poured forth their inmates, who seemed intensely watching the result of this singular *rencontre*, about to take place within cannon-shot of either army.

The marshal and his staff, previously to observing the 12th, were so far advanced that he certainly incurred danger of being intercepted; but with him were some *voltigeurs*, who, on being approached, covered the plain on his left, and kept up a warm tiraillade on the British dragoons, checking their progress when at a short distance from the French staff, and affording time to secure a retreat, of which the Duke of Ragusa availed himself without the least delay. The 12th returned to their quarters, the French infantry to their huts, and everything again became as quiet as before; no further attempt at *reconnaissance* was, however, made by the Duke during the time he subsequently continued in front of the San Christoval position.

The 23rd, at daylight, the enemy's columns were perceived moving from the position of the preceding day, covered by their cavalry. The ground towards which Marshal Marmont was now marching, lay at the distance of two leagues to the right of that he had previously occupied. It was ascertained, later in the day, by Lord Wellington, that some of the French troops had passed the Tormes; in consequence of which movement, Sir Thomas Graham was ordered to cross the river at the Santa Marta ford with the 1st and 7th divisions of infantry, and to interpose his force between that of the enemy now on the left bank, and the town of Salamanca.

On the evening of the 24th, it was resolved to attempt the capture of the two minor forts by escalade. The troops of the 6th division received orders to that effect. Exactly at ten o'clock, Generals Hulse and Bowes proceeded on this service.

From the spire of the cathedral I witnessed the scene that ensued, certainly one of a very brilliant description: the enemy was on the alert; the moon shone bright, rendering the slightest movement discernible. The moment the British troops debouched, an uninterrupted and vigorous fire burst forth from the artillery of the forts, accompanied by incessant discharges of musketry: the valley presented one continued blaze of light. General Hulse attacked La Merced. General Bowes succeeded in rearing some ladders against Gayetano, but could not force an entrance: unfortunately he fell, and the column under his orders lost upwards of 120 in killed and wounded. Of the former, was Captain Sir George Colquhoun of the Queen's Regiment.

The attack by General Hulse proved equally unsuccessful, and hopes of gaining immediate possession were consequently abandoned.

After manoeuvring for some time on the left bank of the river, the French marshal, finding all his attempts at communication with the forts frustrated, recrossed the Tormes.

A supply of ammunition having been received by the allies on the morning of the 26th, renewed efforts were made to complete the reduction of the works. The batteries commenced firing at three in the afternoon, and before sunset, a volume of smoke, ascending from one of the towers of the Convent of San Vicente, proved the success that attended the use of heated shot: portions of the roof of the building also exhibited symptoms of ignition; but the exertions of the garrison for a time again succeeded in checking the conflagration.

During the night, the fire of heated shot was continued: the utmost efforts of the enemy could not effectually subdue the flames which burst forth at intervals: nor did a very heavy fall of rain tend to extinguish them, and at ten o'clock in the forenoon of the 27th, the entire range of building was in a blaze.

The *commandants* of San Vicente and Gayetano at length became alarmed. Flags of truce were displayed, and offers of surrender made,

SALAMANCA

but the moment was too critical to admit of much time for consideration being granted; Lord Wellington limited the period of his acceptance of conditional surrender to five minutes, at the expiry of which, no indication of the imperial flag being immediately lowered becoming visible, the batteries recommenced firing, and the troops advanced to the assault, carrying Fort Gayetano by its gorge, and San Vicente from the fascine battery at its south-eastern front. The garrisons making but slight resistance, the loss sustained by the allies in the ultimate operation was very insignificant.

Thirty-six pieces of ordnance, with eight hundred prisoners, were captured in these works, where were also found a large quantity of stores and ammunition. Their surrender gave great joy to the inhabitants of Salamanca: in the evening the town was illuminated, and rejoicings were heard in every direction; the population crowded the streets; music and dancing occupied a large portion of the lower orders, while the sounds of patriotic festivity were to be heard throughout the whole course of a beautiful and serene night.

Early on the 28th, the Duke of Ragusa, having ascertained the capture of the forts, retired from before the allied army, one of his columns marching on the Valladolid, and another by the Toro road. Thus was this once celebrated seat of learning relieved from the presence of any French troops; nor could the sincerity of the demonstrations of cordiality, so prodigally bestowed on the allies, be for an instant doubted. The natural hatred to the enemy had been increased by the wanton conduct which for years past had excited the strongest feelings of detestation: the ruined state of the public buildings of the town proved the unnecessary devastation that had been committed, and which, in every direction, served to recall circumstances never to be erased from the minds of its inhabitants, keeping alive the dormant, but strongly excited spirit of revenge resulting from such deep and bitterly felt injuries.

When it was ascertained that Marshal Marmont had retired, a *Te Deum* was performed in the cathedral, at which Lord Wellington, accompanied by a numerous body of the officers of his army, attended. The scene was grand and impressive, the spacious noble building crowded to excess, and the ceremony performed with all the pomp and splendour of Catholic worship. The pealing organ never poured its tones over a more brilliant, varied, or chivalrous audience. To describe the variety of groups would be endless; the eye, wandering through the expanse of building, could seldom rest twice on objects of similarity. All the pomp of a great Episcopal seat was displayed on the occasion. Contrasted with the sombre dresses of the numerous unofficiating clergy, the scarlet uniforms of the British were held in relief by the dark Spanish or Portuguese costume.

The Spanish peasant, in all the simplicity and cleanliness of his dress, appeared by the moustached and fierce-looking guerilla; while the numerous *mantillas* and waving fans of the Spanish ladies attracted attention to the dark voluptuous beauties of Castille. It was an enthusiastic and imposing scene; nor was its least impressive effect produced by the quiet, unassuming presence of the great man who, in the career of his glory, knew that by shewing respect to the religious institutions of other countries, he best secured for himself acquired by deference to the customs of a people having an equal right with ourselves to adopt the persuasion or the forms most congenial to their minds, and most consistent with their conscientious views.

Of the clergy present on this occasion, one of the most dignified in manner and appearance was Doctor Curtis, whose perfect knowledge of the language and customs of both kingdoms, enabled him to become essentially useful in all communications with the civil or ecclesiastical authorities of Salamanca.

In the evening, the town was again illuminated, and a ball given by the magistracy to Lord Wellington and his officers, at which the sounds of music had not ceased when the allied army marched in pursuit of the enemy.

At half-past three in the morning, the troops advanced. The centre, composed of the 1st, 5th, and 7th divisions, with General le Marchant's brigade of dragoons, encamped on the heights above Obrado, where the left and right columns also arrived and bivouacked. The whole army occupied a wood extending about three miles in length; the weather was beautiful—the troops in high spirits; everything bespoke cheerfulness. The fortunate commencement of the campaign had inspired confidence, and ardent hopes were entertained of future successes.

On the 30th, the centre column halted at Fuente la Peña, which became the headquarters. The enemy had retired from that village on the preceding day. At Alaejos, on the 1st of July, it was ascertained that we were treading rapidly on the footsteps of the French Marshal, he having left that town at two in the morning with the force collected in front of Salamanca; excepting one division which had marched direct upon Toro.

The 5th division bivouacked on the banks of a stream one league in front of Alaejos: the light cavalry patrolled through Nava del Rey; and the following day the whole army continued its advanced movement; the right column arriving at Dueñas de Medina, the centre at Torrecilla, the left in the valley of Medina, below Torrecilla. The Spanish corps of Don Carlos España occupied Nava del Rey; while the light division and cavalry, having driven the enemy from Rueda, were established in that village with their advanced posts near to Tordesillas.

The army halted on the 3rd, with the exception of the cavalry and light division sent in advance towards the bridge of Tordesillas, and the 3rd division, under General Picton, moved to the left for the purpose of watching the enemy's troops stationed near the fords of the Duero at Polios. The whole of the enemy's army had now passed the river. Tordesillas became the headquarters of the Duke of Ragusa, and his troops were concentrated along the line of the Duero, extending towards Castronuño, with a division still further to their right at Toro.

From the 3rd to the 8th of July, no material alteration took place in the position of the allied army. The enemy had a line of posts close upon the banks of the Duero, watching the fords. The 5th and 6th divisions moved about two miles down the valley of Medina, and encamped on the heights upon the right bank of the Zapardiel rivulet.

Lord Wellington had, at this period, under his immediate orders, ten regiments of cavalry—the Light, 1st, 3rd, 4th, 5th, 6th, and 7th divisions of Infantry; the unattached Portuguese brigades of Generals Pack and Bradford, and the Spanish cavalry and infantry under Don Carlos Españo and Don Julian Sanchez.

From the delay which had taken place, it appeared evident that the commander of the forces had no intention of forcing the passage of the Duero. All active operations were consequently for a time suspended; nor did there seem a probability of renewed hostilities until the French General should repass the river with a purpose of regaining possession of the ground he had lost, important to either army from being a very fertile and productive district.

There were three points in his line at which the enemy might repass the river, and attack the allied army—either by the bridge of Tordesillas, then in a perfect state, by the fords at Polios, or by the repaired bridge of Toro. From the alacrity with which the French worked at the latter, and its being the shortest line from the Duero to Salamanca, it was probable that the Duke of Ragusa would recross his army in that direction, and by so doing come on the left flank of the allies.

The river alone intervening between the armies, any movement, or alteration of position, on the part of the enemy, became immediately known. His slightest change of quarters was vigilantly watched; and, secure of no important offensive operation taking place without sufficient warning, the troops continued quietly stationed in the neighbourhood of the numerous and extensive villages with which this part of Spain is closely studded.

On the evening of the 9th, the 5th and 6th divisions marched from the camp near Foncastin, and bivouacked close to Nava del Rey: from thence General Clinton, with his division, and two squadrons of General le Marchant's brigade of cavalry, moved to Alaejos.

In consequence of reports that the enemy had marched troops towards his right, and the repairs of the bridge at Toro being nearly completed, it became important to extend the allied army to its left. On the 12th, the 7th division marched into Nava del Rey, and the 1st moved from Medina del Campo to Villaverde.

Medina del Campo, still a populous town, is greatly reduced from the consequence it once possessed. In the reign of the Emperor Charles V., it enjoyed great celebrity and commercial importance, being then the place of assembly for one of the largest fairs in Europe.

From the 12th to the 16th, no event of an interesting description varied the then rather monotonous character of the campaign. Not a musket-shot disturbed the tranquillity of the armies. On the forenoon of the latter, nothing appearing to indicate a movement of importance, and being instigated by curiosity to ascertain the operations of the enemy at Toro, I left the encampment of the 5th division, and rode to within about half a mile of the bridge then under repair. The French, accompanied by a number of Spanish peasants, were actively employed in laying planks across the chasms that had been formed by the explosion of its two centre arches. The work, apparently, was in a state of great forwardness: nor did it seem improbable that the reports of the enemy's intention to cross the Duero on the following day would be realised.

The quiet uninterrupted manner in which I was permitted to overlook this operation, induced me to commit to paper the position of the city, with the river and bridge. No French soldier appeared on the left bank; nor did I meet with the slightest obstruction during the course of a rather protracted *sojourn* in the enemy's immediate view. The repair, so elaborately bestowed on the bridge of Toro, was, as became subsequently proved, for the purpose of deceiving the Brit-

Toro

ish general in the line of march to be adopted by the enemy's troops; consequently there could be no jealousy created by the circumstance of an officer sketching the position, or noting down the progress towards completion, of a work to be destroyed the moment its purposes of deception had been carried to their full extent.

In returning to Nava del Rey, I passed the quarters of General Picton's division. The general was then absent from bad health. The personal look and manner of General Picton was stern and cold, as was his conversation on subjects where his individual opinion was at variance with the conduct of others, or opposed to the current of passing events; but, with this unusual appearance of austerity was combined a gentleness and occasional kindness of manner when in society, or without the excitement produced by reference to the more immediate incidents connected with the profession, in which he was undoubtedly enthusiastic. His cool determined bravery in action was strongly contrasted with the irritation sometimes exhibited under other circumstances of command.

It was twilight when I rejoined the 5th division. The day had been one of great activity in the French Army; nor had the tired horse I rode again entered the streets of Nava before two divisions of the enemy had crossed the bridge of Toro—these troops having marched from the neighbourhood of Tordesillas, under the orders of General Bonnèt, who had recently arrived from the Asturias to reinforce the Duke of Ragusa. His division, composed of veteran soldiers, numerous and in high order, had not previously been opposed to British troops. The inactivity, that for a month had characterised the war, now gave place to movements of the deepest interest. The re-passage of the Duero was not the manoeuvre of an army about to prosecute a campaign either by partial affairs, long and distant marches, or operations tending to procrastinate its decided results; the French marshal, evidently confident in his force, seemed determined to come into immediate contact with his opponent.

General Bonnèt, after crossing the river at Toro, and circulating reports that the entire French Army were to adopt the same route, again passed to the right bank of the Duero, broke down the repairs of the bridge, and, having marched all night, rejoined the main body in the act of advancing from Tordesillas.

The motive of the Duke of Ragusa for making this feint, was evidently to occasion an alteration in Lord Wellington's line of operations, that would essentially contribute to the success of a movement, having for its object forcing back the allies from the line of the Duero, and intercepting, if possible, their direct communication with Salamanca.

On the evening of the 17th, Lord Wellington put his army in movement: the 5th division arriving at Canizal, the Light and 4th divisions being at Castrajon, and the cavalry in front of that village. At daybreak, on the 18th, General Leith left Canizal, with his own and the 6th division, in consequence of orders to advance in the direction of Torrecilla de la Orden, situated about a league in rear of Castrajon. While the troops were executing this movement, a heavy cannonade was heard in our immediate front, proceeding, evidently, from an attack on the allied force, at or near to the last-mentioned village.

As was to be expected, the French marshal advanced with rapidity and determination; either the movement on Toro was perfectly useless, or, if otherwise, his only chance of deriving the slightest advantage from it, was pressing on the allies before the different corps of the army were collected on the line of march, which, he had reason to hope, would be in some measure abandoned. Having received orders to proceed in advance, and to ascertain the nature of the attack which had been made, I rode to the infantry encampment near Castrajon, and there found General Cole dismounted, surveying the warm affair in progress between our cavalry and that of the enemy, supported by infantry and artillery: the plain was filled with smoke, while the hostile parties appeared engaged in a very unequal conflict. The British cavalry were outnumbered, and losing ground; nor did there appear any intention on the part of the commander of the forces to send forward the infantry in support; the distance was crowded with the advancing troops of the enemy, and everything indicated the commencement of a very serious affair.

The artillery fire, which had been kept up for a considerable space of time, the galloping about of cavalry, the clouds of dust ascending from the plain, all conspired to make this affair appear of greater importance than from its results, either as to loss of life or immediate consequences, it in reality deserved, It was, notwithstanding, a very animated and interesting scene, evidently the forerunner of great events. When Lord Wellington arrived on the spot, much anxiety prevailed to learn what movement he would direct; the enemy was pressing rapidly forward on both flanks, thereby rendering an immediate change of position necessary. The whole French Army was in movement.

The ground upon which the Light and 4th division stood, was

neither sufficiently extensive, nor otherwise well calculated to afford a good defensive position for the allied army; the strong heights of Canizal were in its rear, and to these the British general determined to retire: the infantry marched in retreat, while the cavalry and horse artillery were ordered to attract the attention, and check the advance, of the enemy.

Wounded dragoons and captured soldiers were arriving from the front in rapid succession, the former exhibiting, in the cuts they had received, the comparatively harmless effect of sabre encounters, when contrasted with the more deadly working of musketry, or thrusts from the straight sword of the French dragoon.

The advance of the enemy on Alaejos turned the left flank of the position at Castrajon; and as at the same time he pressed vigorously on the rear of the column retreating from thence, the line of march towards Torrecilla de la Orden became rather obstructed. The troops, however, retired in the most perfect order; and although, in descending to the banks of the Guareña, the light division was obliged to abandon the great route, and march by lateral footpaths, it was executed with trifling loss, and without the slightest confusion.

The rear of the British divisions had but a few minutes retired from the heights, when they were crowned by the enemy's artillery, directed into the valley now crowded with troops.

The 5th division, unaware of the near approach of the enemy's cannon, had halted to obtain water from the river. This was rendered more desirable by an atmosphere of excessive heat occasioning parching thirst, superinduced by quantities of dust, with which the soldiers were absolutely covered. The first discharges from the enemy's cannon convinced General Leith, that retiring in column under this fire would be attended with considerable loss: he, therefore, directed the brigades to deploy as quickly as possible; which being accomplished, the shot plunged over the lines, occasioning but few casualties, and the division took up its ground on the heights of Canizal.

The junction of the different corps of the allied army had now been secured, and although the whole "Army of Portugal" was in front, the only danger to be apprehended was any unforeseen and rapid flank movement that the French marshal might attempt, for the purpose of interposing between Lord Wellington and Salamanca; nor did any time elapse before an endeavour to turn the position by its left, attracted attention to the part of it where General Cole and the 4th division were stationed. There the Duke of Ragusa passed some troops across the Guareña, at Carteillo, below the junction of the streams, appearing determined, if possible, to force an entrance by that direction into the valley of Canizal.

General Victor Alten's brigade of light cavalry had been engaged for some time with that of the enemy. To his support General Cole marched with General William Anson's brigade, and that of Portuguese troops under Colonel Stubbs. The cavalry encounters had been to a certain extent successful on the part of the allies: but, when General Cole proceeded to charge the enemy's infantry with the 27th and 40th regiments, the French stood with unusual firmness, as if determined to await the encounter at close quarters: the British regiments, however, pressed forward with alacrity, resolution, and discipline, overthrew the enemy, who fled, closely pursued by General Alten's brigade, and two hundred and forty prisoners were secured, about four hundred of the French being left dead or wounded on the plain. General Carrier, of the French cavalry, was taken prisoner on this occasion.

With this affair terminated the enemy's attempts on the left of the allies. His army appeared concentrated directly in front; nor did any hostile movement occur during the after part of the day. Lord Wellington, apparently determined, if attacked, to defend the position he now occupied, ordered some field works to be constructed for the purpose of strengthening it; and at night, the 5th division furnished a working party, which, under the superintendence of Colonel Sturgeon, commenced throwing up cover for its artillery. The night passed in perfect tranquillity; the whole country blazed with the fires of the bivouacs, while in the stillness, voices were heard from one encampment to the other. Daybreak displayed no movement or preparation for battle in the enemy's lines: a pause appeared to have taken place, and the bustle and turbulence that had distinguished the early part of the preceding day seemed to have been succeeded by an unexpected cessation of hostilities.

As day advanced, we anxiously inspected all parts of the French encampment, to observe if any signs of renewed activity were visible, but without being enabled to distinguish the most trivial indication that a change of position was meditated, either to the front or otherwise. The often-resorted-to glasses were closed, with the disappointing declaration that all appeared quiet and immovable. At length, towards evening, it became evident that this stillness was to be interrupted. Marshal Marmont, having in vain assailed the left, now manoeuvred against the other flank of the allies, and marched his whole army by its left towards the plain of Vallesa. In consequence of this movement, the light and 5th divisions got under arms, and marched in a parallel direction with that adopted by the French Army. The light division, under General Charles Alten, being on our immediate right, was the first to move off the ground, and we followed the same route across the country.

With the exception of a short period during the dead of night, the troops continued marching; and at daybreak the whole army were assembled in columns on the plain of Vallesa. The enemy was close opposite, and apparently prepared to try the result of a general action; circumstances, however, soon proved this not to be the intention of the French marshal, who persevered in his flank movement, proceeding along the range of heights on the left bank of the Guareña.

To prevent his communications from being obstructed, an immediate and rapid advance by his right became a matter of necessity on the part of Lord Wellington. When the two armies were thus put in motion, they were within cannon-shot of each other; the French occupying higher ground than the allies: but the space between them was lower than either of the routes, and nothing intervened to obstruct a view of the columns of enemies, that thus continued to pursue their course without the least obstacle to prevent their coming into instantaneous contact; for the slightest divergement from either line of march towards each other, would have brought them within musketry distance.

I have always considered this day's march as a very extraordinary scene, only to have occurred from the generals opposed commanding highly disciplined armies; at the same time each pursuing an object from which he was not for an instant to be abstracted by minor circumstances: the French marshal pressing forward to arrive first on the Tormes; Lord Wellington following his motions, and steadily adhering to the defensive, until substantial reasons appeared to demand a deviation from that course, and the adoption of a more decided conduct. During the day of the 20th, which exceeded in heat those that had preceded it, the British infantry, encumbered with the enormous weight they then carried, had to perform a very long and fatiguing march.

There were occasional slight skirmishes, brought on by the routes approaching each other, or the anxiety of French and allied stragglers to obtain undisputed right of pillage in the unfortunate villages that lay in the intermediate space between the armies: otherwise no spectator would have imagined the two immense moving columns that filled the whole country, and seemed interminable, being lost to the eye in dust and distance, comprised two armies actuated with earnest desires for the destruction of each other, but who, although possessed of numerous artillery and cavalry, were persevering on their way, as if by mutual consent refraining from serious hostility, until arrived at the arena destined for the great trial, to which either was now advancing with confidence and without interruption.

About midday, the rear of the allied army presented a long line of straggling conductors of commissariat stores and private baggage: the space between the armies became at the same time narrowed, rendering it probable an effort would in consequence be made to intercept this unguarded line of march; nor did there appear the least difficulty in the enemy obstructing the route, and sweeping off a large portion of these dilatory followers of the troops. General Bonnèt suggested this measure to the Duke of Ragusa, requesting permission to move down with his division, and attack the rear of the allies: this proposition did not meet the views of the general-in-chief, and was strenuously resisted.

At the same moment some French *voltigeurs* entered a village about equidistant from the lines of march: it was not considered advisable to permit their quiet possession of this point. The 5th division was ordered to halt, and the 8th Portuguese Cazadóres being sent into the town, they soon dislodged the enemy; and a great proportion of the persons for whose safety some apprehensions had been entertained, being now advanced in the line of the column, the infantry again moved forward, the valley soon after widened, the route of the enemy inclining to the left, while that of the allies led direct to the San Christoval position, in front of Salamanca. Before evening the armies had lost sight of each other, and to the satisfaction of the troops, we halted near the village of Pitiegua, with every prospect of being permitted to remain undisturbed during the night.

The men had scarcely time to compose themselves in their bivouacs, or the staff of the respective divisions to occupy the indifferent accommodation which the town afforded, when reports arrived that some French light cavalry were approaching. This appeared a very extraordinary crusade for French cavalry to set out upon; but was so confidently stated, that it became necessary to ascertain the fact. I immediately got upon horseback, and proceeded to the encampment in front of the town. A line of cavalry appeared on the plain, advancing with caution. The artillery of the 3rd division were drawn out, General Pakenham watching the progress of these supposedly hostile horsemen. Having seen the Portuguese cavalry in the morning, I had little doubt, from every circumstance, it was General D'Urban's brigade that now appeared on the plain: they were dressed very similarly to the enemy's *chasseurs à cheval*, and had not been previously seen by the officers of the infantry bivouac.

From whatever cause it proceeded, they advanced with great caution; everything tended to increase the delusion. In the act of riding forward to ascertain their identity, after having approached sufficiently near to perceive General D'Urban, I was returning with the information, when a discharge from the artillery of the 3rd division was poured into the centre of the supposed enemies, and several men and horses rolled on the earth. I galloped back, making signals to cease firing; and having communicated to General Pakenham that it was General D'Urban and his brigade, rode forward to the latter, who appeared astonished at the unexpected reception he had met with. The mistake was explained; and the night passed without further excitement.

At daylight, we marched to the heights of San Christoval, and from thence to the right bank of the Tormes, encamping near to the Santa Marta ford.

The whole of the enemy's army was now on the Tormes, near to Babilafuente, and opposite to the fords on the river at Huerta.

The town of Salamanca presented a very different scene from that we had witnessed on the advance of the army. The happiness and confidence then exhibited by its inhabitants had been changed to gloomy forebodings of what they considered now likely to occur, namely, the retreat of the allied army, and the undisputed possession of the enemy; an enemy naturally exasperated at the manifestations of friendship bestowed upon those to whom he was opposed.

The power and resistless influence of French military force again occupied the minds of the Spaniards: we had, they supposed, obtained a temporary success, occasioned by circumstances connected with the then divided state of the French Army, but when brought together, as in the present instance, it was by them considered irresistible. That we were aware of this fact, and prepared to retire upon Ciudad Rodrigo, was the concluding event connected with this mode of reasoning; that pillage, fire, and sword, would be let loose on them and their families, they deemed the certain consequence attending the reverse of circumstances and the disastrous aspect of affairs.

The eagerness with which the Spaniard questioned, the watchful look, the whispering, the not to be mistaken gesture denoting despondency and want of confidence, all bespoke the agitation and hopeless state of his mind. The delight with which he saw troops moving towards the Santa Marta ford, and the terror displayed when others marched to cross the bridge of Salamanca, proved the anxiety with which he endeavoured to discover, more from circumstances than protestations, what was likely to be the line of conduct adopted by Lord Wellington: the former route being very correctly supposed to lead into contact with the enemy, the other commencing the line of immediate retreat. Many of its inhabitants had deserted the town, which looked gloomy and desolate.

As usual in similar cases, constant reports spread alarm, and ludicrous scenes occurred from its being supposed that the enemy was in the immediate vicinity. So near the track of a large army, it was to be expected that many of its followers would enter the city, and linger within its walls. Frequent orders and repeated messages proved ineffectual in getting subordinate commissariat officers and others to repair to the bivouacs. At length, an officer of the staff, wearied with fruitless endeavours to clear the town of these people, circulated a report that the French cavalry were in the act of entering it: the scene that ensued was very ridiculous; but the *ruse* had the desired effect, and I have seldom seen fear more decidedly exhibited than by some civilians of our own country upon this occasion.

Towards evening, the commander of the forces ascertained that Marshal Marmont had passed the main body of his army across the Tormes by the fords of Huerta, moving by his left to gain the Ciudad Rodrigo road; to counteract the effects of this manoeuvre, he immediately put the allied army in motion. Before darkness had closed in, we had passed the Santa Marta ford, and encamped on the high ground in rear of Calvarassa de Ariba; the 3rd division, the Spanish force under Don Carlos de España, and General D'Urban's brigade of cavalry, being the only allied troops remaining on the Salamanca side of the river.

The 5th division had but a short time arrived at its bivouacs, in rear of an extensive wood, and on the summit of a *plateau*, that, with little variety of altitude, extended from the nearest of two remarkable heights, called the Arapiles, to the bank of the Tormes at the village of Santa Marta, when the appearance of the air bespoke an approaching storm. The rain soon fell in torrents, accompanied by vivid flashes of lightning, and succeeded by instantaneous peals of thunder. A more violent crash of the elements has seldom been witnessed; its effects were soon apparent. General le Marchant's brigade of cavalry had halted to our left; the men, dismounted, were either seated or lying on the ground, holding their horses, who, alarmed by the thunder, started with violence, and many of them, breaking loose, galloped across the country in all directions.

This dispersion, and the frightened horses passing without riders in a state of wildness, added to the awful effect of the tempest; nor was the situation in which we were otherwise placed one of great brightness. For days past the enemy appeared to control our movements, and to force us back without an effort: we were now, in the darkness of night, close to him—but where, or in what direction, was known only to the headquarters, in search of whom officers were constantly passing and re-passing; but with the night closed the gloomy prospects of the drama.

Morning was to dawn on brighter views and nobler deeds: with the light commenced that scene of intense interest,—that, by the British, never to be forgotten day, on which was turned the fortune of the war, which laid the foundation for the career of glory that ultimately liberated Spain, and, by destroying the *morale* of the troops of Napoleon, never afterwards enabled them to cope with the inhabitants of Great Britain with equal confidence, or with a like prospect of success.

Before daybreak, scattered reports of musketry were heard in the direction of Calvarassa de Ariba, in front of which, on the height of Nuestra Senora de la Peña, the enemy had advanced a large body of light troops. When it became perfectly light, the tiraillade grew warm and incessant. Some troops of the 7th division, and General Victor Alten's light cavalry, were engaged in this affair.

The nearest of the Arapiles, which, although considerably higher, is connected with the ridge on which we now stood, had been occupied by the allies on the preceding night: the other hill of that name, of greater altitude, more isolated, and rising from the plain at the angular point formed by the receding of the heights, had not been then considered as important. Early in the morning, however, troops were sent to take possession of it; but the enemy had anticipated this movement, and part of the brigade of General Maucun already crowned the summit, no effort being then made to dislodge him.

Large bodies of the enemy's troops were perceived marching to their left; forming in rear of the Arapiles, and on the skirts of a wood extending towards Alba de Tormes. These columns were considered by General Leith to be within the range of the artillery of his division, which he ordered in advance to a height in front of his position, from whence was obtained a better view of the formation taking place under cover of the Arapiles. Having reached this eminence, Captain Lawson opened his fire with such effect that the nearest of the enemy's troops made a rapid, and not very orderly change of position, proceeding to a distance greatly out of reach of the point where the British artillery were annoying them.

To counteract the galling effects of this attack, the enemy brought forward some guns, which he placed so as to bear diagonally on the height occupied by Captain Lawson; from these, immediately opened a destructive fire, killing and wounding several men and horses, and damaging one of the carriages. Captain Tomkinson's troop of the 16th Light Dragoons had been sent forward to protect the British cannon: it was formed under shelter of the height, and was not exposed to the cannonade now kept up with great spirit.

I was sent down to direct the artillery to retire, and to bring the light dragoons back across the ravine, which was now swept by a shower of balls and howitzer shells. The 16th separated, and galloped back without sustaining serious loss; but I was more apprehensive for the artillery, its carriages of course presenting larger objects, and not moving with the same rapidity: they, however, did not suffer so much as might have been expected, and soon regained the ground on which the division had been the unwilling spectators of this noisy fray.

The day was fine; the sun shone bright,—nor was there any atmospheric obstruction to prevent a clear view of passing events; no haze withheld a distinct observation to the very extremity of the plains upon which the enemy was in movement. Occasional smoke from the firing, and dust, alone created a temporary uncertainty in the view of any movement of either army.

About midday, a force, consisting of not less than 10,000 men, countermarched from near the Arapiles, and formed directly opposite to the 5th division: this column was accompanied by artillery, and had every appearance of meditating an immediate attack. I was ordered to proceed as expeditiously as possible towards the right of the army, to inform Lord Wellington of this demonstration. On being made acquainted with the posture of affairs, he declared his intention of riding to the spot, and directed me to accompany him.

When he arrived at the ground of the 5th division, now under arms, and perfectly prepared to receive the attack, his Lordship found the enemy in the same formation as when he first appeared opposite, but not displaying any intention of trying his fortune by crossing the ravine at that point. The commander of the forces soon became satisfied that no operation of consequence was intended against this part of his line; and he again galloped towards the right, which at that time had become the most interesting and important scene of action.

The French Army was evidently pressing forward to gain the Ciudad Rodrigo road, and the greater proportion of its force had now assembled either to the southward, or to the left of the Arapiles; it consequently became necessary for Lord Wellington to follow, and counteract these movements of his adversary.

The 4th division, and General Pack's brigade of Portuguese infantry, had already arrived to our right of the nearest Arapiles. The 5th division soon after received orders to march in that direction; in executing which we passed close to the rear of the 4th division, taking up ground to its right, and on the same line. At some distance, in rear of the 5th, was stationed the 7th division, under General Hope; while the 6th, commanded by General Henry Clinton, was in line to support the 4th.

The 1st and light divisions continued between the Tormes and the Arapiles height. General Pakenham, with the 3rd division, General D'Urban's cavalry, two squadrons of the 14th Light Dragoons, and the Spanish infantry of Don Carlos España, were posted near to Aldea Tejada; while General Bradford's brigade, and the heavy cavalry of General le Marchant, were immediately on the right of the 5th division, but considerably to its rear: such was the disposition of the allied army at two o'clock in the afternoon of the 22nd. The whole range of heights on the opposite side of the valley, in which the village of Arapiles is situated, was completely covered with the enemy's troops, all in motion; his cavalry and artillery pressing forward, and repelling those of the allies, not towards the line of the army, but in the direction of General Pakenham, then on the flank of both armies.

The British infantry remained for a considerable time without movement, or being assailed by the enemy, who still advanced in column, presenting a similar line of march with that he had adopted on the 20th, and probably anticipating the same results.

From the formation of the ground, the left of General Cole's position was nearer the line of march of the French than any other portion of the British line. It also presented a knoll well calculated for the operations of field artillery; from thence, previous to the commencement of the action, Captain Sympher kept up a constant and well-directed fire against the moving masses of the enemy.

About three o'clock, a force of not less than twenty pieces of artillery were assembled by the enemy on the heights directly opposite to the 5th division. The ground upon which the division stood was flat, and the troops without any means of shelter. It became consequently advisable to make the regiments recline on the field, and, by so doing, avoid in some measure the effects of what was evidently to become a very heavy cannonade. For at least an hour did these brave soldiers immovably support the efforts made to annihilate them by the showers of shot and howitzer shells that were either passing over or *recochèting* through the ranks.

General Leith, on horseback, passed repeatedly along the front of his division, speaking to and animating the men, who earnestly expressed an anxious desire for permission to attack the enemy.

In the progress of this scene the light infantry of either army were busily employed. The village of Arapiles, defended by the Guards, and two companies of the fusiliers, was repeatedly assailed, and the enemy invariably driven back.

At length, the welcome intelligence was imparted that we were no longer to be cannonaded with impunity. Lord Wellington arrived from the right, and communicated to General Leith his intention of immediately attacking the enemy.

It is impossible to describe the energetic exultation with which the soldiers sprang to their feet: if ever primary impulse gained a battle, that of Salamanca was won before the troops moved forward! General Pakenham commenced the action by advancing in four columns, coming direct upon the enemy's left flank, which he vigorously attacked, and drove back in disorder.

General Leith was directed to form his division in two lines, the first of which was composed of the Royal, 9th, and 38th regiments, with part of the 4th regiment from General Pringle's brigade, necessarily brought forward for the purpose of equalising the lines, of which the second was formed by the remainder of General Pringle's, and the whole of General Spry's Portuguese infantry.

When General Bradford's brigade came up, the division was to *appui* itself on his left, march directly up the heights, and attack the enemy's columns. Lord Wellington on this, as on all occasions, gave his orders in a clear, concise, and spirited manner: there was no appearance of contemplating a doubtful result; all he directed was as to time and formation, and his instructions concluded with commands that the enemy should be overthrown, and driven from the field. He then proceeded towards the 4th division. The 5th, formed as he had directed, with its general in front of the centre of the first line, impatiently awaited the arrival of General Bradford; the moment he was in line, General Leith gave the signal, and the whole advanced in the most perfect order. Previously to this movement, he had despatched his *aides-de-camp*, Captain Belshes and Captain Dowson, to different points of the line, in order to restrain any effort at getting more rapidly forward than was consistent with the important object of its arriving in perfect order close to the enemy, and at all points making a simultaneous attack.

In ascending the height on which the French Army was placed, the division continued to be annoyed by the artillery fire from its summit; the ground between the advancing force and that to be assailed was also crowded with light troops in extended order, carrying on a very incessant tiraillade. The general desired me to ride forward, make the light infantry press up the heights to clear his line of march, and, if practicable, make a rush at the enemy's cannon. In the execution of this service, I had to traverse the whole extent of surface directly in front of the 5th division: the light troops soon drove back those opposed; the French cannon were removed to the rear; every obstruction to the regular advance of the line had vanished. In front of the centre of that beautiful line rode General Leith, directing its movements, and regulating its advance. Occasionally every soldier was visible, the sun shining bright upon their arms, while at intervals all were enveloped in a dense cloud of dust, from whence, at times, issued the animating cheer of British infantry.

The confident presence of the enemy was now exchanged for the quiet formation proceeding in his ranks, as preparatives for resisting the evidently approaching shock. His columns, retired from the crest of the height, were formed in squares, about fifty yards removed from the ground, on which, when arrived, the British regiments would become visible. The French artillery, although placed more to the rear, still poured its fire on the advancing troops. In the act of urging forward the light infantry, a ball struck the horse I rode, and, passing through his body, laid him dead on the spot. In this dilemma, I waited until a line approached, and having dismounted an orderly dragoon, proceeded with the general, who continued in the same situation he had occupied when the division commenced its advance; namely, in front of the colours of the 1st battalion of the 38th regiment. That corps, numerous and effective, had joined the army on the previous day, and, being the junior regiment, formed the centre of the first line: its commanding officer, Colonel Greville, having charge of the brigade in the absence of General Hay.

The second line of the division was about a hundred yards in rear of the first; and between these, during the march towards the enemy, Lord Wellington at one time was observing the progress of the attack.

We were now near the summit of the ridge. The men marched with the same orderly steadiness as at first: no advance in line at a review was ever more correctly executed: the dressing was admirable, and spaces were no sooner formed by casualties than closed up with the most perfect regularity, and without the slightest deviation from the order of march.

General Leith, and the officers of his staff, being on horseback, first perceived the enemy, and had time to observe his formation, previous to the infantry line becoming so visible, as to induce him to commence firing. He was drawn up in contiguous columns, the front rank kneeling, and prepared to fire when the drum beat for its commencement. All was still and quiet in these columns;—not a musket was discharged until the whole opened. Nearly at the same moment General Leith ordered the line to fire, and charge: the roll of musketry was succeeded by that proud cheer that has become habitual to British soldiers on similar occasions—that to an enemy tremendous sound, which may without doubt be termed the note of victory.

At this moment, the last thing I saw through the smoke was the plunge of Colonel Greville's horse, who, shot through the head, reared, and fell back on his rider. In an instant every individual present was enveloped in smoke and obscurity. No struggle for ascendency now took place; resistance was vain; the French squares were penetrated, broken, and discomfited; the victorious division pressed forward, not against troops opposed, but a mass of disorganised men, overpowered and flying in all directions. General le Marchant's brigade of heavy cavalry dashed forward on the right flank of the 5th division, while General Pakenham, having overthrown everything before him, added an immense number to the mass of fugitives escaping from this brilliant attack.

Thus, in the short space of less than one hour, the battle was decided; the defeat of the French Army became inevitable. Other divisions and corps of troops participated in the glory of the day, suffered seriously, and nobly upheld the reputation they had previously acquired; but the Battle of Salamanca was in reality won by the 3rd and 5th divisions, General Bradford's Portuguese brigade, the squadrons of the 14th Dragoons, and the heavy cavalry. By the combined attacks of these troops, one-fourth of the French Army was defeated, and driven in confusion on its centre: and ten thousand of the allies, regularly formed, flushed with success, and supported by a large body of cavalry, were on the flank of the enemy's army, every step they advanced adding to his discomfiture, driving him rapidly from height to height, and forcing back an additional crowd of fugitives to annoy and confound their still undefeated comrades.

It will easily be conceived that, in such a state of affairs, the battle was irretrievably lost to the enemy. The attack made by General Pack on the Arapiles was, as might have been expected from the nature of the ground, unsuccessful. The 4th division, so frequently distinguished during the war, attacked the division of General Bonnèt, which, favoured by its position, powerful from its numerical strength, and, as I have previously stated, unaccustomed to encounter British troops, made a firm and gallant resistance, nor could the utmost efforts of General Cole succeed in driving it back. Outflanked, and seriously resisted, he for a time lost ground; but, upon the 6th division moving up in support, the favourable state of the action in that part of the field was restored, and the whole French Army gave way.

When close to the enemy's squares, in the commencement of the battle, General Leith was severely wounded, and reluctantly compelled to quit the field; nearly at the same moment the author of these pages was also wounded, and his horse killed by a musket-ball. Captain Dowson, another of the general's *aides-de-camp*, had his foot shattered by a bullet, and remained all night without assistance on the field. Colonel Berkeley, Major Gomm, Captain Belshes, and Captain George Hay, acting *aide-de-camp* in the absence of his father, composed the remaining officers of the divisional staff on this occasion, and, by their activity and gallantry, greatly conduced to the result of the successful service it had the good fortune to perform.

Having been removed from the field, I cannot detail the future movements of the 5th division on the night of the battle. They, however, consisted solely of pursuit, capturing many of the enemy; and, as a proof that it had penetrated to the very centre of his regiments, Major Birmingham, of the 15th Portuguese, one of the corps of General Spry's brigade, was seen riding forward carrying a French eagle, which he had, during the *mêlée*, torn from the grasp of its bearer.

Colonel Barnes, of the Royal Scots, was shot through the body, leading his regiment in pursuit of the enemy. Colonel Miles, of the 38th, had been previously severely wounded. Never was a more rapid reverse, and seldom a more signal defeat, than had overtaken the French Army, which continued its flight during the night in the direction of Alba de Tormes, unfortunately left without any regular troops of the allied army. Situated as the armies were previous to the action, it would have compromised any force placed in that town; but, could the result have been foreseen, its occupation must have ensured the capture of all the artillery and ambulances, if not the entire destruction, of the French Army.

The small body of irregular Spanish soldiery stationed in Alba fled on the approach of the vanquished army, which, consequently, met with no obstruction in defiling by the bridge at that place. The retreat by the fords of the Tormes, under such circumstances, would have been attended with great difficulty, and a delay fatal to the defeated army; for the unengaged troops of the allies had been marched towards Huerta, and would have obstructed its retreat in that direction; the darkness of night favoured the escape of many soldiers already captured, and enabled others to get away with impunity. Eleven pieces of cannon, two eagles, six stand of colours, and seven thousand prisoners, were ultimately secured. The field of battle was covered with dead bodies of the enemy.

Marshal the Duke of Ragusa was struck early in the action by a howitzer-shell; it broke his right arm, severely wounded him in the side, and incapacitated him from further command. General Bonnèt succeeded, and was also wounded. General Clausel, the next in seniority, met with the same fate; but his hurt was not of a nature making it imperative to resign the charge of the discomfited army, whose retreat he from a litter continued to direct with great judgment and military knowledge. Generals Thomières and Ferret were killed on the spot. General Desgraviers died of his wounds, after having been taken by the allies.

The "Army of Portugal," previous to the action, was composed of eight divisions of infantry, a large body of cavalry, and upwards of one hundred pieces of cannon—a force much superior in numbers to that of the allies. Lord Wellington had under his immediate command seven divisions of infantry, the unattached Portuguese brigades of Generals Pack and Bradford, the Spanish corps of Don Carlos de España, about two thousand cavalry, and from fifty to sixty pieces of cannon: of this force four divisions of infantry, the Portuguese brigades, and part of the cavalry, only were engaged; at the close of the action, the light, 1st, and 7th divisions were entire, and ready to move against the flying enemy.

General le Marchant was the only officer of his rank that fell on the part of the allies; but among the wounded were numbered Marshal Sir William Beresford, Sir Stapleton Cotton, and General Cole. General Victor Allen had been wounded during the skirmish on the height of Nuestra Senora de la Peña in the morning.

The events I have thus very superficially detailed, were of an importance quite disproportioned even to the great occasion itself; and in contemplating the incalculable advantages to be derived from so decisive a victory, particularly in a war of opinion such as then agitated the Peninsula, one of the most striking features is, the pre-eminent station in which it at once placed Lord Wellington: distinguished as he had ever been, there yet remained to be established the climax that annihilated all criticism of his actions, and placed him deservedly beyond the reach of mistrust.

Previous to the Battle of Salamanca, there were persons highly talented, and of sound military acquirement, that supposed the campaign might have been better conducted, and who murmured at the vacillating policy, which, without a blow, led back a brilliant army from the Duero to the Tormes. Salamanca put an end to all these dreams, and, by producing unlimited confidence, enabled the great commander of the allied army to become unshaken by reverses that circumstances, over which he had no control, subsequently rendered inevitable, and to carry with him the full tide of success only to be secured by that feeling, and made irresistible by that impression.

The 22nd of July had been an anxious day in the town of Salamanca. Early in the morning, the firing towards Calvarassa de Ariba gave the inhabitants hopes that the armies were engaged; but as the day advanced, and the sound of artillery and musketry became closer, and evidently approaching the Ciudad Rodrigo road, despondency took possession of the minds of those most deeply interested; the heights near the town, and the roofs of its most lofty buildings, were crowded with persons watching the progress of events, which for hours previous to the serious commencement of the battle wore to them a disastrous aspect; but when the fire became loud and incessant, and gradually more distant from the town, exultation and presages of victory and deliverance succeeded to the recently gloomy prospect of affairs.

General Leith and myself remained the night of the battle in the village of Las Torres, and were the following day conveyed to Salamanca, where we became residents in the house of the Marques Escalla.

The gratitude of the inhabitants of Salamanca on this occasion was not confined to empty expressions, or wild ebullitions of patriotic feeling, but far more substantially and usefully evinced by sincere and zealous exertion to provide for the wants of the wounded, and afford assistance in furnishing the large hospitals, of necessity established after such an action, with every requisite for the comfort of their deliverers, as they designated the troops of the allied army.

The captured cannon, trophies of the victory, were parked in the *plaza*, where were also assembled the column of prisoners, previous to their being marched for the frontier.

Guitars sounded in the streets, patriotic *sequidillas* were composed and sung, the lively noise of *castenets* proclaimed the progress of the fascinating *bolero*. The town exhibited an appearance of the gayest carnival. The wounded being removed from public view, formed no visible contrast to the enlivening scene. The sound of artillery, and note of war, no longer struck upon the ear; boasted achievements, and comparisons between the British and French nations, interspersed with anecdotes alike romantic and improbable, occupied the Spanish population. To have heard what was passing, or observed the feeling expressed, a spectator must have supposed that the great crisis was past; all oppression or exaction at an end, and Salamanca for ever freed from the presence of the detested French.

The whole night of the Battle of Salamanca, the enemy's army continued its flight in the utmost possible confusion. No adequate arrangement to soften the effects of so unexpected and rapid a discomfiture had been made; nor were the circumstances of the war, the line of retreat over so considerable a river as the Tormes, or the probable chance of effecting it unobstructed, likely to produce order or self-possession in the French Army;—an army great under events of successful warfare, but too calculating, and, during the imperial government, too self-confident, to be easily controlled or directed when misfortune occurred, and when the "*sauve qui peut*" principle was in such activity as on the occasion above narrated.

When arrived at Alba de Tormes, all accounts agree in representing its complete disorganisation. It was a mass of fugitives rather than an army, the men having lost their officers; regiments intermixed; many soldiers without arms; all having but one object, that of removal, with the utmost celerity, from the field of battle. The first intention of the general commanding evidently was, to fall back on the "Army of the Centre," led by the king, and advancing from the capital. With this view, the shattered "Army of Portugal" pursued the route to Arevalo. But having received information of Joseph's retrograde movement, which was the instantaneous consequence of his being made acquainted with the result of the action, General Clausel altered his line of retreat. Branching off from his intended route, he entered upon the Camino-real, leading from Madrid to Valladolid, and proceeding directly for the Duero, crossed that river at Tudela: from thence he continued on the road to Aranda, still hoping to form a junction with the troops from Madrid; but, disappointed in that expectation, the defeated army, abandoning its hospitals at Valladolid, precipitately retired upon Burgos.

Having thus driven the army immediately opposed to him from the field, and rendered it incapable of speedily resuming an offensive attitude, Lord Wellington resolved to move towards the south, where the Army of the Centre, numerically weak, and unsupported by any other force, could neither check his progress, nor prevent his victorious troops from obtaining possession of the capital, and the temporary control over a large portion of the Spanish territory. Joseph Bonaparte, aware of the fatal disaster that had befallen the numerous and highly effective army he meditated to reinforce, lost no time in retracing his steps; and, having passed the Puerta de Guadarama, again appeared in Madrid.

General Clinton, with the 6th division, and some of the battalions most reduced in numbers during the progress of the campaign, were stationed at Cuellar, to hold in check the remains of the Duke of Ragusa's army, while the main body of the allies marched towards the centre of the country. Lord Wellington arrived at San Ildefonso on the 9th, and on the two following days, crossed the mountain passes of Guadarama and Naval Serrana, descending like a torrent on the plains of New Castille.

On the night of the 11th of August, after reconnoitring the allied army, and ascertaining its force to be disproportioned to what they could possibly present effectual resistance to, the *soi-disant* king and his major-general, Marshal Jourdan, quitted Madrid, marching on Aranjuez, after placing two thousand men in the fort constructed in the grounds of the ruined palace of the Retire.

The garrison, although well provisioned and appointed, was committed to a certain sacrifice. No French engineer could have doubted the impossibility of the fort holding out for any length of time, even against the means Lord Wellington could bring against it: being relieved was not within the reach of probability. It remains, therefore, to be accounted for, on what principle the French officers in command determined to compromise so considerable a body of excellent soldiers, without any apparent advantage to be gained by pursuing a system which, in the forts at Salamanca, under much more favourable circumstances, had proved fallacious.

On the morning of the 14th, the Retire surrendered, when one hundred and eighty-nine pieces of cannon, two thousand and fifty-five officers and privates, nine hundred barrels of powder, twenty thousand stand of arms, above two millions of musket-ball cartridges, and two eagles, were captured by the allies. A very considerable *dépôt* of cables and cordage of every description was also found within the work, and in the grounds of the Casa del Campo. It was determined to employ these materials in repairing the bridge of Almaraz, in a manner similar to that previously adopted at Alcantara. The fractured arch of the former being of much greater span, it consequently made the successful application of this mode of repair more decided, giving at the same time to the ingenious work a more extended character. The chasm to be passed by the rope-repair at Almaraz was one hundred and forty-three feet. The network was completed in the new museum at the Retiro, under the superintendence of Captain Todd, of the Royal Staff corps.

The reception of Lord Wellington and his army in the metropolis of Spain was, as might have been expected, extremely cordial and enthusiastic. The authorities of the city, supported by the unanimous voice of the population, considered the Palacio Nuevo as the only becoming residence for the British general, and to it he was escorted amidst the cheers and benedictions of the people.

A few short years had, in this volcanic period, occasioned a rapid and singular change in the ruling inmates of the palace of the Spanish monarchy. The weak, good-natured, and prejudiced Carlos IV., the intriguing, dissolute, and selfish Maria Louisa, the erring, vulgar, and ignorant Prince of Peace, retired from the scene to be succeeded by Joseph Bonaparte, alike incapable, under any circumstances, of conducting the affairs of this great country, as he was of conquering the undivided allegiance of his subjects. To replace his brother on the throne, after the Battle of Baylen, and subsequent events had occasioned his absence from the capital, the Emperor Napoleon visited Madrid, and the apartments of the Palacio Nuevo were momentarily subjected to his eagle glance. For nearly four years after this memorable visit, Joseph preserved a semblance of royalty, and passed the greater portion of his time, at Madrid. The Battle of Salamanca again occasioned his abrupt removal from the capital, and the distinguished commander of the allied army for a short period inhabited the palace of the Bourbons.

The effects of the recent victory were speedily demonstrated by the alteration of circumstances attending the enemy's troops in every part of the Spanish territory. It had shaken the whole fabric of French domination to its very base; nor did the power of Napoleon in the Peninsula ever recover from the shock.

The siege of Cadiz raised, the army of the Duke of Dalmatia on its march to the north, the Andalusias liberated, the army of Cataluña and Valencia paralysed, the guerilla force tripled,—all resulted from the successful termination of that important battle. But the times were not those of lassitude or inactivity; and before Marshals Soult and Suchet had recovered from the astounding information that Lord Wellington was in possession of the capital and the whole centre of the country, he was again on his way to Old Castille, there to oppose the reinforced "Armies of Portugal" and "of the North," and lay siege to the Castle of Burgos.

On the 17th, 18th, and 19th of the month, four divisions of the army, namely, the 1st, 4th, 5th, and 7th, marched from Madrid to the Escorial: the light and 3rd divisions, with part of the cavalry, continuing quartered in the capital and its vicinity. Having left General Cole, with his division, in New Castille, the 1st, 5th, and 7th divisions crossed the Guadarama, and proceeded on their route to Cuellar, where, having formed a junction with General Clinton, the whole force moved towards Burgos.

Sir Rowland Hill received orders to march on Toledo; by which movement a large force became concentrated on the Tagus, covering the approach to the capital from the southern parts of Spain.

General Leith left Salamanca on the 19th, taking the route to Lisbon. During his absence from the army, I determined to continue in Spain, and to solicit service as formerly; when acting with the Spanish Army, I had procured information of the enemy's motions in Estremadura. Lord Wellington consented to employ me, and I only awaited restoration from the effects of the wound received at Salamanca to proceed in any direction he might be pleased to consider my presence of the slightest utility.

Accompanied by Staff-Surgeon Emery, who had received orders to proceed for Madrid, I left Salamanca on the 24th of August, travelling in a *berlina* of the most cumbrous and uneasy description, but drawn by powerful and active mules. We had secured this conveyance for the whole journey; and being still unable to mount on horseback without difficulty, this was the only means by which, for some time, I could have removed from the dullness of Salamanca. Having halted, on the evening of our departure, at Ventosa, we next day passed through Peñranda—a considerable town, in which the principal building, formerly the residence of the Duques de Frias, had been converted into a cavalry barrack by the French Army. After a very sultry day we arrived at Fontiveros, and on the 26th partook of the hospitality of the Cura of Blascho Sancho, whose house had been the temporary residence of Joseph Bonaparte, where he received information of Marshal Marmont having been defeated, and from whence he commenced his retrograde movement on Madrid.

After passing the Venta of Almarza, we entered the Camino-real. At the summit of an ascent several miles in length is Labajos, a large village; the country from Salamanca to Labajos is bare and uninteresting: neither woods nor vineyards vary the uninterrupted level, on which the cornfields, after the harvest, become parched by the excessive heat, presenting to the traveller an appearance of an arid and unproductive district.

The next village of importance on this route is Villacastin; from thence we slowly prosecuted our journey, arriving in the evening at Las Navas de San Antonia, where the ravages of French visitation were even more than ordinarily visible. On the morning of the 28th, we reached the Fonda de San Rafael, romantically situated at the entrance to the Guadarama pass. The scenery there becomes very beautiful, the mountains assuming the boldest and most picturesque forms, the effect of which is greatly improved by their being clothed to the summits by forests of pines.

The *fonda*, or inn, formerly one of the stages of the royal family in their journeyings to the north, was now much dilapidated and destroyed. It evidently had been the most extensive and respectable establishment of its kind I had yet seen in Spain, but now presented a very ruinous and decayed aspect. Immediately after leaving the *fonda*, the road commences a gradual ascent, winding up the face of the mountain, until, arriving at the lion on its summit, the widely extended plains of New Castille appear in view, and Madrid is seen in the distance. It is difficult to conceive more beautiful mountain-scenery than the sierra presents in crossing the pass.

The descent to the southward is more steep and precipitous than that towards Old Castille, but the same wild luxuriant scenery gives interest to the route, which winds amongst stupendous rocks, under the shade of chestnut and oak-trees of gigantic growth. At the foot of the mountain stands the village of Guadarama, and to the right, at the distance of a mile, is situated the convent palace of the Escorial. A league in advance of Guadarama we left the Camino-real, and struck into the Segovia road, on which is the Fonda de la Trinidad—in ruins, but the post-house afforded us shelter for the night.

The country from La Trinidad to the capital is cultivated, but without wood, until near the Pardo, when woods, in great luxuriancy of foliage, line the road to the gates of Madrid. For a league previously to entering the city, the approach passes between walls, and is ornamented by trees of great magnitude: on its right runs the River Manzanares.

Madrid has undergone great and to be regretted changes since I formerly visited it: the inhabitants now comprised a class of persons perfectly distinct from those most distinguished in the days when the Bourbon court passed most of the year in uninterrupted sameness within its walls. Most of the *grandees* had fled on the approach of the French armies, and those who, espousing an opposite line of policy, had adhered to the fortunes of the French dynasty, had also left the capital, as the natural consequence of the reverse it had recently experienced; with few exceptions, therefore, the higher orders of Spanish society no longer graced it with their presence: it had consequently ceased to exhibit in the *salons*, and on the Prado, the highly aristocratic appearance which distinguished the city in 1808.

Of the few great families continuing to reside in Madrid, on the entrance of the allies in 1812, that of Rivella Gijeda was eminent for amiability and superiority of style. The *condessa*, representative of a very distinguished family, and a *grandee* of Spain, had married the provincial Marques de Cañallejas.

Don Carlos España had, on the entrance of the allies, been appointed governor of the city—a situation, under the circumstances, of very considerable difficulty, and in the exercise of which few persons could have given satisfaction. Intrigue, jealousy, and distrust, on the part of the Spaniards, rendered, in his instance, the distinction very unenviable: so many conflicting events, tending to harass and annoy a soldier taken from the ranks of his profession to exercise at the time so vexatious an authority, worked on a mind naturally irritable; and I am satisfied no period of Don Carlos's life was ever considered by him less congenial to his feelings than that which he passed in the house of the Marques de St. Iago as governor of Madrid.

Lord Wellington left the capital on the 1st of September, and the headquarters were at Valladolid on the 9th. The army of Portugal, reinforced, and, in some measure, again restored to an effective state, had, during the absence of the main body of the allied army in New Castille, made several advances towards the cantonments of General Clinton, without attempting any serious attack; but, upon receiving intelligence of the divisions from the capital having formed a junction with the 6th, it fell back, offering no resistance to the direct and undisputed march of the British General upon Burgos.

From the period of the allies obtaining possession of the capital to Lord Wellington's leaving it for the north, no French force of any description approached to disturb the quarters of the army in that city.

Joseph, with the "Army of the Centre," lingered on the left bank of the Tagus, from the evacuation of Madrid to the 16th of August, on which day he marched from Ocaña, taking the route of Valencia, then the headquarters of the Marshal Duke of Albufera.

By the division of his force, and leaving so large a portion of it in New Castille, as also the subsequent movement of Sir Rowland Hill on Toledo, Lord Wellington ensured either the retaining possession of Madrid, or occasioning the liberation of the whole southern territory of the Peninsula by the removal of the armies holding it in subjection, these now forming the only force in Spain capable of effectually driving back the allies, and thereby restoring for a short period the centre of the kingdom to the sway of Joseph Bonaparte. In either case, great advantage to the general cause must ensue, and the movement most likely to be decided on by the French generals, and which they afterwards carried into execution, was probably, although attended with the retreat of the allies, that most conducive to the final success of the war. Andalusia, by the talent and exertions of the Duke of Dalmatia, had been more universally reduced to subjection, and was less inclined to dispute the point of French domination, than any other part of Spain.

His arrangements for its civil government were daily becoming matured, and Seville represented, at the time of the Battle of Salamanca, more the seat of a viceroy, than the quarters of an enemy's general. All these advantages, every exertion he had made permanently to fix the people in their allegiance to the brother of the idol of the French Army, were at once to be foregone. Seville was abandoned; the siege of Cadiz raised; battering artillery destroyed; and the Army of the South, loaded with spoils, reluctantly moved, in conjunction with the king and Marshal Suchet, to outnumber the allied force on the Tagus and the Manzanares, and compel it to resign the great advantages derived in a war of opinion from the influence attached to the British being in possession of the capital.

While these extensive preparations were completing in the south, we remained quiet and undisturbed at Madrid. A numerous and formidable army was there and in its neighbourhood assembled, composed of the light division; the second, under the orders of General Chowne; the 3rd, commanded by General Pakenham; the 4th, by General Cole; the Portuguese division of General Hamilton; Sir William Erskine's division of cavalry; and the Spanish force; while the British troops from Cadiz, commanded by Colonel Skerrett, were daily expected.

At Palencia, on his route to the north, Lord Wellington was joined by the army of Gallicia, commanded by General Castaños; and on the 9th of September he entered Burgos. The castle, well situated for defence, had been fortified with considerable care and ingenuity, but was not a work calculated to resist a regular force if accompanied by the adequate means for reducing it. So much impressed with this idea was General Souham, that, previously to leaving Burgos, he asked General Dubreton, the newly appointed governor, whether he could hold out for ten days, and his answer was one of a very doubtful nature.

The artillery provided for the siege of the castle of Burgos was the same that had been in battery against the forts at Salamanca; and if defective in numbers and force upon the former occasion, it became doubly insufficient when brought against a much more formidable work, ably, resolutely, and skilfully defended.

The extreme hardships endured by the troops conducting the siege, the severe loss therein sustained, the numerous instances of devotion and gallantry displayed, have been so often and fully detailed by eye-witnesses to the facts, that I shall not attempt a connected recapitulation of the events which occurred in the course of the persevering efforts made to reduce the place. The weather, during the sojourn of the allies before Burgos, was unfavourable to a degree: rain, accompanied by violent gales of wind, continued to obstruct and annoy the troops, exposed at the same time to a galling and constant fire.

The operations of the siege were confided to the 1st and 6th divisions, under the orders of Generals Campbell and Clinton, with the Portuguese brigades of Generals Pack and Bradford; most of the regiments suffered severely. In the various assaults, mining operations, escalades, repulsing sorties, and tirailladed, which took place, the troops displayed unwearied assiduity, and. unceasing exertion: the loss was proportioned to the arduous nature of the service.

In attempting to carry the exterior line of the enemy's works by storm, on the night of the 22nd of September, Major Laurie, of the 79th regiment, was killed, and Captain M'Kenzie Fraser, of the Coldstream Guards, severely wounded.

At three o'clock on the morning of the 8th of October, a sortie took place, rendered memorable by the fall of Major Cocks, commanding in the trenches, and who, with his accustomed energy, had assembled the guard and workmen to force the enemy back into the covered way.

Long distinguished as an active officer of light cavalry, Major Cocks had commenced his career as a field-officer of Highland infantry, in charge of the light battalion of Colonel Stirling's brigade, with great success and renown. On the morning of the 19th September, he drove in the enemy's advanced posts, and in the evening of the same day led the attack that placed the allies in possession of the important hornwork of San Michael, which he gallantly carried with a loss of four hundred men. During the future operations against the place, previous to the night of the 8th October, no opportunity of distinguishing himself was permitted to escape; his name carried with it the assurance of service being brilliantly executed wherever it became his duty to be present.

In detailing the events of the occasion on which the army lost this really promising officer, Lord Wellington has paid the following tribute to his merits.

"At three in the morning of the 8th, we had the misfortune to lose the Honourable Major Cocks, of the 79th, who was field-officer of the trenches, and was killed in the act of rallying the troops who had been driven in. I have frequently had occasion to draw attention to the conduct of Major Cocks, and in one instance very recently, in the attack of the hornwork of the castle of Burgos, and I consider his loss as one of the greatest importance to this army, and to His Majesty's service."

Colonel Jones, of the engineers, was severely wounded in conducting the arrangements for the assault of the third or outer line, on the morning of the 4th of October.

In his excellent work, *The Sieges in Spain*, Colonel Jones mentions the singular difference in feeling occasioned from wounds inflicted by grape-shot, to those of any other species of missile used in modern warfare. After detailing what occurred during the night of the 25th September, he states:—

> It was remarked here, as it had been on former occasions, that a wound from a grape-shot is less quietly borne than a wound from a round-shot or musketry. The latter is seldom known in the night except from the falling of the individual; whereas the former not unfrequently draws forth loud lamentations.

On the night of the 20th October, the siege of Burgos was raised, the covering army retired, and the whole force marched in the direction of the Duero.

The "Army of Portugal," once more become effective and powerful, outnumbered the allied divisions under the immediate direction of Lord Wellington. The disposition of his force and that of the enemy no longer admitted of carrying on operations so widely extended; or of continuing so distant from each other as were the corps of the commander-in-chief and that under Sir Rowland Hill. The object in gaining possession of the castle of Burgos, was more to destroy the great *dépôt* for the enemy's "Army of Portugal," than from any importance attaching to the work itself, it being in reality of little consequence with reference to the general success of the allies. But, al- though the French armies now had it in their power to transfer the scene of action from that part of Old Castille, and Burgos consequently became removed from the line of operations, Lord Wellington with reluctance abandoned an object, for the attainment of which the army had made such unwearied exertions.

On the arrival of the Duke of Dalmatia, with the "Army of the South," seventy thousand men were assembled at Valencia, in readiness to march, and recover possession of the capital. From the moment this great reunion of force was known at Madrid, the public mind became agitated; constant reports of military operations that never occurred, doubtful opinions as to the stability of the allied power in the capital, an anxious desire on the part of persons in the interest of Joseph Bonaparte to witness the arrival of the French troops, all denoted the approach of more interesting events and unsettled times, than for six weeks past had agitated the numerous, divided, and, upon occasions, turbulent population of the Spanish metropolis.

The Duke of Dalmatia was, under these circumstances, the leader in whom the French party appeared to have the greatest reliance. The King, Marshal Jourdan, and the Duke of Albufera, were unnoticed. The question usually put, in a significant tone and manner, bespeaking a sup- pressed opinion that we had better prepare for removal, was "*Unde esta Soult?*"

Although the favourite marshal had commenced his march on the 15th of September, it was not before the 23rd of the following month, that, united with the "Army of the Centre," he appeared on the bank of the Tagus. This loss of valuable time was in some measure occasioned by the spirited resistance of a small body of Spaniards garrisoning the castle of Chinchilla, which place it was considered of importance to reduce, before proceeding towards the capital. The arrival of the enemy's army occasioned the British force then on the left bank of the Tagus being withdrawn; Sir Rowland Hill, to cover Madrid, placed the troops in position on the River Jarama, having his headquarters at Cienpozuelos.

The army, under his command, on this occasion, was numerous, and highly appointed in every arm. It comprised the Light, 2nd, 3rd, and 4th divisions of infantry; the Portuguese division, under General Hamilton; the Spanish corps of General Morillo; the cavalry of Sir William Erskine; and General Victor Alten's brigade of Light dragoons.

Had the continued successful progress of the war permitted that a trial of strength should take place on the Jarama, nothing under a very powerful army could have driven back the allied force above enumerated. But events had greatly altered the situation of the contending armies: the delay occasioned by the protracted defence of Burgos, the evacuation of Andalusia by the French troops, and the concentration for the recovering possession of the capital, rendered it absolutely necessary to yield to circumstances, and that Sir Rowland Hill should retire, and join Lord Wellington's army in the north.

The reasons for raising the siege of the castle of Burgos appearing conclusive, and the "Army of Portugal," now reinforced, superior in numbers, and pressing on the allied force, rendering a change of operations necessary, during the night of the 21st of October, Lord Wellington crossed the Arlanzon, and at five o'clock on the morning of the 22nd, the rear-guards were retired. This movement was so judiciously conducted, that the enemy was in ignorance of the final march of the allies from before the place until the evening, when his whole army, amounting to thirty thousand infantry, a large body of cavalry, including twelve hundred *gens-d'armes à cheval*, with one hundred pieces of artillery, passed the river, and advanced in pursuit.

On the following day, the right of the allies marched to Torquemada, and the left to Cordovillas. The enemy's army pressed forward rapidly; having frequent encounters with the rear-guard and the guerilla corps marching on the flanks of the allied troops. On one occasion, the partisan soldiers of Don Julian Sanchez, having been defeated, rode back towards the flank of the rear-guard of General Anson's brigade of light cavalry, and some squadrons of the enemy, following up in pursuit, intermixed with the British dragoons before they were aware of the immediate presence of the French cavalry. This produced some confusion, occasioning also a delay before they became disengaged, that enabled the enemy to bring up a superior force. He was charged by General Anson and General Bock's brigades, near the Venta del Poso, but without success.

The British and German cavalry yielding to numbers and to the *élite* of the French Army,—for the *gens-d'armerie* composed a considerable part of the force engaged,—were forced back upon the light battalions of the German Legion, commanded by Colonel Halkett. These regiments, being formed into squares, repelled the repeated charges made against them; stood unshaken, occasioning great loss to their opponents; and, as is generally the case when service is really well performed, suffered in a comparatively trifling degree.

On the 24th, the army arrived on the Carrion, having its right at Dueñas, and left at Villa Muriel. During the following day, the enemy crossed the river; but were attacked, and driven back by the 5th division, then under the command of General Oswald. Some Spanish troops co-operated in this attack on the enemy, and in the act of rallying a regiment that had given way, General Alava was severely wounded.

Don Miguel Ricardo de Alava, a naval officer, and nephew to the admiral of that name, who was second in command of the Spanish fleet at Trafalgar, had served, as is customary in the Spanish service, with rank in the army corresponding to that held in the other profession. He was consequently a major-general, had long been at the British head-quarters, and enjoyed the confidence of Lord Wellington.

Brave, active, and intelligent, General Alava was a universal favourite with those officers of the allied army who were fortunate enough to form his acquaintance; his subsequent manly and honourable conduct, during the unfortunate struggles of his devoted country, give him an additional claim to respect from all parties, whatever their political sentiments may have been.

The allied army crossed the Pisuerga at Cabezon on the 26th. On the following day, during a cannonade, Colonel Robe, a very distinguished officer of artillery, was severely wounded.

General Souham passed the Carrion on the 27th, forming his army on the heights near Cigales; on the 28th, he extended his right, manoeuvring in that direction, and intending, if possible, to force across the Pisuerga by the bridges of Simancas and Valladolid. These bridges were defended by the 7th division, under Lord Dalhousie, who had recently joined the army, and been appointed to its command.

Colonel Halkett, with his brigade, encountered the enemy at Simancas, but being overpowered, he exploded the bridge, and retired. The passage of the Pisuerga thus secured from the enemy, Lord Wellington crossed the Duero, on the 29th, by the bridges of Puente de Duero and Tudela, both of which were subsequently destroyed, as also those at Cabezon, Valladolid, Tordesillas, and Quintanilla.

On the 30th, Lord Wellington placed his army in position on the heights between Rueda and Tordesillas. The enemy had worked diligently at the repair of the bridge, and the position of both armies made it probable that the future line of operations would be similar to that adopted by the allies and the army of the Duke of Ragusa previously to the battle of Salamanca. At all events, the British general had secured his uninterrupted retreat upon Salamanca.

The day on which the army from Burgos arrived at Rueda, it was announced to the troops in or near to Madrid, that an immediate change of quarters would take place; and, on the following morning, the whole, having passed from out the capital by the Puerta de San Vicente, moved, in one column, upon the great route towards the Escorial. During the halt, which took place on the 1st of November,

I accompanied General Pakenham to visit the palace, the most extensive building we had ever seen, rendered more impressive from being surrounded with all the gloom of the wildest mountain scenery.

The Escorial, seated at the base of the Sierra de Malagon, forming a bold and rugged portion of the line of mountain embracing the chain extending from the Sierra de Avila to that of the Carpentanos, is very romantically situated: the venerable trees growing in luxuriance, and displaying their natural beauties, are in majesty corresponding to the magnificent edifice which they surround and adorn.

The desolation that had overtaken the Convent Palace, and the wild aspect of the neglected and deserted grounds, added to the solemn grandeur of the scene; nothing could be more impressive than were, at this time, both the exterior and the innumerable spacious apartments of the ruined Escorial. The proud trappings of the Bourbon Palace; the rich and gorgeous spoils of South America; the decorations of the great convent chapel; the well-stored refectory; the splendid gallery, containing the noblest specimens of the Italian and Spanish schools;—all had vanished. The Madonna of Raffaelle, the Sebastian del Piombo, the Venus of Velasquez, no longer graced its walls.

The mausoleum of the royal family alone remained perfect. We descended into this splendid pantheon, and stood by the sarcophagus containing the ashes of the Emperor Charles V. The remains of the Spanish monarchs are deposited in urns composed of black marble, supported on claws of bronze; these are formed with great simplicity and plainness, the name of the personage whose ashes it contains being inscribed on the front of each in golden characters. The wantonness of French spoliation had not visited this grand cemetery.

Passing from the pantheon, we visited the galleries, the cells, apartments of state, the cloisters, terraces, the chapels, and spacious courts of this immense edifice,—all had been appropriated to the accommodation of troops. Cavalry horses had occupied the lower portion of the building, while the blackened walls and scathed floorings of the apartments, proved the frequent fires lighted within them to cheer the sojourns of French infantry.

On the 2nd of November, the army from Madrid resumed its march to the north. The whole force had now been assembled in one column, and proceeded to ascend the Guadarama mountain.

At the Escorial, Sir Rowland Hill did me the honour to request I would act as his *aide-de*-camp during the progress of the retreat. I consequently joined his headquarters, and accompanied him over the pass, arriving in the evening at Espinar, where he remained for the night.

The army continued its march during the 3rd, without being molested by the pursuit of the enemy, headquarters being established at Labajos. On the morning of the 4th, was ordered to remain with General Cole, who commanded the rear-guard of the army, until he received certain information of the enemy's motions; and about ten o'clock in the forenoon I left Labajos, with intelligence of his having passed the Guadarama and driven in the cavalry posts at Villacastin.

When Marshal Soult entered Madrid, and ascertained the recent movement of the allies, he determined to march instantly in pursuit; and so earnest was he in urging this movement, that he directed the "Army of the South" not to enter the capital, but, defiling along the banks of the Manzanares, that it should take the direct route for the Guadarama.

At three o'clock on the morning of the 5th, Sir Rowland, having received intelligence that the enemy's armies were rapidly advancing on his rear, ordered me to proceed without delay to the head-quarters of Lord Wellington at Rueda, and communicate to his Lordship the course of events on the Aduja. I was immediately on horseback, and from Villanueva de Gomez, passing through Arevalo, arrived at ten o'clock, after travelling a distance of fifty-two miles.

I found Lord Wellington inhabiting a very indifferent quarter in the village of Rueda, but, notwithstanding the reverse he had sustained, apparently in the same excellent spirits, the same collected, clear, distinct frame of mind, that never varied or forsook him during the numberless embarrassing events and anxious occasions that naturally occurred to agitate a commander during the long and arduous struggle which he conducted with such firmness and judgment.

After questioning me on the local situation of the several divisions of Sir Rowland Hill's corps, and the points to which the enemy's army had advanced, his lordship wrote a despatch, directing me to deliver it with the least possible delay. Having been instructed by the General that I should find his headquarters during that night at Fontiveros, I posted by Medina del Campo, arriving at the former in the evening, after being absent fifteen hours, and having performed a journey of eighty-eight miles.

The weather, during the 6th, was particularly favourable. Cantaracilla became Sir Rowland's headquarters; and on the following day his army arrived at Alba de Tormes.

Never was a retreat conducted with less confusion, or more trifling annoyance from a pursuing enemy, than that of the allies from Madrid to the Tormes. The marches were not of excessive length, nor did the French troops come up with or harass the infantry; only the rear-guards of cavalry were engaged, and that very slightly.

On the morning of the 8th, during a storm of wind and rain, the light, 3rd, and 4th divisions, the guards, and Colonel Skerret's brigade from Cadiz, with Sir William Erskine's division of cavalry, defiled across the Tormes by the bridge of Alba. On the same day, the army of Lord Wellington from Burgos arrived on the San Christoval position in front of Salamanca.

General Hill, with his staff, remained during the day in Alba, receiving constant reports of the enemy's approach. On the following morning, he learned that a French marshal had reached Cantalpinos, and was marching troops from thence towards the fords of the Tormes. Sir Rowland ordered me to proceed with a patrol of cavalry, for the purpose of ascertaining this movement. When near to Babilafuente, a column appeared descending from the height on which that village is situated, directly towards the fords near to Huerta. Continuing in observation of this advance, to ascertain the description of force of which it was composed, upon perceiving that a brigade of cavalry was accompanied by infantry and artillery, I considered it important to proceed direct to Lord Wellington.

Having, therefore, written a note to Sir Rowland Hill, and directed the dragoons to return with it to Alba, I set forward alone, and, urging my horse, rode the twelve miles in an hour. The commander of the forces immediately proceeded to the height above Aldea Lengua, commanding a view of the plains extending towards Alba, and from whence the enemy's movements towards the river were perceptible. In returning by its left bank, I met Sir Rowland, who, with the 2nd division, excepting the brigade of General Howard, was marching to prevent the passage of the enemy by the Encinas and Huerta fords.

The allied army, now assembled on the Tormes, with its headquarters in Salamanca, was the most numerous Lord Wellington had yet collected under his immediate command during the war. It was composed of nine divisions of infantry, exclusive of the Spanish corps acting with it, of about six thousand cavalry, and from sixty to seventy pieces of cannon. To this numerous and brilliant force was opposed the united troops of the enemy, composing the armies of the "South," under the Duke of Dalmatia; that of the "Centre," commanded by Marshal Jourdan; and of "Portugal" and the "North," by Generals

Souham and Caffarelli; the whole being under the nominal control of Joseph Bonaparte, ninety thousand strong, including ten thousand cavalry, and accompanied by two hundred pieces of artillery.

In the course of the 10th, the enemy's whole army appeared on the Tormes; on his left was Marshal Soult, who pressed forward to force the allies from Alba, and obtain possession of the bridge. Twenty pieces of ordnance opened upon the devoted town; shells descending, crashed through the roofs of the houses, showers of balls swept along the streets, while occasional parties of *voltigeurs*, rushing forward, endeavoured to avail themselves of the consternation they supposed must have resulted from the bombardment to which the town had been subjected. They were invariably met, and bayoneted back.

General Howard, and the brave regiments of his brigade, were neither to be intimidated by noise, nor forced from their posts by the desultory attacks of French *voltigeurs*; and the enemy's general, spectator to this violent assault on the open and unsheltered quarters of three British regiments, ordered back the troops employed, and desisted from the hopeless attempt of gaining possession of the place without bringing on a much more serious affair. It is only necessary to mention, that the regiments in Alba were the 50th, commanded by Colonel Stewart; the 71st, by Colonel Cadagon; and the 92nd, by Colonel Cameron, to account for the gallant repulse of the enemy on the above occasion.

Although the French Marshal retired his artillery, and a large portion of the infantry that had appeared in the immediate vicinity of the town on the preceding evening, he continued to support a constant fire of light troops, both during the night and on the morning of the 11th. About eight o'clock, I was sent into Alba to ascertain the state of affairs, and convey the report of General Hamilton to Sir Rowland Hill. I found the troops posted in the way best calculated to derive shelter from the ruined houses. The effects of the cannonade were everywhere visible; but as the enemy had now ceased to fire artillery on the town, the number of casualties had much decreased; the soldiers obtaining cover and protection from the musketry fire, which was still kept up with considerable spirit. Having been assured by General Hamilton that he had no doubt of maintaining his post, and that he had not suffered so much as might have been expected, I rejoined the General on the heights above Carpio.

On the afternoon of the 11th, a numerous staff visited the enemy's quarters, and reconnoitred the fords of the river. From the honours paid by the troops, we conjectured that the *soi-disant* king, accompanied by the marshals and senior officers, was present. When the escort approached the several cantonments the bands played, and the troops got under arms; while the distinctly heard roll of drums denoted the compliments paid to the higher ranks of the French Army.

No visible alteration of position or movement had taken place in the enemy's army, when, early on the 12th, Lord Wellington arrived on the heights opposite to Alba, and from thence closely examined the line of country and situation of the French troops. From the town of Alba, extending up the right bank of the Tormes, is one continued dense forest, as far as the eye can reach. It being possible that, under cover of this wood, a concealed movement might have taken place, and the right flank of the allies be thereby turned, Lord Wellington ordered me to proceed and ascertain whether any of the French troops had marched to their left, or crossed unperceived. In the execution of this service, he desired me to take a patrol of the 13th Light Dragoons, and, ascending the river as far as Salvatierra, cross over and come down on the enemy's bivouacs, in the direction of Alba, feeling my way, until the extension or not of his troops was ascertained.

At Salvatierra, the only intelligence to be obtained of the enemy was of a negative description, namely, that none of his troops had passed at or near to that place. I therefore crossed the Tormes, and, following a road through the centre of the forest above mentioned, advanced towards the village of Galinduste. When near to that place we met a peasant, who, on being questioned, stated that he had seen French cavalry there in the morning, but they had, he believed, since retired. As it was a matter of doubt, I considered it advisable, before proceeding, to send him into the town, thereby ascertaining the fact.

Not being confident in the integrity of the person thus employed, the moment he had disappeared, I struck off the road, desiring the men of the 13th to remain quiet among the nearest trees. If the Spaniard returned alone, of course we should then discover ourselves if accompanied, we might penetrate into the recesses of the wood. In a brief space of time, the Spaniard again appeared, informing me of the enemy having left Galinduste, and retired in the direction of Alba.

From the *alcalde*, I learned that no French force had passed through his town, nor had any troops moved towards the upper line of the Tormes. This was so far satisfactory; but, determined still further to ascertain whether any movement to his left had occurred, taking a guide from Galinduste, we pushed forward in the direction of Alba without obstruction, or meeting any of the enemy's patrols, until arrived within two leagues of that place, and consequently at a short distance from the left of the French Army. It was neither safe nor necessary to advance further; therefore, in the middle of the night, I forded the Tormes, and, having left ray escort at the quarters of General Long, rode direct for Salamanca, there to inform Lord Wellington as to the result of my observations.

It was reported on the 13th, that the enemy was preparing to pass the Tormes by the fords above Alba: but during the day no movement to that effect was observable.

On the following morning, I was ordered to the heights above Carpio, there to watch the line of the river, and report the enemy's motions hourly to Lord Wellington: it was no longer doubted that he would cross the Tormes, and come on the right flank of the allied army. Upon arriving at the high ground, from whence what was passing in the valley became distinctly observable, I perceived troops crossing over. From that time the French Army denied without intermission. Apparently, the fords were of a description not admitting of very rapid passage. The infantry moved across temporary truckle bridges, in single files; while the cavalry and artillery forded the stream a short distance higher up its course.

The moment Lord Wellington had ascertained the passage of the river, he marched the 2nd division, under General Chowne, and all the cavalry within his reach, to attack the troops already crossed; but the force now arrived on the left bank was too numerous, and had become too firmly posted, to admit of any impression being made by the portion of the allied army thus brought against it: and his Lordship desisted from any serious attack, confining his operations to cannonading the columns of cavalry within his reach. The whole cavalry of the "Army of the South" had passed the river; General Bonnemain's brigade was on the right, and with it was Marshal Soult. The infantry were formed on the strong line of heights near to Mozarbes, and the undisputed passage of the Tormes, by the whole of the enemy's army, was secured.

Under these circumstances, it became absolutely necessary to assemble without delay the allied army on the left bank of the river. Orders were, consequently, despatched to the divisions on the San Christoval position, and to the Portuguese brigades of Generals Pack and Bradford, at Aldea Lengua and Cabrerizos, to cross the river, and move to the ground near to the Arapiles.

The morning of the 15th dawned on the allied army occupying the field of its former glory. Sir Edward Paget, with the 1st division, was on the right at Aldea Tejada, near to the spot from whence General Pakenham and the 3rd division marched to commence the battle of Salamanca. The 2nd division, composed of ten British battalions, strong in numbers, and brilliant in appearance, looked forward with anxiety to a struggle on that field, where, on a former occasion, the rest of the army had been so successfully engaged. It was formed in line at the base of the Arapiles, and its ranks looked impenetrable.

Early in the morning, the commander of the forces and Sir Rowland Hill were on the heights, from whence an extensive view of the plain to the right and left is to be obtained: in front, the uneven nature of the ground, it being also partially covered with wood, obstructed the prospect, and concealed the enemy's position. Everything appearing quiet, Lord Wellington mounted on horseback, and galloped forward to reconnoitre.

The morning had been tempestuous to a degree, the wind blew with violence, and it rained heavily. We were anxiously pacing along the summit of the ridge, a great number of staff-officers being there assembled, awaiting the presence of the commander-in-chief, when, through the mist and drizzling rain, he was perceived rapidly returning to the Arapiles. The curiosity of all was greatly excited to know the result of his observation, and what probably would occur. Being with Sir Rowland Hill when his Lordship came up, I heard his communication to him, as also his opinion of the hopeless prospect that any direct movement against us would be attempted. Orders were soon after issued for the removal of everything from Salamanca, and that the army should march towards the Valmusa.

It is impossible to conceive more unfavourable weather for the commencement of a retreat: the roads had become extremely deep from the effects of the great quantity of rain that had fallen; nor did there appear the slightest prospect of alteration in the cold, damp, boisterous season that had set in. Notwithstanding, the army retired without confusion. That the change of circumstances, so rapidly produced by the French general's manoeuvring to cut off the communication of the allies with Ciudad Rodrigo, did not occasion great difficulty, where the encumbrances of so large an army, and an extensive *dépôt*, had to be withdrawn from such a town as Salamanca, and put in immediate line of march, proved the excellent arrangement of its commander.

When afterwards with the French Army, I was questioned by its officers, whether the removal from Salamanca, and suddenly decided upon retreat, had not been attended with confusion or inconvenience; and when replied to in the negative, they were loud in praise of Lord Wellington's qualities as a general.

Having crossed the Valmusa by different routes, the allied army, on the night of the 15th, bivouacked in the extensive woods on its northern bank. The troops were without cover, and drenched with rain. The following morning the march was resumed: the enemy following with a large body of cavalry and infantry, but without attempting to make any serious impression even against the rear of the army.

On the 17th, the enemy's cavalry and horse artillery appeared on the heights to the right, and domineering the passage of the River Huebra at San Muñoz; from thence they cannonaded the light division, occasioning considerable loss. Towards evening, an extraordinary event occurred, namely, the second in command of the army being taken prisoner on the line of march between two divisions of the troops. To account for the possibility of this happening, it is necessary to describe the nature of the country through which the army was retiring. A broad and level road is, in most parts, conducted through forests of ilex, obscuring a prospect of the surrounding scenery, and presenting to sight only the dark foliage of the trees, or portions of the route extending from one turn to another, so that to travellers those persons within a very limited distance are alone perceptible.

The extreme depth of the road, and inclement state of the weather, at this particular time, had occasioned a space to intervene between the line of march of the 5th and 7th divisions; anxious to restore the compact order of the column, Sir Edward Paget proceeded to the rear of the leading division, and before he met the head of the next body of infantry, a detachment of light cavalry rushed from the wood, and carried him off, soon becoming lost to observation in its recesses. Had the enemy's cavalry acted with enterprise and judgment, these woods might have afforded opportunities of prosecuting more extensive annoyance to the retreating army, their motions being completely concealed until arrived close upon the flanks of the passing column.

The only occasion on which I have ever seen French troops press upon the rear of a British force, as if they were not restrained by some feeling of respect for those retiring, was at Castrejon and in the valley of Canizal, during Marshal Marmont's advance, previous to the Battle of Salamanca.

The column under the orders of Sir Rowland Hill was, on the evening of the 18th, encamped on the banks of a rivulet near to the village of Tenebron. At daybreak on the following morning, I was on horseback, with orders to put in motion the 3rd, 4th, and General Hamilton's divisions of the army; after which, returning to Tenebron, I accompanied the General to Ciudad Rodrigo, where Lord Wellington had established his headquarters. The retreat, thus concluded, had been attended with considerable hardship to the troops, not so much from the excessive length of the marches, as the particularly unfavourable state of the weather, the scarcity of provisions, and wretched quality of the roads, rendered, by the violent rains and the numerous carriages of every description passing along them, almost impassable.

The soldiers, throughout the march from the Tormes to the Agueda, had been very scantily and irregularly supplied with provisions, frequently obtaining no other subsistence than that afforded by the chestnuts which grew in profusion during the whole progress of the route. Forage for the horses was also extremely scarce, and difficult to be procured. Although attached to the staff of an officer commanding a column of the army, when we arrived at Ciudad Rodrigo, the horses I had brought in the highest condition from Madrid were reduced to a nearly unserviceable state. Before concluding the memoranda noted from recollections of this retreat, the only one during the campaigns in the Peninsula that can be compared with that of Sir John Moore in 1809, I shall briefly state what appear to me the most striking difference in their features, and may, in some measure, lead to a correct estimate of the relative dangers and hardships of each.

The season was decidedly more unfavourable, and the cold more intense, during the campaign in Gallicia, than in the close of that just narrated; but unusual severity of weather also prevailed during the latter.

The country through which Lord Wellington moved was incomparably more dangerous, more susceptible of affording scope for manoeuvre and the harassment of a retreating force, than that from Astorga to Coruña; lateral roads branched off in every direction; cavalry could act in all parts of the country; there were no mountain positions to defend; nor were the flanks of the retiring columns ever secure.

The roads in both cases were excessively bad, but, from its formation, the flat country, and clay soil through which it was conducted, the one just travelled was the most fatiguing and least passable.

The marches in the latter case were never of an unreasonable length, consequently within the scope of the physical powers of every class of soldiers.

During the retreat in Gallicia, the troops were never so long without a supply of provisions as some corps of Lord Wellington's army on the present occasion. In conclusion, Lord Wellington possessed two essential advantages; first, in the experience of his army; inured to campaigning, the troops had learned to neutralise difficulties, and instead of sinking under, to combat hardships. They had also, from habit and success, ceased to contemplate the French soldiers with opinions of their invincibility; and without questioning the proved bravery of Sir John Moore's army, it will not be denied, that in 1812, British troops learned the approach of the enemy's cavalry with very different sensations from those created in 1809 by the appearance of his hussars and *chasseurs* when galloping along the Camino-real, leading to Bembibre or to Calcabelos; not that they were then met with wavering or undecided conduct, but the practice of habitual warfare can alone make men view conflict with enemies either with indifference or as a familiar occurrence.

Arrived on the Agueda, the campaign was ended. The French Army had desisted from pursuit, and the allied force was immediately sent into cantonments.

Sir Rowland Hill fixed his headquarters, on the night of the 19th, at the village of Zamarra, where he remained until the 21st, marching on that day to Robleda, a town gloomily situated in a wild, uncultivated country, to the north of the Sierra de Gata. On the 28th, Sir Rowland marched to cross the *sierra*, and descend into Spanish Estremadura. The road over the mountain-pass is steep and rugged, conducted in many places between rocks, impracticable for carriages, and only adapted for foot passengers and the mules of the country.

The scenery, on descending the southern declivity of the sierra, becomes very delightful and picturesque; the town of Gata, situated near to its base, and embosomed in wood, although insignificant in extent or population, looks cheerful and prosperous.

In the valley advanced from Gata, elevated on precipitous and commanding ground, stands the ruined castle of Santivaños el Alto. Rising from the surrounding plain, encircled by the windings of a river, and surmounting grounds shaded by the noblest trees, there are few situations in any country more strikingly beautiful, or more dignified by natural advantages, than the castle of Santivaños.

On the 29th, we halted at Moraleja, and on the 30th, Sir Rowland established his headquarters at Coria.

I have omitted to notice in its proper place the circumstance of General Ballesteros, actuated by feelings of jealousy and dislike to the idea of foreign control, having disobeyed the orders of the Regency, by which he was directed to consider Lord Wellington as general-in-chief of the Spanish armies, and report to him accordingly. The first indication of his resistance was continuing inactive, instead of marching his army to harass the flank of the enemy, advancing from Valencia to Madrid.

That such a feeling could or did exist in the breast of many Spanish officers, alike ignorant and self-conceited, is not a matter of wonder; but that so intelligent and useful a person as General Ballesteros had proved himself, should permit childish personal feeling to obstruct the important execution of his duty, appears inexplicable. Had this circumstance occurred during times of comparative tranquillity, however much the disobedience must have been reprehensible, there might have arisen by possibility some excuse; but in the present case, not only to paralyse the operations of the army under his command, but endanger the success of a campaign, by deranging a part of the system on which it was to be conducted, bespoke a weakness and erring judgment inconsistent with his previously distinguished conduct. This pertinacity was deservedly punished by deportation from the command of the army of Andalusia, and imprisonment in the fortress of Ceuta.

Both armies were now in cantonments; the allies gaining strength, unmolested, and perfecting in discipline, in health, and equipment; the enemy constantly subjected to predatory warfare, harassed by civil and military enemies, daily reducing in numbers, with but slight prospects of reinforcement.

Thus the period of cessation from active warfare was attended with very opposite results to the parties soon again to engage in the great struggle, now in the fifth year of its endurance.

Lord Wellington's headquarters were once more established at Fuenteguinaldo, on the left bank of the Agueda. Valladolid had become the principal station of the "Army of Portugal." Joseph Bonaparte returned to Madrid. The headquarters of the "Army of the Centre," commanded by Comte D'Erlon, were at Arganda, his troops occupying the environs of the capital and the country towards Guadalaxara.

Marshal the Duke of Dalmatia, with the "Army of the South," cantoned in the valley of the Tagus and in La Mancha, had his headquarters in Toledo, his advanced guard and light cavalry being stationed at Daimiel, Almagro, Manzanares, and Villarubia, de los Ojos.

View near Payo

CHAPTER 6

Battle of Vittoria

During this period of inactivity, Lord Wellington visited Cadiz, for the purpose of personally communicating with the Spanish Government, on assuming the command of the Spanish armies, and, to adjust the arrangements for prosecuting the successful and decisive campaign he afterwards made. In travelling across the country from the banks of the Agueda to Andalusia, passing near to Coria, he took the opportunity of inspecting various battalions of Sir Rowland Hill's corps. At Cadiz, his reception was of a very flattering description; his entrance was expected with the most enthusiastic anxiety, the highest authorities of the country meeting him on his route, and conducting him in triumph along the ramparts that had been prepared for the uninterrupted passage of the *cortège* assembled to do honour to the British general.

Accustomed, in their own country, and from the habits of the French marshals, to find a commander-in-chief placing much importance in outward show or gaudy parade, the Spanish Regency and members of Cortes met with surprise the great leader of the allied army, accompanied by Lord Fitzroy Somerset, and one orderly dragoon! They had the good sense to form a still higher opinion of the man, from this habitual simplicity of appearance; his uncompromising mind, great military talent, and undaunted firmness of purpose, affording more substantial claims to respect than are to be derived from the trappings not unfrequently displayed to withdraw attention from the vacancy or insignificance that reigns within.

The presence of Lord Wellington occasioned in the town of Cadiz an uninterrupted series of *fêtes*: the government, the army, the Spanish nobility, all were emulous to testify their respect and attachment.

The *grandees* of Spain, most of whom the circumstances of the war, and occupation of their estates by the French armies, had compelled to adopt the town of Cadiz as a temporary asylum, gave a, *fête* on the occasion, which was celebrated with unusual splendour. On that night, in the centre of the beauty and the chivalry of Spain, the Duque de Frias rose, and addressed the following *Soneto*, composed by himself, to the illustrious guest, whom they recognised with pride and satisfaction as the Duque de Ciudad Rodrigo.

> *Soneto.*
> *Vuelves, O Duque, a la sangrienta arena,*
> *A la arena de honor, que al Galo espanta,*
> *De la gloria immortal morada santa,*
> *Y de las huellas de tus triunfos llena.*
> *Cierra, vence, destroza; y en cadenas*
> *Del Vandalo el poder hunda tu planta,*
> *Ese torpe padron de infamia tanta,*
> *Y el Aguila Imperial arroja al Seina.*
> *En tanto empero que el pendon Britano*
> *Por ti en el trono de las Lises brilla,*
> *Unido al Espanol, y al Lusitano,*
> *La ofrenda admite que con fe sencilla*
> *Hoy a la faz dal pueblo Gaditano*
> *Te dan 'los ricos hombres de Castilla.*'[1]

Translation:
Thou returnest, O Duke! to the ensanguined arena: to the field of honour, theatre of Gallic dismay, and of thy undying glory; on every part of which thy triumphant path hath left enduring and hallowed traces. Close with the foe, conquer and destroy him. Low in the dust, let thy heel trample on the enchained Vandal's power, the patron of infamy and crime, and to her native Seine beat back the Imperial Eagle.
While for thee Britannia's banner, united with Spain and Lusitania's, floats with brilliant lustre over the throne of the Lilies, accept the offering of respect which this day, with unaffected faith and zeal, is given in presence of the people of Cadiz by "The Nobles of Castille."

From amidst these demonstrations of respect and attachment, Lord Wellington again proceeded to his army, which was daily gaining strength, and in active preparation for the great campaign that ensued, and which decided the Peninsular War.

Sir Rowland Hill's headquarters continued at Coria; where great

---
1. The ancient designation of the Spanish *grandees*.

sameness rendered this period of inaction very uninteresting: no excitement of any description occurred; day after day passed without the slightest variation of incident, the natural dullness of the town adding to the *ennui* of this tiresome life. At length, after having experienced the kindness and hospitality of the general for six weeks, I was ordered to La Mancha, to communicate information of the movements of Joseph Bonaparte and the Duke of Dalmatia.

The evening of the 7th of January I passed at Ceclavin, with Colonel Leith and the officers of the 31st regiment: crossing the Tagus by the Barca de Consejo on the following morning, and arriving at Brozas, the headquarters of the cavalry division of Sir William Erskine; from thence, the route passing through Caceres, I visited the Marques de Santa Marta, and at Truxillo, received from General Morillo letters for the Spanish authorities, whom it was probable I should encounter on my route.

General Morillo, with all his roughness and his ignorance, was an enthusiastic admirer of everything English. Throughout the whole course of his various services during the war, he evinced a strong and marked feeling of attachment and respect for the troops of that country. He had raised himself from the lowest ranks by his enter- prising courage and cordial exertion in forwarding every scheme or measure calculated, as he conceived, to resist French domination. He had obtained considerable authority over the division of Spaniards under his immediate orders; his courage was undoubted, his devotion to Sir Rowland Hill, with whom he had long served, unbounded. Under these circumstances, this officer, in most respects a very ordinary man, became known to the army, and his name identified with some degree of distinction.

General Morillo is one of those instances where an individual may give a false impression of higher powers, until elevated beyond the rank of respectably exercising subordinate command, and placed in supreme authority. When left to his own resources, he alternately exhibited the harshness and iron hand of weakness, or the vacillating decision of inferior talent raised beyond its sphere, until, in a political crisis of his country, he descended to the insignificance from whence he had so adventitiously arisen.

On the 15th, I was at Guadalupe; at Castelblanco on the 17th; the 18th, at Anchuras; at Navalucillas on the 19th; and on the 21st returned to Castelblanco, after having travelled over many intricate bad roads, in the dreary mountains of Toledo.

Seated with the *cura* of Anchuras, and discussing the popular topics of the day, I had the satisfaction of seeing Lord Tweeddale enter. Tired of the monotony of inactive life, he had followed my path into the mountains, and in search of that professional variety in which he delighted, determined to dedicate a short space of time in wandering about the neighbouring quarters of the enemy.

On the 23rd, we again returned to Guadalupe, a large and populous town, situated in the centre of the sierra bearing that name; deriving its importance from the extensive and opulent monastery, formerly the object of many a pilgrimage; and from its local situation, fortunate enough to have escaped the devastation attending French visitation to most buildings of a similar class throughout the Spanish territory.

The friars of the order San Geronimo, in number upwards of one hundred, are very richly endowed. The building is spacious; the image of "*Nuestra Señora de Guadalupe,*" to whose shrine kings and princes, from most of the countries of Europe, have for ages performed pilgrimages, filled the coffers of the convent; by the powerful influence of her assistance, encouraging others to adopt the salutary expedient of invoking that aid, which was never done without an offering proportioned to the means of the suppliant for her favourable consideration.

This celebrated image is placed in a recess above the altar of the convent chapel. The town of Guadalupe is very irregularly built, the streets dirty and ill paved, and the inhabitants of an inferior order; it has the appearance of being constructed solely for the convenience of the convent, and is the largest town I had yet seen in Spain of that description.

Having ascertained that Guadalupe was too remote a station to expect any very authentic information of the enemy's movements, we resolved to proceed nearer to the quarters of Marshal Soult's army, and, on the 27th, were at Alias; on the 28th, at Castelblanco; on the following day, crossed the Guadiana, and entering the province of La Mancha, passed the night in the village of Aguda; were at Saceruela on the 30th, and on the 31st, at Abenojar.

On the 2nd of February, Lord Tweeddale and myself proceeded towards Corral de Calatrava, in which town resided one of those partisan officers from whom General Morillo had been accustomed to receive information, and who was now instructed to assist me in learning the movements executed by the enemy's troops. When arrived within half a league of Corral, we received intelligence of its being occupied by a detachment of French cavalry, and consequently struck off the main road; and, directed by the Spanish Captain Calvo, followed the mountain tracks leading to the castle of Calavassos, situated on an eminence overhanging the Guadiana.

Having adopted measures of precaution for receiving timely notice of the enemy's approach, we became inhabitants of the castle for the night, and at daybreak, on the morning of the 3rd, rode to a height overlooking Corral, from whence we could discover the departure of its visitors, who, about noon, marched in the direction of Ciudad Real. When they had sallied forth we mounted and entered the town, but were soon apprised of the reappearance of the enemy; and, upon ascending a slight acclivity to the westward, observed about thirty of the enemy's *chasseurs à cheval* advancing towards the village at a rapid pace. They patrolled through the street, and some pistol-shots were exchanged with those most advanced. Having questioned its inhabitants regarding the detachment that had passed the night in Corral, these horsemen again departed, adopting the same route as their companions had previously done, and we saw them no more.

Distributed over the face of the country as the enemy's foraging parties evidently were, it became, absolutely necessary to advance with caution, ascertaining the direction in which we were least likely to encounter the detachments of cavalry constantly in motion, at the same time hovering about the neighbourhood of his quarters, and thereby arriving at a knowledge of his precise situation and movements.

On the 4th, we arrived at Valverde, with the intention of penetrating still further into La Mancha, but were informed by the *alcalde*, that the French were in Ciudad Real, which being distant only six miles, it was considered advisable to change our route; and, in consequence, continuing on the right bank of the Guadiana, we entered the large and populous village of Piedrabuena.

Resolving to visit Andalusia, Lord Tweeddale left me on the 6th, and arrived at Cordova on the 11th. On the forenoon of the former day, after ascertaining the departure of the enemy's troops from Ciudad Real, I passed the Guadiana, and entered that town. I was received with a restraint and ill-dissembled reluctance that convinced me the French were not far distant; and to the Spaniard who accompanied me it was explained, that receiving a British officer with cordiality would be reported by the persons in their interest immediately on the return of the enemy, which was confidently expected, and would produce, under these circumstances, effects of a ruinous character to them and their families.

When made acquainted with this state of public feeling, I determined to remain a brief space of time in the capital of La Mancha. Having, therefore, examined the chief magistrate, and obtained, as I conceived, the requisite information to guide my movements, I rode to Miguelturra, distant a quarter of a league; and which may almost be considered a suburb of the former town.

In Ciudad Real, seated on a level of great extent, in the centre of a highly cultivated country, is a handsome town, containing a large population. The buildings are spacious, the streets wide and regular; eight convents, and an hospital for the sick, are within the city, which is surrounded by an old Moorish wall. In no part of Spain does the olive grow in greater luxuriance than in the vicinity of this place.

The province of La Mancha, one of the richest in Spain, produces corn, wine, and oil, in great abundance: it became, in consequence, a favourite quarter of the French troops, and had for months supplied the wants of Marshal Soult's army.

Piedrabuena, situated on the confines of the province of Toledo, and on the right bank of the Guadiana, was not only at some distance from, but also to the westward of, the usual line of country subjected to the visits of the enemy's foraging parties. I, therefore, remained in that town, making excursions in the neighbourhood, and employing the peasantry to procure information of any movements that might take place in the French quarters.

On the 14th, I rode to Fernan Caballero and Malagon; the latter a large and populous town, containing a Franciscan and a Carmelite monastery; from thence to Fuentelfresno, seated at the base of that part of the chain of mountains of Toledo extending to the sources of the Guadiana, and on the 15th, passed through Malagon and Porzuna, on my return to Piedrabuena; but when near the latter, was informed of an enemy's detachment having arrived there in the forenoon. I had therefore only left the alternative, either to retrace my steps, or pass in the dark near to Piedrabuena, and proceed to Luciana, situated at the confluence of the Rivers Ballaque and Guadiana.

Having adopted the latter expedient, and favoured by the obscurity of the night, I followed a route down the ravine between the town and the ruined castle of Miraflores, which being only removed a short distance from the French sentinels, was attended with some chance of obstruction. Fortunately we passed unnoticed, and at Luciana I found my horses and servants, who had made a precipitate and not very orderly retreat, on the approach of the enemy's detachment. It was composed of cavalry and infantry, marching with the sole object of levying contributions; which having effected, they departed, taking the route towards Ciudad Real.

On the 20th, I crossed the Guadiana, and arriving at Ciudad Real, learned that the French were in Miguelturra, much too near to admit of a prolonged *sojourn* in the former, which, at this period, was seldom many hours without a visit from some of the enemy's troops.

A Spaniard, placed on the Ciudad Real road to give me information, returned to Piedrabuena early on the morning of the 24th, with a report that a detachment had passed the river during the night, and were marching direct to the town. He was immediately despatched on the line from whence he came, and others' sent to the different routes by which the enemy could approach; but the short space of time that intervened from receiving the intelligence to the appearance of the dreaded visitors, made it evident their vicinity had been from the first beyond a matter of doubt, and that the *vigilant* messenger had actually seen them previous to his primary communication. In a few minutes the people were perceived running in all directions, in great agitation and alarm, while the cry of "*Los Franceses! Los Franceses!*" echoed from every quarter.

The consternation of my host, Don Vencislaus, was extreme. The crisis was to him overpowering; his mind wavered under the circumstances of anxiety and alarm. Instead of being active in forwarding the removal of evidences that a British officer had been received beneath his roof, he bewailed the fate that awaited him; and I left him pacing from one apartment to another, apparently reduced to helpless childishness. His family, assisted by their constant visitor, the Sangrado of the village, shewed greater presence of mind; and the moment I had departed, closed the front gateway, thereby occasioning some delay in parleying with the French officer, who was kept thundering for admittance until the apartment I had deserted no longer appeared to have been recently occupied. When, on the following day, I returned to Piedrabuena, Don Vencislaus claimed for himself great praise in having effected the speedy removal of my baggage from French observation; and I was too happy in having it restored in safety to question the agency by which that had been accomplished.

After the alarm they had received, it would not have been surprising that this family should have expressed some degree of reluctance at again admitting so dangerous a visitor; but, on the contrary, I was welcomed with, if possible, greater kindness than formerly: nor was a repetition of the late scene either anticipated or dreaded.

Until the 7th of March I continued, with slight variation, at Piedrabuena, when, receiving information that the enemy had broke up from his cantonments in Almagro and its neighbourhood, I proceeded to that city.

Almagro is a very fine town, built with regularity, and situated in a beautiful country. Its inhabitants appeared delighted at the departure of the enemy; the streets were crowded with musicians and people dancing; guitars sounded in every direction, the sprightly *"seguidilla"* of La Mancha being in accordance with the cheerfulness that seemed to pervade all ranks.

The losses sustained by the Emperor Napoleon in his disastrous campaign of Moscow, occasioned, at this period, the withdrawal of the Duke of Dalmatia and a large body of the veteran troops composing the army in Spain; their presence being important in the ranks of the new levies that soon after brilliantly commenced their career on the field of Lutzen.

The Duke of Dalmatia, having made over the command-in-chief of his army to Comte Gazan, left Toledo on the 1st of March, entering Madrid on the following day, with a numerous staff and 8000 men. On the 3rd, the Marshal continued his route towards Valladolid; from thence, crossing the frontier, he was speedily at his master's side, on the plains of Saxony.

The great diminution in numerical strength occasioned by these drafts from the French force, made a concentrated movement necessary. The troops of the "Army of the South "were consequently finally withdrawn from La Mancha, and the whole of that fertile province relieved from the presence of the enemy. At Daimiel, on the 9th, I ascertained the march of the light cavalry in the direction of the Tagus. At night, having returned to Ciudad Real, the departure of the enemy from all parts of La Mancha being confirmed, and my presence in that province no longer of the slightest utility, I resolved to proceed across the mountains of Toledo, and again come near to the quarters of the enemy's troops.

Having passed through Alcoba and Retuerta, after travelling a steep and intricate mountain road, I descended to Navalucillos, there establishing a direct communication for intelligence with the capital. This was carried on through the medium of the Madrid *Gazette*, the circulation of which to the provinces had not been interrupted by the French authorities; and on its margin, written with invisible characters, until subjected to the process by which they became legible, were conveyed the remarkable events occurring at the court of Joseph Bonaparte.

A *Gazette*, received on the morning of the 19th, communicated the final departure of the Court, having taken place on the 17th; on which day King Joseph, attended by the ministers O'Farrel, Urquijo, and Azanza, and escorted by his guards, several regiments of cavalry, with a numerous convoy of persons in the French interest, left Madrid.

Joseph departed privately by the gate leading to the Casa del Campo, and having, at the Puerta de San Vicente, joined the cavalcade there awaiting his presence, the whole proceeded to Valladolid, arriving in that city on the 23rd. Upon ascertaining the departure of the French court, I sent an express direct to Lord Wellington with the intelligence.

The "Army of the South" continued its movement towards the capital, and upon the 26th of April, the headquarters proceeded from Toledo to Madrid. Everything denoted want of confidence on the part of the enemy. The circumstances of the war became completely changed; nor was it possible for the Emperor Napoleon longer to bestow upon the Spanish struggle that incessant supply of troops rendered necessary by the immense losses sustained during the contest. The consequences of Moscow became felt on the banks of the Tagus: his armies no longer contemplated the possession of extensive territory in the Peninsula, but, condensing, and prepared to act upon the defensive, awaited the commencement of the campaign, which it was evident Lord Wellington would have the means of prosecuting with a numerous and very efficient army.

After years of constant fighting and extremely harassing service, the French officers had become aware of the superficial benefit derived from defeating Spanish troops; the discomfiture of whom had equally ceased to create surprise, or produce depression, in the minds of the population. It was the universal voice, of a great people exerted in resistance, and supported by the powerful aid and countenance of Great Britain, with which they had to contend; in battling against whom, they had only conquered the ground on which their armies stood, when the whole strength of France, and the united force of a large portion of the Continent of Europe, led by Napoleon in person, formed the tremendous instruments for subjugating a refractory people.

Now, reduced in numbers, and harassed by the partisan warfare in active operation against them, they had to contend against the feeling of confidence derived from the slight success attending the protracted and strenuous efforts of the French emperor to conquer the resistance of eleven millions of inhabitants; added to which, their opponents, possessing details of the fatal losses sustained in the Russian campaign, were animated and encouraged by the novel sight of troops returning to France, instead of pouring, as previously, through the passes of the Pyrenees, to aid in that coercion which the presumption of a great mind had erringly supposed could be applied with success to a people in arms.

The enemy's troops evacuated Talavera de la Reyna on the 3rd of April; the vanguard and light cavalry of Comte Gazan's army were quartered in Bargas, Olias, and Mocejon. Not a French soldier remained upon the immediate bank of the Tagus, with the exception of the 12me *Légère*, and one hundred and fifty *chasseurs à cheval* that accompanied General Maransin, and still lingered at Toledo. There appeared a great reluctance in abandoning the fertile country in the neighbourhood of that city; nor were the French detachments within its walls without serious apprehensions of being subjected to attacks from the numerous guerilla parties that infested the whole country. To prevent the possibility of surprise, the gates at the bridge of San Martin, and that of Alcantara, were *barricadoed*.

For some days I continued to reside at Polan, anxiously expecting the departure of the enemy from Toledo, and receiving constant reports from that city of his probable movements. Secure in the certainty of no wandering detachments venturing on the roads in the neighbourhood, I made daily excursions to the heights, from whence the town was seen at the distance of half a mile; there the French soldiers were distinctly observed moving about, without being permitted to come from out the walls, and having the appearance of troops in a besieged fortress. Such was the influence produced on enemies' minds, by the terror attending guerilla warfare.

At length, on the night of the 10th, General Maransin left Toledo; and at daylight on the following morning, I was on horseback, crossed the Tagus, and entered the city accompanied by the *intendant* of the province, who had been for some days the companion of my wanderings, and had occasionally exhibited involuntary expressions of restlessness, with reference to what he considered the too close neighbourhood of enemies' troops.

Toledo, decayed in its importance, and greatly reduced in population, is nevertheless a noble town. Seated on a conical hill, its streets descend either to the banks of the Tagus, or to the level ground towards Olias, in the direction of Madrid. On the summit of the height, and conspicuously overlooking every quarter of the city, stands the ruined Alcazar, whose roofless walls, towering above all other buildings, and seen at a great distance, possess a distinguished appearance, beyond what is usually obtained by even the residences of princes, when identified with the exterior forms of masonry included in the view of a great city. The cathedral spire, the convent tower, or the domes of many churches, all appear beneath the eye; the Alcazar alone claims pre-eminence in majestic and impressive effect.

Erected by, and for years the favoured residence of, the Emperor Charles V., it remained for the French Army to destroy this palace, the interior of which was reduced to ashes during the campaign of 1809.

The cathedral is a very splendid edifice; its interior much the richest in florid decoration that I observed in Spain. Being the seat of the primate, all the ordinances of Catholic worship were in it performed with great dignity and magnificence. During Easter, I had frequent opportunities of witnessing the ceremonies, and have never seen anything equalling in splendour the gorgeous and costly, the dignified and impressive celebration. It wanted a combination of circumstances to invest the scene with the interest imparted to that on a former occasion in the cathedral of Salamanca, but in pomp and richness it was infinitely superior.

The Cardinal de Bourbon, Archbishop of Toledo, had long been an exile from his palace, which became for months the residence of Marshal Soult, and from it General Maransin had the previous day taken his departure. Without any pretension to architectural beauty, it is a spacious and convenient residence, situated in the principal street, and nearly opposite the great entrance to the cathedral.

The inhabitants of Toledo expressed much satisfaction at the departure of the French, and the majority, apparently, with sincerity; at the same time there were many partisans of the unpopular cause, who, either really interested in the enemy's success, or doubtful of the part to espouse, preserved a sullen demeanour, but were alike harmless and incommunicative.

Having received intelligence of the events passing in the north of Europe, detailing the successes of the allied powers, and decadence of the French imperial influence, I considered it important to communicate to the inhabitants of New Castille, as extensively as possible, information so much calculated to inspire hopes of a successful termination to the war of resistance which they had so long waged with persevering, but doubtful advantage.

For this purpose, having procured a translation of the most important paragraphs, a proclamation issued from the Toledo press, and thousands of copies were put into immediate circulation. They were read with avidity; and to prevent the possibility of a doubt as to the author, I despatched copies in my own name to General Maransin, General Leval, at Madrid, and to the headquarters of the "Army of the South." So important did General Maransin consider the removal of the impression produced by the circulation of this document, that, upon his return to Toledo, he published an answer to it, endeavouring to contradict what he was aware must have a pernicious effect in a country, only waiting for reverses to encourage a more general armament against him.

On the evening of the 27th of April, I was informed that the enemy was again approaching the town, and that I must prepare for departure. Soon after this unwelcome communication, clouds of dust appeared on the road leading from Olias: on their nearer approach, a detachment of French cavalry, followed by a column of infantry, became visible. On horseback, having the Tagus to protect me from being cut off by any of my enemies making a *détour*, and across which river there was no difficulty of effecting an escape, I remained a spectator to the movements on the plain. When arrived within about a quarter of a mile from the city, the cavalry left the column, and rapidly trotted forward to the gate. I then quitted the town, and passed the night at Polan.

On the following morning, when on the Sierra de Los Palos, directly over Toledo, I received the proclamation of General Maransin, and having affixed a reply to several copies, dated them from the heights, and prevailed upon a Spaniard to place them on the gates of Toledo. This mode of life was extremely interesting. The constant sight of, and almost communication with, the enemy, produced excitement; while the fact of an officer, removed one hundred and fifty miles from the nearest troops of his country, being enabled to continue in safety close to the quarters of an enemy's army for months, proved the current of popular opinion to be decidedly in favour of the cause of which he was the partisan. On the 6th of May, the muleteers travelling the route towards Polan, informed me that the French troops were preparing for departure. Subsequent travellers from Toledo communicated the march of General Maransin, when I immediately proceeded to occupy his quarters.

During the absence of the French at this time, some of the minor guerilla parties from the neighbourhood entered the town, and expressed a desire to close the gates against any subsequent arrival of French troops. This proposal being made to the magistracy, a meeting of the junta of Toledo was immediately called, at which I was invited to be present. It was urged by some of the most influential persons, that resistance, without adequate means to render it effectual, would be attended with most pernicious effects, exasperating the enemy, occasioning hardship and distress to the inhabitants in the event of an entrance being forced; and also, that the partisans within the city were neither sufficiently numerous nor disciplined to defend the town. The prudence of this view was evident; and it was decided not to permit any appearance of resistance, but rather to request the guerillas would, on an enemy's approach, betake themselves to the scenes from whence they had arrived to display their zeal and promised determination.

The quarters of the enemy's light cavalry being so near, few days passed without our seeing some of them moving about in the distance; but none advanced to the walls of Toledo until the forenoon of the 9th, when a detachment was seen deliberately marching direct to the gate. Previous to their arrival, it became evident they accompanied a flag of truce: numbers flocked to the parley, and the horsemen, having reined up without the walls, conversed for some time with the Spanish civilians that had presented themselves. Waiting, at the upper part of the town, the result of this visit, a peasant arrived in great haste, stating that the French officers had inquired for me, and, upon being informed I was in the town, had despatched him with a request that I would come down and converse with them.

This I had no hesitation in doing; and upon reaching the barrier, with difficulty penetrating the crowd collected, I checked my horse close to those of two officers of the 2nd, or Chamboran Hussars. Civilities having passed, I was anxious to become acquainted with the object of their visit, but it being made apparently from pure curiosity, and to ascertain whether a British officer really was in Toledo, I put a stop to the communication, bade them *adieu*, returned into the town, and they speedily disappeared on the route from whence they came.

On the forenoon of the 11th of May, General Maransin, accompanied by the 45me regiment of the line, and a squadron of the 5me Chasseurs à Cheval, again entered Toledo. I had become so accustomed to these "exits and entrances," that they produced slight annoyance beyond that of leaving agreeable quarters for others of a less cheerful description.

The society of Toledo had suffered essentially from the changes produced by the war; still it was not devoid of interest, and custom had attached me to the habits of a town where I had received so much kindness and attention. An intercepted letter from General Maransin to General Leval, communicated his intention of taking me prisoner with the least possible delay.

Not considering Polan very safe quarters, I determined to remove two leagues further into the country; and having taken the usual ride to the Sierra de Los Palos, proceeded at night to Fuentelcaño, a country house, surrounded by wood, and at some distance from any of the principal lines of communication. Having left the Intendant of Toledo in this apparently secure retreat, I made daily excursions, returning in the evening, and by my reports restoring that confidence in the mind of the Spanish functionary which solitude and a lack of cigars had nearly destroyed. In returning from the heights above Toledo, on the 16th, I became so unwell as to determine me not to proceed further to the rear than Polan.

I consequently sent a messenger with the information to Fuentelcaño, and made preparations for securing, as I believed, timely information, should the enemy make an excursion in that direction during the night. An Andalusian, who had for some time been employed in procuring information, was stationed on one of the roads, while a Spanish sergeant undertook to watch the only other leading towards Toledo. These persons were instructed to advance a league from the town, and occupy heights from whence they, without difficulty, could, unperceived, ascertain the approach of any body of troops moving along the respective routes. Had this duty been either vigilantly or honestly executed, there could not have existed the slightest danger; either of these persons might, without difficulty, have reached Polan so much sooner than a column of troops, that perfect facility would have been given to effecting escape. Relying on these arrangements, I retired for the night.

About one in the morning, my rest was disturbed by receiving a communication of some movements on the part of the enemy, but not from Toledo, or in any direction to compromise my personal safety. It was past nine o'clock in the evening, when General Maransin became acquainted with the circumstance of my having resolved to continue for the night at Polan. He immediately resolved to detach and surprise me. In ignorance as to the force he believed had for some time been hovering about his quarters, and apprehensive of the neighbouring guerillas, he ordered an unusually numerous detachment to be paraded in marching order: it consisted of a squadron of the *5me Chasseurs à Cheval*, with 300 of the *45me* of the line. His *aide-de-camp*, Captain Acoste, was directed to accompany this promenade, and soon after sallied forth on the route for Polan.

At the distance of a league from that village is a *venta*, or inn, whose inhabitants were secured, to prevent an alarm being communicated. This being accomplished, the troops advanced until near to the town, when the cavalry left the road, and in patrols closed the different routes leading from the houses; the infantry marched direct to the street forming the entrance from Toledo. Having secured the roads by which escape was practicable, the French *aide-de-camp* impressed a peasant from the first habitation at which he arrived, menacing him with instant death if he did not without delay lead to the quarter I had occupied during my frequent visits to Polan; and where, from the information received, he doubted not I then was. About two o'clock, a violent knocking was heard at the outer gateway, which speedily gave way before the force applied to break it down, and soon after the court was filled with French infantry.

The house, although spacious, was but of one storey in height; the windows were slightly elevated from the court, which, of considerable extent, was surrounded by a lofty wall. There could not for an instant be a doubt as to what had happened; the enemy's troops had succeeded in surprising me, and a last but hopeless effort at escape was the sole alternative. Extinguishing the lamp which burnt in my room, I locked the door, retiring into a chamber to the back of the house, the entrance to which I also secured, and attempted to force through a window, the only one in the apartment, which I had not previously inspected, but which proved to be closely grated with iron bars.

No other egress presenting itself, my fate became inevitable. The whole range of windows in front of the house gave way with a loud crash, as the butt-ends of the French muskets were directed through them. I heard my bedchamber fully occupied, while noise, confusion, and loud conversation marked the progress of rapid and anxious search. At length, violent blows, applied in rapid succession, completely demolished the door that obstructed a sight of their prey; when, perceiving no possibility of escape, I walked forward, surrendering to Captain Acoste, and at the same time making a request that he would order the soldiers forth from the house, and permit the completion of that toilet, which had been commenced under such hurried and inauspicious circumstances.

Having secured the principal object of their visit, the soldiers proceeded to the stable, and then to the dormitory of an English groom, the only individual accompanying me, from whence some of them returned, reporting their search to have been vain, and that he had escaped. This appeared very improbable, as any previous warning of the arrival of these unwelcome visitors was out of the question, nor could his unnoticed departure be accounted for, more particularly after the house had become so completely beset by enemies. At length, some of the French *voltigeurs*, with much gaiety and laughter, produced the unfortunate *palefrenier*, who, in the terror of the occasion, had considered his mattress much better placed over than under his person: now brought forth, he soon recovered his serenity, and even smiled at the merriment raised at his expense by the volatile and laughter-loving soldiers.

The cavalry parties were now recalled, and the squadron formed in the street fronting where we then were. The soldiers, having returned from plundering the village, brought with them provisions and numerous animals of burden, which were collected in the court. The officers assembled in the room I had previously occupied: conversation commenced; we were no longer enemies; and in the course of two hours were seated at a substantial repast of viands prepared for the occasion, and to which ample justice was done before these warriors would move on their return. I was closely questioned on the subject of troops, whether I had any British soldiers in the neighbourhood, or guerilla parties, at my immediate disposal? to both of which I could, with perfect truth, answer in the negative.

These to me most interesting events had passed with a rapidity precluding much thought or serious contemplation of the reverse that had befallen me; nor was it until we had quitted Polan that all the annoyance flashed in full force upon my mind. The French officers had treated me with great cordiality. Some of the soldiers, when removed from the restraint of their presence, were not so considerate, jeering me on the situation I had unwillingly obtained in their society; and, as the Spanish white wine elevated their already buoyant spirits, insisting on my unqualified assent to the fact, that "*Les Français sont des braves gens.*" At my intercession, the French *aide-de-camp* prevented any further destruction to the house or furniture; and the unfortunate agriculturist to whom it belonged seemed to consider himself, under the circumstances, treated with considerable lenity.

The troops being again formed, we sallied forth, and, amidst clouds of dust, entered upon the road to Toledo. Mounted upon one of the animals taken from the inhabitants of Polan, and accompanying the officers at the head of the infantry, I commenced this journey, having previously perceived two officers of *chasseurs* on my captured horses, essaying their powers of action to the amusement of their companions in arms.

The detachment proceeded without halt or interruption to the *venta* above mentioned, where the soldiers again regaled themselves, and where my thoughts became directed to the possibility of escape. Upon the heights, near to the city, the road is conducted between walls, bounding the orangeries of some villas belonging to the inhabitants of Toledo. It occurred to me as possible, by watching an opportunity, when unperceived, to leap one or other of these walls, and penetrate into the thicket beyond; but the escort were too vigilant to permit a chance of success in any such attempt; nor did I conceive it, under the circumstances, worthy of a trial, the failure in which would inevitably be accompanied by a shower of musket-balls.

On our arrival in the town, I was immediately taken to the palace of the archbishop, and presented to General Maransin. His manner, at first distant and reserved, became softened by degrees, and restored to what appeared his natural and usual demeanour. The impression occasioned by the circumstances under which we had met, became removed, and in the course of an hour a conversation was in progress with all the appearance of confidence existing between officers of the same army, and long accustomed to familiar discourse. The general had for some time commanded the vanguard of Marshal Soult's army, had long served in Spain, and in the commencement of 1812 was attacked by General Ballesteros, near to Cartamo, and defeated; the troops under his orders, amounting to about 3000, flying in the direction of Malaga.

He had an appearance of intelligence and activity, was aged about forty, had the manners of a gentleman, and seemed not devoid of information. A baron of the empire, his military rank was that of "*Général de Brigade*;" but under his immediate orders at this time, were the light cavalry of General Soult (brother to the marshal), consisting of the Chamboran hussars, the 5me and 10me *Chasseurs à Cheval*. The 12me *Légère*, and 45me regiment of the line, composed the infantry of the vanguard, and the only French troops now on the banks of the Tagus.

Accompanied by an officer of the *état major*, I was permitted to pay visits in the town, returning to the palace at six, where the general was attended by several of his officers, and a very sumptuous dinner was served up. In the evening, the other members of his family having retired, I had an unconstrained conversation with the French baron. For upwards of an hour we paced along the spacious and elegant salon of the archbishop, discussing the leading topics, rendered interesting in the progress of the Spanish warfare, with a frankness on his part that occasioned my surprise. Whether it proceeded from having me in his power, and consequently conceiving that no detriment to the imperial cause could result from his open and candid avowal, certainly he was more communicative than either circumstances demanded, or our relative situations warranted.

The campaign in Russia, the frightful sufferings of the Grand Army, the hopeless state of affairs in the Peninsula, the imbecility of Joseph Bonaparte, or the military talents of Lord Wellington, were alike subjected to the unreserved remark, the eulogium, and, occasionally, to the bitter invective, of the French general. A stranger, overhearing the conversation, would rather have supposed it carried on by officers of the same family, than by a person of rank in one army, and a prisoner brought to his quarters, after having instigated the inhabitants of the country to rise, and cut off the supplies on which the existence of the other depended.

General Maransin, without hesitation, admitted the difficulties and losses to which the French armies in the Peninsula were subjected; the faulty arrangements made under existing circumstances, and the improbability of reinforcements, at a time when the guerilla system was of all others most harassing and destructive. The departure of Marshal Soult he considered an event much to be deplored, and calculated to have a serious effect on the *morale* of his army.

On the following morning, it was arranged that we should proceed to Olias, there to meet General Soult. At nine, I was at the palace, and prepared to depart. General Maransin ordered the horses to be led, and we passed on foot through the streets. Whether occasioned by the circumstance of a person whose presence had in some measure become familiar to them, being carried away in captivity, or some other undefined cause, I know not, the whole population of Toledo crowded to their windows and the entrances of their houses. The general, surprised at the numerous assemblage, stated that he now saw its inhabitants for the first time. There was something allied to apprehension in the hurried step with which he escaped from the gaze of so numerous a body of enemies. When without the walls, and mounted on horseback, he reverted to the scene, it was to descant upon the curiosity so unusually displayed by the great population of Toledo.

Arrived at Olias, we were conducted to the quarters of the colonel commanding the 5me *Chasseurs à Cheval*, and introduced into a large room, where had previously assembled General Soult, his *aides-de-camp*, and the officers of the regiment.

General Pierre Soult had neither a gentlemanlike nor soldierly appearance. Gross and unwieldy in his person, no prepossession of manner tended to remove the extremely unfavourable impression; he had all the look of a *parvenu* of the vulgarest and lowest description. After a *déjêuné à la fourchette* of the most substantial kind, I was ushered into the cabinet of the officer acting as chief of the staff, and by him informed that, upon giving my parole of honour, I might become immediate master of my motions; that is, in selecting any portion of the French Army with which to continue, either accompanying the 5me *Chasseurs*, or, by proceeding to Madrid, partake of its society. It never occurred to the Frenchman that this offer would be rejected; consequently, when, from resolutions previously formed, he was made acquainted with the fact that I would not give my parole, he started from his seat, and, without losing a moment, acquainted General Soult with the determination.

The difficulty which had notoriously occurred in effecting any exchange during the earlier period of the Peninsular War, had induced me rather to adopt the chance of making an escape than become bound by an engagement that, once entered into, of course precluded taking the advantage of any such fortunate opportunity were it to occur. It was with these views, and in ignorance of the harsh measures likely to result from refusing what had ever been considered a matter of usual practice, and of consequent indulgence, that I subjected myself to every chance of the most serious annoyance.

The first communication made on the occasion was, that as the only motive for withholding my parole naturally must be the hope of escaping, especial care would be taken to prevent success, and instant death accompany the attempt. An escort was then ordered; the officer commanding received his instructions, and I was directed to depart. In the street were drawn up about fifty of the 5me; a horse being brought and mounted, two *chasseurs* unslung their carbines, placing themselves on either side; an officer rode near; we were preceded by an advanced guard, and in this formation entered upon the level and sandy plains leading to Illescas.

The officer in charge of the detachment communicated to me, soon after leaving Olias, that in the event of the slightest deviation from the route on my part, the *chasseurs*, holding my bridle, were instructed to discharge their carbines into my body, and that if any guerilla party, either from accident or design, appeared to obstruct our passage, I was to be despatched as a preliminary measure. It is unnecessary to describe the anxious feeling with which I hoped and trusted that no partisans would cross our path; it was decreed that we should pass unmolested. At one part of the route my anxiety became extreme; a cloud of dust, evidently arising from a body moving rapidly along the road, appeared behind us, but, on approaching, proved to proceed from a troop of the 10me *Chasseurs*, despatched, soon after our departure, to investigate into the progress of their companions, and whether the rescue they doubted not I anticipated had in reality been attempted.

At Illescas, on our arrival, were assembled the officers of the *état major*, and with them the evening was passed in courtesy and apparent cordiality. When the hour of retiring for the night sounded, the officer, having instructions on the subject, accompanied me to where, I was informed sneeringly, it had been arranged I should repose. The night was extremely dark. After passing through several streets of the populous town, we reached the *corps-de-garde* of the 12me *Légère*, and, on entering, discovered a bed prepared in one corner of the chamber. The soldiers were strolling about, but evidently aware of the prisoner destined to come under their charge.

Upon taking leave for the night, after wishing me every comfort in this novel habitation, the officer, in bitter irony, added, that no doubt could exist as to my uninterrupted and secure slumbers, they being under the safeguard of the brave grenadiers of the 12me *Légère*, who would not for a moment leave me. This mode of surveillance was persevered in until the 20th, when General Soult, arriving at Illescas, ordered an escort to proceed forthwith and deliver me over to the authorities at Madrid.

At Illescas, during the short period of my remaining, I experienced great civility and kindness from the French officers, particularly Colonel St. Laurent, of the *10me Chasseurs*, with whom most of the time was agreeably passed. His quarter seemed the rallying point of many French officers. In it was constantly assembled a numerous society. The weather was brilliant, and in the garden was placed the superb band of his regiment. On one of these occasions, I had an opportunity of witnessing the constant terror in which the enemy's troops were kept by the guerillas. The colonel had passed the forenoon in shooting, and not returning at the accustomed hour, the anxiety expressed was great, the surmises as to what had happened, various; but the predominant feeling was, that he had fallen into the hands of guerillas. It was stated, that nothing could be more hazardous than the slightest wandering from the immediate quarters of the troops; that, sooner or later, his sportsmanlike propensities would occasion to the army a very serious and much-regretted loss. At length the anxiously expected colonel made his appearance, having seen no guerillas, and but few partridges; his uninterrupted good humour continued to enliven the society, and the evening passed very agreeably.

The impression made on these officers by the disastrous Russian campaign, the detailed reports of which had circulated throughout the army, appeared to carry with it an increased confidence in the prowess of the French arms, their misfortunes being exclusively attributed to the effects of climate; while the extraordinary military talents of Napoleon suffered no diminution in the estimation of these devoted and enthusiastic admirers. Accounts of the battle of Lutzen had just been received, but it remained uncertain whether the emperor had commanded in person. The details of that very important action were yet unknown in the "Army of the South," and by these officers it was conjectured that Prince Eugene, left in charge of the wreck of the "*Grande Armée,*" had gained what they were led to suppose a splendid victory.

This circumstance afforded an opportunity for questioning the opinions entertained as to the character and acquirements of the prince, the answers to which were unanimously favourable. Disposed to attribute his rank and situation more to the connexion with Napoleon than to personal merit, I was met with decided contradiction. Eugene was declared to be equally distinguished as an officer and beloved as a man; his Russian campaign had been brilliant in the extreme, displaying courage and unshaken firmness; as to instruction, I was informed, "*Il a fait toutes les belles campagnes de l'Empereur.*"

Subsequently written narratives of the days of Borodino, and of Malo-Yaroslawetz, prove these officers had formed a correct estimate of the gallant soldier, whose name, identified with valour and unshaken chivalrous fidelity, must ever adorn the annals of the French Army. It will hereafter be considered not the least enviable glory of Prince Eugene, that, under all circumstances of adversity, he evinced undeviating respect, he proved the devotion of honour, the imperishable principle of gratitude inherent in an amiable mind, and fought to the last for the expiring fortunes of the man,

Who, born no king, made monarchs draw his car.

Of their enthusiastic confidence in the Emperor Napoleon, the following may be considered as a specimen. Conversing on the continental wars, some events of danger or difficulty to the French armies were noticed, accompanied by reasons for the almost impossibility of extrication. Upon demanding an explanation as to the means resorted to in these disastrous circumstances, and what restored the position of the Grand Army, Colonel St. Laurent merely said, "*L'Empereur étoit là,*" conceiving that fact to embrace conclusive reasons for military success being obtained even under the most improbable chances of victory, or the most perilous occurrences of war.

It was on the 20th of May, that, having taken leave of Colonel St. Laurent, accompanied by a detachment of his regiment, I entered Madrid; upon the Prado encountering the Generals Leval, Fonblanaque, and Vinot, nothing could be more repulsive than my reception, particularly by the former, whose countenance bespoke most indignant feeling. General Leval then commanded the troops in the neighbourhood of the capital; and being the senior officer present, he addressed me. The conversation was laconic on his part, not complimentary, and in substance as follows:

General Leval. What is your name?

Answer. Andrew Leith Hay.

Gen. L. What rank?

Ans. Captain and *aide-de-camp.*

Gen. L. Is it you who have published proclamations against the emperor, and sent them to me by express?

Ans. It is.

Gen. L. Very pretty productions they are! I am surprised that an officer of a civilised country should have put his name to such things.

Ans. I am not aware of their being in any respect unworthy of a British officer.

Gen. L. These publications, sir, will cost you dear; in the meantime, you will go to prison, there to remain until your fate is decided.

This dialogue, unexpected, and certainly unsatisfactory, was no sooner concluded, than the general directed Colonel Prévost, one of his *aides-de-camp*, to escort me to his quarter, there to write an order by which General Hugo, the Governor of Madrid, might be directed in his mode of proceeding. We entered the Calle Alcala, and in the house of the Marques de Alcanizas the billet was indited, consigning me to the dungeons of the Retiro. In the low dark room wherein I was placed, were already confined ten Spanish prisoners of the worst class. Its solitary window, closely grated with iron bars, admitted but an inadequate portion of fresh air.

From this horrid receptacle we were never permitted to go forth, and for three days I was subjected to the miseries attendant upon such a situation. The weather was at this time extremely sultry, adding to the annoyance that became almost insupportable. At length, repeated remonstrances produced a relaxation in the severity with which General Leval had considered it consistent with propriety to visit the sins committed against the power he knew to be on the wane; and on the fourth day after being immured in the Retiro, the adjutant of the place arrived with instructions to remove me, not to liberty, but to a less horrid place of confinement. Delighted to obtain egress from so disgusting a scene, I eagerly followed the French officer across the Prado, and through the Calle de Atocha to the Carcel de la Corte.[2] When placed in a tolerable, though gloomy apartment, I considered the change of the most favourable description.

Previous to departing, Monsieur Dubois informed me that I would not be permitted to leave the apartment, or communicate with any person whatever, excepting my servant and the keeper of the prison; nevertheless, it was a paradise compared to the habitation I had just left; and for three days, nothing occurred to interrupt the monotony that reigned within the walls of the spacious Carcel. Its keeper had re-

---

2. Prison of the Court.

sisted my repeated entreaties that he would connive at escape; alleging his perfect willingness, but well-founded terrors for the consequences. From him I learned the prevailing reports that the French troops and partisans were on the eve of leaving Madrid, which became confirmed by a visit from the *adjutant de la place* on the evening of the 26th, with an intimation that I must be in readiness to accompany a convoy destined to move from the capital on the following morning.

At daybreak, on the 27th, a guard of infantry appeared at the prison gate, demanding that I should be delivered up to them; we then joined the column already formed, and moved towards the Puerta de San Vicente. No animal of any description had been provided to transport us, or convey the scanty supply of wearing apparel appertaining either to myself or servant. Remonstrances were vain; it was evidently intended that I should in every respect be treated with unusual harshness, nor was it a befitting time either to attempt obtaining redress, or to exhibit any outward indication of the annoyance having produced a deep impression.

An officer, at my request, permitted my servant to mount one of the baggage wagons of his regiment; and I proceeded on foot with the 88me of the line, forming the guard of a very numerous cavalcade that now issued from the walls of the capital. Madrid, on this morning, presented one of those remarkable scenes incident to the war; the bustle attending a march of troops being accompanied by the confused departure of a portion of its population, whose political opinions during the struggle now rendered it unsafe to remain behind. Persons of rank, forced from their hitherto comfortable homes, were intermixed with all orders of the community, and alike contemptuously treated by the French troops.

Quantities of carriages, cars, wagons, or laden mules, were urged onward to join the cavalcade, while numerous groups of the remaining population witnessed these departures with silent, but expressive contempt. One of the groups in the line of march consisted of my former companions in the Retiro, wretched in appearance, and some of them incapable of undergoing any great degree of bodily fatigue. Their lamentations or declarations of inability were listened to with stoical indifference, and the bayonets of the amused French soldiery goaded them forward on their way.

Near to the village of Guadarama the convoy halted for the night: the fields became covered with the motley encampment; women and children, that had previously never slept without the substantial walls of their habitations, now had to derive shelter from the vehicles in which they had travelled, and in which, crowded and comfortless, they were destined to pass the night. On the open field, without covering of any description, in the bivouac of the 88me regiment, I remained for the duration of the halt.

On the 28th, we ascended the Guadarama mountain, encamping upon its summit; a more stormy, wet, and boisterous night I have seldom witnessed. The lofty and exposed situation in which we were placed, of course increased the comfortless feeling produced by the inclement state of the weather: even the French infantry, accustomed to campaigning in all its least desirable features, expressed their unqualified horror at the night. Unprepared to obtain either shelter or rest from being possessed of the customary habiliments under similar circumstances, and the ground streaming with moisture, I was constrained to refrain from a recumbent posture, and was also prevented by the guard from moving in search of a tree to afford shelter from the piercing wind or incessant rain.

Thus circumstanced, the approach of day was looked forward to with the utmost anxiety. A more comfortless or miserable night can hardly be imagined, or one more calculated to impress with gloomy ideas. At break of day, the wretched bivouac was abandoned, and the cavalcade commenced its descent towards Old Castillo. Near to the Fonda San Rafael, General Leval, with his staff, passed the convoy, which pursued the Segovia road, while he advanced on that of Espinar.

Near to Segovia an encampment was again formed for the night; although in the open field, application to the inhabitants having produced some articles of bedding, affording shelter from the rain, which fell heavily, it was passed by me in comparative luxury.

The town of Segovia, romantically situated, must ever be interesting from many associations; its splendid aqueduct is one of the grandest remains of antiquity in the Peninsula; and the castle, seated on a lofty and precipitous rock, forms an object alike conspicuous and noble. As a state prison, it long possessed celebrity, and its walls have at different periods become the receptacles of misfortune, or of crime.

There is a gloomy magnitude about the castle of Segovia, which, added to its elevated and domineering situation, appears to have eminently adapted it for the twofold purposes of striking terror, and, in most cases, ensuring security to the persons of unfortunates who too frequently became its inmates.

A portion of the romantic life of the favourite Duke de Ripperda was passed within its walls.

The aqueduct, one of the noblest monuments to the munificence and taste of the Emperor Trajan, is composed of a double row of nearly 160 arches, extending across the valley containing the large and populous town. That of Lisbon is alone superior to it, either in extent, loftiness, or grandeur of effect.

General Hugo, the *ci-devant* Governor of Madrid, now commanded the troops escorting the convoy, which he evidently considered—that is, the Spanish portion of it—a great incumbrance: the contemptuous and uncourteous manner in which he treated his allies was manifested by a demeanour equally harsh and unnecessary. Travelling as I now did in the covered car of a Spanish family, and in the centre of the line of carriages, many opportunities were given for observing the conduct of all parties. To the applications of those under his protection, with the exception of his own immediate friends, the general was invariably repulsive, and frequently rude.

Many of the higher orders of Spaniards seemed overcome by the misery of their situation: on one occasion, when descending from his carriage to facilitate its passage over a rough and steep part of the road, I overheard a Spanish *marques*, with an expression of countenance not to be misunderstood, say to the ladies of his family accompanying him, that death would be preferable to the indignity and misery to which he was subjected. When, in the mornings, this motley assemblage was to be put in motion, unaccustomed to military habits, ill prepared for renewed exertion, and in some cases oppressed with sickness, the persons scattered over the plain were rallied, and urged forward by the threats or taunting jeers of the French soldiery. Whatever might have been their conduct, it was impossible not to feel for these people, becoming, as they were, expatriated for having espoused the cause of others, from whom they now received only *opprobrium*, and by whom they were considered with the utmost contempt.

Arrived at Cuellar, on the 31st of May, its prison became my residence; and the first house I had been permitted to enter since leaving Madrid. A more wretched habitation cannot well be imagined; its insecurity also so manifest, that a guard of infantry was ordered to accompany me, a sentinel from which remained constantly in the same apartment. From the commencement of this march, not a moment had passed during which relaxed vigilance on the part of my guards had presented the slightest chance of effecting an escape. When travelling on foot, I was kept close to the column of infantry; when in a carriage, it was surrounded by them; at night in the bivouacs, a sentinel was placed at my head; and when at intervals he dozed with his arms in hand, others were awake, or strolling about the remoter parts of the camp, to have given an immediate alarm.

Prison walls were rendered doubly secure by being guarded, and all hope vanished of accomplishing what was the object of my incessant and anxious thoughts. On the 2nd of June, after marching without intermission, except for very brief periods, during the preceding day and night, we arrived in the vicinity of Valladolid, but were not permitted to enter within its walls; and having crossed the Pisuerga, encamped on the right bank of that river. The main body of the "Army of the South," having passed the Duero by different routes, were assembled in the neighbourhood of the city: everything bespoke the rapid and continued retreat of the French Army. Two hours were alone permitted as the duration of rest for the convoy near to Valladolid, and at the expiry of that time the whole were again in motion. We were now identified with the "Army of the South," and moved in conjunction with its divisions.

The precipitation so evident in these movements, although attended with personal inconvenience, was too certain an indication of the storm overtaking the enemy's armies, not to afford a person situated as I was great exultation; and when in the bivouac of the 2nd June, an immense train of artillery, accompanied by its ambulances, passed to the rear, I demanded with no slight degree of satisfaction, where these cannon were directed, perceiving at the same time a despondency of manner in the French officers, as they hesitatingly declared it to be but the result of a change of quarters. During this day's march we passed through the populous village of Cigales, crowded with French soldiery, and then the temporary headquarters of Joseph Bonaparte. Induced by the apparent magnitude of the town promising a plentiful supply, and being destitute of provisions, I sent my servant, mounted on a pony, purchased the day preceding, with instructions to proceed to the market, but return as expeditiously as possible; from that moment I never either saw or received authentic information as to what became of him.

The frequent and various inquiries fruitlessly made, the length of time subsequently passed with the French Army, the facility of ascertaining the existence of a person of his class with our own, after rejoining it, having all proved unsuccessful in gaining the slightest insight regarding his fate, adds to the probability of his having been robbed and murdered. A circumstance occurred during the next day's march, which had a most suspicious appearance, and tended to corroborate that impression.

One of the soldiers of the 88me regiment, who had the day before fallen in rear of his company, upon again joining, without being questioned, informed me that he had seen my servant, and been directed by him to state that he would rejoin me on the following day. In the first place, he could not speak French; and, secondly, being mounted, could without difficulty have been with me before a straggling and fatigued soldier; nor was it probable he would have sent any such message. No doubt remains in my mind of his having been put to death, and the soldier of the 88me an accessory to the fact. I regretted the loss of this man extremely; he had long been with me, remaining voluntarily and uncomplaining during the little enviable period of existence we had just passed with the French Army.

Prevented from visiting the other parts of the line of march, I had yet only obtained an insight of the habits and discipline of the French Army, from observing what passed in the 88me regiment. In marching, the French soldiers of that corps observed no kind of regularity, nor did the officers appear to consider it necessary to urge a constant attendance in the ranks of their companies; the men, intermixed and confused, left their companions, and straggled into the villages on the route, without interruption, or being questioned on returning. Occasionally, soldiers were absent for days, but invariably again appeared; and proved by their style of marching, that falling in the rear had been more a matter of inclination than of necessity.

Upon arrival at the different bivouacs, the soldiery appeared freed from all restraint, immediately in parties preparing provisions, or making arrangements for their individual comforts: no time was lost in parading. To a casual observer, discipline appeared neglected, but when called into line, or to the performance of duty, nothing could be more orderly and regular than the demeanour of these veteran soldiers.

On the 6th, the convoy arrived at Burgos, and for a short space of time halted in the suburb on the bank of the Arlanzon. From thence I was conveyed to the prison, and received by its keeper with cordiality and kindness; for the first time on our route the presence of French soldiers was not deemed necessary, and I enjoyed the solitude to which I was consigned, the more that, independent of the restraint, my accustomed companions had not been of a class I should have wished to select.

On the morning of the 10th, I left the prison of Burgos, taking the route for Breviesca.

The French armies were now in full retreat, and it was understood that Lord Wellington was rapidly advancing. A sergeant of the 10th Hussars, taken in an affair at Morales, joined the column of prisoners, and from him I learned with satisfaction the brilliant commencement of the campaign.

The Life Guards, and Royal Horse Guards, had joined the army; nineteen regiments of British and German cavalry crossed the Douro; the allied infantry, recruited, re-equipped, and perfectly efficient, was accompanied by a numerous and brilliant force of artillery; a practised commissariat, and ample means of transport, facilitated the movements of the formidable army now in progress to attack the weakened, and, in some respects, disheartened ranks of the enemy. Numerous bodies of Spanish troops moved in line with the allied army, and the most formidable of the guerilla leaders were acting in immediate concert with Lord Wellington.

From the banks of the Douro at Lamego, the Agueda at Ciudad Rodrigo, and the Alagon at Coria, the different corps of the allied army marched to complete that grand movement of concentration subsequently so fatal to the French Army. Advancing in the finest season of the year, through rich and plentiful countries, following the footsteps of a retreating, and already in idea discomfited, enemy, the allies had cheering and *riant* prospects. That these were fully realised, history will unerringly record.

At Burgos, what a different scene was presented to the British general from that preceding his retreat the former year! Accompanied by four divisions of infantry, and five brigades of cavalry, he reconnoitred that stronghold of the French Army. The rapid retreat of the enemy, and explosion of those works that had occasioned such endless exertion and lamented loss to the assailing troops, were the immediate consequences.

Joseph Bonaparte, with the "Army of the Centre," led the retreat of the enemy's troops towards the Ebro; then followed the "Army of the South;" and, lastly, that of "Portugal." At Breviesca, the prisoners were placed in the church. One of the stone niches of a chapel in its interior, served as my couch for the night; nor did a prospect of any other destiny await me at the time, than being marched to some of the French *dépôts*. At daybreak, several *gens-d'armes* arrived to apprise the numerous inhabitants of the church of their immediate march. These sounds had scarcely reached my ears, when, rising from the cold marble dormitory I had occupied, the welcome intelligence was communicated, that orders had been received, countermanding my further progress.

Delighted beyond measure, and awaiting the result of this alteration, I again occupied the recess in the chapel wall, and soon after became a solitary inhabitant of the parochial church. Prisoners and guards had disappeared; the loud and rapid talking of the French soldiery, intermixed with the occasional eloquence of my native country, died away, and the sound of the closing gate, as the last person left the interior, reverberated in loud echoes through the spacious building.

That I should have been selected from others proceeding to France, originated in the desire of Comte Gazan of restoring to liberty a captain of French artillery, taken at Badajos. This he expected to accomplish by agreeing to an exchange; and the preceding evening had written to General La Martinière, *chef d'état major* of the "Army of Portugal," ordering my detention at Breviesca until his arrival.

Footsteps were again heard within the porch, and soon after a *gen-d'arme* appeared, directing me to follow him; whither was matter of conjecture, from which I was speedily relieved, by being conducted into a small vaulted chamber, without a single article of furniture of any description. Its floor was covered with straw, apparently not of the cleanest description, and the confined heat within was excessive: the inhabitants of the straw, rejoicing in the presence of a victim, flew up, and commenced recreating on my limbs; insects of a similar class have seldom bit more voraciously, or continued their attacks with greater perseverance. This place was worse than the Retiro, and only wanted its inmates to render it totally insupportable.

Desirous of relaxing the severities sought to be heaped on a British officer, the Baron D'Orsay, colonel of the 122me of the line, soon after visited my dungeon. His presence, very stylish appearance, and gentlemanlike manner, inspired me with immediate confidence, and left no doubt of removal from the horrid place to which malignity had consigned me. The baron, without hesitation, agreed to my liberation on parole; and the adjutant of his regiment proceeded with me for the purpose of procuring a quarter in the town. Unfortunately, that selected was exactly opposite to General La Martinière's, who was perceived pacing the length of his apartment, in conversation with other officers, and apparently not in a very agreeable turn of mind.

He considered the presence of a British officer very offensive; a *gend'arme* was directed to remove me from his sight, and to continue my companion until further orders.

The look and appearance of this French general is fresh in my recollection. I have seldom seen hatred more strongly depicted than in the occasional glances of his bloated countenance, as, turning towards the window from whence I surveyed him, he seemed to regret that inflicting summary punishment was not within his jurisdiction. In the French Army it was notorious the marked dislike to the English manifested on all occasions by this officer, upon whom beating appeared not to have produced the usual effect, that of creating respect. In the street at Breviesca was the last time I ever had the misfortune of seeing him.

Baron D'Orsay expressed regret at the prejudices of his superior officer, exhibiting in his conduct the not-to-be-mistaken difference between a person born a gentleman, and the soldier raised beyond his sphere. The baron, descended from an old and distinguished family, had lived in the best society; his appearance was particularly handsome, his politeness perfectly natural and unconstrained. For two days I partook of a hospitality, that appeared sincerely bestowed; conversation became unreserved, and on his part very entertaining. Perfectly acquainted with the habits and customs of the imperial court, the anecdotes concerning its personages were to me most interesting. Baron D'Orsay was at the Tuileries when Napoleon paid the great and well-merited compliment to Marshal Ney, and used the expression that has so justly been attached to his name.

It was after his return from the fatal campaign of Moscow that the court was assembled. Never had the emperor appeared in the midst of a more brilliant circle: the Prince of Moskwa was late in arriving, but, on being perceived, Napoleon, turning to the nobles and the marshals by whom he was surrounded, exclaimed, "*Voilà le brave des braves!*" The French Army cherished the saying: it was the greatest compliment ever paid by their victorious leader to one of his lieutenants; nor was the correctness of the application for a moment questioned.

The 122me regiment formed part of the division Bonnèt, and was particularly noticed by the Duke of Ragusa for its gallant conduct at the Battle of Salamanca. The disasters of that day seemed to have made a deep impression on the French Army; but, unlike other occasions of defeat, I never heard an attempt made to deny the fact, or to account for its having taken place, by any of those fallacious or unfounded reasonings usually resorted to for the purpose of explaining away or palliating discomfiture. The Battle of Salamanca, it was admitted, had been lost by the "Army of Portugal;" that most of its generals had been either killed or wounded, its ranks reduced, whole regiments nearly annihilated, and the impression on the minds of the soldiery greater than on any former occasion. The conduct of different corps became subject of criticism, and the Baron D'Orsay, with all the *esprit* of a gallant and zealous officer, seemed delighted at the supposition of General Bonnèt's division having been noticed in the British Army for its vigorous and determined conduct.

On the 14th, the headquarters of the "Army of the South" arrived at Breviesca, and I was soon after ordered to attend the general-in-chief, Comte Gazan. Having passed through the street crowded with soldiery, and replied to the interrogatories of the guard, I was ushered into the presence of the general, who appeared to be holding a species of *levée*. Having, from the officer accompanying me, ascertained my identity, he immediately commenced animadverting on my conduct at Toledo, and those proclamations which appeared to have given such umbrage to the French Army.

His lecture appeared to be more one of necessity than inclination; it was couched in very different terms from those of General Leval, and a kindliness of manner bespoke no personally hostile feeling on the part of Comte Gazan. Combating the truth of the news from Germany, he talked slightingly of the allied powers, and concluded by assuring me, "*Si l'Empereur a perdu une armée, il a encore une autre*" The most agreeable part of the interview was its *finale*, when the *comte* stated, that in consequence of an application from Lord Wellington, he would propose an officer now in England as an exchange, offering, at the same time, to forward a letter from me requesting this might be agreed to, and if it was so, promising I should be immediately sent to the advance posts.

On the 16th, during the march of the "Army of the South "from Breviesca to Pancorbo, Colonel Arnaud, first *aide-de-camp* to the general-in-chief, rode up in the line of march, expressing his surprise at the non-appearance of the allies. What could have become of Lord Wellington? The French troops, in full retreat, were permitted to move leisurely along the great route, without being harassed or urged forward; not a carriage of any description being lost: to him it appeared inexplicable. The mystery was destined to be solved without delay.

At Comte Gaza's, on the 16th, I met a numerous party of the officers of his army, amongst others, the Generals Darriceau, Marti, and Reymond. The *comtesse*, who accompanied her husband, seemed to regret Seville and the change from Andalusia. Nothing but the approach to France appeared cheering in her estimation: harassed by the movements of the army, and the consequent discomforts, she was heartily tired of campaigning; a child, three years old, the *nameson* of Napoleon, appeared to occupy her devoted attention.

At Pancorbo, I again met General Maransin, and passed the day with him. The whole army were assembled at or near to the town. Situated on the great route from Bayonne to Burgos, it is defended by a fort, elevated on a steep and rocky height; the valley is very narrow, scarcely affording space for the road, and rapid mountain-stream, that, rushing past, is in perfect unison with its surrounding scenery, which is characterised by the wildest and most rugged features of uncultivated nature.

During this period of slow retrograde movement on the part of the enemy's army, Lord Wellington had been actively employed. He passed the Douro on the 1st and 2nd of June, the Carrion on the 7th, and the Pisuerga on the 8th, 9th, and 10th; and, having concentrated his numerous and brilliant army, reconnoitred Burgos on the 12th, occasioning the abandonment of that place, as previously noticed; after which the allies, unobstructedly advanced to the banks of the Ebro. The routes to the left of the great communication from Burgos to Vittoria were considered by the French generals impracticable for the movement of an army. Reports from peasantry, and personal acquaintance with the localities, tended to confirm this belief, adding to the surprise occasioned by the non-appearance of the allies on the direct line of their immediate retreat.

Notwithstanding these supposed insurmountable difficulties, the British generals unhesitatingly marched forward, and having turned the strong pass of Pancorbo, all the obstructions between it and Miranda, and the right flank of the enemy's armies, he crossed the Ebro by the bridges of San Martin, Rocamonde, and Arenas. This very judicious, ably executed, and highly effective movement, became known at the French headquarters on the evening of the 18th, when General Gazan learned, with astonishment, that the whole allied army were on the left bank of the river.

This was probably the most masterly movement made during the Peninsular War, either with reference to the object meditated, the difficulties attending its execution, or the consequences produced by its success. All the confident and matured arrangements of the French Army were at once overset; hurry and confusion followed the knowledge of what had happened, and an immediate night march was the consequence. Drums beat in all directions; cavalry filed past: while the town of Pancorbo, crowded with the unwieldy ambulances containing plunder accompanying the army, presented a scene of strange confusion.

Having left a garrison of 800 men in the fort, Comte Gazan marched his army direct upon Miranda, which continued to be the headquarters of the "Army of the Centre." There we arrived before daybreak, but were permitted a very brief interval of rest. I was now in charge of two mounted *gens-d'armes*, but permitted to ride in any part of the column of march most congenial to my wishes: by this means, opportunity was afforded of seeing, at different times, the whole French Army. As the Franco-Spanish court moved with these troops, there was a great display of uniform: the civil departments of the army, officers attached to the household, or the Spanish ministers, were alike loaded with embroidery; the general officers, even in the forenoons, constantly wore their uniforms.

Accompanying the "Army of the South," numerous ladies, dressed *en militaire*, and on horseback, having forsaken the plains of Andalusia, followed the fortunes of their Gallic lovers. The assemblage was motley in the extreme; nor could it be doubted that habits of luxury, added to the facility of procuring transport in a country where every animal was by them considered the property of the first military person that secured it, had to a great degree encumbered the French armies; a circumstance that did not escape the animadversion of the superior officers themselves.

Of the cavalry, the heavy dragoons, dressed in green, with brass helmets, were superior troops to the other classes of the same army serving in Spain. The *Chasseurs à Cheval*, except in uniform, varied little, either in quality or appearance, from the hussars; both were mounted on a slight, not very compact, species of horse; each of these regiments possessed a *"compagnie-d'élite."* The *chasseur* regiments under the imperial government were variously dressed; and of the hussars, not two corps were in uniform alike. The horse artillery, habited in light blue, braided with black, appeared in a high state of equipment and discipline.

Of the infantry there were but two classes,—the light regiments and those of the line. To each battalion of the latter were attached a company of grenadiers, and one of *voltigeurs*. And to the light regiments were also added companies of the former. No soldier was armed with a rifle in the imperial party.

The *voltigeurs* performed the duties of light troops, while the regiments denominated *légère*, most frequently acted in line.

Of the different corps in the French Army, none appeared more efficient than the artillery. The brigades accompanying the three armies, I had, on this occasion, an opportunity of observing, were invariably well appointed—horses, carriages, accoutrements, all seemed in perfect order.

The *gens-d'armerie à cheval*, at this time numerous in Spain, and selected from the *élite* of the cavalry regiments, were fine in appearance, frequently acting in a body; and with the distinction to be expected from veteran soldiers. Their long blue clothing, cocked hats, and broad buff belts, gave them a very distinct appearance from any other class of French cavalry. The *élite* of the dragoon regiments, wearing furred grenadier caps, were men of great stature and martial appearance.

The discipline of the troops seemed not of the strictest description; nor did the regimental officers apparently preserve that control so necessary for its support. The same line of distinction between men and officers was not so sedulously observed as in the British Army, arising in great measure from the opposite modes of composition, the conscription conveying to the ranks persons of family; and occasionally the private or non-commissioned officer being from a superior grade of French society to the officer placed over him. As a proof of this species of unmilitary equality existing in the imperial armies, I have witnessed a sergeant of infantry walking in familiar conversation with, and his arm locked in that of, his officer.

But with all this apparent laxity, it was impossible to see the French armies without being impressed with the perfect manner in which the duties were invariably performed; ever in readiness, the soldier was instantaneously put in motion when occasion demanded celerity of movement. Under the most unenviable circumstances, custom had inured him to the practice of endeavouring, as far as possible, to provide for diminishing the want of comfort that prevailed; and, instead of staring about to discover all the miseries of his bivouac, he had probably already half-unroofed the nearest habitation for the purpose of composing his fire, before a British soldier, under similar circumstances, would have taken off his accoutrements.

When the blaze was kindled, and his knees and *schakos* in close contact with the crackling wood, a shrug of the shoulder denoted the commencement of a long tirade of complaints, which, until the fire was lighted, and the soup in a state of preparation, he had neither time nor inclination to think of or to compose.

In marching, the French infantry appeared indefatigable: their progress was equally remarkable for the rapidity with which they passed over the ground, or the distances performed, encumbered by long and heavy great coats, which were constantly worn; the soldiers, not satisfied with the burdens they were necessitated to carry, were occasionally seen conveying articles of a superfluous description, sometimes not of the lightest kind. In the line of march, I have observed roulette tables borne on the shoulders of the soldiery.

To render the carriage of foils less irksome, they were occasionally strapped close to the short sword of the grenadier, while several circular Spanish loaves of bread, perforated with a cord through their centres, and slung over the cross-belts, hung dangling at his back.

After a long and fatiguing march of thirty-two miles, the "Army of the South" entered Vittoria on the evening of the 19th. A more crowded town has seldom been witnessed: the court of Joseph Bonaparte, his guards, the various convoys from the interior, the headquarters of the "Army of the Centre," and some of the cavalry, already occupied its buildings, or added to the confusion in the streets; the numerous staff and civil departments of Comte Gazan's army, formed a most embarrassing addition to this already very unmanageable assemblage.

The convoy with which I had left Madrid had not yet proceeded beyond Vittoria; nor did it appear to have been the primary intention of the enemy to abandon the country on the left bank of the Ebro, and many of the Spanish refugees had consequently hoped the capital of the province of Alava would, for a time, terminate the very unwilling pilgrimage they had from necessity been induced to make. The passage of the Ebro by the allied army awakened the military and civil authorities from these dreams; and upon visiting some of the Spanish families with whom I had previously been acquainted, they were found making preparations for accompanying the cavalcade destined to move the following day on the road to Bayonne.

At night, Vittoria was illuminated in honour of the *soi-disant* king. As this was the result of orders, and either French officers or their adherents inhabited every house, there could be no difficulty in accounting for this tribute of respect. During the evening and night, the armies were placed in position, covering the town; peasants were compelled to assist in throwing up temporary field-works, into which were conveyed upwards of one hundred pieces of artillery.

The whole of the convoys, excepting that of the king, and the baggage immediately appertaining to the different armies, left Vittoria on the morning of the 20th, defiling by the route leading to Irun; the carriages and wagons extended as far as the eye could reach, winding through the rich and beautiful valley.

Vittoria is situated on rising ground, surrounded, at a considerable distance, by an amphitheatre of mountain. With the exception of the height upon which the city is built, the country in its immediate neighbourhood is level, and of slight elevation. Extending along the north-west front of the town, at the distance of a mile, runs the Zadorra, a considerable stream, over which are erected several bridges; to the south-west the lofty and extensive heights of Puebla communicate with the high grounds domineering the route leading to Pampeluno: while on the directly opposite side of the valley, which in that particular part becomes more widely displayed, rise the eminences above the villages of Gamarra Mayor and Abechuca.

The situation of Vittoria is particularly picturesque and beautiful. At the period I am detailing, everything about it had become eminently interesting from the situation of two powerful armies having arrived in close contact, under circumstances that rendered it nearly a matter of certainty that its neighbourhood must become the arena of very serious conflict.

During the morning of the 20th, great excitement, attended with feverish and unsteady feeling, seemed to have taken possession of the inhabitants and their numerous visitors. They had ascertained the near approach of the allied army, and in the act of occupying so extensive a position as that selected by Marshal Jourdan, great activity and constant movement were perceptible; troops passed through the town, and the sound of artillery and carriage wheels became incessant. The immense convoy that had left Vittoria appeared to have produced but little effect in relieving the crowded state of the town, the streets still presenting scenes of the utmost confusion, without any effort being apparent, by which order was sought to be restored.

In the midst of this chaos, an *aide-de-ca*mp of Comte Gazan arrived, with orders that I should immediately proceed to his headquarters. This most welcome intelligence was communicated by a colonel of the *état major*, who directed me to prepare for departure, and intimated his intention of accompanying me to the residence of the general-in-chief. On leaving Vittoria, to the left of the fine avenue of trees leading into the city, my attention was directed to the reserve parks of the French armies. In point of number I had never seen so many pieces of field artillery assembled, nor can I conceive anything more regular, beautifully arranged, or in better order, than was this very imposing display of cannon.

The French colonel particularly called my attention to this sight, and, as if determined it should be my last impression of the imperial army, ordered my eyes to be bound up immediately after. We soon arrived at the village of Ariñez, where I was presented to the officers of the *état* major, and conducted to the house occupied by the general-in-chief. Having passed the night in completing the arrangement in position of the army under his orders, Comte Gazan had retired to obtain some repose, previous to the renewal of fatigues which he had every reason to anticipate. Madame Gazan, and the officers of his staff, were assembled in the *salon*, and with them I remained until the general appeared.

In the morning, Colonel Alexander Gordon, *aide-de-camp* to Lord Wellington, had arrived at the advanced posts, with a letter from his Lordship, agreeing to the exchange proposed by Comte Gazan; who, faithful to his promise, determined at once that I should be conveyed to the nearest of the allied troops. During the time occupied in preparing an escort, the French officers conversed with great cheerfulness, and apparent cordiality; and Madame Gazan, considering it an impossible contingency, ironically requested, in the event of her being captured by the allies, that I would exert my good offices to obtain for her a favourable reception. This sally occasioned considerable mirth, which was not diminished upon my departure, an event witnessed by the whole staff.

Mounted on a very diminutive horse, my eyes bound up, the appearance of a low and small cocked hat then worn by the British Army, and the constant subject of derision in that of the enemy, all contributed to complete, in their opinion, a most grotesque figure; nor were the French officers very restrained in the mirth thereby drawn forth. They, however, closed the scene by protestations of kindness and good wishes. I was too happy at the prospect of rejoining my companions, to be either hurt or affected by the amusement produced at my expense, and, after repeated *adieus*, quitted the presence of those careless and apparently happy persons.

As we were about proceeding to the quarters of the allied army, considerable pains had been taken in the selection of an escort: it consisted of detachments from the *élite* of the 2nd Hussars, and *21me* regiment of *Chasseurs à Cheval*: an officer of the *état major*, and a trumpeter, completed the *cortège*. The moment we had passed the last French *vidette*, the bandage being removed, I had an opportunity of observing my companions, and noticed the broken, rugged, but picturesque, country through which we were advancing. At length, in a valley shaded by trees, a piquet of Portuguese cavalry appeared, upon observing which, the French trumpeter began to exert his lungs, and a white pocket handkerchief was waved as an emblem of peace.

All proved ineffectual; the piquet, alarmed at the array evidently approaching direct to their post, treated with disregard the signals made, and, mounting with precipitation, galloped back, circulating a very unfounded alarm in the infantry camp. Under these circumstances it became necessary to advance with caution, until we encountered troops inclined to remain, and discover that it was merely a flag of truce paying this unexpected, and apparently, to the Portuguese, not very welcome visit. In noticing this precipitate and very unsoldierlike conduct in a small detachment of Portuguese cavalry, I do it without the slightest intention of casting any reflection that can attach generally to the troops of that service. I have previously stated my humble tribute of respect for their undeviating good conduct on every occasion, wherein I had opportunities of witnessing their demeanour in contact with the enemy; only rendering more remarkable the uncommonly manifest dislike to hostile encounter shewn by the detachment on the above detailed occasion.

The appearance of officers of the allied staff coming to ascertain what had happened, and to whom the object of the flag of truce was explained, rendered it unnecessary for the French escort to proceed, and after some conversation, we took leave, the enemy's detachment almost immediately after being lost to sight among the wooded knolls, situated between the positions of the armies.

Having obtained information from Captain Owen, of the 18th Hussars, one of the officers whom curiosity had drawn to the front, relative to the situation of the nearest troops, I proceeded to the encampment of the 4th division; and having met Sir Lowry Cole, walked on with him towards the headquarters. On arriving at the house inhabited by the commander of the forces, I had the satisfaction of meeting Sir Rowland Hill, Marshal Beresford, Colonel Rooke, and Lord Charles Fitzroy. An *aide-de-camp* having communicated my arrival from the enemy's army, I was immediately received by Lord Wellington, and, with delight, communicated to him the information derived from a residence with the imperial troops. The important fact of the French generals being determined to make a stand in their present position, from every circumstance I considered perfectly decided, and adduced reasons for that opinion.

Having marched with the different armies, obtained information from each, and learned probably more than was intended of their relative situations and numerical strength, my observation, although defective, carried with it a certainty of authenticity seldom to be derived by a commander-in-chief on the eve of fighting a general action.

General Gazan had intrusted me with a letter for Lord Wellington, in which was stated his having, according to agreement, restored me to liberty; but that, until the officer, with whom the exchange had been made, left England, I must continue on parole, and not serve in any capacity against France.

This was not agreeable; but to have been exchanged under any circumstances was an instance of good fortune: it was the first Lord Wellington had been enabled, without difficulty, to effect with the French Army, and proceeded in all probability from the great desire felt by a general-in-chief to ensure the liberation of a person in whom he felt particularly interested. That Comte Gazan acted on such impulse there can be no doubt; but the whole course of his conduct and manner towards me was kind and considerate.

In consequence of this arrangement, I was destined to be present in the battle, about to take place, merely as a spectator. Late in the evening, accompanied by Lord Charles Fitzroy, I rode to the quarters of Sir Rowland Hill, and anxiously anticipated the great events now with certainty to occur on the succeeding day.

It was rather a singular coincidence of circumstances, that the intelligence of the Emperor Napoleon having, in Germany, concluded an armistice on the 4th of June, should have arrived at Vittoria in time to be, for the first time, communicated as an authenticated fact by a British officer to his commander the day preceding the great battle that ensued.

The morning of the 21st of June was extremely brilliant: a clearer or more beautiful atmosphere never favoured the progress of a gigantic conflict. The corps of Sir Rowland Hill marched in the direction of the great road leading from Burgos to Vittoria, crossing near to La

The Battle of Vittoria

Puebla, the same route which I had, two days previously, travelled with the French Army. Sir Rowland, being intrusted with the service of turning the left flank of the enemy, commanded on the extreme right.

The French armies occupied the extensive line of country from the heights of La Puebla on one hand, to those above Gamarra Mayor on the other. The "Armies of Portugal and of the South" were in the first line, that of the "Centre," with the cavalry, being in reserve; the whole force were, with few exceptions, on the left bank of the Zadorra, and in front of the town of Vittoria.

In the centre, and near to the village of Gomecha, considered the most vulnerable part of the position, had been placed in battery a large proportion of the enemy's cannon. His front was protected by the Zadorra, and to the rear, the great route leading to Bayonne, and that towards Pampeluna, seemed to assure means of retreat, in case of eventual disaster. Communications from one part of the French position to another were direct, and not liable to obstruction. The low grounds near to Vittoria affording the only field for cavalry operations, there, at the commencement of the action, a large body was assembled, and for many hours remained in a state of inactivity. The great error of the French position was extent, more particularly when opposed by an army sufficiently numerous to manoeuvre at the same time against all parts of its line.

In the morning, Sir Rowland Hill's corps, having arrived close to the Miranda road, halted between it and a mill upon the Zadorra; from thence he detached General Morillo, with part of the Spanish division, to attack the left flank of the enemy's army, and drive him back from the commanding heights of La Puebla. Under cover of a wood, the Spaniards mounted the steep ascent, and on its summit became immediately engaged with the enemy: a desultory and constant fire of musketry continued for some time to proceed from nearly the same spot, proving the slight impression made on the enemy's position. General Morillo had led this attack with his accustomed gallantry, and although twice wounded, declined quitting the field; but requested reinforcements.

Sir Rowland ordered Colonel Cadogan, with part of the brigade under his temporary command, to ascend, and secure the success of the attack. Thus assailed, the enemy, alarmed for the safety of that flank, detached troops from the centre of his line, who, meeting the British and Spanish force, now established on the very summit of the

La Puebla heights, a warm and severely contested action took place. Pressing forward at the head of his brigade, Colonel Cadogan was mortally wounded by a musket ball. In a hopeless state as to the possibility of recovery, no attempt was made to carry him from the field, where, enthusiastic to the last, he requested removal to a situation from whence he could gaze on the triumphant progress of companions with whom he had so frequently participated in victory.

His fall was deeply regretted, affording a striking example of the uncertainty attending all human events, and the fallacy of dependence on what is considered most desirable. The evening previous to the battle, when informed that it would certainly take place, his exultation was unbounded: going into action as the commander of that noble brigade appeared the climax of his wishes, and the forerunner of distinction: before the conflict terminated, he was numbered with the dead!

A brigade of the 2nd division, consisting of the 28th, 34th, and 39th regiments, under Colonel O'Callaghan, was ordered to carry the village of Subijana de Alava—a service speedily accomplished, notwithstanding the determined resistance of the enemy. Advanced as Subijana was, its occupation, previous to a general movement in the whole line, occasioned Colonel O'Callaghan's being exposed to the repeated and strenuous efforts of French troops to recover possession of the village, which he, however, gallantly maintained for a length of time before the centre and left of the array had closed up in a manner enabling the commander of the forces to make his attack general and decisive.

Several divisions of the army had passed the night at a considerable distance from the field of battle, the roads to which occasioned delay not previously calculated upon; consequently the attack on the French left commenced earlier than was necessary, could it have been ascertained with accuracy when the centre divisions would by possibility be brought into action.

It being probable, from having so recently left the French Army, that there might be some points on which Lord Wellington would wish to question me, with the approbation of Sir Rowland Hill, I proceeded, soon after the firing commenced, to his Lordship, and had the honour of being with him during the whole course of this most eventful day.

The headquarters staff, when I rode up, were stationed on an eminence considerably elevated above the line of the Zadorra, on its right bank, and nearly opposite to the village of Ariñez. Lord Wellington was on foot, with his glass, surveying the whole extent of either army, and particularly the progress of the contest on the heights of La Puebla.

Dressed in a short gray great coat, closely buttoned over his embroidered Spanish sash, a feathered hat alone denoted his rank; but, upon approaching, the greatest stranger could not long have remained in ignorance of his presiding over the destinies of Britain, Portugal, and Spain.

Upon a remark being made that the troops of Sir Rowland Hill did not seem to be making much impression on the enemy's left, Lord Wellington declared the contrary to be the fact, and that he saw the Highlanders advancing. It was with no slight degree of exultation I heard this tribute to my countrymen; and with my glass perceived the waving tartans of the 92nd, as the soldiers of that distinguished regiment marched along the ridge of the La Puebla heights in pursuit of the enemy. Distant as they were, in imagination I conceived they trode with unusual firmness, and, on the mountain summit, emulated the unconquerable qualities of their ancestors.

The repeated and severe attacks to which the troops in Subijana de Alava were subjected, increased anxiety for the arrival of the centre columns; more particularly as the smoke of Sir Thomas Graham's artillery proclaimed the battle having also commenced on the left. At length, it was reported to Lord Wellington, that Lord Dalhousie had arrived at Mendonza, with the 3rd and 7th divisions. The light and fourth divisions had already crossed the Zadorra, by the bridges of Nanclaus and Tres Puentes. These were speedily followed by Sir Thomas Picton and Lord Dalhousie; upon which the battle became general.

At the moment of the allied divisions passing the river, was exhibited one of the most animating scenes ever beheld: the whole country appeared filled with columns of troops: the sun shone bright: not a cloud obscured the brilliant and glowing atmosphere. From right to left, as far as the eye could reach, scarcely the most diminutive space intervened between bodies of troops, either already engaged, or rapidly advancing into action; artillery and musketry were heard in one continued uninterrupted volume of sound, and although the great force of French cannon had not yet opened upon the assailants, the fire had already become exceedingly violent.

Soon after passing the river, General Colville's brigade of the 3rd division encountered a considerable body of the enemy's troops, which it speedily defeated; but, in the eagerness of pursuit, and in some confusion, met, on the summit of a ridge, two lines of French infantry, regularly formed, and prepared to receive it. Elevated as we were, this situation of affairs was very distinctly perceptible, nor could a rational doubt exist relating to the fate of the assailants. It was remarked by the commander of the forces, who expressed his expectation of some disaster in consequence occurring, but with a coolness and self-possession only to be acquired by an inward confidence of having the means speedily to remedy the anticipated temporary repulse. He continued to observe the irregular advance of these troops, and beheld, with surprise, this crowd of gallant soldiers at once vanquish formation and discipline, sweeping before them the array that, circumstanced as they were, appeared calculated to produce annihilation.

The village of Ariñez was vigorously defended, and for a time the enemy successfully resisted every effort made to obtain possession of it. The 88th, so often distinguished in the gallant achievements of the 3rd division, was repulsed, and the town ultimately carried by the 74th and 45th regiments. On an eminence above this village, Lord Wellington, in the midst of the musketry fire, gave orders for future operations; it was the only period during the day that there appeared a very doubtful struggle; and it is but justice to declare, that, in this instance, the "Army of the South" fought with great determination.

I must here relate a circumstance, insignificant in importance with reference to the progress of events, but conclusive as to the self-possession and perfect coolness of Lord Wellington.

Immediately after the repulse of the first attack on Ariñez, when musket balls were flying about him in all directions, his Lordship, wishing to despatch an order, turned round and directed me to proceed with it, when, instantly recollecting the situation in which I was placed, he said, "No, you cannot do it;" and another officer, who had just come up, was intrusted with the message. What renders this anecdote more striking is, that in the bustle of such a scene, when the success of an attack appeared for a moment doubtful, when from the midst of fire and smoke he had detached every officer previously with him except myself, his mind continued so unshaken by events, and in such a perfect state of equanimity, as to remember the circumstances under which was placed so insignificant a person.

Soon after the above-mentioned occurrence, General Alava, and some of the confidential officers of his staff, on returning, expressed alarm at the exposed situation in which he then was, but without effect; he continued issuing orders from nearly the same spot, until Ariñez was in possession of the British line, and the enemy in full retreat towards Vittoria.

It was after the abandonment of the first position, that the French artillery, formerly mentioned as having been placed in rapidly constructed field works, opened on the advancing columns of the allied army. Through this tremendous fire Lord Wellington had to pass, as he galloped to the right of his army for the purpose of ascertaining the state of the battle in that direction. His route being in a nearly parallel line, he ran the gauntlet of about eighty pieces of cannon, and fortunately escaped untouched.

In passing through the village of Ariñez, I interrogated a wounded French soldier of the *12me Légère*, and from him learned that the advanced guard of the "Army of the South" had been there engaged, and suffered severely.

The enemy had hitherto retired in perfect order; nor was it until the abandonment of its artillery commenced, that the French Army lost its formation. At this period of the action, the allies were advancing in the most beautiful style. Lord Wellington having ascertained the progress of affairs on his right, arrived on an eminence to the south of the great road, and about a mile from Vittoria. He there observed confusion in the enemy's ranks on a plain close to the town, and sent for Colonel Grant, who, soon appearing at the head of his brigade of hussars, advanced along the Camino-real at a rapid pace. In passing, he received orders to branch off to his left, and charge the enemy's flying troops. Reports every moment arrived of the quantity of captured cannon, and that the enemy was hurrying through the town, and giving way in every direction.

To prevent their being immediately used, the French cannon were, in many instances, thrown into the ditches and narrow ravines, where, overturned and mixed with tumbrils and the bodies of dead or wounded soldiers, they presented unusually marked indications of defeat; undoubted proofs of the wreck of an army, and evidences of the consequently secured victory already obtained. A long train of carriages, wagons, and animals of burden, were now seen issuing from Vittoria. Upon observing the line on which they moved, Lord Wellington expressed surprise, and interrogated me respecting the direction of the road to Irun, which he correctly supposed led more to the left. On being informed that this mass of fugitives were on the

Pampeluna road, and that Sir Thomas Graham must have cut off their retreat on that conducting direct to Bayonne, he urged the pursuit with increased animation.

At this moment, the second division, in line, extending up the ascent of the heights to the right, had a most brilliant appearance. Having conquered every obstacle, and driven the enemy from its immediate front, it had been halted, and only awaited orders to move forward in pursuit of further triumphs. At its head was Sir Rowland Hill, the same on all occasions, undeviatingly attentive to the particular service with which he was intrusted: from that he never permitted his attention to be for a moment distracted, invariably performing his duty in the most distinguished and satisfactory manner.

The enemy's troops having entirely disappeared from in front of Vittoria, the commander of the forces proceeded towards that town, for the purpose of urging forward the different columns of his victorious army. Such a scene as the town presented has been seldom witnessed; but no time was permitted either to investigate into, or correct, the chaos that therein reigned. Every step we took proved the decided nature of the *déroute* that had overtaken the French Army. Cannon, overturned carriages, broken down wagons, forsaken tumbrils, wounded soldiers, civilians, women, children, dead horses and mules, absolutely covered the face of the country; while its inhabitants, *and others*, had commenced, diligently commenced, the work of pillage.

Seldom on any previous occasion had so rich a field presented itself. To the accumulated plunder of Andalusia were added the collections made by the other armies; the personal baggage of the king, Fourgons having inscribed upon them in large characters, "*Domaine Extérieur de S. M. l'Empereur*," wagons of every description; and a military chest containing a large sum, recently received from France, for payment of the troops, but which had not yet been distributed; jewels, pictures, embroidery, silks, everything that was costly and portable, seemed to have been assiduously transported, adding to the unmilitary state of these encumbered armies.

Removed from their frames, and rolled up, some of the finest Italian pictures from the royal collections were found in the Imperials of Joseph Bonaparte's carriage.

At one period of the pursuit, an officer of Lord Wellington's personal staff, having carried an order towards the left of the army, on returning, brought with him a long Spanish blade, about a third of which from the point was covered with blood. This had been found on the field, and was, from its singularity of shape, recognised as the sword of Lord Tweeddale. During the confusion, and in the eagerness of pursuit, he had, at the head of some heavy dragoons, penetrated into a lane filled with the enemy's cavalry, and became outnumbered and over- matched at a time when extrication was impracticable. With that determination which marked his conduct on every emergency, he charged the French dragoons, and was overwhelmed in the *mêlée*. Insensible, and trampled underfoot, a considerable time elapsed before he was discovered, when, bruised and wounded, he was withdrawn from among the heaps of dead men and horses that encumbered the narrow road.

While these events were in progress on that part of the field where the commander of the forces led the pursuit, the left of the allies, under Sir Thomas Graham, had been obstinately resisted by the "Army of Portugal," whose divisions, strongly posted, and prepared for defensive operations, occupied very favourable ground, and outnumbered the troops opposed.

Notwithstanding the gallant resistance made by the French infantry, they were beat back; and about noon compelled to abandon the important object of defending those points covering the Bayonne road, and which being forced, not only effectually prevented the adoption of that line of retreat, but endangered the whole position, subjecting the French Army to the extraordinary situation of being turned on both flanks, while an attack of the first magnitude was directed against its centre. No action was ever more general than that of Vittoria: all parts of the enemy's army were assailed nearly at the same moment, and the impression made was everywhere satisfactory.

In the morning, advancing by the great route from Bilbao to Vittoria, Sir Thomas Graham found the enemy strongly posted on the heights above the village of Abechuco; from whence, however, he was speedily removed by General Oswald, having under his orders the fifth division, General Pack's brigade, the Spanish troops of Colonel Longa, and General Anson's brigade of cavalry.

Soon after obtaining possession of the heights, the troops marched to assault the *barricadoed* towns of Gamarra Mayor and Abechuco. Great pains had been taken to strengthen these places, and they were by the enemy occupied as *têtes-de-po*nt for the passages of the Zadorra.

The former was stormed by General Robinson's brigade of the fifth division, which, advancing in columns of battalion, regardless of a heavy and destructive fire of artillery and musketry, pursued its steady, orderly, and not to be obstructed, course, without returning a shot, and at the point of the bayonet forced back the enemy, who retired in confusion, with the loss of three pieces of cannon. Although in possession of the town, General Robinson was not in sufficient force to carry the bridge, on the opposite end of which the enemy had rallied. Fresh troops moved to his support. General Hay's brigade reinforced the assailants, and the contest became of the warmest and most destructive description. Repeated and violent efforts were made to recover possession of the village; but these were rendered unavailing by the unshaken gallantry of the fifth division. The bridge of Gamarra and its vicinity, exhibited proofs of the pertinacity with which both parties had contended; it was covered with dead bodies, and in every respect bore marks of a tremendous conflict. In these affairs the fifth division had nearly five hundred men killed or wounded.

Colonel Fane, of the 59th, and Colonel Campbell, of the Royal, were included in the number of the latter. The former died a few days after, universally regretted; the latter recovered, notwithstanding the dangerous appearance of a very severe musket wound on the head.

It was on the bridge, zealously urging the attack, that Captain George Hay, of the Royal, was mortally wounded: he was transported to Vittoria, where General Hay, after executing the service of the day, passed the whole night in searching for the quarters of his son, and only discovered them to learn that he had a few minutes previously expired.

The village of Abechuco was carried by the light battalions of the German Legion, under Colonel Halkett, supported by General Bradford's brigade, and assisted by the fire of Captain Ramsay's troop of horse-artillery, and a brigade of guns, under Captain Dubourdieu. The enemy does not appear to have considered this point of equal importance with the possession of Gamarra Mayor, nor were similar efforts made either to maintain or to recover the bridge, which, near to Abechuco, also afforded means of passing the Zadorra. In the line of operations, there were no less than six bridges across that stream, over which some portion of the allied army passed. That on the road leading from Burgos enabled Sir Rowland Hill's corps to gain the left bank. Sir Lowry Cole, with the fourth division, passed by the bridge of Nanclaus; the light, at Tres Puentes; Lord Dalhousie and Sir Thomas Picton crossed between Tres Puentes and Abechuco; Sir Thomas Graham's corps by those of Abechuco and Gamarra Mayor: of these, only the two latter were obstinately defended.

The French Army rallied at no point of its line; nor was there the slightest effort made, after passing Vittoria, to check the rapid pursuit of the allies. To escape seemed then to have become the sole object. Its artillery, at first captured in lesser numbers, became at once entirely abandoned; an impression of the impossibility of removing it had become general in all parts of the field, over whose widely extended and uneven surface the artillerymen were seen flying, after having left their cannon to be captured by the nearest advancing troops.

Never previously had so large a body of British artillery been engaged as at Vittoria; and there were casualties in every brigade.

Chapter 7

Pampeluna Blockaded by the Allies

When a considerable distance advanced on the Pampeluna side of Vittoria, Lord Wellington rode to the summit of a knoll, from whence the line of the retreating army was perceptible for upwards of a mile. It is impossible ever to forget the scene opened to view upon gaining the ascent. The valley beneath represented one dense mass, not in column, but extended over the surface of a flat containing several hundred acres. On this spot the now confused multitude were obstructed by their own irregular and precipitate efforts at escape; little movement was discernible, and inevitable destruction seemed to await a crowd of not less than twenty thousand people. Immediate orders were sent for horse-artillery, and in a few minutes Captain Ross's troop, regardless of roads, had crowned the summit of the commanding height, from whence he showered down balls and howitzer shells upon the terrified masses, now urged into efforts at accelerated flight by the slaughter around.

The necessity of passing across the country after its progress had been interrupted by Sir Thomas Graham, and the nearly impracticable state of the road leading from the Irun to the Pampeluna line of communication, occasioned a confusion and delay that insured the capture of the heavy baggage and the reserve artillery.

Never did the commander of the allied army appear so anxious to strike a terrific blow against the enemy; and in the midst of such exhilarating, such apparently satisfactory circumstances, when the full tide of success seemed to crown his exertions, there appeared a feeling of regret at the supposition of the imperfect destruction that had overtaken the armies opposed to him. Probably this proceeded from the comparatively speaking small number of prisoners that met him in his victorious advance; but the nature of the country, the absence of all encumbrance, the rapid disappearance of the French battalions, rendered it out of the question to capture a number at all proportioned either to the killed and wounded, the complete state of *déroute*, or the loss of *matériel*, which had resulted from the battle.

When Lord Wellington closed the pursuit, which he had personally led, it was at a distance of two leagues from Vittoria, and even then he reluctantly desisted, darkness preventing the possibility of any further favourable result. Thus, during the action, three leagues of country had been traversed, on every portion of which different scenes had been enacted. Some estimate may be formed of the fatigues of a general-in-chief under such circumstances, when it is recollected that Lord Wellington had been on horseback, with a short interval, since daylight in the morning; that his mind must have been in constant active excitement; and it was nine at night before he returned to Vittoria.

The town, which, two days previously, I had witnessed lighted up in honour of Joseph Bonaparte, was now blazing with illumination for his total discomfiture. Order had in some measure been restored; and when Lord Wellington and his staff directed their wearied horses along the streets, although extremely crowded, no great irregularities appeared in progress. Soon after entering the town, one of the *aides-de-camp*, who had previously arrived, informed me, that among the French equipages left on the field, was that of Madame Gazan; and being the only person in the army with whom she was acquainted, numerous inquiries had been despatched, trusting anxiously that I would befriend her in the unlooked-for disastrous situation she then was.

I immediately proceeded to wait upon her. A more unenviable situation can scarcely be imagined; but, with the sprightliness and unconcern of her country, she did not appear feeling it to the fullest extent. In the confusion occasioned by the rush of carriages, and the near approach of the firing, a *gen-d'arme à cheval* rode up, proffering his assistance to the wife of his general. Her first impulse was securing the safety of her child, which the soldier undertook to be answerable for; and, having placed the boy before him, rode off, soon disappearing in the crowd. General Darriceau, wounded, and retiring from the field, rode up, and spoke to her; but attempt at extricating her carriage would have been fruitless; and in it she remained until surrounded by the British cavalry. On being brought back to Vittoria, she proceeded to the house of two Spanish ladies, her former acquaintances, and there I found her residing.

At her request, I visited the *dépôt* of prisoners, from whence her servants were restored. I then placed her remaining carriage in safety, endeavoured to quiet her fears for the safety of her child, assured her there could be no doubt of Lord Wellington admitting of immediate return to her husband; after which, having procured a guard, I placed sentinels at the entrance of her quarters, to prevent intrusion, and took leave for the night.

Very early on the morning of the 22nd, I accompanied Madame Gazan to the spot where the equipages had been arrested in their flight on the preceding day; and where she very erroneously entertained hopes of recovering some of the spoils, which, having travelled from Andalusia, loaded three wagons, and enriched the inhabitants of Alava and the stragglers from the allied army. The field was strewed with manuscripts, broken trunks, or shattered carriages; but, naturally, not a vestige remained of anything worthy the trouble of transporting it thence. Being speedily convinced of this fact, we returned to Vittoria, and soon after followed the route of the army towards Salvatierra.

Considering it my duty, and feeling happy in the opportunity of in a slight degree returning the kindness of Comte Gazan, by securing the safety of his wife, I remained near to her carriage, or rode within sight of it during the course of the forenoon. Lord Wellington desired me to request Madame Gazan would dine with him on the 22nd. At the accustomed hour, I accompanied her to his Lordship's. The evening passed very agreeably: she was in every respect treated with the utmost courtesy, and the following morning rejoined her husband and her child.

The march from Vittoria to Salvatierra was unlike what might have been expected immediately to succeed so decisive a victory as that of the preceding day. None of the enemy's troops were visible giving animation to the way; all had disappeared: so effectually had the French Army escaped, that, during the intervening space, not a shot was fired. The advancing columns beheld not an enemy against whom could be renewed the revelry of the 21st.

Lord Wellington, having at first pursued on the direct track of the enemy's armies, considered those defeated at Vittoria so completely subdued, that he despatched some light troops in the direction of Roncesvalles, and the light, 3rd, 4th, and 7th divisions, with Colonel Grant's and Colonel Ponsonby's brigades of cavalry, marched towards Tudela de Ebro, hoping to intercept the retreat of General Clausel, who, in full march to reinforce, had received the unwelcome tidings of the battle. The 5th and 6th divisions, with the household cavalry, had marched by another route, to ensure his capture; but, by extraordinary exertion, he succeeded in effecting an escape, under circumstances of great peril, thereby supporting the military character deservedly obtained by saving the wreck of the Duke of Ragusa's army after Salamanca. Despairing of being enabled to effect anything decisive against a corps retreating with such rapidity, and whose route to join the army of Cataluna, under the Duke of Albufera, now became unobstructed, Lord Wellington turned towards the Pyrenees; and having left the indefatigable Mina to follow up the retiring column of the enemy, he established the headquarters near to Pampeluna.

Previously to passing the frontier, after the Battle of Vittoria, the enemy placed General Cassan, with a numerous garrison, in the strong fortress of Pampeluna, which, on the arrival of the allies, became blockaded by the troops under Sir Rowland Hill.

Sir Thomas Graham, having been detached on the Bayonne road, for the purpose of beating back the corps of General Foy, and compelling him to evacuate the Spanish territory, came up with that general, strongly posted in the walled town of Tolosa; and having manoeuvred to secure the success of his attack, he blew open the gates with artillery, forcing a passage into the place. Darkness alone favoured the retreat of the enemy, who pursued his route across the Bidassoa, without any further attempt at resistance.

The fort of Santa Engracia at Pancorbo, having surrendered on the 1st of July, (1813), to the Spanish Army of the Condé de la Bisbal, with the exception of the garrisons of Pampeluna and San Sebastian, not a French soldier continued in arms within the whole extent of the northern provinces of Spain. Of four hundred thousand men that had entered the Peninsula to enforce its subjugation, the diminished army of Marshal Suchet, and the two garrisons above stated, alone remained!

Pampeluna, the ancient Pompeiopolis, founded by Pompey the Great, is, in modern days, an extensive city, and one of the strongest fortified places of the Peninsula. Situated on a perfect level, it is not commanded by any domineering or neighbouring height. The citadel, built at the southern extremity of the works, is, from the exterior, little perceptible, the parapets of its walls being on a level with the surrounding plain, and consequently in great measure protected from the effects of breaching batteries. This formidable place the commander of the forces prepared to besiege, but subsequently resolved to reduce by blockade.

Lord Dalhousie, with the 6th and 7th divisions, was, in the first instance, intrusted with the operations; and the investment being rendered perfect, nine redoubts were constructed on eminences encircling the town, at a distance of twelve or fifteen hundred yards. Major Goldfinch, of the engineers, superintended the completion of these works, which were garrisoned and armed with some of the French field-artillery captured at Vittoria.

The probable re-advance of the French Army, for the purpose of withdrawing the garrisons, rendering it important to assemble the whole British force on the immediate frontier, Lord Dalhousie delivered over the conduct of the blockade to Don Carlos España, who, with a force of about nine thousand Spaniards, was intrusted with that important service.

Pampeluna

CHAPTER 8

Termination of the Peninsular War

Not being permitted to serve with the army, I left Sir Rowland Hill's headquarters at Orcayan, on the 2nd of July, taking the route for Madrid; resolved to remain in that city until apprised by the military secretary that the cartel, restoring me to unrestricted liberty, had arrived from England.

In the evening, I entered Tafalla, one of the minor cities of Navarre; and the following day, having crossed the Ebro, near to Peralta, remained for the night in the large and populous town of Cintruenigo. The limited portion of territory on the right bank of the Ebro, appertaining to the kingdom of Navarre, is populous and highly cultivated; the walled cities of Calahorra and Alfaro rising from the plain in the immediate vicinity of the river, give an imposing appearance to the landscape. Having entered the province of Soria, near to Cervera, and passed through Agreda on the 4th, I halted at Paredes, continuing my journey the following morning through the fertile plains of Guadalaxara. On the 7th, I visited the fine town of Alcala de Henares, and in the evening arrived at Madrid.

The day after thus again entering the capital, I became an inmate of the house of Rivella Gijeda, and experienced that kindness and hospitality with which the *condé* and *condessa* had ever greeted the English. During the period that had intervened since the departure of the allied army in 1812, they had continued to reside in Madrid, notwithstanding the suspicion and dislike expressed by the French authorities in consequence of their well-known sentiments. In detailing some incidents that had occurred during the winter, one instance of presumptuous feeling seemed to have afforded great amusement. Soon after the French repossessed the capital, an *aide-de-camp* of Joseph Bonaparte, in the arrangement of quarters, became domiciled in their house; but upon his master being made acquainted with the fact, he declared that no officer of his household should inhabit a quarter that had been the residence of the Prince of Orange! and, to the satisfaction of the family, he was compelled to betake himself to other apartments.

The Battle of Vittoria had occasioned so great a change in public opinion, and the return of the French court was now believed to be so improbable, that many of the *grandees*, who had considered themselves in a species of exile at Cadiz, adopted the resolution of returning to the capital.

By these accessions to the society, the Tertullas at the house of Rivella Gijeda became more numerous and more brilliant, while report announced the daily arrival of powerful and influential families; but Madrid still wanted the Medina Celis, the Altamiras, the Ossunas, or the Infantados. The old Duchess of Ossuna and Benevente remained at Cadiz; but her more enterprising daughter, the beautiful Marquesa de Santa Crux, had returned to grace that society in which she had formerly moved with distinguished *éclat*.

Many of the French party still lurked in Madrid, but preserved a caution in their conduct proportioned to the hopeless state of the cause to which, from mistaken policy, they had adhered and become the partisans.

The Spanish Government, on learning the great events that had occurred in the north, expressed its unbounded gratitude to Lord Wellington, conferring on him the additional title of Duque de Vittoria, and possession of the beautiful estate of Soto de Roma, near to Grenada. When the favour of the Prince of Peace with the Spanish Bourbons was at its height, he had appropriated to himself two of the most valuable estates in Spain; one of which, having been conferred upon Marshal Suchet by the Emperor Napoleon, formed the title of his dukedom; the other was now bestowed, as above stated, on the successful leader of the allied army.

The temporary cessation of hostilities in Germany had, of course, occasioned a brief period of relaxation from that conflict which Napoleon, notwithstanding his losses in Russia, had maintained with nearly unimpaired vigour, and with the unsubdued and terrifying impression naturally attached to that stupendous military genius, which, until the snows of the north taught a lesson of humility, had led the armies of France from triumph to triumph, occasioning in the nations of Europe a feeling of terror greater than ever previously attached to mortal name.

The armistices on former occasions concluded by this extraordinary man, either in Italy, the scene of his early glory, under the walls of Vienna, or when in possession of the capital of the great Frederick, had invariably been preludes to the humiliation of his adversaries; and although misfortune had diminished his means, and the battles of Lutzen and Bautzen had not been of the decisive character, or partaken of the overwhelming results that attached to those of Marengo, Austerlitz, or Jena, still there was an impression created by the circumstance of the Russian and Prussian cabinets being desirous to conclude a suspension of arms, calculated to mislead regarding the real posture of affairs, and to induce a belief that Napoleon, on the eve of concluding a peace with those powers, would once more be enabled to direct his undivided energies to the Peninsular War.

Under these circumstances, nothing could have been better timed than the Battle of Vittoria: the same courier that conveyed to his brother a notification of the armistice, might, in returning to Napoleon, have been the bearer of intelligence announcing the total defeat of his armies, and the circumstance of his being driven from the territory, that no longer, in the most trivial respect, acknowledged his supremacy. One month deferred, the armies on the Ebro would have been reinforced by sixty thousand men, and thereby have become too powerful to admit of the great impression created by the energetic and well-timed advance of the allied army.

It is to be conceived with what mingled feelings of disappointment and irritation the ruler of France learned the course of events at the base of the Pyrenees, and that his brother and his generals no longer prosecuted the war in Spain, but, defeated and shaken in confidence, had sought shelter in the plains of Gascony. Accustomed as he had been to receive reports from the Peninsula little calculated to give satisfaction, or to confirm his impression of the invincible qualities of those troops which he had personally ever led to certain victory, so extensive and alarming a reverse as that now made known must have been as unexpected as it was disastrous; but with all the promptitude of a person born to command, instead of yielding to gloomy circumstances, he issued orders for a bold effort to counteract the tide of war, to recover the ground lost by Vittoria, and to awaken to energy, as he conceived, the dormant spirit of his soldiers. Troops marched from the interior to reinforce, artillery from the *dépôts* completed the equipment, and the Marshal Duke of Dalmatia was intrusted with full powers to conduct the renewed hostilities, and retrieve the errors of his predecessors.

General Gazan resumed his situation as chief of the staff; the army, divided into three corps, commanded by Comte Reille, Comte D'Erlon, and General Clausel, with a reserve under General Villatte, and three divisions of cavalry, prepared to force the passes of the mountains, and march to relieve Pampeluna. Upon assuming the command of the "Army of Spain," Marshal Soult issued a proclamation in imitation of those spirit-stirring productions by which Napoleon was accustomed to call forth the enthusiastic admiration of his soldiers; but the essential quality calculated to give effect was wanting. When the emperor, by the roll of the drum, called attention to his emphatic words, the troops knew that he would fulfil the promise of leading them to victory; and that knowledge gave effect to the concise but brilliant announcement of his intentions, and what he expected from them. When the Duke of Dalmatia's proclamation appeared, it was that of an ordinary man promising more than he could perform, and as such was received by those to whom it was immediately addressed.

The blockade of Pampeluna, which commenced on the 25th of June, was from that date strictly enforced.

Lord Wellington, after reconnoitring San Sebastian on the 12th July, gave orders for the siege. Trenches were opened on the evening of the 13th, and the works against the place proceeded with regularity; the troops employed to reduce it being the 5th division, commanded by General Oswald, and the Portuguese brigades of Generals Bradford and Wilson; the whole under the orders of Sir Thomas Graham, who was intrusted with the conduct of the siege.

The first operation of importance that occurred was obtaining possession of the convent of San Bartolomeo, which was carried on the 17th by the 9th regiment, three companies of the Royal Scots, and some detachments of Portuguese infantry.

On the 23rd, two practicable breaches having been formed, the houses in their vicinity also on fire, and the flames rapidly increasing, it was decided to assault the place; but from circumstances that were considered important, its execution was deferred until the 25th; at five o'clock on the morning of which day, the 5th division was assembled, and ready to move from the trenches. Soon after, a mine was exploded, destroying a considerable length of the counterscarp and glacis; it also occasioned a momentary panic in the garrison, from which the assailing party were enabled to reach the breach before the enemy had suf-

RONCESVALLES

ficiently recovered to maintain a concentrated and well-directed fire.

The ground over which the British had to pass in their progress to the ruined wall, was extremely difficult; masses of rock, covered by seaweed, intervening, while pools of water assisted in obstructing the progress of the troops. The breach was flanked by towers of considerable altitude, from whence issued a galling and destructive fire of musketry. Notwithstanding these difficulties, the troops gained the summit of the breach, but were there received by so violent a discharge of grape, shells, and musketry, as to occasion very serious loss. Confusion resulted from the impossibility of forcing forward; and after the fall of Major Fraser, and the capture of Lieutenant Jones, the conducting engineer, the attempt was abandoned, and the troops recalled into the trenches, having sustained a loss of about five hundred men.

Many wounded men lay upon the ascent to the breach, or were extended on the rocky sands at its base. Unable to move, and exposed to the fire which still continued on the part of the enemy, these brave soldiers must have remained in a very fatal situation, had not Captain James Stewart, of the Royal Scots, with great gallantry and perseverance, gone forward, regardless of personal exposure, and succeeded in arranging a truce for a sufficient period to admit of their being removed to the trenches, or carried prisoners into the body of the place.

During these operations, the allied army, exclusive of the troops employed in the siege of San Sebastian and the blockade of Pampeluna, was posted to defend the passes in the Pyrenees. Sir Rowland Hill, on the extreme right, occupied the pass of Roncesvalles, with General Byng's brigade of British infantry; and the troops of General Morillo, having General Pringle's brigade, in the valley of Bastan; while the Portuguese division of the Condé de Amarante, and General Walker's brigade of the 2nd division, were encamped near to the summit of the Maya pass.

General Cole, with the 4th division, at Viscarret, one league in rear of Roncesvalles, was in reserve to Sir Rowland Hill.

The 3rd division, under Sir Thomas Picton, supported the troops at Maya.

The 6th division was also in second line at San Estevan. The light and 7th divisions were at Vera and Echelar. The Spanish division of General Longa kept up the communication between Vera and the 1st division, which, with the army of General Giron, was on the great *chaussée* leading to Bayonne, or on the heights to its immediate right.

The allied force, thus stationed, covered a great extent of country, intersected by mountain and valley, in many respects difficult of access, or of rapid communication. The only means of penetrating being by the great routes leading across the Pyrenees, it was evident the French marshal might select a line, and conduct a force quite disproportioned to any that could be speedily assembled at a particular point, for the purpose of resistance. This occasioned an almost certain success to assailants in the first instance; but from the nature of the country, and means of concentration afforded by retirement, it was improbable that superiority would for any prolonged period accompany the advance of an enemy.

The 25th of July was not only rendered remarkable by the failure of San Sebastian, but was the date of commencement to those operations of Marshal Soult against the allied positions, by which he hoped to relieve Pampeluna, and again penetrate to Vittoria. On that day, the Duke of Dalmatia having assembled a large force at St. Jean Pied de Port, ascended the Pyrenees, and soon after daybreak, with the utmost impetuosity, attacked General Byng's brigade on the summit of the Roncesvalles pass. Unawed by the presence of from thirty to forty thousand enemies, that distinguished officer maintained his ground; nor could the utmost efforts of the French marshal force back the brave regiments under his orders. Hour after hour passed away, and the assailants were still completely checked. Upon no occasion did the same number of infantry ever arrest for such a period so overwhelming a force.

Sir Lowry Cole moved up with the 4th division in support, and for nine hours, these troops effectually blocked up the passage, impeding the progress of the enemy; nor was it until late in the afternoon, that, by manoeuvre, and turning the position, which necessarily occasioned the retreat of the British infantry, Marshal Soult was enabled to pass the mountain road he had not succeeded in forcing by direct attack.

Towards evening of the same day, Comte d'Erlon, with two divisions of his *corps d'armée,* attacked the brigades of the 2nd division, under Generals Walker and Pringle, stationed on the Maya pass. The enemy for a time advanced unperceived, and a very serious conflict took place. Sir William Stewart, who had that morning gone to Roncesvalles, on his return, heard the firing, and hastened to the spot; with his accustomed gallantry, he rallied the troops, and, regardless of superiority of numbers, repeatedly charged the enemy.

Supported by General Barnes, the 2nd division maintained for seven hours an unequal but determined contest with the enemy. In this very serious attack, many of the British regiments suffered severely. Colonel Fenwick, of the 34th, was severely wounded; as were Colonel Hill and Captain Grant, of the 50th. Colonel Cameron, Majors Mitchel and Macpherson, with sixteen other officers of the 92nd, were also included in the list of wounded. Aware of the events at Roncesvalles, Sir Rowland Hill retired this portion of his corps to Irurita.

Informed, during the night of the 25th, as to the retrograde movement by the right of his army, Lord Wellington gave immediate orders to suspend the further prosecution of the siege of San Sebastian, and left Lezaca to conduct that operation of concentration, by which alone the French Army could be effectually checked. Some idea may be formed of the extensive nature of the position, the centre and right of which had been attacked, and of the time required to traverse the mountain and valley in his route, when it is related that, anxious as he must have been, and active as on every occasion he was proverbially esteemed, it was not until the morning of the 27th that his presence gave confidence to the allied force assembled in position near to Huarte, within a short distance of Pampeluna.

The 3rd and 4th divisions were in the act of taking up their ground when the commander of the forces arrived. The enemy, ranged on the mountains in front, soon after attacked an important height, defended by part of the 4th division, but without success. On its summit, troops of the three allied countries fought with distinction. The 40th British regiment, the 4th Portuguese, and the Spanish battalions of El Principe and Pravia, for two days repelled the repeated attempts made to dislodge them.

Sir Stapleton Cotton, with the British cavalry, was to the right of Huarte; the enemy also displayed a large force of that arm, but from the unfavourable nature of the country, no collision took place.

In the act of taking up its position on the morning of the 28th, the 6th division was attacked, and General Pack, then commanding it, severely wounded. It was from the village of Sorauren the enemy advanced on this occasion, and a more ill-advised movement has seldom been made. From the position of the allies, he was assailed in front, both flanks and rear, and, of course, driven back with enormous loss.

It was subsequent to this repulse that the brave 4th division was subjected to a general attack along the range of heights occupied by its troops.

The only reverse during the day was occasioned by a height, on which was posted the 10th Portuguese Infantry, having been carried. This success on the part of the French general was momentary. Lord Wellington sent the 27th and 48th regiments to charge the enemy, and they not only drove his troops from the eminence, but with the bayonet dislodged those to its immediate left. The repeated charges this day made by the regiments of Sir Lowry Cole's division, particularly the 40th, 7th, 20th, and 23rd, ensured the brilliant execution of the service on which they were employed, and added to their former well-earned renown. A favourable termination to the contest in the Pyrenees became no longer doubtful; every hour added to the improved situation of the allied army; fresh troops came into line; nor did there appear a chance of the Duke of Dalmatia being in any respect enabled to carry his boasted intentions into serious effect. He must, when subsequently called upon to defend the territory of France, have bitterly repented the loss of gallant soldiers fruitlessly expended during the actions in the mountains.

Despairing of being enabled to relieve Pampeluna, and determined to vary his line of operations, on the evening of the 28th, Marshal Soult sent back his artillery, wounded, and the other incumbrances of his army, to St. Jean Pied de Port. On the 30th, the allies became the assailants, and forcing up the crests of mountains, fording rivers, penetrating almost impervious woods, and following the tide of success with singular audacity and enterprise, beat back the French troops from position to position, until the British colours were again posted on those grand eminences from whence are displayed the plains of Gascony.

Had Marshal Soult commenced these operations without pretension, had he assumed the command under usual circumstances of service, his failure might have passed without severe animadversion; or had his military character been supported by a series of scientific or skilful movements, although unfortunate, posterity would not have withheld the meed of praise; but when placed in command with the presumptuous intention of rectifying the errors of others, proclaiming that he was to do so, and supported by great devotion and undoubted gallantry on the part of his troops, the result of the battles in the Pyrenees will establish the facts, that, as a leader, he was not a Napoleon, and that the loss of the Battle of Vittoria might be attributed to other causes than the incapacity of the imperial commanders on that occasion.

As a natural consequence of fighting in the description of country on which these affairs took place, the loss in both armies was very considerable. This must ever be the case in modern warfare in a mountainous country, where the advantage derived from situation will generally be in favour of the inferior quality of troops. To ascend heights resolutely defended, is, on most occasions, a disadvantage not easily overcome, and when surmounted, naturally attended with the severest loss; but, being possessed of them, inferior troops may occasion a murderous ascent to others whom, in the end, they have no prospect of successfully resisting. In the battles of the Pyrenees, the localities were as above described; while the assailants and the attacked, which circumstances occasioned to be alternately the fate of either army, were entitled to be considered troops of the first quality: consequently, the repeated and varied conflicts could not fail to be of a determined and most sanguinary description.

During the retreat of the enemy, General Barnes, with his brigade of the 7th division, became particularly distinguished; he attacked a very superior force, posted on high and difficult ground, proving at the same time the spirit of his battalions, and the dejected feeling produced by repeated reverses on the minds of the enemy's troops.

Over the passes of the Pyrenees, the enemy's army again descended from whence it came; Comte D'Erlon, with his corps, marching by Maya, while General Reille retired by Roncesvalles, and General Clausel by Echelar. Not a soldier in arms, of Marshal Soult's army, continued in the territory of Spain.

Lezaca once more became the British headquarters; and the allied army resumed nearly the same position it had occupied previous to the advance of the French marshal.

Encamped on the romantic heights, and in the beautiful valleys, of the Pyrenees, the troops remained inactive: it was improbable that any renewed attempt would be made, having a similar object to that on the late occasion so signally frustrated; nor was it likely that any movement in advance by the allied army would take place previous to the fall of San Sebastian and Pampeluna.

Upon Lord Wellington's return to Lezaca, the siege of the former was directed to be urged with renewed vigour. The ordnance and stores, which the uncertain state of affairs in the Pyrenees had occasioned being embarked, were, on the 5th of August, relanded at Passages. Subsequent arrivals of battering cannon and ammunition having augmented the force of heavy artillery to one hundred and seventeen pieces, no doubt existed of the army being possessed of

SAN SEBASTIAN

means to ensure a speedy reduction of the fortress; and the engineer and artillery arrangements being in a state of forwardness, on the 24th of the month the attack recommenced.

The town of San Sebastian is situated on a peninsula, at the extremity of which, washed by the tempestuous sea of the Bay of Biscay, rises a remarkable conical rocky height, called Monte Orgullo, upon the point of whose summit stands the citadel or castle of La Mota: the whole extent of this singular eminence is distinctly separated from the town by an outer line of defence at its base; while batteries, erected on the southern ascent, aid and protect the defences in the main body of the place. The town, previous to the siege, contained a large population; the entire space within the works being closely built upon, and numerously inhabited; the streets regular; its *plaza* spacious, and the houses handsome and commodious.

The principal road leading from the place to the castle-keep is conducted from the convent of Santa Teresa to the Mirador battery, situated on a rocky point at the eastern extremity of the ridge, and from thence to that Del Principe, of still greater altitude, and nearly on a line with the battery De la Reyna.

The convent of Santa Teresa, the arsenal, and the battery of St. Elmo, occupy the northern line of the town; and, consequently, are its nearest points of communication with the castle rock.

The eastern defences of San Sebastian are washed by the River Urumea; the western by the ocean; the southern, or land front, stretching across the isthmus, is about 350 yards in extent, having a flat bastion in its centre, strengthened by a hornwork, with a counterscarp, covered way, and glacis: but the defences running on to the peninsula, and facing to the east, consist of a single rampart wall, exposed to the range of sand hills on the right bank of the Urumea, at a distance of from 500 to 1000 yards.

At the southern extremity of the isthmus, distant some hundred yards from the glacis, rise the heights upon which stand the convent of St. Bartolomeo; in rear of these, ground was broken for the left of the attack, and the convent stormed and carried, as formerly mentioned, by the troops of the 5th division.

One hundred and fifty yards nearer the town, on the road leading from Ernani, is the suburb of St. Martin, and on a point of the isthmus stretching to the east, is situated the ruined village of Santa Catalina, from whence a bridge formerly communicated across the Urumea to the towns of Renteria and Passages.

To the eastward of the castle, distant about a thousand yards from the keep, and enfilading its defences, is the island of Santa Clara, of considerable altitude, and naturally very inaccessible.

At nine on the morning of the 26th, by signal, the batteries opened with a general salvo from fifty-seven pieces of ordnance; which fire being kept up during the day with spirit and precision, rapidly reduced to ruins the defences against which it was directed.

During the night a detachment of infantry, commanded by Captain Cameron of the 9th regiment, and conducted by Captain Henderson of the engineers, stormed and carried the rocky island of Santa Clara.

Captain Cameron executed this service with his accustomed gallantry. At the head of the grenadiers of the 9th, he had long been a participator in the brilliant services of that excellent regiment.

While these operations were in progress, the blockade of Pampeluna had been carried on with great assiduity and success; it must be considered highly creditable to the engineers who planned and arranged the measures for rendering it complete, as also to the troops employed in the investment, that, notwithstanding the near approach of the enemy's army, no sortie was ever permitted to make a great impression, nor was there the slightest communication in any respect established between the garrison and the frontier.

At Madrid, the Battles of the Pyrenees occasioned much exultation, increased by an impression that the Spanish troops therein engaged had taken a distinguished and creditable part; but the anxiety formerly evinced on any victory or disaster, had in great measure subsided. Vittoria, it was conceived, had given such a blow to the French power in Spain, that Joseph Bonaparte's return to the capital was a speculation no longer entertained; nor was it contemplated that any current of events would enable the enemy's troops ever to regain the ascendant, or to penetrate into the centre of that country from whence they had been driven under circumstances of such exemplary defeat.

The capital gradually resumed its former appearance; the Prado again became crowded; the theatres well attended; the opera once more graced by the presence of the Spanish aristocracy; the amphitheatre for the bullfights delighted the population of Madrid; and the continuation of the war appeared to be forgotten. The hotel of the Prince of Peace was in a state of preparation to receive the regency, and report announced their early arrival from Cadiz.

From the midst of these scenes I was recalled, by the receipt of a letter enclosing my cartel of exchange, and announcing that as Captain Cheville, of the artillery, had been sent to France, no further obstacle prevented my serving with the army. On the 27th of August, I left Madrid, and once more crossed the Somasierra, arriving on the following day at Burgos; on the 29th at Vittoria, where I remained the 30th and 31st, with General Alava; and at twelve o'clock at night of the 1st September, reached San Sebastian. From some officers of the 4th regiment, I learned that the town had been captured by assault on the previous day.

Sir James Leith having, on the 29th, resumed the command of his division in the trenches, to him was confided the immediate conduct of the storm, and direction of all the troops therein employed.

Lord Wellington, after closely reconnoitring the breaches, on the afternoon of the 30th, gave orders that the place should be assaulted at eleven o'clock on the following morning.

At two o'clock a.m. of the 31st, three mines were exploded by the British engineers, blowing completely down the sea-wall facing to the west. Workmen were immediately employed, and before ten o'clock a sufficient passage for the troops had been secured; the debouches from the trenches were also completed.

Sir Thomas Graham had from the first conducted the siege of San Sebastian, and, consequently, directed the whole force now prepared to enter on the desperate service of assaulting that fortress; but the immediate command of the storm was vested in Sir James Leith. Having confided to the general of the 5th division the direction of the attack to the left of the Urumea, Sir Thomas passed that river, and during the day overlooked the progress of the troops, and directed the fire from the batteries on the right of the attack.

In addition to the great breach, a lesser one had been formed in the same curtain, nearer to its extremity in the direction of the St. Elmo battery. It being determined that these should be assailed at the same moment, arrangements were made to that effect.

Some irritation having been occasioned by the failure of the assault on the 25th of July, an erroneous impression was formed that a party of volunteers from other divisions of the army would have the effect of stimulating the troops of the 5th to more strenuous exertion, and thereby ensure the success of the assault. The officers and soldiers of the 5th division required not such emulous incitement, but could entertain no jealous feelings in acting with those brave men who had spontaneously answered an appeal made to their zeal and enterprise, and now appeared ready to contend for distinction in the execution of a service universally known to be to a degree hazardous and sanguinary.

The morning of the 31st was unfavourable for the early practice of the British artillery; a heavy mist shrouded the town, and it was between eight and nine o'clock before objects became so clearly displayed as to admit of their being struck with precision. At that hour, however, the batteries opened, and continued firing until the troops debouched to commence the assault.

Exactly at eleven o'clock, the advance of the 5th division issued from the trenches. General Robinson's brigade had on this occasion the post of honour, and was destined first to mount the great breach, followed by the column of detachments, which was directed to its right, assailing the lesser one, in co-operation with some Portuguese troops of the 5th division.

The distance from the mouth of the trench to the great breach was about one hundred and eighty, and to the other, two hundred and twenty yards; from the low state of the tide, a considerable breadth of strand presented a tolerably wide and unobstructed passage.

The enemy, in hopes of occasioning great loss to the advancing column, and of intercepting its passage by forcing forward masses of ruined masonry, had mined under the sAllent angle in the covered way of the left demi-bastion of the hornwork. No sooner had the first troops appeared, than an explosion took place, which blew down a considerable extent of the wall immediately in front of which they were advancing, burying in its ruins the soldiers then in the act of passing. Fortunately, these mines were rather prematurely lighted, depriving them of the destructive effects that must have resulted had the main body of the column arrived at the spot.

Unchecked by this circumstance, General Robinson's brigade unhesitatingly advanced to the breach, and, regardless of a fire which burst forth from every direction, steadily, and in perfect order, ascended to its crest; upon gaining which, dangers and difficulties appeared but commencing. In addition to an incessant musketry fire from the hornwork, from the traversed rampart of the curtain, and the ruined houses directly in front and numerously occupied, the batteries De la Reyna, Del Principe, and Mirador, poured down showers of grape, round-shot, and shells. All this might have been passed through by some of the survivors, had it been possible to force an entrance; but, upon arriving on the crest of the breached curtain, it was ascertained that, although the ascent had been rendered practicable by the effect of artillery, the passage from thence into the town was more difficult than at the commencement of the siege.

The wall of San Sebastian, on the summit of which the 2nd brigade of the 5th division now stood, had an elevation, varying from sixteen to thirty feet, from the level of the town: its interior had been strengthened by a retaining wall, which, adding to the thickness and security of the curtain, was as perfect and as perpendicular as ever; the houses built against it had been removed to increase the difficulties of entrance, and small portions of their ruined partitions alone, connected with the reverse of the breach, could have afforded the slightest facility in aiding a descent to the level of the town: these being under the immediate fire of loophooled houses directly opposite, at a distance of less than forty yards, and from whence issued a constant discharge of musketry, rendered it a matter of certain death making the attempt. Under these circumstances it will appear evident, that forcing an entrance into the street from the direct front of the breach was perfectly impracticable; to proceed along the curtain on either of its flanks, became consequently the only means of penetrating into the place.

To force its way along the ramparts at the left of the breach, now became the object of the 5th division; but the troops were there met with apparently unconquerable difficulties: the enemy had constructed traverses, which, extending across the *terre-plein,* at short distances from each other, admitted but one individual to pass at a time; behind these were stationed French grenadiers, who, themselves in a great measure protected from fire, deliberately put to death the gallant soldiers who had temerity to attempt forcing a passage, and who, in addition to these nearly insurmountable obstructions, were from all points exposed to a body of fire, sustained with incessant violence, and directed with fatal precision.

Sir James Leith, previously to the advance of the troops, had consulted Sir Richard Fletcher respecting the selection of a situation from whence he might be best enabled to direct the progress of the storm, and was by the chief engineer recommended to place himself on the strand in front of the debouche from the trench, and rather nearer to the breach than that part of the hornwork exploded by the enemy at the commencement of the assault; there Sir Richard accompanied him, and continued, regardless of the heavy fire of all descriptions to which they were completely exposed.

The enemy had directed so great a body of fire against the mouth of the trench, that Sir James Leith found it necessary to send an officer of his staff with instructions to have the debouches cleared from the obstruction occasioned by the dead and dying that choked up the passage.

Soon after doing so, he was beat down by a blow on the chest, either from the rebound of a plunging shot, deadened by having struck the earth, or by a fragment of rock. Completely stunned, and for a short time insensible, the officers near him believed the injury to be fatal; but he soon recovered his respiration and recollection, and, resisting the wishes of his staff that he should retire, continued to issue orders with the utmost energy and self-possession, although so weakened by the effects of the blow as to support himself with difficulty, almost dropping to the earth as he enthusiastically cheered forward the troops. General Robinson had been severely wounded, and one-half of his brigade lay extended on the breach, the moment of arrival at its summit being that either of certain death or of grievous injury.

The brave detachments from the light, 1st, and 4th divisions, nobly upheld the character of their respective corps, making the most strenuous exertions to effect a lodgement, but hitherto in vain. They suffered considerably, but not in proportion to the troops of the 5th division.

The infallibility of British troops, when opposed to those of other countries, had ever been a decided opinion of Sir James Leith's, and experience had confirmed him in an impression not to be shaken even by the disastrous appearance of the attack above narrated. During its worst aspect he continued confident of eventual success, and ordered supports to issue from the trenches as rapidly as could be effected, without producing confusion, or crowding the already numerously covered ground, so arduously and so gloriously contested.

For two hours had the troops, with the utmost perseverance, continued to struggle for entrance into the town, not one minute of which elapsed without the fall of many of the bravest men, and at the termination of that period the capture of the place appeared as distant as ever; while the whole extent from the mouth of the trench to the crest of the breaches was thickly strewed with dead bodies, or persons writhing under severe and dangerous wounds. In the centre of this scene of destruction, in which not a soldier had receded or evinced an inclination to give way, Sir James Leith continued, animating the men by his presence and example, addressing words of encouragement as they passed. The soldiers, with increased energy, stepping over the bodies of their fallen comrades, rushed to the murderous ascent.

Remaining nearly stationary for so long a period, and exposed to such a fire, it was almost impossible to suppose he could escape untouched. In the act of directing support to be poured from the trenches, a shell bursting close to him tore the flesh from the back of his left hand, at the same time breaking the arm in two places. The shock was so violent as to overcome his remaining strength, and in the act of falling he was supported by his *aide-de-camp*, Captain Belshes. Soon after, fainting from loss of blood, he reluctantly permitted the officers of his staff to conduct him from the animating but tremendous scene. In passing through the trenches, he met the 9th regiment pressing forward to join in the assault. The soldiers recognising their general, whose individual exposure had ever cheered and encouraged them, they spontaneously promised not to desist from exertion until the place had fallen. In detailing the events of the assault, Sir Thomas Graham bears the following honourable testimony to the services of Sir James Leith:

> Lieutenant-General Sir James Leith justified, in the fullest manner, the confidence reposed in his tried judgment and distinguished gallantry; conducting and directing the attack, till obliged to be reluctantly carried off, after receiving a most severe contusion on the breast, and having his left arm broken.

A detachment of Portuguese troops, under Major Snodgrass, forded the Urumea, and joined the troops on the lesser breach, while another column, commanded by Colonel Macbean, also crossed from the right attack, and proceeded to the main point of assault.

These troops passed the river under a tremendous fire, preserving a compact and beautiful order; but their arrival and their efforts produced no decidedly beneficial effect.

It now appeared that every exertion which skill could suggest, or bravery make conclusive, had been repeatedly and unsuccessfully applied; fresh troops added to the loss, without affording any well-founded prospect of eventual success, and the hopes of all concerned in the storm were materially shaken. In this desperate state of affairs, Sir Thomas Graham consulted with the senior officer of artillery, and they concurred in the propriety of an attempt to make a last effort, by directing the whole ordnance of the right attack against the curtain, to the left of the great breach, and consequently close over the heads of the allied troops on the crest of the ruined masonry.

In this novel, but, in the present case, fortunately beneficial system of supporting an attack, it is difficult to determine which is most admirable, the resolution and self-confidence that proposed the measure, or the conduct of the British artillery that carried it into immediate and perfectly accurate execution.

In Colonel Dickson, Sir Thomas Graham had the assistance of an officer who, in the early stages of the Peninsular War, had displayed talents and energy that, previous to its close, placed him in the first ranks of his profession.

No sooner had these officers decided on the arrangement, than forty-seven pieces of heavy ordnance opened from the Chofre sand-hills on the high curtain, above the breach in its demi-bastions. The effect was soon visible: the enemy, unable to support so violent a cannonade, retired from the prominent stations which success had emboldened him to occupy, and his musketry fire was in a great measure beat down.

Upon Sir James Leith being wounded, the command of the 5th division devolved upon General Hay. General Oswald, although superseded in command by the return of the former to the army, volunteered his services, and assisted at the assault. As a spectator, he continued with Sir James Leith, exposed to the full effect of the enemy's fire, and was wounded during the operations.

About twenty minutes after the commencement of the artillery fire from the right, an explosion took place on the rampart of the curtain to the left of the great breach, occasioned by the bursting of shells having set fire to a quantity of combustibles there collected. Previously to the assault, a great number of fire-barrels, hand-grenades, and live-shells, had been heaped at intervals in rear of the traverses, for the purpose of being instrumental in destroying the assailants. These igniting in succession along the whole line of the wall, in a great measure cleared it of defenders, striking terror into the survivors. The favourable moment was seized with alacrity by the troops. Colonel Greville, at the head of General Hay's brigade, was already on the crest of the breach, and the Royal Scots, under Colonel Barnes, with the 38th, commanded by Colonel Miles, had the good fortune to force past the nearest traverse, and establish themselves on the curtain. The 9th, under Colonel Cameron, being the rear regiment of the brigade, came up immediately after.

The traverse nearest to the breach was composed of a barrel filled with earth, having at its side towards the horn work a brass cannon. The spaces between the cask and parapet next to the town, also between it and the gun, were closed up, the only passage along the curtain being close to the exterior wall, and that capable of admitting but one person at a time. Through this narrow entrance San Sebastian was taken, by the officers and men of General Hay's brigade having succeeded in forcing themselves; the brave garrison, however, returned to the charge, and still endeavoured to resist; but a footing once obtained, the British regiments pressed forward, driving their opponents from space to space, until they bayoneted them down the flight of steps leading from the cavalier bastion into the town.

Exulting in hard-earned success, the soldiers eagerly rushed forward. The garrison having abandoned the hornwork, and withdrawn from the retrenchments in front of the breach, some of the infantry, no longer restrained by the musketry fire, descended by the ruined fragments of the houses, while the whole extent of the curtain was crowded with soldiers anxiously advancing to enter the streets in pursuit of the discomfited enemy.

During the progress of these occurrences the Portuguese detachments had carried the lesser breach, and the success of the storm at all points became certain. The close of the most serious part of this very desperate service was accompanied by an elemental crash of the grandest description. Thunder rolled, as if, by comparison, to render insignificant the sublimest of earthly sounds; lightning flashed, and rain fell in torrents. Although the walls had been carried, the capture of the town was by no means completed. Obstacles of a very serious nature presented themselves, and the garrison, resolute to the last, appeared determined to persevere in resistance.

During the progress of the siege and intermediate blockade, General Rey had directed the streets to be strongly barricaded in every direction. This had been carried into effect in the most substantial manner. Materials from the ruined houses assisted in constructing traverses of a formidable description. These stone barriers were defended by cannon, forming part of their line across the streets. They were also loopholed, and behind them were posted the reserves of French infantry. From each and all of these, after repeated contests, the enemy was driven; the allies gradually gaining possession of the town, with the exception of the convent of Santa Teresa, in front of which the brave 9th regiment suffered severely in the act of overcoming the last effort of the garrison, previous to its retiring into the castle. Six hundred and seventy prisoners were taken.

Thus, at three o'clock in the afternoon, terminated a struggle protracted for four hours, and maintained by all parties with distinguished gallantry and perseverance. On no occasion had any troops more appalling obstacles to overcome than the allies, and no garrison could have supported a more honourable or more resolute resistance than that by which the assailants were met and obstructed.

Sir Richard Fletcher, after having conducted, as chief engineer of the army, the various sieges during the Peninsular War, was not destined to witness the termination of that of San Sebastian. A short time previous to Sir James Leith being wounded, he was pierced through the heart by a musket ball, near to the spot which he had himself selected as their station during the storm. Five other officers of engineers were either killed or wounded during the assault; of these, Captains Rhodes and Collyer fell on the summit of the breaches.

Five hundred of the assailants killed, and fifteen hundred wounded, attested the destructive fire of the enemy. Of these, thirteen hundred and seventy-six belonged to the British regiments of the 5th division, ninety-nine to detachments from the guards, one hundred and five from thirteen battalions of the light and 4th divisions, and fifty-four to the German Legion. The remainder of the above mentioned aggregate number comprised the loss of the Portuguese troops on the occasion.

A very extensive mine, charged with twelve hundredweight of powder, was discovered under the great breach after the place was taken. Fortunately, by some accident, the enemy had failed in exploding what would inevitably have blown into the air the hundreds of men at every period of the assault within reach of its effects.

The 5th division had, with that of so many other brave officers, to lament the fall of Colonel Crawford of the 9th, of Majors Werge of the 38th, Kelley of the 47th, and Scott of the 59th regiments.

Of the detachments, Major Rose of the 20th, in command of those from the 4th division, was severely wounded near the summit of the lesser breach, from whence he was precipitated from a height of nearly thirty feet to the level of the town, and killed on the spot.

Colonel Hunt of the 52nd was wounded leading forward the volunteers from the light division. General Robinson had been compelled to retire, from a severe wound in the face, after having, in the most gallant manner, led his brigade to the crest of the breach.

Colonel Cameron of the 9th, and Colonel Piper of the 4th, were also wounded.

The effect produced by the artillery fire, so fortunately determined upon by Sir Thomas Graham, was terrific. Colonel Jones, in his luminous account of the siege, states, that "on inspecting the defences, it was found that the tremendous enfilade fire on the high curtain, though only maintained for twenty minutes, had dismounted every gun but two. Many of these pieces had their muzzles shot away, and the artillerymen lay mutilated at their stations. Further, the stone parapets were much damaged, the cheeks of the embrasures knocked off, and the *terre-plein* cut up, and thickly strewed with headless bodies; in short, the whole land-front had, from the effects of the cannonade, been rendered a scene of destruction, desolation, and ruin."

What must have been the original obstacles, when a scene, thus described, only partially shook difficulties opposed to the entrance of the troops? And what praise is too great for the gallant garrison of San Sebastian? A more desperate defence has seldom been recorded, or one more calculated to uphold the military character of the nation to which the undaunted soldiers within its walls belonged.

No sooner had the town been secured to the allies than a scene of the most ferocious pillage commenced—the usual result of a successful storm, and one of the barbarisms of war. The original motive for permitting such excess is self-evident, being intended as an incitement to exertion, by holding out a prospect of individual enrichment. This, to mercenary soldiers, must have had considerable effect, and may have been deemed important in accelerating the fall of strongly fortified places; but with an army zealously officered and well disciplined, the duty in the trenches ought to be reduced to a certainty of steady labour, without the aid of individual stimulus; and in the act of assault, it is to be questioned whether the minds of men can be so abstracted from its dangers and difficulties, as to continue exertion for the purpose of obtaining plunder; nor do I believe, had the interior of Badajos or San Sebastian been barren forts, that the troops who captured them would have relaxed one iota in those glorious exertions which, if not conclusive as to skilful attack, must ever be allowed in a signal degree to have displayed undisputed examples of the bravery, the perseverance, and the unconquerable energies, of British soldiers.

Having succeeded, the troops were, of course, admitted to the immemorial privilege of tearing the town to pieces. It was on fire in many places, and a dreadful scene of devastation ensued, rendered additionally to be deplored from the unfortunate inhabitants being friends and allies to the lawless soldiery now revelling in every species of excess.

The same day that the allies were engaged in the storm, Marshal Soult made one of those unsuccessful efforts to relieve the place, for which his professional career in the Peninsula had been so conspicuous. Passing the Bidassoa with a large portion of his army, he attacked the position of the Spanish divisions under General Freyre, and was repulsed.

The Spaniards, encouraged by the support of a British division on either flank, and being placed on very commanding ground, met the attack with firmness, and withstood the shock of the enemy; but renewed efforts on the part of the French were supported by an increased body of troops, and some uncertainty momentarily prevailed. At that critical instant, Lord Wellington arrived on the heights of San Marcial. His presence renewed confidence, and gave animation to the troops, who, directed by his masterly judgment, without the assistance of any other force, drove the enemy back into the territory of France. This was the last effort made by Marshal Soult to invade the Spanish territory, and it is rather a singular circumstance, that it should have been repelled exclusively by the native troops; thus presenting, during the long and eventful war, a victory at Baylen, and a *finale* at San Marcial, highly honourable to the national character, while the intermediate military incidents, with few exceptions, and wherein the soldiers of the country were alone concerned, present a series of misfortunes essentially produced by want of confidence, accompanied by laxity of discipline and lamentable misrule.

Although the town of San Sebastian had fallen, the enemy's garrison, that escaped from the effects of the storm, and sought refuge in the castle, appeared determined to procrastinate that surrender, now become inevitable; but, persevering in the gallant spirit with which the defence had been conducted, they resolved to delay to the last moment delivering up so important an obstacle to the further progress of the campaign and the advance of the allied army.

On the 1st of September, everything being again quiet on the immediate frontier, Lord Wellington arrived in the trenches, and there decided upon the measures to be adopted for the speedy reduction of Fort La Mota.

Batteries were ordered to be constructed against the castle defences, while a constant fire of mortars reduced in numbers the soldiery, unprotected from their effects by casemates of any description.

Desirous of seeing the state of affairs in the town, on the morning of the 2nd, I left Sir James Leith's quarter, and walked along the isthmus, and through the trenches, until arrived at the spot where the general had been wounded. The scene from thence was most impressive: the whole ascent of the breach was covered with dead bodies. During the intervening day, circumstances had not permitted their being interred; stripped and naked, therefore, they now lay on the ground where they had individually fallen, but in such numbers, that on a similar space was never witnessed a more dreadful scene of slaughter. Behind this impressive foreground rose columns of smoke and ashes, and occasionally, through the vapour, was to be distinguished the towering castle-keep, from whence, and from its batteries, issued at intervals an artillery discharge, or irregular and half-subdued musketry fire: above all this was distinguishable the thunder of the British mortar batteries, as, from the right attack, they poured shells upon the devoted rock, whose surface became furrowed and torn up by their repeated explosions.

Having walked up the face of the breach, I proceeded along the curtain, which presented a scene of indescribable havoc and destruction. The heat from the blazing houses was excessive; and from the midst of this mass of fire was at intervals to be heard, the noise created by soldiers still busied in adding to the miseries that had overtaken the devoted town. Never was there in the annals of war a more decided case of annihilation than that of San Sebastian: the buildings all having communication, and being very closely arranged, ensured the conflagration becoming general; roofs falling, and the crashing of ruined walls that rolled down, and, in some cases, blocked up the passage in the streets, it was rendered more impressive from the obscurity occasioned even at midday by the dense cloud of smoke that shrouded this scene of ruin and desolation.

After descending the great flight of steps leading from the curtain, in the centre of this chaos, I found General Hay, blackened with smoke and dust, not having had a moment's rest, and still busily employed in restoring order to the troops, or in vainly endeavouring to obstruct the unquenchable flames that surrounded him in every direction.

In the sort of *plaza* fronting the entrance from the isthmus to the town were erected halberds. These emblems of preparation for punishment exhibited, in not-to-be-mistaken terms, the difficulty attending the restoration of order, when so fearfully outraged as in the result of a successful storm.

The convent of Santa Teresa, being the building in immediate communication with the enemy, was occupied in its lower part by a party of the 9th regiment, while the upper stories were inhabited by French infantry. In arriving at its principal entrance fronting to the east, it became necessary to pass across a street running at right angles, and exposed to an enfilade fire from the castle and the exterior lines of wall encircling the face of the rock. To prevent the casualties occasioned by this exposed route, the street, towards the height, had been hastily barricaded by casks, mattrasses, and dead bodies, affording protection from the fire of musketry, and effectually obstructing the sight of the unerring marksmen at a short distance from the spot. Towards evening, General Hay, Captain James Stewart, and myself, having passed through several parts of the town, crossed the *plaza*, and proceeded towards the northwest angle of the place.

When we arrived at the traverse above described, I proceeded to visit, the 9th regiment in the convent, while Captain Stewart proposed detailing to General Hay his views of dislodging the enemy from the upper part of the building, and of rendering less obnoxious a fire from the French sentinels stationed on the slope of the hill. For this purpose, he led the general to the bulwark, and, clambering up, proceeded to point out the situation of the enemy's posts, as also what he recommended concerning them. A French sentinel, not fifty yards distant, on perceiving two officers reconnoitring, took a deliberate aim, and firing, his ball entered Captain Stewart's left temple, passing directly through his head. He continued in a state of insensibility for some minutes, and then expired.

Sir Thomas Graham, very properly considering that General Rey ought to have arrived at the conclusion, in which the unanimous voice of either army must have supported him—namely, the fruitlessness of further resistance, he, early in the afternoon of the 3rd, sent a flag of truce, with proposals to negotiate. Several hours were given to enable the French governor deliberately to make up his mind, and we were informed that, at the expiry of the period, a salvo from the mortar batteries would announce the recommencement of hostilities. Considerably elevated, and at the distance of about two miles from the Chofre sand-hills, Sir James Leith's quarter was admirably situated for seeing in perfection those large masses of destruction as they passed through the air.

The French general continuing obstinate, a flight of shells, exactly at the hour indicated, following each other in rapid succession, was perceived sailing through the firmament. In the darkness that prevailed, nothing could be more fallacious than the impression created, as our eyes followed them, by the fuses in their rotatory motion. Instead of passing through the air with the velocity and impetus they in reality possessed, in appearance they were majestically and slowly pursuing their course.

It was now evident that General Rey would not surrender until the batteries in preparation opened against the castle. Of these, the most considerable was constructed in the hornwork of the place, occupying nearly the length of its *terre-plein*, and prepared for the reception of seventeen twenty-four-pounders. This powerful battery was armed by cannon brought across the Urumea, and was destined to fire upon and breach the batteries of Mirador and De la Reyna.

Arrangements having been completed for a very energetic attack upon the castle defences, and it being understood the batteries would open on the morning of the 8th, at half-past nine I was in the hornwork with Colonel Dickson: the artillerymen were at their posts, everything in readiness, and, at ten o'clock, by preconcerted signal, fifty-nine pieces of heavy ordnance commenced a rapid and terrific fire. Standing in the battery, close in rear of the twenty-four pounders, from whose mouths issued an incessant and deafening sound, the noise of the other batteries was inaudible; but, in looking around, columns of smoke ascended in all directions, while dust and fragments of stone, flying from the masonry of the Mirador, indicated the perfect direction and overpowering effect of the British artillery.

The enemy, apparently astonished at the tremendous nature of the cannonade, tardily returned the fire by a few discharges from the battery De la Reyna; but, perceiving the feeble effects of this last effort, it was speedily discontinued; while every half hour we had the satisfaction of perceiving, that in a short space of time the Mirador must be beat down sufficiently to admit of its being assaulted. Nothing could be better directed, or more constantly sustained, than the fire from the great battery in the hornwork.

About one o'clock a flag of truce appeared flying on the battery of Mirador, and the firing ceased. The Chevalier Songeon, colonel and *chef d'état major* of the garrison, soon after descended into the town, where, having met Colonel de Lancey, Colonel Dickson, and Colonel Bouverie, nominated by Sir Thomas Graham to negotiate on the part of the allies, the terms were speedily arranged, by which the garrison surrendered prisoners of war; and at four o'clock in the evening the Mirador and battery Del Gobernador were occupied by British troops.

The following morning, the garrison marched out with the honours of war. At its head, with sword drawn, and firm step, appeared General Rey, accompanied by Colonel Songeon, and the officers of his staff; as a token of respect, we saluted him as he passed. The old general dropt his sword in return to the civilities of the British officers, and, leading the remains of his brave battalions to the glacis, there deposited their arms, with a well-founded confidence of having nobly done his duty, and persevered to the utmost in an energetic and brilliant defence.

Thus terminated the final operations against San Sebastian, a fortress not of the first order, but capable, as had been proved, of a protracted defence, when skilfully and resolutely conducted.

After an expenditure of 70,000 rounds of ammunition, the place fell, not from its defences being rendered useless, or its garrison intimidated, but from being assaulted by irresistible troops; nor would any other infantry in Europe have penetrated into the town under similar circumstances. Nothing but the most ardent perseverance, the most determined courage, and perfect confidence in those leading them, enabled the British battalions to conquer difficulties that must have effectually obstructed ordinary men.

In the progress of the siege, three thousand five hundred of the allies were killed or wounded; and of a garrison originally numbering three thousand four hundred, only fifty-seven officers, with twelve hundred and forty-four men, were in a state to follow their gallant governor to the glacis, and deposit those arms they had used so creditably, during the long and arduous service of resisting a powerful force, straining every nerve to gain possession of the place.

As usual in sieges, the allied army lost some of its best officers and soldiers before San Sebastian. In the field, there is a more equal chance of casualty attending the enterprising or nerveless, and, in fact, the latter is, of the two, most likely to be cut off, in consequence of performing duty tardily or with apathy, affording time for the destructive efforts of adversaries. In sieges, the bravest, most energetic, or most talented, come necessarily in the immediate front of danger, and, being so, are most frequently disabled.

On the evening of the 9th September, the Spanish ensign floated over the ruined walls of San Sebastian, while a constantly spreading conflagration, of ten days' endurance, had not yet completed the total destruction of its devoted town. The scenery in its neighbourhood is picturesque and beautiful in the extreme: great variety of ground is enlivened by luxuriant orchards and extensive olive plantations, while broken and precipitous rocky heights occasionally give variety to a landscape closed by the magnificent background of the Pyrenees.

For three weeks subsequent to the fall of the castle, nothing of importance occurred near to San Sebastian. Wishing to see the romantic country, and to ascend one or other of the passes into France, on the morning of the 29th I left Sir James Leith, and, passing across the Urumea, joined General Pack, who, recovered from his wound, had resolved to proceed in the same direction, for the purpose of resuming the command of his brigade of the 6th division, stationed at Maya. We determined to adopt the route by Lesaca, and remained on the night of the 29th at Oyarzun, on the great road to Bayonne, and then the headquarters of Sir Thomas Graham. From thence to Lesaca, the route, passing through a valley of considerable extent, arrives at the base of the great mountain of Haya, or of Quarte Couronnes, when, gradually ascending, it winds through ravines and over eminences covered with magnificent trees. In one of the most sequestered spots of this wild and beautiful country was encamped the brigade of Lord Aylmer; the white tents of the troops strongly contrasting with the dark foliage of the chestnut and ilex, while the soldiers, variously employed, enlivened a scene naturally of sombre character.

At Lesaca, we were disappointed of seeing the commander of the forces, who had the day previous gone to Roncesvalles to inspect the position occupied by the right of his army. But, determined to await the return of Lord Wellington, we passed the day with Colonel Campbell, and the officers of his personal staff, joining a numerous party, over whom the Prince of Orange presided. This was the last time I ever saw General Pakenham—a person equally beloved and respected by the army—one of those officers whose natural element appeared to be amidst the smoke and fire of a field of battle, but whose manner in society was blended with unusual kindness and gentleness of demeanour.

Having remained three days at headquarters, we arrived, on the 4th, at Maya. General Pack's quarter was situated in the valley directly under the pass leading into France; and in a village to his right, a short distance further removed from the frontier, was General Colville, with the headquarters of the 6th division, the other British brigade being in the immediate vicinity.

On the 6th I rode to Roncesvalles, then the headquarters of Sir Rowland Hill, and beheld, with admiration, that scene of chivalrous and poetic celebrity.

The abbey, seated at the foot of the pass, is surrounded by the habitations of the abbots, forming a considerable village. That of the prior, erected by government, and calculated to shelter travellers crossing the frontier, is spacious and convenient. While towards France the scenery is bold and majestic, it assumes, in the direction of Pampeluna, a tamer but not less beautiful character: the valley of Burguete, rich in cultivation, and ornamented by the finest wood, is extended beneath the eye, and the sun illuminating its varied tints, rendering them more striking from being contrasted with the sombre appearance of Roncesvalles, while the dark masses of pines and forest trees clothing to its summit the grand mountain barrier, partially hid in mist and vapour, give increased magnitude to objects naturally of a stupendous description.

Immediately from the abbey of Roncesvalles, the great route commences a gradual ascent, terminated at the summit of the Altobiscar mountain, from whence a descent of three leagues leads to the town of St. Jean Pied de Port.

From the loftiest part of the road a magnificent view is presented to the traveller. To his right appear, in great variety and majesty, the range of Pyrenees towards Jaca, including the Pic du Midi and other conspicuous features of the chain. In advance, to the left, extends the French coast, with the city of Bayonne, forming a splendid break in the otherwise unvaried line; directly in front, and displayed to a great distance, appear the fertile plains of Gascony; while, in the immediate vicinity of the route, valleys, rendered impervious by luxuriant foliage, cataracts, rocks, and the wilder accompaniments of splendid mountain scenery, are visible in constant and endless variety.

It was on the 7th of October, 1813, that Lord Wellington invaded France; and it fell to the lot of the 5th division to be the first British troops whose colours waved over the "sacred territory" of Napoleon. The regiments crossed the Bidassoa with the utmost regularity and firmness, regardless of the depth of water, or of a fire poured by the enemy from the opposite bank. General Robinson passed the river on foot at the head of his brigade, and, in the midst of a shower of musketry, supported by artillery, up to the middle in water, pressed forward, and in the exhilaration of the occasion, increased by enthusiastic cheering, and the bands of the regiment playing the national anthem, established his brave soldiers on the soil hitherto unvisited, during the

Pyrenees from the summit of the Roncesvalles pass

reign of Napoleon, by the horrors of war.

Three times did defensive positions appear crowded with the enemy's troops endeavouring to check the advance of General Hay's brigade, and as often did success attend the assaults made upon them. As it is the last occasion on which I shall have to notice the services of the 5th division, it may be permitted me to revert to those deeds which entitled its battalions to as ample a meed of praise, and as just a claim to gratitude from their country, as any portion of the Peninsular army. Whether in defending the heights of Busaco, in scaling the walls of Badajos, in leading the victorious attack at Salamanca, in driving back a pursuing enemy at Villa Muriel, in forcing the passage of the Zadorra at Vittoria, in storming and taking San Sebastian, or in planting the British ensign on the French imperial territory, their conduct was equally conspicuous for gallantry, devotion, and discipline.

Although many years are now passed since this body of troops have been separated, and it may be supposed mature consideration of what they were, and of their achievements, must be tempered with some degree of moderation as to the enthusiastic recollections with which I revert to those scenes, yet the contrary effect is produced in my mind; and while, with increased feelings of respect, I feel honoured in the good fortune of having served with those gallant soldiers, I at the same time unequivocally record my belief, that, commanded by a general possessing the confidence of his army as Lord Wellington did, and led as they had invariably been, there is nothing within the scope of human powers which might not have been accomplished by the 5th division.

The Bidassoa, forming for several leagues the boundary of the countries, rises in the valley of Bastan, from whence, after rather a circuitous course, it runs into the sea near to Fuentarabia. On its right bank, Sir Thomas Graham, with the 1st and 5th divisions, and some Portuguese troops, had established a footing not subsequently assailed by the enemy. While the left of the allied army were thus prosecuting the war, and had commenced offensive operations on the enemy's territory, the centre and right continued in a state of comparative inaction. And it may afford some idea of the various circumstances under which corps of the same army on an extensive line may be placed, when it is stated, that the same day on which Sir Thomas Graham passed the Bidassoa, the officers of Sir Rowland Hill's corps had races on the plain of Burguete, which were conducted without the slightest knowledge of, or reference to, the contest in progress near the coast, or any prospect of being interrupted by the movements of an enemy.

The great wooden bridge of Irun, on the Bayonne road, had been destroyed by General Foy's corps on its retreat after the Battle of Vittoria; but the allies, having a pontoon train with the army, a communication was restored immediately after their encampment on the right bank of the Bidassoa.

The Duke of Dalmatia had established his headquarters in St. Jean de Luz, with his army strongly intrenched, extending from the coast to St. Jean Pied de Port. The position of Lord Wellington's army was as follows:—

The 1st and 5th divisions, with the brigade of Lord Aylmer, the Portuguese of Generals Bradford and Wilson, and the Spanish force of General Giron, encamped in France, extending to the great mountain of La Rune: the light and 4th divisions occupied the heights in front of Vera: the army of reserve of Andalusia, with the 7th British division on their right, near to Echelar: the 3rd division between Echelar and Maya: the 6th in position at the latter, with Sir John Hamilton's Portuguese division in reserve, at Ariscoon: one brigade of the 2nd division at Alduides, the remainder of that division, and the Spanish corps of General Morillo, were at Roncesvalles: the cavalry in rear of the army, were principally cantoned in the valley of the Ebro: headquarters removed from Lesaca to Vera.

Aware of the hostile movement which, on the fall of Pampeluna, would immediately take place, Marshal Soult commenced the formation of an intrenched camp, extending along the course of the Nivelle, from St. Jean de Luz by Serres and the heights of Ainhoe, until it rested on a minor chain of the Pyrenees, north-east of the Maya pass. On the left bank of the river, formidable redoubts strengthened the mountain of La Petite Rune; while the heights of Ascain, protected by numerous works, covered the passages of the river for a considerable extent, and were *appuied* on those of Ainhoe, stretching to the eastward, and completing the defences in communication with those to the extreme left of the French Army.

In front of the right of this very formidable position, in advance of Andaye, and with their left resting on the shores of the Bay of Biscay, were encamped the 1st and 5th divisions of the allied army. Fieldworks strengthened the ground thus occupied, and a large force of British artillery was prepared to resist any effort that might be made to force back the allies from the right bank of the Bidassoa. On the 25th of October, having returned from Roncesvalles, Lord Charles

FitzRoy and myself entered France from Irun, and proceeded along the great *chaussée*, until arrived at the position of the troops. From thence, accompanied by General Robinson, I rode to the advanced posts, in close contact with those of the enemy, and there distinctly perceived the numerous retrenchments in progress to render his position as invulnerable as possible.

On the same day, General Cassan proposed terms for the surrender of Pampeluna, now reduced to the last extremity by a lengthened and rigorously observed blockade; but the allies, aware of the circumstances under which the garrison must necessarily be placed, determined not to accede to the proposition, and the French governor persevered in resistance until his last day's supply of limited rations was in process of distribution to the troops. At length, on the 31st of October, he surrendered the place, which, with its defences in a perfect state, a garrison of 4000 men, and 200 pieces of ordnance mounted on its walls, became the almost bloodless prize of the allied army.

Thus was wrested from the imperial troops their last stronghold in the northern provinces of Spain; and with that event may be said to have closed the Peninsular War.

After having imperfectly traced some of the most important events attending the triumphant career of the Duke of Wellington, I cannot conclude a narrative, which has throughout been dedicated to the relation of achievements, insuring to his name a renown which posterity will not deny, and from which historians will find it difficult to detract, without adverting to his latest, most memorable, and most glorious triumph,—without feeling all the enthusiasm of a soldier for his successful commander, when, by a recent and meritorious action, he adds to former celebrity and fame.

It is possible, that among the various conflicting sensations produced by events during a career, affecting in opposite degrees the situation of most individuals, not only in this country, but throughout Europe, reasons may be adduced for his successes, not withholding admiration, but claiming either for his army, or adventitious circumstances favoured by fortune, a large portion of the merit derived from a long and uninterrupted course of victory. It is also possible that the events of his military life may be so identified with the conduct of others, or the relative situation of states and armies, as that an undivided opinion of individual merit may be withheld; but in that never-to-be-forgotten measure of peace and conciliation, where, regardless of early and erroneous impressions, for the safety and happiness of his country he placed himself in front of the battle of public opinion, and fearlessly removed the darkest stain on the annals, the most portentous cloud that ever threatened the constitutional liberties, of England—in that act of justice, wisdom, and sound policy, he stands unrivalled and alone; and history will not fail to admit, that the celebrated military leader of Great Britain, the only man in the empire who could have achieved the bloodless and decisive victory over prejudice, superstition, and ignorance, added the noblest wreath to the immortal chaplet that encircles his brow, when he entwined his laurels with the moral triumph of religious liberty.

Appendix.

No.1
BATTLE OF SALAMANCA
REPORT OF MARSHAL THE DUKE OF RAGUSA TO THE MINISTER AT WAR.

Tudela, July 31.

Monsieur,

The interruptions of the communications with France since the opening of the campaign, having prevented me from giving you the successive accounts of the events which have passed, I shall commence this report from the moment at which the English began operations; and I am going to have the honour to place before you, in detail, all the movements which have been executed, to the unhappy event that has just taken place, and which we were far from expecting.

In the month of May I was informed the English army would open the campaign with very powerful means: I informed the king of it, in order that he might adopt such dispositions as he thought proper; and I likewise acquainted General Caffarelli with it, that he might take measures for sending me succours, when the moment should have arrived.

The extreme difficulty in procuring subsistence, the impossibility of provisioning the troops, when assembled, prevented me from having more than eight or nine battalions in Salamanca; but all were in readiness to join me in a few days.

On the 12th of June, the enemy's army passed the Agueda: on the 14th, in the morning, I was informed of it; and the orders for assembling were given to the troops. On the 16th, the English army arrived before Salamanca.

In the night between the 16th and 17th, I evacuated that town, leaving, nevertheless, a garrison in the forts I had constructed; and which, by the extreme activity used in their construction, were in a state of defence. I marched six leagues from Salamanca; and there, having collected five divisions, I approached that town; I drove before me the English advanced posts, and obliged the enemy's army to shew what attitude it reckoned upon taking; it appeared determined to fight upon the fine rising ground, and strong position, of San Christoval.

The remainder of the army joined me; I manoeuvred round that position, but I acquired the certainty that it everywhere presented obstacles difficult to be conquered, and that it was better to force the enemy to come upon another field of battle, than enter into action with them upon ground which gave them too many advantages; besides, different reasons made me desire to prolong the operations, for I had just received a letter from General Caffarelli, which announced to me, that he had collected his troops, and was going to march to succour me, whilst my presence would have suspended the siege of the forts of Salamanca. Things remained in this state for some days, and the armies in presence of each other; when the siege of the forts of Salamanca was vigorously recommenced.

On account of the trifling distance which there was between the French Army and the place, and by means of the signals agreed upon, I was every day informed of the situation of the place. Those of the 26th and 27th informed me the forts could still hold out five days; then I decided to execute the passage of the Tormes, and act upon the left bank. The fort of Alba, which I had carefully preserved, gave me a passage over that river, a new line of operations, and an important point of support. I made dispositions for executing this passage, on the night between the 28th and 29th.

During the night of the 27th, the fire redoubled; and the enemy fatigued with a resistance, which to them appeared exaggerated, fired red hot balls upon the fort. Unfortunately, its magazines contained a large quantity of wood; it took fire, and in an instant the fort was a vast fire. It was impossible for the brave garrison who defended it, to support at the same time the enemy's attacks, and the fire which destroyed the defences, magazines, and provisions, and placed the soldiers themselves in the most dreadful situation. It was then obliged to surrender at discretion, after having had the honour of repulsing two assaults, and causing the enemy a loss of more than 1300 men, *viz*. double their own force. This event happened on the 28th, at noon.

The enemy, having no further object in his operations beyond the Tormes, and, on the other hand, everything indicating that it would be prudent to await the reinforcement announced in a formal manner by the Army of the North, I decided on re-approaching the army of the Douro, secure of passing that river, in case the enemy should march towards us; and there take up a good line of defence, until such time as the moment for acting on the offensive should appear.

On the 28th, the army departed, and took a position on the Guareña; on the 29th, on the Trabanjos, where it sojourned. The enemy having followed the movements with the whole of his forces, the army took up a position on the Zapardiel; and on the 2nd it passed the Douro at Tordesillas, a place which I chose for the pivot of my motions. The line of the Douro is excellent; I made in detail every disposition which might render sure a good defence of this river; and I had no cause to doubt my being able to defeat every enterprise of the enemy, in case they should attempt the passage.

The 3rd, being the day after that on which we passed the Douro, he made several assemblages of his forces, and some slight attempts to effect this passage at Polios, a point which for him would have been very advantageous. The troops which I had disposed, and a few cannon shot, were sufficient to make him immediately give up his enterprise.

In continual expectation of receiving succours from the Army of the North, which had been promised in so solemn and reiterated a manner, I endeavoured to add by my own industry to the means of the army. My cavalry was much inferior to that of the enemy. The English had nearly 5000 horse, English and German, without counting the Spaniards, formed into regular troops; I had no more than 2000. With this disproportion, in what manner could one manoeuvre his enemy? How avail oneself of any advantage that might be obtained? I had but one means of augmenting my cavalry, and that was by taking the useless horses for the service of the army, or such as belonged to individuals who had no right to have them, or from such as had a greater number than they are allowed.

I did not hesitate making use of this means, the imminent interest of the army, and the success of the operations, being at stake: I therefore ordered the seizure of such horses as were under this predicament; and I likewise seized a great number which were with a convoy, coming from Andalusia; all upon estimation of their value, and making payment for them. This measure executed with security, gave, in the space of eight days, 1000 more horsemen; and my cavalry reunited, amounted to more than 3000 combatants. Meanwhile, I no less hoped to receive succours from the Army of the North, which continued its promises, the performance of which appeared to have commenced, but of which we have not seen, hitherto, any effect.

The eighth division of the Army of Portugal occupied the Asturias; these troops were completely isolated from the army, by the evacuations of the provinces of Leon and Benevente: they were without succours, and without any communication with the Army of the North; because on the one side the Trinçadores, who should have come from Bayonne, could not be sent to Gijon: and on the other side, the general-in-chief of the Army of the North, although he had formally promised to do so, had dispensed with throwing a bridge over the Deba, and there establishing posts.

This division had been able to bring only very little ammunition, for want of means of carriage; and this was in part consumed: nor did they know how to replace it. Its position might every moment become more critical, and the enemy seriously occupied himself with it; inasmuch as if it were still thus isolated, it would remain entirely unconnected with the important events which were taking place in the plains of Castille. General Bonnèt, calculating on this state of matters, and considering, according to the knowledge he has of the country, that it is much easier to enter than depart out of it, according as the enemy might oppose the entrance or departure, he decided on evacuating this province, and on taking a position at Reynosa. There, having learned that the Army of Portugal was in presence of the English array, and that they were on the point of engaging, he did not hesitate in putting himself in motion, and rejoining it. Strongly impressed with the importance of this succour, and with the augmentation which my cavalry was about to receive;

not having learned anything positive further concerning the Army of the North; and being besides informed of the march of the Army of Gallicia, which, in the course of a few days, would necessarily force me to send a detachment to repulse them, I thought it my duty to act without delay. I had to fear that my situation, which was become much meliorated, might change by losing time; whilst that of the enemy would, by the nature of things, become better every moment.

I, therefore, resolved on recrossing the Douro: but this operation is difficult and delicate; it cannot be undertaken without much art and circumspection, in presence of an army in condition for battle. I employed the days of the 13th, 14th, 15th, and 16th of July, in making a number of marches and countermarches, which deceived the enemy. I feigned an intention to turn by Toro, and turned by Tordesillas, making an extremely rapid march. This movement succeeded so well, that the whole army could pass the river, move to a distance from it, and form itself, without meeting with a single enemy.

On the 17th, the army took a position at Nava del Rey. The enemy, who was in full march for Toro, could only bring two divisions with celerity to Tordesilla de la Orden; the others were recalled from different parts to reunite themselves.

"On the 18th, in the morning, we found these two divisions at Tordesilla de la Orden. As they did not expect to find the whole army joined, they thought they might, without peril, gain some time. Nevertheless, when they saw our masses coming forward they endeavoured to effect their retreat to a ridge which commanded the village to which we were marching.

We had already reached them. If I had had a cavalry superior, or equal, to that of the enemy, these two divisions would have been destroyed. We did not, however, pursue them the less with all possible vigour; and, during three hours' march, they were overpowered by the fire of our artillery, which I caused to take them in the rear and flank, and which they could, with difficulty, answer; and, protected by their numerous cavalry, they divided themselves to reascend the Guareña, in order to pass it with greater facility.

Arrived upon the heights of the valley of Guareña, we saw that a portion of the English army was formed upon the left bank of that river. In that place the heights of that valley are very rugged, and the valley of a middling breadth. Whether it was necessary for the troops to approach the water, on account of the excessive heat, or whether it was for some other cause of which I am ignorant, the English general had placed the greater part of them on the bottom of the valley, within half cannon-shot of the heights of which we were masters; I, therefore, upon arriving, immediately ordered a battery of forty pieces of artillery to be planted, which in a moment forced the enemy to retire, after having left a great number of killed and wounded upon the spot.

The army marched in two columns; and I had given the command of the right column, distant from that of the left three-quarters of a league, to General Clausel. Arriving upon this ground, General Clausel, having few troops before him, thought he was able to seize upon the two rising grounds upon the left bank of the Guareña, and preserve them; but this attack was made with few troops, his troops had not halted, and scarcely formed; the enemy perceived it, marched upon the troops which he had thus thrown in advance, and forced them to retreat. In this battle, which was of short duration, we experienced some loss. The division of dragoons, which supported the infantry, vigorously charged all the English cavalry; but General Carrier, a little too far advanced from the 13th regiment, fell into the enemy's power.

The army remained in its position all the night of the 19th; remained in it all the day of the 20th. The extreme heat and fatigue experienced on the 18th, rendered this repose necessary, to assemble the stragglers.

At four in the evening the army resumed its arms, and defiled by the left to proceed up the Guareña, and take a position in front of Olmo. My intention was, at the same time, to threaten the enemy, and continue to proceed up the Guareña, in order to pass it with facility; or, if the enemy marched in force upon the Upper Guareña, to return by a rapid movement upon the position they should have abandoned. The enemy followed my movements.

On the 20th, before day, the army was in motion to ascend the Guareña; the advanced guard rapidly passed that river, at that part where it is but a stream, and occupied the commencement of an immense piece of ground, which continued, without any undulation, to near Salamanca. The enemy endeavoured to occupy the same ground, but could not succeed: then he attempted to follow a parallel rising ground, connected with the position they had just quitted, and which every where offered them a position, provided I should have marched towards them. The two armies thus marched parallel with all possible celerity, always keeping their masses connected, in order to be every moment prepared for battle.

The enemy, thinking to be beforehand with us at the village of Cantalpino, directed a column upon that village, in the hope of being before us upon the rising ground which commands it, and towards which we marched; but their expectations were deceived. The light cavalry which I sent thither, and the 8th division, which was at the head of the column, marched so rapidly that the enemy was obliged to abandon it: besides, the road from the other plain approaching too close to ours, and that which we had, having the advantage of commanding it with some pieces of cannon, judiciously placed, greatly annoyed the enemy; for a great part of the army was obliged to defile under this cannon, and the remainder was obliged to repass the mountains to avoid them.

At last I put the dragoons in the enemy's track. The enormous number of stragglers which were left behind, would have given us an opportunity of making 3000 prisoners, had there been a greater proportion between our cavalry and theirs; but the latter, disposed so as to arrest our pursuit, to press the march of the infantry by blows from the flat sides of their sabres, and to convey those who could no longer march, prevented us. Nevertheless, there fell into our hands between 300 and 400 men, and some baggage. In the evening, the army encamped upon the heights of Aldea Rubio, having its posts upon the Tormes. The enemy reached the position of San Christoval.

On the 21st, having been informed that the enemy did not occupy Alba de Tormes, I threw a garrison into it. The same day I passed the river in two columns, taking my direction by the skirts of the woods, and established my camp between Alba de Tormes and Salamanca. My object in taking this direction was to continue the movement by m left, in order to drive the enemy from the neighbourhood of Salamanca, and fight them with greater advantage. I depended upon taking a good defensive position, in which the enemy could undertake nothing against me: and, in short, come near enough to them to take advantage of the first faults they might make, and vigorously attack them. On the 22nd, in the morning, I went upon the heights of Calbaraca de Abajo, to reconnoitre the enemy. I found a division which had just arrived there; others' were in march for the same place. Some firing took place for the purpose of occupying the posts of observation, of which we respectively remained masters. Everything announced that it was the enemy's intention to occupy the position of Tejares, which was a league in the rear of that in which he then was, distant a league and a half from Salamanca: they, however, assembled considerable forces upon this point; and, as their movement upon Tejares might be difficult if all the French Army was in sight, I thought it right to have it ready to act as circumstances required.

There were between us and the English some isolated points, called the Arapiles. I ordered General Bonnèt to occupy that which belonged to the position we ought to take; his troops did so with promptitude and dexterity. The enemy ordered theirs to be occupied; but it was commanded by ours at 250 *toises* distance. I had destined this point, in the event of there being a general movement by the left, and a battle taking place, to be the pivot and point of support of the right to all the army. The first division had orders to occupy and defend the ridge of Calbaraca, which is protected by a large and deep ravine.

The 3rd division was in the second line, destined to support it, and the 2nd, 4th, 5th, and 6th, were at the head of the wood *en masse*, behind the position of Arapiles, and could march equally on all sides; whilst the 7th division occupied the left head of the wood, which formed a point extremely uneven, and of very difficult access, and which I had lined with twenty pieces of artillery. The light cavalry was charged to clear the left, and place itself in advance of the 7th division. The dragoons remained in the second line to the right of the army. Such were the dispositions made towards the middle of the day.

The enemy had his troops parallel to me, extending his right by leaning towards the mountain of Tejares, which always appeared to be his point of retreat.

There was, in front of the ridge occupied by the artillery, another vast ridge, easy of defence, and which had a more immediate effect on the enemy's movements. The possession of this ridge gave me the means, in case I should have manoeuvred towards the evening, of carrying myself on the enemy's communications on Tamames. This post, which was otherwise well occupied, was inexpugnable; and in itself completed the position which I had taken. It was, besides, indispensably necessary to occupy it, seeing that the enemy had reinforced his centre, from whence he might push forward *en masse* on this ridge, and commence his attack by taking this important point.

In consequence, I gave orders to the 5th division to take position on the right extremity of this ridge, the fire from which exactly crossed that from Arapiles; to the 7th division, to place itself in a second line to support this; to the 2nd, to hold itself in reserve to the latter; and to the 6th, to occupy the ridge at the head of the wood, where a large number of pieces of artillery were yet remaining. I gave like orders to General Bonnèt, to cause the 122nd to occupy a point situated between the great ridge and the point of Arapiles, which defended the entrance of the village of Arapiles; and, finally, I gave orders to General Boyer, Commandant of the Dragoons, to leave a regiment to clear the right of General Foy, and to push the three other regiments to the front of the wood, on the flank of the second division, in such manner as to be able, in case the enemy should attack the ridge, to attack them by the right of this ridge, while the light cavalry should charge his left.

The most part of these movements were performed with irregularity. The 5th division, after having taken the post assigned to it, extended itself on its left, without any cause or reason. The 7th division, which had orders to support it, marched to its position; and, in short, the 2nd division was still in the rear. I felt all the consequences that might result from all these irregularities, and I resolved in remedying them myself on the spot, which was a very easy matter, the enemy not as yet having made any movement at all. At the same time, I received the report of the enemy having caused fresh troops to pass from his left to the right; I ordered the 3rd and 4th divisions to march by the skirts of the wood, in order that I might dispose them as I found needful. It was half-past four o'clock, and I went to the ridge, which was to be the object of a serious dispute; but at this moment a shell struck me, broke my right arm, and made two large wounds on my right side: I thus became incapable of taking any part in the command.

The precious time which I should have employed in rectifying the placing of the troops on the left, was fruitlessly passed; the absence of the commander gives birth to anarchy, and from thence proceeds disorder; meanwhile the time was running away without the enemy undertaking anything. At length, at five o'clock, the enemy, judging that the situation was favourable, attacked this ill-formed left wing with impetuosity. The divisions engaged repulsed the enemy, and were themselves repulsed in their turn; but they acted without concert and without method. The division which I had called to sustain that point, found themselves in the situation of taking part in the combat without having foreseen it.

Every general made extraordinary efforts to supply, by his own particular dispositions, such as were on the whole requisite; but if he could attain it in part, yet he could not attain it completely. The artillery covered itself with glory, performed prodigies of valour, and in the midst of our losses caused the enemy to suffer enormously. He directed his attack against Arapiles, which was defended by the brave 120th regiment, and was there repulsed, leaving more than 300 dead on the spot.

At length, the army retired, evacuated the ridges, and retired to the skirts of the wood, where the enemy made fresh efforts. The division Foy, which by the nature of the business was charged with the covering the retrograde movements, was attacked with vigour, and constantly repulsed the enemy. This division merits the greatest eulogy, as does likewise its general. From this moment, the retreat was effected towards Alba de Tormes, without being disturbed by the enemy. Our loss amounted to about 6000 men, *hors de combat*.

We have lost nine pieces of cannon, which, being dismounted, could not be carried off; all the rest of the baggage, all the park of artillery, all the *matériel* belonging to the army, having been brought away.

It is difficult, M. *le Duc*, to express to you the different sentiments which agitated me at the fatal moment, when the wound which I received caused my being separated from the army. I would with delight have exchanged this wound for the certainty of receiving a mortal stroke at the close of the day, to have preserved the faculty of command; so well did I know the importance of the events which had just taken place, and how necessary the presence of the commander-in-chief was at the moment when the shock of the two armies appeared to be preparing, to give the whole direction to the troops, and to appoint their movements. Thus, one unfortunate moment has destroyed the result of six weeks of wise combinations, of methodical movements, the issue of which had hitherto appeared certain, and which everything seemed to presage to us that we should reap the fruit of.

On the 23rd, the army made its retreat from Alba de Tormes, on Peneranda, taking its direction towards the Douro: the whole of the enemy's cavalry harassed our ear-guard, composed of the cavalry of the 1st division. This cavalry fell back, and left the division too much engaged; but it formed itself in squares to resist the enemy. One of them was broken, the others resisted, and especially that of the 69th, which killed 200 of the enemy's horse by the bayonet; after this time they made no attempt on us.

General Clausel has the command of the army, and has taken such measures as circumstances require. I am going to have myself transported to Burgos, where I hope, by repose and care taken, to recover of the severe wounds that I have received, and which afflict me more from the dire influence which they have had on the success of the army, than from the sufferings which they have caused me to endure.

I cannot do sufficient justice to the bravery with which the generals and colonels have fought, and to the good disposition which animated them in that difficult circumstance. I ought particularly to mention General Bonnèt, whose reputation has been so long established. I should likewise name General Taupin, who commanded the 6th division. General Clausel, though wounded, did not quit the field, but to the end gave an example of great personal bravery. The generals of artillery particularly distinguished themselves.

On this day, unfortunate as it has been, there are multitudes of traits worthy of being noticed, and which honour the French name. I will collect them, and solicit from His Majesty rewards for the brave men who have deserved them. I ought not to defer mentioning the conduct of the brave Sub-Lieutenant Guillemot, of the 118th regiment, who sprung into the enemy's ranks to obtain a flag, which he seized, after having cut off the arm of the person who carried it: he has brought this flag into our ranks, notwithstanding the severe bayonet wound he has received.

We have to regret the loss of the General of Division Ferey, dead of his wounds; of General Thomières, killed upon the field of battle; and of General Desgravièrs. Generals Bonnèt and Clausel, and the General of Brigade Menne, are wounded.

I beg your Excellency to receive the assurance of my high consideration.

Signed (with the left hand),
The Marshal Duke of Ragusa.

No. 2

LIST OF THE ALLIED ARMY ON THE 30TH OF AUGUST, 1813.

GENERAL IN CHIEF,

Field-Marshal the Marquess of WELLINGTON, K.G.

Quarter-Master-General, Sir GEORGE MURRAY, K.B.
Adjutant-General, Sir EDWARD PAKENHAM, K.B.
Chief Engineer Lieut.-Colonel, Sir RICHARD FLETCHER.
Senior Officer of Artillery, Lieut.-Colonel DICKSON.

CAVALRY.

Lieut.-General Sir STAPLETON COTTON, K.B.
Assistant Adjutant-General Colonel ELLEY.
Major-General Lord EDWARD SOMERSET.

    1st Life Guards.
    2d Life Guards.
    Royal Horse Guards (Blue).

Major-General WILLIAM PONSONBY.
>   5th Dragoon Guards.
>   3d Dragoons.
>   4th Dragoons.

Major-General FANE.
>   3d Dragoon Guards.
>   1st or Royal Dragoons.

Major-General BARON BOCK.
1st Dragoons, King's German Legion.
2d Dragoons, King's German Legion.

Colonel GRANT.
>   10th Hussars.
>   15th Hussars.

Major-General VANDELEUR.
>   12th Light Dragoons.
>   16th Light Dragoons.

Major-General LONG.
>   13th Light Dragoons.
>   14th Light Dragoons.

Major-General VICTOR ALTEN.
1st Hussars, King's German Legion.
18th Hussars.

Brigadier-General D'URBAN.
>   1st Portuguese Dragoons.
>   11th Portuguese Dragoons.
>   12th Portuguese Dragoons.

Brigadier-General OTWAY.
>   4th Portuguese Dragoons.
>   10th Portuguese Dragoons.

Brigadier-General MADDEN.
5th Portuguese Dragoons.
8th Portuguese Dragoons.

INFANTRY.

FIRST DIVISION.

Lieut.-General Sir THOMAS GRAHAM, K.B.
Assistant Adjutant-General, Lieut.-Colonel BOUVERIE.
Assistant Quarter-Master-General, Colonel UPTON.

Major-General HOWARD.
1st Guards (1st battalion.)
1st Guards (3d battalion.)

Major-General Honourable EDWARD STOPFORD.
Coldstream Guards.
3d Guards.

Colonel HALKETT.
1st light battalion German Legion.
2d light battalion.
1st battalion of the Line, German Legion.
2d battalion.
5th battalion.

SECOND DIVISION.

Lieut.-General Sir ROWLAND HILL, K.B.
Lieut.-General Sir WILLIAM STEWART, K.B.
Assistant Adjutant-General, Lieut.-Colonel ROOKE.
Assistant Quarter-Master-General, Lieut.-Colonel Honourable A. ABERCROMBY.

Major-General WALKER.
50th regiment.
71st.
92d.

Major-General BYNG.
   3d regiment.
   57th.
 Provisional ⎰ 31st.
 Battalion. ⎱ 66th.

Colonel O'CALLAGHAN.
28th regiment.
34th.
39th.

PORTUGUESE DIVISION.

Lieut.-General HAMILTON.
2d regiment of the Line.
14th.
5th.
5th Caçadores.

Brigadier-General CAMPBELL.
4th Portuguese regiment.
10th.

Colonel ASHWORTH.
6th Portuguese regiment.
18th.
6th Caçadores.

THIRD DIVISION.

Lieut.-General Sir THOMAS PICTON, K.B.
Assistant Adjutant-General, Lieut.-Colonel STOVIN.

Major-General BRISBANE.
 45th regiment.
 74th.
 88th.

Major-General the Honourable CHARLES COLVILLE.
 5th regiment.
 83d.
 87th.
 94th.

Portuguese Brigade.
9th regiment of the Line.
21st.

FOURTH DIVISION.

Lieut.-General, Honourable Sir LOWRY COLE, K.B.
Assistant Adjutant-General, Lieut.-Colonel BRADFORD.

Major-General ANSON.
27th regiment.
40th.
48th.
Provisional { 2d (Queen's).
Battalion. { 53d.

Major-General ROSS.
7th Royal Fusileers.
20th.
23d.

Brigadier-General HARVEY.
11th Portuguese regiment.
23d.
10th Caçadores.

FIFTH DIVISION.

Lieut.-General, Sir JAMES LEITH, K.B.
Assistant Adjutant-General, Lieut.-Colonel BERKELEY.
Assistant Quarter-Master-General, Lieut-Colonel GOMM.

Major-General HAY.
1st Royal Scots.
9th regiment.
38th.

Major-General ROBINSON.
4th (King's Own) regiment.
47th.
59th.

Major-General SPRY.

3d Portuguese regiment of the Line.
15th.
8th Caçadores.

SIXTH DIVISION.

Lieut.-General HENRY CLINTON.
Assistant Adjutant-General, Lieut.-Colonel TRYON.
Assistant Quarter-Master-General, Major VINCENT.

Major-General PACK.

42d Royal Highlanders.
79th.
91st.

Major-General LAMBERT.

11th regiment.
32d.
36th.
61st.

Portuguese Brigade.

8th regiment of the Line.
12th regiment of the Line.
9th Caçadores.

SEVENTH DIVISION.

Lieut.-General the Earl of DALHOUSIE, K.B.
Assistant Adjutant-General, Lieut.-Colonel D'OYLEY.

Major-General BARNES.

6th regiment.
Provisional { 24th.
Battalion.   { 58th.
Chasseurs Britannique.

Colonel MITCHELL.

51st regiment.
68th.
82d.

Major-General Le Cor.
7th Portuguese regiment of the Line.
19th.
2d Caçadores.

LIGHT DIVISION.

Major-General Charles Baron Alten.
Assistant Adjutant-General, Major Marlay.
Assistant Quarter-Master-General, Major Stewart.

Major-General Kempt.
43d regiment.
95th (1st battalion).
95th (3d battalion).

Major-General Skerret.
52d regiment.
95th (2d battalion).

Portuguese Troops attached to the Light Division.
20th regiment of the Line.
1st Caçadores.
3d Caçadores.

UNATTACHED BRITISH BRIGADE.

Major-General Lord Aylmer.
76th regiment.
84th.
85th.

UNATTACHED PORTUGUESE BRIGADES.

Major-General Bradford.
13th regiment of the Line.
24th.
5th Caçadores.

Brigadier-General Wilson.
1st regiment of the Line.
16th.
4th Caçadores.

ROYAL STAFF CORPS.

Lieut.-Colonel, Honourable R. L. Dundas.
Lieut.-Colonel Sturgeon.

STAFF CORPS OF CAVALRY.

Lieut.-Colonel Scovell.

The 60th regiment (5th battalion), and the regiment of Brunswick Oels, attached in companies to the different brigades of the army.

No. 3

Proclamation of Marshal Soult.

(To Be Read at the Heads of Companies in Each Regiment.)

23rd July, 1813.

Soldiers!

The recent events of the war have induced His Majesty the Emperor to invest me, by an Imperial Decree of the 1st inst., with the command of the armies of Spain, and to honour me with the flattering title of his 'Lieutenant.' This high distinction cannot but convey to my mind sensations of gratitude and joy; but they are not unalloyed with regret at the train of events which have, in the opinion of His Majesty, rendered such an appointment necessary in Spain.

It is known to you, soldiers, that the enmity of Russia, roused into active hostility by the eternal enemy of the continent, made it incumbent that numerous armies should be assembled in Germany early in the spring. For this purpose were many of your comrades withdrawn. The emperor himself assumed the command; and the arms of France, guided by his powerful and commanding genius, achieved a succession of as brilliant victories as any that adorn the annals of our country. The presumptuous hopes of aggrandisement entertained by the enemy were confounded. Pacific overtures were made; and the Emperor, always inclined to consult the welfare of his subjects, by following moderate councils, listened to the proposals that were made.

While Germany was thus the theatre of great events, that enemy, who, under pretence of succouring the inhabitants of the Peninsula, has in reality devoted them to ruin, was not inactive. He assembled the whole of his disposable force—English, Spaniards, and Portuguese—under his most experienced officers; and relying upon the superiority of his numbers, advanced in three divisions against the French force assembled upon the Duero. With well provided fortresses in his front and rear, a skilful general, enjoying the confidence of his troops, might, by selecting good positions, have braved and discomfited this motley levy.

But, unhappily, at this critical period, timorous and pusillanimous counsels were followed. The fortresses were abandoned and blown up; hasty and disorderly marches gave confidence to the enemy; and a veteran army, small indeed in number, but great in all that constitutes the military character, which had fought, bled, and triumphed in every province of Spain, beheld with indignation its laurels tarnished, and itself compelled to abandon all its acquisitions—the trophies of many a well-fought and bloody day. When at length the indignant voice of the troops arrested this disgraceful flight, and its commander, touched with shame, yielded to the general desire, and determined upon giving battle near Vittoria, who can doubt—from this generous enthusiasm—this fine sense of honour—what would have been the result, had the general been worthy of his troops? had he, in short, made those dispositions and movements which would have secured to one part of his army the co-operation and support of the other?

Let us not, however, defraud the enemy of the praise which is due to him. The dispositions and arrangements of their general have been prompt, skilful, and consecutive. The valour and steadiness of his troops have been praiseworthy. Yet do not forget that it is to the benefit of your example they owe their present military character; and that whenever the relative duties of a French general and his troops have been ably fulfilled, their enemies have commonly had no other resource than flight.

Soldiers! I partake of your chagrin, your grief, your indignation. I know that the blame of the present situation of the army is imputable to others,—be the merit of repairing it yours. I have borne testimony to the emperor of your bravery and zeal. His instructions are to drive the enemy from those lofty heights which enable him proudly to survey our fertile valleys, and chase them across the Ebro. It is on the Spanish soil that your tents must next be pitched, and from thence your resources drawn. No difficulties can be insurmountable to your valour and devotion. Let us, then, exert ourselves with mutual ardour; and be assured, that nothing can give greater felicity to the paternal heart of the emperor, than the knowledge of the triumphs of his army—of its increasing glory—of its having rendered itself worthy of him, and of our dear country.

Extensive but combined movements for the relief of the fortresses are upon the eve of taking place. They will be completed in a few days. Let the account of our success be dated from Vittoria,—and the birth of his Imperial Majesty be celebrated in that city: so shall we render memorable an epoch deservedly dear to all Frenchmen.

Soult, Duc de Dalmatie,
Lieutenant de l'Empereur.

No. 4

FRENCH MARSHALS.

In the foregoing narrative, frequent mention has, of course, been made of the Marshals of France under Napoleon, they having occasionally been designated by those titles, the reward of military renown, and sometimes by their family sirnames; it may, therefore, not be deemed improper attaching to the work a brief notice of those distinguished officers, of whom no less than fifteen participated in the precarious fortunes of the Peninsular War, and of that number thirteen have ceased to exist.

Alexandre Berthire, the constant companion of Napoleon during his campaigns as Emperor of the French, previous to the Abdication of 1814, was born at Versailles, in 1753. The earlier part of his military career was passed with General La Fayette in America. Subsequently he served in the revolutionary armies, with but minor distinction, until the commencement of the memorable campaign of 1796, when the young general-in-chief of the army of Italy appointed him chief of his staff, and elicited those talents for detail, afterwards so eminently conspicuous. Created a Marshal of the Empire, he was also elevated to the dignities of Prince of Neufchatel, and of Wagram, Vice-Constable, Grand Dignitary of the Empire, Senator and Counsellor of State, Major-General of the Grand Army, Grand Eagle of the Legion of Honour, Grand Dignitary of the Iron Crown, and of the Imperial Order *De la Réunion*, Grand Cordon of the Order of the Duke of Hesse, Grand Commander of that of Westphalia, Knight of St. Joseph of Wurtzburg, of the Golden Eagle of Wirtemburg, of the Crown of Saxony, Grand Cross of the Order of St. Henry of Baden, and St. Etienne of Hungary, Knight of the Black Eagle of Prussia, and of the Imperial Russian Order of St. Andrew. Marshal Berthier's services in Spain were confined to the short visit paid to that country by Napoleon in 1808, and the commencement of 1809.

Andrew Massena, a native of Nice, was born in 1758, and from the ranks of the French Army rose to great distinction. His last eminent campaign, as general-in-chief, was that of Portugal, being the only one in which he participated during the Peninsular War. Marshal Massena became Duke of Rivoli, and Prince of Essling.

*Joachim Mura*t, the first cavalry officer of his day, and a man of the most brilliant courage, was born in 1767, being son to the vintner of a village named Bastide-Frontonier, in Guienne. From being a private of *chasseurs*, he became an officer, and having attracted the attention of General Bonaparte, soon rose to distinction beneath his fostering and discriminating genius. There was a chivalrous and romantic feeling about the character of Joachim Murat, which, added to his noble personal appearance, the eccentric splendour of his dress, and dauntless demeanour, admirably calculated him for leader of the French cavalry, who, inspired by his courage, and following the nodding of his snow-white plume, as it invariably led the charge against an enemy, were enabled to perform brilliant services, and create impressions, that, under a less energetic leader, would never have produced similar effects.

Napoleon's opinion of his brother-in-law is, by Lord Ebrington's *Narrative of Conversations at Elba*, couched in the following terms:

> *C'est un bon militaire: c'est un des hommes les plus brillants que j'ai jamais vu sur un champ de bataille. Pas d'un talent supérieur, sans beaucoup de courage moral, assez timide même pour le plan des opérations; mais le moment qu'il voyoit l'ennemie, tout cela disparoissoi—c'étoit alors le coup-d'œil le plus rapide, une valeur vraiment chevaleresque. D'ailleurs, une belle homme, grand, bien mis, et avec beaucoup de soin—quelquefois une peu fantasquement; enfin, un magnifique Lazzarone.*

Marshal, Grand Duke of Berg, and King of Naples, this brave soldier shared the fate of his only compeer in the French Army.

Jean Baptiste Jourdan was born at Limoges, in 1762. As General-in-chief of the army of the Sambre and Meuse, he acquired a distinction that obtained for him the rank of Marshal. As Major-General of the French armies in Spain, his career was one of misfortune and error; want of confidence on the part of the troops bespoke his lack of military knowledge, while subsequent vacillation of purpose denoted his failure in political consistency and undoubted mediocrity of mind.

Jean Lannes, son of a Norman mechanic, was born in 1769. Like many other distinguished soldiers, he was indebted for his elevation to the penetrating judgment of Napoleon, who having once adopted an impression of his military talent, advanced him to the highest honours of his profession,—Marshal, and Duke of Montebello. He was killed by a cannon-shot at Aspern, in 1809.

Jean-de-Dieu Soult was born at St. Aurans, in Languedoc, in 1769. He entered the service as a private of artillery, and in the first republican campaigns obtained considerable distinction: under Hoche. and Jourdan, and Lefevre, he increased his reputation; in 1794, was made *Général de Brigade*, and in 1798, General of Division. His career in Spain was marked by gaining the Battle of Gamonal, by losing that of Coruña, being surprised and defeated at Oporto, defeated at Albuhera, in the battles of the Pyrenees, on the heights of San Marcial, and in every subsequent action with the allied army on the territory of France. Marshal Soult was created Duke of Dalmatia, and his conduct, commanding a corps of the grand army, under Napoleon, on many occasions, was most distinguished.

Pierre Francois Charles Augereau was born at Paris in 1757; having passed several years in the ranks of the French Army, he retired, and became a fencing-master at Naples; but, in 1792, returning to revolutionary France, again became a private soldier, and in four years was a General of Division.

Possessed of some talent, and no principle, but undoubted bravery, the Marshal Duke of Castiglione is alike celebrated for his gallantry, his rapacity, his perfidy, and his treason.

Jean Moncey was born at Besançon, in 1754. He was appointed successively, by the Emperor Napoleon, First Inspector General of Gendarmerie, Grand Officer of the Empire, Marshal, Grand Eagle of the

Legion of Honour, and Duke of Conegliano.

Jean Baptiste Bessières, born in 1768, was another example of a man of subordinate rank having attracted the attention of his great master, and becoming one of the most distinguished officers of the French Army. In command of the cavalry of the Imperial Guard, Marshal Bessières obtained frequent and deserved distinction. His victory at Rio Saco was probably the most important, in point of time and circumstances, that occurred during the war. As Duke of Istria, his name will ever be honourably remembered; as also the premature termination of his career by a cannon-ball at the Battle of Lutzen.

Francois Joseph Lefebvre, an Alsacian, was born in 1755. He, in early life, became sergeant in the French Guards. At Fleurus, he established a great reputation, and subsequently became Grand Eagle of the Legion of Honour, Marshal of France, and Duke of Dantzic.

Michael Ney, one of the bravest soldiers that ever existed, was born at Sarrelouis, in January 1769. He entered very young into the regiment Colonel-General of Hussars, and, passing rapidly through all the subordinate ranks, was, in 1794, appointed Adjutant-General by Kleber, under whose orders he subsequently acquired that reputation for audacity and talent, matured during the numerous campaigns he afterwards served.

In 1796, after a very glorious affair on the Rednitz, he was promoted, on the field of battle, to the rank of *Général de Brigade*, and the following year to that of General of Division. On the assumption of the imperial dignity by Napoleon, he was elevated to the distinction of a Marshal of France, Grand Officer of the Legion of Honour, Duke of Elchingen, and subsequently Prince of Moskwa. On two occasions, Marshal Ney commanded the rear-guard of retreating armies with distinguished *éclat*: first, in Portugal, under Massena, where, by his gallantry and judgment, he materially contributed to the safety of the French Army; and, secondly, in that never-to-be-forgotten service of terrific suffering, that unquestionable trial of everything which constituted firmness, the retreat from Moscow, in which the name of the Duke of Elchingen shines with unrivalled glory.

Columns of troops, rear-guard after rear-guard, dwindled into insignificance, or utterly vanished from his grasp; but the unbroken spirit, the romantic and chivalrous gallantry, of Michael Ney, rose as difficulties increased; and the icy rigours of insufferable cold, the livid bodies of his companions bleaching in the gale, the incessant fire of enemies, the hurras of barbarian adversaries, and the almost impenetrable snows of a Russian winter, were but stimuli to exertion, and instead of depressing his energies, or weakening his judgment, added fire and ardent feeling to that iron mind and undaunted heart that nothing human could, in the execution of military duty, either vanquish or *appal*.

Edward Adolphe Casimir Joseph Mortier, one of the most celebrated Generals of the Republic, was, by the Emperor, elevated to the rank of Marshal; he was also nominated a Grand Officer of the Empire, Grand Eagle of the Legion of Honour, and created Duke of Treviso.

Suchet, a native of Lyons, the most successful of the French Generals in the Peninsula, made the campaigns of Italy under Napoleon, by whom he was nominated Inspector-General of Infantry, Governor of the Imperial Palace of Lacken, near to Brussels, Grand Eagle of the Legion of Honour, Marshal of France, and Duke of Albufera.

Frederic Louis Marmont, born at Chatillon in 1774, was *Aide-de-Camp* to Napoleon during his first Italian campaign, and commanded the artillery of the French Army at Marengo: subsequently elevated to the rank of Marshal, he commanded one of the corps of the Grand Army, and, in Spain, succeeding the Prince of Essling in the Army of Portugal, he lost the battle of Salamanca, and proceeding to France for the recovery of his wounds, did not return to the Peninsula. His subsequent history is well known; it is for his conscience to determine whether he did, or did not, infamously betray his benefactor. Marshal Marmont was, by the Emperor Napoleon, created Duke of Ragusa, and nominated Grand Eagle of the Legion of Honour!

Victor, an old and intrepid soldier of the Revolution, commanded a *corps d'armée* at Marengo, served in Spain during several years, was nominated Grand Eagle of the Legion of Honour, Marshal of the Empire, and Duke of Belluno.

www.ingramcontent.com/pod-product-compliance
Lightning Source LLC
Chambersburg PA
CBHW030219170426
43201CB00006B/133